MW01518937

Anglo-American Relations and the Transmission of Ideas

Transatlantic Perspectives

Series Editors: Christoph Irmscher, Indiana University Bloomington, and Christof Mauch, Ludwig-Maximilians-Universität, München

This series explores European and North American cultural exchanges and interactions across the Atlantic and over time. While standard historical accounts are still structured around nation-states, *Transatlantic Perspectives* provides a framework for the discussion of topics and issues such as knowledge transfer, migration and mutual influence in politics, society, education, film and literature. Committed to the presentation of European views on America as well as American views on Europe, *Transatlantic Perspectives* offers room for the publication of both primary texts and critical analyses. While the series puts the Atlantic World at centre stage, it also aims to take global developments into account.

Anglo-American Relations and the Transmission of Ideas

A Shared Political Tradition?

Edited by Alan P. Dobson and Steve Marsh

berghahn

NEW YORK · OXFORD

www.berghahnbooks.com

First published in 2022 by
Berghahn Books
www.berghahnbooks.com

Library of Congress Cataloging-in-Publication Data

Names: Dobson, Alan P., editor. | Marsh, Steve, 1967- editor.
Title: Anglo-American relations and the transmission of ideas : a shared
 political tradition? / edited by Alan P. Dobson and Steve Marsh.
Description: English-language edition. | New York : Berghahn, 2022. |
 Series: Transatlantic perspectives ; volume 6 | Includes bibliographical
 references and index.
Identifiers: LCCN 2021052743 (print) | LCCN 2021052744 (ebook) | ISBN
 9781800734791 (hardback) | ISBN 9781800734807 (ebook)
Subjects: LCSH: United States--Relations--Great Britain. | Great
 Britain--Relations--United States. | United
 States--Civilization--British influences. | Great
 Britain--Civilization--American influences. | Ideology--United
 States--History. | Ideology--Great Britain--History. | Political
 culture--United States--History. | Political culture--Great
 Britain--History.
Classification: LCC E183.8.G7 A673 2022 (print) | LCC E183.8.G7 (ebook) |
 DDC 327.73041--dc23/eng/20211221
LC record available at https://lccn.loc.gov/2021052743
LC ebook record available at https://lccn.loc.gov/2021052744

British Library Cataloguing in Publication Data

A catalogue record for this book is available from the British Library

ISBN 978-1-80073-479-1 hardback
ISBN 978-1-80073-480-7 ebook

Contents

Illustrations

Introduction

Alan P. Dobson and Steve Marsh

Cogito, ergo sum

—René Descartes

as we know, there are known knowns; there are things we know we know. We also know there are known unknowns; that is to say we know there are some things we do not know. But there are also unknown unknowns – the ones we don't know we don't know. And if one looks throughout the history of our country and other free countries, it is the latter category that tend to be the difficult ones.

—Donald Rumsfeld: US Secretary of Defence 2001–6

For the seventeenth-century French philosopher René Descartes, the act of thinking was the existential precursor of all else, the only thing he could be certain of. It was the evidence of self. From his 'I think therefore I am' proposition necessarily flowed many questions. How am I similar or different to others? How do individual thinking-selves differ from collectives of thinking-selves? How does like-thinking impact the behaviour of individuals and polities? Such questions have often driven thinkers in Britain and the United States in surprisingly similar directions. British and American governments, too, have responded to such thought and challenges in not dissimilar ways, despite the American republic first being defined in opposition to the British monarchy. As we shall see, good correspondence and friendship between Britain and its former colonies were not easy to sever.[1] Interestingly, since then, some of the thinking on both sides has fallen into Donald Rumsfeld's category of known unknowns. For example, we know intuitively that political ideas and concepts have an impact, but exactly how and to what extent is often opaque, to say the least. And in investigating this kind of known unknown there is always the possibility of revealing previously unknown unknowns. Such concerns are important because Anglo-American policymakers have frequently lauded the uniquely positive implications of a 'common cast of mind' for co-operation. British Prime Minister Harold Wilson put matters thus in January 1975 at a summit meeting with President Gerald Ford: 'We don't have, you know, to spend about fifty minutes in every hour arguing about first principles, arguing about trying to convince one another. They are thoroughly practical and that's why you get six times as much results out of an hour of discussions such of the kind we've had.'[2] It is the sharing of these first principles, or the question of how there came to be a common cast of mind, that is the focus of investigation here.

John Winthrop's City upon a Hill through Thomas Jefferson's Empire of Liberty and Ronald Reagan's Evil Empire speech suggest that the United States, more than Britain, has overtly styled itself upon ideals that inform practice. And those ideals are often characterized as forming part of America's exceptionalism. For example, such a notion of exceptionalism is at the heart of Louis Hartz's iconic thesis set out in *The Liberal Tradition in America*.[3] Yet rarely are such ideals uniquely American or alien to Britons. Famous first principles enshrined in the US Constitution and political and legal practice as a guide for the new republic, including due legal process, political representation and inalienable rights to life, liberty and property, were effectively inherited from the motherland. A shared commitment to democratic government and the rule of law help explain the Anglo-American underpinning of some of the great experiments in collective security and international law and organization. Furthermore, first Britain and later the United States have evinced a common commitment to spreading their ideals abroad, sometimes contentiously so, as in relation to Anglo-Saxon supremacy, the white man's burden and forcible democratization.

It was over three hundred years after Descartes discovered certainty as a thinking self that Donald Rumsfeld pondered the knowledge that thinking might bring in his (in)famous 'known knowns' speech. While 'unknown unknowns' most troubled Rumsfeld, known knowns could evidently be worked with or legislated against. Anglo-American relations, especially since the Second World War, have largely fallen into the latter category. That is not to say there have been no surprises: Suez, Skybolt, President Nixon's opening to China, British withdrawal from east of Suez, the US invasion of Grenada and experience with President Donald Trump were all unanticipated. Nevertheless, for the most part, knowledge of one another's culture, society, politics, foreign-policy objectives and so forth has been unusually strong. Reciprocal learning has been facilitated by the English language and has been accumulated over centuries of shared experiences and interpenetration at all levels of society. How and to what effect political ideas and values play out in international affairs may well be more difficult to explain than, for example, power and national self-interest, but this should not preclude exploration of their role.

Numerous opinion polls have revealed consistently high levels of popular affiliation between Britons and Americans. Also, from the Second World War and Churchill's invocation of the special relationship in his 1946 Fulton speech,[4] Anglo-American foreign policies have exhibited unusually high levels of correlation. This phenomenon has been attributed in part to the so-called layered cake of transatlantic bureaucratic intermeshing, so much so that some scholars argue that there is a distinctive Anglo-American style of diplomacy.[5] Indeed, in 1982, former US Secretary of State Henry Kissinger spoke explicitly of how the wartime habit of intimate, informal collaboration became 'a permanent practice'. He emphasized, too, that 'The ease and informality of the Anglo-American partnership has been a source of wonder – and no little resentment – to third countries. Our post-war diplomatic history is littered with Anglo-American "arrangements" and "understandings," sometimes on crucial issues, never put into formal documents.'[6]

One might fairly assume from the above, then, that this book about the impact on Anglo-American relations of ideals, thought, political values and transatlantic reciprocal learning at multiple levels of government and society would sit comfortably in the mainstream of analyses of the special relationship. Yet this is not the case. Instead, a longstanding predominance of realist approaches in international relations (IR) and diplomatic history has caused consideration of such 'first principles' to be eschewed in favour of rational calculations of mutual utility based on more apparently tangible factors such as power and national interest, and detailing changes in the quantity and quality of functional co-operation over time. Such approaches appeal to many scholars because they appear to be scientific in a soft sense, marked by observations regarding clearly defined self-interest and calculations about, and the deployment of, visible power in what appear to be clear cause-and-effect relationships.

Realists range from Thucydides to Machiavelli, from Carl von Clausewitz to E.H. Carr, from Hans J. Morgenthau to Kenneth Waltz and John Mearsheimer. The roll call is impressive and it should be clearly noted that it includes eminent historians as well as IR scholars. In his classic work of realism, Hans J. Morgenthau remarked that: 'A realist theory of international politics will ... avoid the ... popular fallacy of equating the foreign policies of statesmen with his philosophy or political sympathies, and of deducing the former from the latter.'[7] Realism metamorphosed through many stages, later emerging as structural or neorealism, as it was sometimes called, with key exponents such as Kenneth Waltz and John Mearsheimer presenting a quasi-scientific theory of how states behave.[8] For Mearsheimer, the component and determining variables are an anarchic or non-hierarchical international system; the offensive military capability of all states; chronic uncertainty about state intentions; the paramount goal of the survival of the state; and the rationality of state action.[9]

With regard to realist historians, or at least those heavily influenced by realism, many who have studied the Anglo-American relationship over the past half-century have foregrounded utilitarian interest: scholars such as Christopher Thorne, C.J. Bartlett, John Dumbrell, John Bayliss, Ian Clark, Jonathan Colman, Sylvia Ellis, Nigel Ashton, James Ellison and David Reynolds.[10] And while some would agree with Bartlett's caveat that 'hard-headed calculations in both Washington and London in response to the grim realities of power politics do not wholly explain the remarkable Anglo-American relationship which developed after 1941', the pervasive emphasis on the hard calculation of interests abides among many historians.[11] One can with considerable plausibility assert and illustrate direct cause and effect between the pursuit of self-interest rationally calculated, the rational deployment of power to pursue chosen ends and the results that ensue. It is far more difficult to quantify the impact of ideas upon decisions and actions.

All forms of realism, be they in historical or IR scholarship, are reductionist in that they seek to identify the key dynamics that move international affairs and determine their outcomes while relying heavily on the notion of rational actors. Of course, there are different disciplinary motivations. Like other theories applied in IR, realism has the laudable objective of trying to improve the way the international system operates and, above all, avoid war. In this sense, there is a practical and prescriptive policy aspect to realism in IR. History is no less abstract in its assumptions than science; what could be more abstract than trying to study the past, which, by definition, has gone? Well, it has gone except for the evidence left in the present to suggest what the past may have been: memory, conventions, ways of thinking, institutions and artefacts, images and contemporary written evidence. For many historians, especially when dealing with interstate relationships, the reasons of actors, those who make decisions with important political, economic and strategic consequences, are of major importance. Where realism bites is in the dominant assumption that individuals and governments act rationally in the definition and pursuit of national interests and that therein there is little scope for intangible factors such as ideals, values and senses of affinity to influence behaviour.

All of this gives rise to some potentially serious problems for the approaches adopted by the contributors to this book. However, there is good reason to develop alternative perspectives on Anglo-American relations. First of all there is a combination of the so-called cultural turn in international history and the weaknesses in (neo-)realist explanatory narratives exposed by the end of the Cold War. For Richard Ned Lebow, neorealism had 'denuded Realism of its complexity and subtlety, appreciation of agency and understanding that power is most readily transformed into influence when it is both masked and embedded in a generally accepted system of norms'.[12] Lebow noted, too, that in the later stages of Morgenthau's intellectual journey, values and beliefs are re-entered into the calculus of how states operate in the international system. This would seem more akin to the work presented here, although significant differences remain.[13] Concomitantly, Akira Iriye et al.'s argument that the 'cultural turn' raised a 'fundamental question of the relationship between a country's cultural system and its behaviour in the international system' gained ground.[14] For the likes of Alexander Wendt, this meant that a more thorough understanding of historical causation could be formed by considering the hard realities of geopolitics in the context of the cultural discourses that shape identity and imagination.[15]

Secondly, as we have argued elsewhere, there are limitations to what Steve Smith and Martin Hollis refer to as the 'outside' style of explanation adopted by writers such as Morgenthau. One might be tempted to say that the outside is not as wide-ranging as the word might suggest, with the scope of focus being reduced by assumptions regarding what are judged to be important determinants or variables.[16] Equally, one might suggest that it is a serious error to take interests as rational givens. Self-interest for suicide bombers consists in a rational route to heaven through their violent actions, but this could never be a rational action for a non-believer or for a believer with a different route map to heaven. One person's rationality is determined differently to that of another. This is an extreme example, but it illustrates the importance of interrogating ideas and their function in helping to shape international affairs. What comes to be seen as an interest is often moulded by common beliefs and values, which usually lead to the establishment of common interests. This is a mutually and self-reinforcing dynamic. And it is important to note that once one appreciates these takes on rational action, interests and sentiments, they change the way usable power is conceptualized and its use determined.

Consider, for instance, a bitter row in the early 1990s between Britain and the United States over the latter's desire to replace the ailing airlines TWA and Pan Am with American and United Airlines at Heathrow Airport, which was, at the time, the busiest and most important international hub in the world. The situation was complex, but essentially Britain had an unassailable advantage because of an American commitment made during negotiations in 1980 that restricted them to two airlines at Heathrow, which should be TWA and Pan Am or their corporate successors.[17] As neither American nor United Airlines had any corporate connection with Pan Am or TWA, the British response to demands that they be allowed to enter into Heathrow was to say yes, of course, but you have to pay. It was not something that the airlines had an automatic right to.

The Americans were incandescent. Paul Wisgerhof of the US State Department suggested by-passing Britain altogether and angrily declared: 'I don't think we need the UK if we have an open-skies agreement with Germany. And my personal preference would be to tell Mr. Rifkind [UK Secretary of State for Transport] and Mr. Moss [UK Under Secretary for International Aviation, Department of Transport] to go stuff it.'[18] Not the kind of language one might expect from a diplomat. And ill feeling towards Britain was not confined to the State Department. For example, Cyril Murphy of United Airlines was equally outraged and particularly angry at the British press, of which he said 'it was like this is our chance to get even for the American Revolution'.[19] The whole affair was clearly pretty bad; it is remarkable that it happened when British and American forces were fighting shoulder to shoulder in the First Gulf War.

Rather surprisingly, more even-tempered views were expressed in the US Department of Transportation. Maybe institutional memory in that department stretched back to the Bermuda 1 Anglo-American Air Service Agreement of 1946, when the boot was on the other foot and Americans ruthlessly extracted concessions from the British.[20] Whatever the case, there was a kind of understanding regarding how the United States and Britain related to each other that had been temporarily eclipsed among State Department officials and US airline executives because of the anger into which they had been tipped by the Heathrow succession rights talks. Paul Gretch, Director of the Office of International Aviation, US Department of Transportation, after all the difficulties he had experienced at first hand in the recent talks, still felt that 'the UK would be the preferred partner in Europe to get where we want to go'. One reason for this was hard-headed calculation, because Britain was the largest European market for US airlines. The other reason had more to do with those 'first principles': 'I don't know that the Germans really share our views philosophically. I think deep down the UK does.'[21]

The point of this aside is to underscore what, at the start of this introduction, seemed self-evident: that, contrary to central tenets of realism, first principles do seem to matter in Anglo-American relations. None of us contributors seek to devalue realism in our contributions. Rather, we seek to expand analytic horizons beyond the relatively narrow confines of realism writ large. As C.A.W. Manning put it many years ago: 'Actually it is right choosings that we want, between concrete alternatives, not rightness as opposed to wrongness, in the abstract.'[22] Manning was no realist, being instead a founding member of the English School that tried to reconcile realism with idealism/liberalism, but the point is well made concerning the world of practice. And one of the overriding principles of practice is guidance that works, as opposed to a search for often esoteric truths.

This book, then, seeks to encourage a rebalancing of scholarship on Anglo-American relations by approaching historical truth – or, if that is too highfalutin, accuracy – through an invocation of the world of ideas. It is a collective endeavour that starts from a common assumption: important political, economic and strategic decisions can be better understood when they are contextualized within the various and often intersecting traditions of thought, values, ideas and practices that prevailed contemporaneously. By interrogating the notion of a shared Anglo-American political tradition stretching back to the founding of the American republic and beyond, we hope to deepen understanding of the nature and conduct of Anglo-American relations through to the present and, in doing so, reveal the importance of some of the known unknowns. Necessarily, this brings us to a few final observations about focus and structure. What do we mean when we speak of an Anglo-American political tradition? Much scholarship has already sought to identify the American and British political traditions. For example, the British political tradition is often seen as resting primarily on a set of nineteenth-century ideas centred on particular appreciations of governance and democracy, which draws on a rich history embracing romanticized views of Anglo-Saxon democracy, the Magna Carta and the Bill of Rights. A.H. Birch's *Representative and Responsible Government*[23] advanced a view of this tradition as an aggregate of ideas of representation and responsibility that emphasizes accountability to Parliament, conservative notions of responsibility, and prudent leadership. The following year, Samuel Beer added collectivism to this debate, along with strong government and high levels of continuity.[24] For their part, Michael J. Oakeshott emphasized rationality in non-ideological pragmatism[25] and Jack Greenleaf the dominant and interacting ideas of collectivism and libertarianism.[26] The primary manifestation of these ideas is the so-called Westminster model of governance, organized around historical continuity – actual or constructed – and the principle of parliamentary sovereignty and evinced in an elitist form of top-down government.[27] However, the idea of a dominant British political tradition is still far from uncontested. Mark Bevir and R.A.W. Rhodes, for instance, argue the case for the importance of contested political traditions in understanding British politics.[28] Similarly, the health or otherwise of the Westminster model itself in Britain continues to divide opinion.[29] With regard to the American political tradition, a common starting point is Richard Hofstadter's *The American Political Tradition and the Men Who Made It*. It is unfortunate that Hofstadter's interests did not stretch to the significance of women in the American political tradition, an omission that has only recently begun to be amended by scholars such as Sue Davis and Lisa Pace Vetter.[30] Notwithstanding the importance of Hofstadter's omission, his characterization of the American way of political life still has value. He asserts a strong sense of continuity in core values, which can now be seen also to incorporate contributions by women, and he presents it as being founded on certain principles commonly regarded, consciously or subconsciously, as essential components of Americans' daily lives. As to what these might be, Hofstadter claims that there is consensus amongst competing traditions on the rights of property, a philosophy of economic individualism and the value of competition. For the political scientist Louis Hartz, this way of life is encapsulated in republicanism and liberalism, which constitute the dominant ideology of the United States.[31] Hartz goes so far as to claim that this tradition is uniquely American – a claim we have challenged elsewhere in favour of seeing commonalities in the American and British traditions.[32] Many component strands of American thought are evident in key eighteenth-century documents drafted as the US republic developed, including the Declaration of Independence, the Constitution, *The Federalist Papers* and the Bill of Rights. And this written part of the tradition is perhaps the United States' most significant departure from Britain. At the core of the tradition is the constitution and the practice of judicial review, which seeks to prevent laws being applied that contradict or are incompatible with the constitution. Nothing in Britain is comparable to judicial review, given the overriding principle of parliamentary sovereignty. But such differences do not, as this volume amply demonstrates, create a chasm that prevents dialogue, understanding and a cross-fertilization of ideas.

As with its British counterpart, the American political tradition has necessarily evolved over time. In recent years, for instance, US domestic politics have been marked by increasing tension between modern conservatism and liberalism. More controversially, some scholars have identified in the American political tradition darker strands of thought associated with liberalism and republicanism. Consider, for instance, what Rogers M. Smith has termed a political tradition of ascriptive inegalitarianism, whereby, from the colonial period through the Progressive Era, full US citizenship was denied to various populations on the grounds of race, ethnicity or gender.[33]

These notions of a distinctive American and British political tradition are important to our work, but they also lie at the opposite end of the analytic spectrum to our primary concern. Whereas they emphasize the national and the particular, we are concerned with ascertaining aspects of commonality, mutual learning and the transatlantic sharing of ideas and practices. In short, we need a richer understanding of political tradition. Cast in this light, it is important to appreciate first that political tradition is not necessarily state-centric. S.N. Eisenstadt, for instance, argued that:

Tradition can perhaps best be envisaged as the routine symbolisation of the models of social order and of the constellation of codes, the guidelines, which delineate the limits of the binding cultural order, of membership in it, and of its boundaries, which prescribe the 'proper' choices of goals and patterns of behaviour; it can also be seen as modes of evaluation as well as of the sanctioning and legitimation of the 'totality' of the cultural and social order, or any of its parts.[34]

Dig a little further into political tradition and it becomes apparent that it is a slippery concept, so much so that some have deemed the pursuit of an analytic definition worthless.[35] Fortunately for our purposes, it is sufficient to identify certain characteristics, functions and processes of political traditions, accepting as we do that these can be and are contested. Starting from first principles, the concept of 'tradition' derives from the Latin word *tradere*, meaning to transmit or hand over for safekeeping. In line with Eisenstadt, emphasis can therefore be placed on the content and/or the process of transmission that provides for political-cultural continuity. In addition, political traditions are seen as being broadly structured at mental, behavioural and institutional levels. Mamina Natalia Alekseevna, for instance, proposes the following. The mental level consists of political symbols, myths and stereotypes. These help to form the image of political reality and authority, as well as values and norms, which influence political behaviour. The behavioural level includes models of conduct and patterns of action, including political habits and rituals. Finally, the institutional level reflects historical features of interaction between branches of power and relations between a state and society.[36]

On reflection, one might feel that these latter-day theorists are not saying much more than might be generically teased out of Edmund Burke's writings on his conception of the organic state. For Burke, the good polity was one with unbroken continuity that developed organically over time. Here, organically refers to change that comes about in a piecemeal manner in response to problems and dysfunctionalities in society. Change is a bottom-up rather than a top-down process that adjusts politics and governmental practice in order to deal pragmatically with problems that arise. According to this understanding of politics, institutions are more than just functioning bureaucracies: they embody aspects of wisdom from the past that are transmitted institutionally to the present in the way that they manage affairs. Of course, Burke made assumptions about what we would see as being specific to a form of conservatism, for example his views on fallen man and the limits of rationality, and that order was the prerequisite for the establishment and enjoyment of legally granted civil rights. Nevertheless, strip those away and one is still left with the idea of continuity, of a dialogue or conversation about politics that addresses different and emerging problems, adjusting the political, economic and social landscapes over time. And such dialogues and conversations can take place between differing political doctrines, as well as within specific doctrines. However, clearly, there are limits to the differences that can be tolerated within a tradition. The idea of National Socialism, evident in Germany in the 1930s and 1940s, could not sit alongside liberalism within a single tradition. Furthermore, the idea of a revolutionary tradition seems oxymoronic. So, a political tradition is characterized by continuity and change, dialogue and conversations between and within different political doctrines, although these are bounded by certain limits, and it retains a familiar language, fundamental values and similar style that would enable one to travel back in time and still be understood. Our argument here is not only that someone who is British and someone who is American could travel back in time in their own respective traditions and grasp what was going on and feel more or less at home, but also that if they crossed over into each other's traditions, they would still feel the same. An anecdote recounted by an old friend and mentor, Warren Kimball, illustrates what we mean here. During a stopover at Heathrow with a group of other American historians after conferencing in the Soviet Union during the Cold War, one of his American colleagues, while refreshing himself, declared: 'It's good to be home!'

It is this broad appreciation of political tradition that we adopt in this book. This approach sets the book apart from some previous investigations of an Anglo-American political tradition based on narrower parameters of political thought.[37] More importantly, this appreciation is apposite for our particular objectives. We are not solely interested in identifying shared patterns of thought. Rather, we also seek insight into how that thought is transmitted and operationalized consciously and subconsciously through ideas and habits of organization and co-operation.

Organization and Chapter Overview

The structure and contributions to this book are determined by these research questions and our reading of political tradition. Of course, no single text can comprehensively examine all aspects of Anglo-American political ideas, which is significant in itself. Consequently, our approach has been to sample the transatlantic transmission of ideas by including carefully selected and commissioned chapters organized around three themes: political philosophy, institutions – broadly defined – and representations of an Anglo-American political tradition. The first section comprises four chapters, the first two of which are dedicated to demonstrating the continuity of the changing American republic as it came into being and gradually developed. Kristin

Cook begins by identifying features of the bonds that were preserved through revolution and those that were lost in the act of political severance. She interrogates how it is that the political bands were severed, while the tradition remained. Drawing upon a wide range of transatlantic pamphlets, memoirs and accounts, she demonstrates how undercurrents of sensibility, security and statecraft persisted and ensured an enduring relationship. In so doing, she assigns particular significance to the language of correspondence that frames the final 1783 Treaty of Peace (Paris).

Gavin Bailey then examines the legacies of two British thinkers who both had an important and long-lasting impact on what was to become the United States: Thomas Paine and Edmund Burke. In his intricate account of the interplay between the radicalism of Paine and the conservatism of Burke, Bailey demonstrates how Paine's radicalism was tempered by the Burkean embedding of exceptionalism and constitutional power in custom, alongside the evolution of a complementary continuum of Anglo-American shared ideals and national co-operation that would have dismayed Paine.

Alan P. Dobson and Reed Davis develop the reciprocal impact of ideas further in their analyses of two of the most important underlying political ideologies in both countries, namely liberalism and conservatism. They consider probably the most continuous and robust conversations within and between doctrines shared by Britain and the United States, exemplifying in the process how political traditions can tolerate highly divergent political narratives and values. Dobson even goes so far as to claim that it is liberalism that does more than any other doctrine to set the agenda in both countries: you are either seduced by liberalism or react against it. From John Locke to Ronald Dworkin and A.C. Grayling, he traces how the Liberal agenda has developed and interacted across the Atlantic, producing an ongoing dialogue that interrogates the notion of freedom, the legitimate scope of government, how to reconcile the individual and the community, and the difficulties faced by government in a multicultural society of individuals who struggle to find a sense of collectivism from which authority can issue for concerted government action. Davis sets out to plumb the depths of Anglo-American conservatism in order to determine in what ways, if any, Anglo-American conservatisms have come to be alike. Comparing Edmund Burke and Russell Kirk and considering important strands of libertarianism, neo-conservatism and contemporary conservative populism, he highlights interesting parallels and an intersecting of ideas.

The second section of the book consists of three chapters that explore the institutions of slavery, empire and international law. In doing so, it engages with two ephemeral issues and what one imagined until recently would be and may still turn out to be a permanent issue. One of the huge, puzzling anomalies of history is the question of how slavery and imperialism could coexist in societies that espoused the values of liberalism. In the end, they could not and maybe that speaks to our contention that while different political doctrines can coexist in a political tradition, there are limitations to what one can embrace and survive. Slavery clearly falls into the irreconcilable category and eventually prevailing values led to its demise, but how this came about and how each nation conceived of the process says much about the interactions between them. David Ryan makes a similar argument about the anomaly of imperialism; the Anglo-American political tradition and the associated philosophical ideas coexisted with the systemic engagement with imperialism that denied, limited and subverted these ideas elsewhere in the world. It is difficult to determine the extent to which the former relied on the latter; American freedom was very much predicated on various forms of expansion. At the heart of the US Anti-Imperial League was the charge that such expansion subverted US values. But one suspects either the values of liberalism prevail and imperialism expires, or imperialism triumphs, liberalism withers away and the American political tradition changes into something radically different. This would be an existential threat to the Anglo-American political tradition, unless Britain, perhaps carried along by the United States, travelled the same route.

In their examination of slavery, Clive Webb and David Brown explain how the two countries challenged one another by each claiming that their own political culture better embodied the ideals of democracy and individual liberty. This is a story of clashing perspectives, though it is centred on issues that loomed large in each society and that prima facie seemed incompatible with democracy. Not surprisingly, they accused each other of hypocrisy. Americans criticized the British for opposing slavery while continuing to assert their imperial dominance over other nations. Conversely, the British attempted to claim the moral high ground by contrasting the supposed benevolence of empire with the barbarism of slavery in the American South. Each country therefore acted as a foil for the other as they competed to assert their moral and political superiority. Webb and Brown's exploration of slavery concludes by showing how the rise of racial Anglo-Saxonism in the late nineteenth century did as much to divide the two nations as it did to unite them.

David Ryan takes up the institution of empire, touched on by Webb and Brown, and explores the similarities and differences between American and British conceptions of empire. He examines the place of empire in both cultures, from denial to acknowledgement to nostalgia, and considers the thinking within the British and American spheres on empire, formal and informal, on civilization and conceptions of barbarism, on progress and order, and on the justifications of and opposition to empire.

David Clinton turns to the broader issue of international law and institutions and identifies three important features that Britain and the United

States seem to have in common, which, as he effectively demonstrates, are not wholly compatible. First, what Arnold Wolfers called the difference between a Continental emphasis on the necessity of the state and an Anglo-American foregrounding of debate about the best way of applying accepted principles of morality to the field of foreign policy. Second, a heightened emphasis on international freedom of action and a corresponding disinclination to subject national decision-making to supranational control. And third, the attitudes towards international law developed by both countries on the basis of being great powers. Taken together, the result has been a sharing of legal tradition that is quite distinctive in nature.

The final section deals with concepts of identity: namely Anglo-Saxonism, the Anglosphere and the special relationship. The first two are obviously close-ly connected. The racial aspect of Anglo-Saxonism is carefully catalogued by Robert Hendershot through an assessment of the evolving applications of the concept, particularly during and after the Great Rapprochement at the end of the nineteenth century. He reveals how the intersections of nationalism, racism, progressivism and exceptionalism culminated in a unique Anglo-American alliance during the First World War. And while the emphasis on such racial language waned in the mid- and late twentieth century, its leg-acy endures. David Haglund explains how time mellowed hostile American conceptions of the British as 'the other' and then, in the bitterly contested years of American neutrality (1914–17), a national identity crisis pitted Eng-lish-Americans against German and Irish Americans. The outcome of this clash of civilizations was the emergence of a widespread identification with inheritances from Britain, which was critical for the eventual emergence of the Anglo-American special relationship, buttressed by what we now refer to as the Anglosphere. However, as he also demonstrates, that Anglosphere is now under threat and may be coming to an end as a result of the damage done during the presidency of Donald Trump. Finally, in his chapter, Steve Marsh considers bilateral Anglo-American summit meetings between prime ministers and presidents to explore the importance of political tradition to the special relationship. First, he examines the discursive construction of the special relationship itself through textual analysis of speeches and commen-tary around certain summits. Second, he analyses how political traditions are used to justify the special relationship 'in action'. Particular attention is paid to selected wartime summits.

The combined impact of this scholarship strongly suggests that the Anglo-American special relationship is one of deeply embedded ways of thinking, understanding and values. These are at the heart, or indeed are the heart, of the relationship. They conjure up an understanding of the highways and by-ways of practice that is lacking in many studies on power and interest and even the immediate reasoning that prompts action. Our understanding of political actions, be they in the economic, social, cultural or defence domain, is given more nuance through a better appreciation of the basis from which political leaders and officials arrive at the decisions they make. Taken together, these chapters do more than complement an understanding of shared security, economic and political interests; they demonstrate the means by which such interests are formulated, articulated and promoted.

Alan P. Dobson, currently Honorary Professor at Swansea University, has held Chairs at Dundee University and St Andrews (honorary) and fellowships at the Norwegian Nobel Institute, Saint Bonaventure University (Lenna), where he held a senior research fellowship, and Baylor University (Fulbright). He has written extensively on Anglo-American relations, international civil aviation and the Cold War strategic embargo. His most recent book is *A History of International Civil Aviation* (Routledge, 2017). He is currently working on a book about the United States, Britain and Canada at the Chicago International Civil Aviation Conference 1944. In 2014, he won the Virginia Military Institute's Adams Centre annual Cold War Essay prize. He founded the Transatlantic Studies Association in 2002 and chaired it until 2013 and is editor of both the *Journal of Transatlantic Studies*, which he founded in 2003, and the *International History Review*.

Steve Marsh is Reader in International Politics at Cardiff University, United Kingdom. His principal research interests lie in post-Second World War international politics, with a particular focus on American foreign policy and Anglo-American relations. His latest book, co-edited with Robert M. Hendershot, is *Culture Matters: Anglo-American Relations and the Intangibles of Specialness* (Manchester University Press, 2020).

Notes

1. See chapter 1 by Kristin A. Cook.

2. Bodleian Library, MS Wilson, 1263, Transcript of Prime Minister's Q&A session at the National Press Club Luncheon, 31 January 1975.

3. Louis Hartz, *The Liberal Tradition in America* (New York: Harcourt, Brace & World, Inc., 1955).

4. Cf. Alan Dobson and Steve Marsh (eds), *Churchill and the Anglo-American Special Relationship* (London: Routledge, 2016).

5. See, for instance, Alison Holmes, 'Transatlantic Diplomacy and "Global" States', in Alan Dobson and Steve Marsh (eds), *Anglo-American Relations: Contemporary Perspectives* (London: Routledge, 2013), 105–28.

6. Henry Kissinger, 'Reflections on a Partnership: British and American Attitudes to Postwar Foreign Policy', 10 May 1982, available at https://larouchepub.com/other/2002/2901_kissinger.html.

7. Hans J. Morgenthau, *Politics Among Nations: The Struggle for Power and Peace*, 5th edn (New York: Alfred A. Knopf, 1973), 6–7.

8. Kenneth N. Waltz, *Man, the State, and War: A Theoretical Analysis* (New York: Columbia University Press, 1959).

9. John J. Mearsheimer, 'Structural Realism', in Tim Dunne, Milja Kurki and Steve Smith (eds), *International Relations Theories: Discipline and Diversity*, 2nd edn (Oxford: Oxford University Press, 2010), 79–80.

10. Christopher Thorne, *Allies of a Kind: The United States, Britain and the War against Japan* (London: Hamish Hamilton, 1979); C.J. Bartlett, *The Special Relationship: A Political History of Anglo-American Relations since 1945* (London: Longman, 1992); John W. Dumbrell, *A Special Relationship: Anglo-American Relations in the Cold War and After* (London: Macmillan, 2001) and 2nd edn, *A Special Relationship: Anglo-American Relations from the Cold War to Iraq* (London: Palgrave Macmillan, 2006); John Baylis, *Anglo-American Defence Relations 1939–1984* (London: Macmillan, 1984); Ian Clark, *Nuclear Diplomacy and the Special Relationship: Britain's Deterrent and America, 1957–1962* (Oxford: Oxford University Press, 1994); Jonathan Colman, *A 'Special Relationship'? Harold Wilson, Lyndon B. Johnson and Anglo-American Relations 'at the Summit', 1964–1968* (Manchester: Manchester University Press, 2004); Sylvia Ellis, *Britain, America, and the Vietnam War* (Westport, CT: Praeger, 2004); Nigel Ashton, *Kennedy, Macmillan and the Cold War: The Irony of Interdependence* (Basingstoke: Palgrave 2002); James Ellison, *The United States, Britain and the Transatlantic Crisis: Rising to the Gaullist Challenge, 1963–68* (Basingstoke, Palgrave, 2007); David Reynolds, 'A "Special Relationship"? America, Britain and the International Order Since the Second World War', *International Affairs* 62(i) (Winter 1985/86), 1–20, and 'Roosevelt, Churchill, and the Wartime Anglo-American Alliance, 1939–1945: Towards a New Synthesis', in Hedley Bull and William Roger Louis (eds), *The Special Relationship: Anglo-American Relations Since 1945* (Oxford: Clarendon Press, 1986), 17–43.

11. Bartlett, *Special Relationship*, 2.

12. Richard Ned Lebow, 'Classical Realism', in Dunne et al., *International Relations Theories* (Oxford: Oxford University Press, 2016), 59.

13. The English School of IR also comes to mind, with scholars such as C.A.W. Manning, Hedley Bull, Herbert Butterfield and Martin Wight trying to bridge the divide between realism and idealism/liberalism. See, for example, Hedley Bull, *The Anarchical Society: A Study of Order in World Politics* (London: Macmillan, 1977).

14. Akira Iriye, 'Culture and Power: International Relations as Intercultural Relations,' *Diplomatic History* 3(2) (1979), 116–18; Thomas Field, 'Transnationalism Meets Empire', *Diplomatic History* 42(2) (2018), 305–34, at 306.

15. Alexander Wendt, *Social Theory of International Politics* (Cambridge: Cambridge University Press, 1999), 21, 60, 371; Thomas Zeiler, 'The Diplomatic History Bandwagon: A State of the Field', *Journal of American History* 95(4) (2009), 1053–73.

16. See Martin Hollis and Steve Smith, *Explaining and Understanding International Relations* (Oxford: Clarendon Press, 1991), 3, and Alan P. Dobson and Steve Marsh (eds), *Anglo-American Relations: Contemporary Perspectives* (London: Routledge, 2013), 5–8.

17. 'Bermuda 2' – Air Services Agreement Between the Government of the United States of America and the Government of Great Britain and Northern Ireland, including amendments through 1980, Annex 7, *London Airports*, 69. Copy courtesy of US Department of Transportation. The 1980 amendments are often referred to as Bermuda 2.5.

18. Author interview with Paul Wisgerhof, Director, Office of Aviation Negotiations, US State Department, Washington, DC, 4 April 1991.

19. Author interview with Cyril Murphy, Vice President for International Affairs, United Airlines, Chicago, 1 July 1991.

20. Alan P. Dobson, *Peaceful Air Warfare: The United States, Britain and the Politics of International Aviation* (Oxford: Clarendon, 1991), 173–211.

21. Author interview with Paul Gretch, Director of Office of International Aviation, US Department of Transportation, 4 April 1991.

22. C.A.W. Manning, *The Nature of International Society* (London: Bell and Sons, 1962), 123.

23. A.H. Birch, *Representative and Responsible Government* (London: Unwin, 1964).

24. Samuel Beer, *Modern British Politics* (London: Faber and Faber, 1965).

25. Michael J. Oakeshott, *Rationalism in Politics and Other Essays* (Indianapolis, IN: Liberty Fund, 1991).

26. W.H. Greenleaf, *The British Political Tradition: The Rise of Collectivism*, vol. I (London: Methuen, 1983(; W.H. Greenleaf, *The British Political Tradition: The Ideological Heritage*, vol. II (London: Methuen, 1983); W.H. Greenleaf, *The British Political Tradition: A Much Governed Nation*, vol. III (London: Methuen, 1987).

27. R.A.W. Rhodes, *Understanding Governance: Policy Networks, Governance, Reflexivity and Accountability*, Public Policy and Management (Philadelphia, PA: US Open University, 1997).

28. Mark Bevir and R.A.W. Rhodes, *Interpreting British Governance* (London: Routledge, 2003); Mark Bevir and R.A.W. Rhodes, *Governance Narratives* (London: Routledge, 2006). See also M. Hall, *Political Traditions and UK Politics* (Basingstoke: Palgrave Macmillan, 2011).

29. See, for instance, Jeremy Richardson, 'The Changing British Policy Style: From Governance to Government?', *British Politics* 13(2) (June 2018), 215–233; Special Issue of *Governance* 29(4) (2016), 467–571.

30. Sue Davis, *The Political Thought of Elizabeth Stanton: Women's Rights and the American Political Traditions* (New York: New York University Press, 2008); Lisa Page Vetter, *The Political Thought of America's Founding Feminists* (New York: New York University Press, 2017).

31. Hartz, *The Liberal Tradition in America*.

32. See, in particular, Alan P. Dobson, 'Anglo-American Political Culture', in Robert Hendershot and Steve Marsh (eds), *Culture Matters: Anglo-American Relations and the Intangibles of 'Specialness'* (Manchester: Manchester University Press, 2020), 108–30.

33. Rogers M. Smith, *Civic Ideals: Conflicting Visions of Citizenship in U.S. History* (New Haven, CT: Yale University Press, 1999).

34. S.N. Eisenstadt, *Tradition, Change and Modernity* (New York: John Wiley, 1973), 139.

35. Stephen Eric Bronner, *Ideas in Action: Political Tradition in the Twentieth Century* (Lanham, MD: Rowman and Littlefield, 1999), 9.

36. Mamina Natalia Alekseevna, 'Political Traditions: The Concept and Structure', *Modern Research of Social Problems* 4 (2013), 366–80.

37. See, for instance, Lee Ward, *The Politics of Liberty in England and Revolutionary America* (Cambridge: Cambridge University Press, 2004).

Bibliography

Alekseevna, M.N. 'Political Traditions: The Concept and Structure', *Modern Research of Social Problems* 4 (2013), 366–80.

Ashton, N. *Kennedy, Macmillan and the Cold War: The Irony of Interdependence*. Basingstoke: Palgrave 2002.

Bartlett, C.J. *The Special Relationship: A Political History of Anglo-American Relations since 1945*. London: Longman, 1992.

Baylis, J. *Anglo-American Defence Relations 1939–1984*. London: Macmillan, 1984.

Beer, S. *Modern British Politics*. London: Faber and Faber, 1965.

Bevir, M., and R.A.W. Rhodes. *Governance Narratives*. London: Routledge, 2006.

_____. Interpreting British Governance. London: Routledge, 2003.

Birch, A.H. *Representative and Responsible Government*. London: Unwin, 1964.

Bronner, S.E. *Ideas in Action: Political Tradition in the Twentieth Century*. Lanham, MD: Rowman and Littlefield, 1999.

Bull, H. *The Anarchical Society: A Study of Order in World Politics*. London: Macmillan, 1977.

Clark, I. *Nuclear Diplomacy and the Special Relationship: Britain's Deterrent and America, 1957–1962*. Oxford: Oxford University Press, 1994.

Colman, J. *A 'Special Relationship'? Harold Wilson, Lyndon B. Johnson and Anglo-American Relations 'at the Summit', 1964–1968*. Manchester: Manchester University Press, 2004.

Davis, S. *The Political Thought of Elizabeth Stanton: Women's Rights and the American Political Traditions*. New York: New York University Press, 2008.

Dobson, A.P. 'Anglo-American Political Culture', in Robert Hendershot and Steve Marsh (eds), *Culture Matters: Anglo-American Relations and the Intangibles of 'Specialness'*. Manchester: Manchester University Press, 2020, 108–30.

_____. Peaceful Air Warfare: The United States, Britain and the Politics of International Aviation. Oxford: Clarendon, 1991.

Dobson, A.P., and S. Marsh (eds). *Anglo-American Relations: Contemporary Perspectives*. London: Routledge, 2013.

_____. Churchill and the Anglo-American Special Relationship. London: Routledge, 2016.

Dumbrell, J.W. *A Special Relationship: Anglo-American Relations in the Cold War and After*. London: Macmillan, 2001, and 2nd edn: *A Special Relationship: Anglo-American Relations from the Cold War to Iraq*. London: Palgrave Macmillan, 2006.

Eisenstadt, S.N. *Tradition, Change and Modernity*. New York: John Wiley, 1973.

Ellis, S. *Britain, America, and the Vietnam War*. Westport, CT: Praeger, 2004.

Ellison, J. *The United States, Britain and the Transatlantic Crisis: Rising to the Gaullist Challenge, 1963–68*. Basingstoke: Palgrave, 2007.

Field, T. 'Transnationalism Meets Empire', *Diplomatic History* 42(2) (2018), 305–34.

Greenleaf, W.H. *The British Political Tradition*, 3 vols. London: Methuen, 1983 and 1987.

Hall, M. *Political Traditions and UK Politics*. Basingstoke: Palgrave Macmillan, 2011.

Hartz, L. *The Liberal Tradition in America*. New York: Harcourt, Brace & World, Inc., 1955.

Hofstadter, R. *The American Political Tradition and the Men Who Made It*. New York: Vintage Books, 1948.

Hollis, M., and S. Smith. *Explaining and Understanding International Relations*. Oxford: Clarendon Press, 1991

Holmes, A. 'Transatlantic Diplomacy and "Global" States', in A.P. Dobson and S. Marsh (eds), *Anglo-American Relations: Contemporary Perspectives*. London: Routledge, 2013, 105–28.

Iriye, A. 'Culture and Power: International Relations as Intercultural Relations', *Diplomatic History* 3(2) (1979), 116–18.

Lebow, R.N. 'Classical Realism', in T. Dunne et al., *International Relations Theories*. Oxford: Oxford University Press, 2016, 58–77.

Manning, C.A.W. *The Nature of International Society*. London: Bell and Sons, 1962.

Mearsheimer, John J. 'Structural Realism', in T. Dunne, M. Kurki and S. Smith (eds), *International Relations Theories: Discipline and Diversity*. 2nd edn. Oxford: Oxford University Press, 2010, 79–80.

Morgenthau, Hans J. *Politics among Nations: The Struggle for Power and Peace*. 5th edn. New York: Alfred A. Knopf, 1973.

Oakeshott, M.J. *Rationalism in Politics and Other Essays*. Indianapolis, IN: Liberty Fund, 1991.

Reynolds, D. 'A "Special Relationship"? America, Britain and the International Order since the Second World War', *International Affairs* 62(i) (Winter 1985/86), 1–20.

_____. 'Roosevelt, Churchill, and the Wartime Anglo-American Alliance, 1939–1945: Towards a New Synthesis', in H. Bull and W.R. Louis (eds), The Special Relationship: Anglo-American Relations Since 1945. Oxford: Clarendon Press, 1986, 17–43.

Rhodes, R.A.W. *Understanding Governance: Policy Networks, Governance, Reflexivity and Accountability*. Public Policy and Management. Philadelphia, PA: US Open University, 1997.

Richardson, J. 'The Changing British Policy Style: From Governance to Government?', *British Politics* 13(2) (June 2018), 215–233. Also in special Issue of *Governance* 29(4) (2016), 467–571.

Smith, R.M. *Civic Ideals: Conflicting Visions of Citizenship in U.S. History*. New Haven, CT: Yale University Press, 1999.

Thorne, C. *Allies of a Kind: The United States, Britain and the War against Japan*. London: Hamish Hamilton, 1979.

Vetter, L.P. *The Political Thought of America's Founding Feminists*. New York: New York University Press, 2017.

Waltz, K.M. *Man, the State, and War: A Theoretical Analysis*. New York: Columbia University Press, 1959.

Ward, L. *The Politics of Liberty in England and Revolutionary America*. Cambridge: Cambridge University Press, 2004.

Wendt, A. *Social Theory of International Politics*. Cambridge: Cambridge University Press, 1999.

Zeiler, T. 'The Diplomatic History Bandwagon: A State of the Field', *Journal of American History* 95(4) (2009), 1053–73.

PART I

Origins

Chapter 1

'This Golden Band'

A Heritage of Anglo-American Correspondence

Kristin A. Cook

Were I a man of fortune, I would offer a gold medal, to the man who should produce the most instances of the friendship of Great Britain towards this country from 1600 to 1813.

—John Adams, Letter to Thomas McKean, Quincy, 31 August 1813

Is all this to be at an end? Is this golden band of kindred sympathies, so rare between nations, to be broken forever? Perhaps it is for the best; it may dispel an illusion called the John Adams Cantos … But it is hard to give up the kindred tie!

—Washington Irving, 'English Writers on America', 1820

At the beginning of the Second World War, Ezra Pound wrote a sequence of ten poems called the John Adams Cantos, numbered LXII to LXXI within a larger project of 'documentary poetics'.[1] Composed in some haste from 1938 to 1939, the Adams Cantos marked Pound's profound and laboured attempt to understand well-ordered government and reflected his struggle to condense political chaos into narrative unity and order.[2] Writing of early Atlantic statesmen such as Thomas Jefferson and John Adams, Edward Bancroft and Sir Edward Coke, Pound used modernist verse to put American history through its paces, testing the limits of eighteenth-century democracy, documentary insight and narrative succession.[3] Building upon epistolary fragments and snippets of his college notes on colonial history, the poems erect a dense textual edifice and cultural obelisk that occupies a central position in the overall activity of Pound's corpus.[4]

Tearing a page from John Adams's 1813 correspondence with moderate politician Thomas McKean, cited in the epigraph above, Pound's concluding 'Canto LXXI' closes the sequence by capturing Adams's post-revolutionary call to record the 'native' political history.[5] In so doing, Pound reveals a long-running historiographical debate over the reality and substance of British-American friendship.[6] Through this fragment of transatlantic writing, Pound deploys the history of the letter itself to signify a fractured Anglo-American exchange. And from such material he activates 'a still workable dynamo', as it were, for the wartime living.[7] As David Ten Eyck observes of Pound's work, 'The material record upon which knowledge of the past depends does not simply serve a memorial function'.[8] It is not (quoting Pound) 'merely something lost in dim retrospect, a tombstone, tastily carved, whereon to shed dry tears or upon which to lay a few withered violets'.[9] Rather, his use of transatlantic history offers 'possibilities of revival, starting perhaps with a valorisation of our cultural heritage'.[10] Looking to the written record as fertile ground for discussing Anglo-American heritage, this chapter identifies key features of British-colonial friendship that troubled and turned the course of revolution. In so doing, it explores related undercurrents of sensibility, security and statecraft that surfaced through the act of political severance. Showing that 'shared values' somehow survived this pivotal juncture, this study transposes Pound to ask: how is it that the political bands were severed, while a 'workable' tradition remained? Where within the shared 'material record' do we yet perceive rhetorical and discursive patterns of friendship and union that date back to the colonial pre-war period? And what does this signify? Drawing upon a wide range of transatlantic pamphlets, memoirs and accounts, I perform close literary analyses to demonstrate the significance of these themes to our understanding of Anglo-American cultural and political life. Moreover, I use eighteenth-century tools of sympathetic discourse to explore complex operations of friendship and reciprocity transmitted through political exchange. In this manner, I foreground a heritage of British-American amity as the *political art of correspondence*, suggesting that, although fractured in space and form, as in Pound's poetry, the substance of an amicable 'illusion' nevertheless finds continuity and special prepossession in enduring ties of good government.[11]

In the following discussion, I will argue that the end-of-war Treaty of Peace (Paris) between Britain and America, signed in 1783 and ratified by the Continental Congress in 1784, sanctioned more than political severance or independent constitutionalism. Rather, it pronounced a new domestic covenant of trust that would inform real cords of alliance down to the present.[12] While Winston Churchill might have repackaged the deal post-1945, building new muscle around Anglo-American unity and defence, the origins of this trust go back much further. I herein suggest that the sinews of enduring relations must be interpreted in light of the post-revolutionary 'Peace' and with respect to a written record of sociopolitical interactions and literary instruments forged within the crucible of independence. These indicate the resilience and robustness of enduring common values and cultural norms. The current discussion will thus explore the following: eighteenth-century 'correspondence' as a vehicle of political ideation; the sympathetic imagination as a cultural mediator across transatlantic identity channels; and the cultivation of an overlapping heritage space as a cultural consequence of the ensuing accord, preserving a political arena for future Anglo-American amity, growth and consensus. In discussing the last of these themes, I make an interpretive return to Pound, whilst adapting John Rawls's notion of 'overlapping consensus' and Martha Nussbaum's fine discussion of political emotions in the history of liberalism.[13]

In assessing a range of kindred transmissions, this chapter will serve as a foundational study for the present volume, whilst orientating itself to address issues of myth-making, remembrance and identity raised in an earlier collection published by the editors, *Churchill and the Anglo-American Special Relationship* (2017) – here drawing discussions of the special relationship between Britain and America back to interpretive features of Enlightenment thought and revolutionary/new national co-ordinates.[14] As the reader will see, I approach the legacy of fellowship between the two nations as less a matter of geopolitical strategy and more akin to J.M. Barrie's storied game of shadows, invented in the interplay between the youthful Peter Pan and his severed sense of self: where an *idea* of shared identity is foremost; where *imagination* is central; and where any *re-pair*ed material continuity must be ever darned at the toe. 'If he [Peter] thought at all', or so the story goes, '… it was that he and his [severed] shadow, when brought near each other, would join like drops of water, and when they did not he was appalled. … Fortunately [Wendy] knew at once what to do. "It must be sewn on," she said … and [she] sewed the shadow on to Peter's foot.'[15]

Shared Identity and Severance: 'Wounded Thro' a Thousand Pores'

To understand the legacy of Anglo-American correspondence, we might as well begin with Rip Van Winkle, who, after waking from a twenty-year slumber in the Kaatskills, strides unknowing and unknown into 'the election' and finds himself a stranger to the republic.[16] 'Does nobody know poor Rip Van Winkle?', Rip cries, seeking sound intelligence.[17] 'Alas! Gentlemen', he implores, 'I am a poor, quiet man, a native of the place, and a loyal subject of the king, God bless him!' Whereon a general outcry besets the 'tavern

politicians' –'A tory! A tory! A spy! A refugee! Hustle him! Away with him!' –
until new order is restored.[18] At this point, Rip, a man now woefully dazzled
out of his time, is enjoined to share his tale with the tribe. He soon undertakes
the telling and is corroborated by an 'ancient inhabitant of the village', through
whom we feel the power of an 'ancient legend' rising to transmit its account.[19]
To quote Rudyard Kipling in later years, 'Then there arose – according to
the story – a masterless man, one who had taken no part in the action of his
fellow, who had no special virtues, but who was afflicted – that is the phrase –
with the magic of the necessary word.'[20] The facts being thus secured, the
election subsequently resumes and '*Rest in Peace*' (Rip) wanders forth from the
mountains, bearing his tale into new political life.

So where does Rip's tale take us? In Washington Irving's nineteenth-century short story, our attention is first drawn to the garish split in colonial self-
identity – and from there to a logical transference of the old known self from
one political reality into the next, via mythical cords of 'family resemblance'
and consanguinity.[21] Rip's character emerges as a loyal subject of King George
III, the old rifle still fitted to his shoulder, only to be suddenly metamorphosed
into a near democratic relation. And this not by political art only (as with the
tavern sign that is magically transformed to represent General George Washington instead of King George), but by correspondence in *type*, his erstwhile
character evolving to meet now independent progeny and likewise accumulat-
ing their new world of hereditary interests.[22] It would seem that by sleeping
through the revolution, Rip has literally drifted into his ideal form of self-
governance: he gains all the liberal rights of liberty, without ever surrendering
the old stock. Poking fun perhaps at John Locke's observation that '[p]eople
are not easily got out of their old Forms', Irving here demonstrates, by sheer
sleight of hand, that it might be quite 'an easie thing to get them changed', or
to propel folks to 'quit their old Constitutions': simply create a new dramatic
unity.[23] Constitutional crises, after all, are an art of the pen.[24] And the result
for Rip is a newly doubled character. 'As to Rip's son and heir', Irving writes,
'who was the ditto of himself, seen leaning against the tree, he was employed
to work on the farm, but evinced a hereditary disposition to attend to anything
else but his business.'[25] Rip meanwhile 'took his place once more on the bench
of the inn door and was reverenced as one of the patriarchs … and a chronicle
of the old times "before the war"'.[26]

To appreciate the power of this symmetry, we turn first to an Enlightenment field of sensibilities underpinning early Atlantic fellowship.[27] For sur-
facing in Irving's short story is the calm Anglo-American pursuit of political
'mirroring', or the idea of 'good [political] representation' as a matter of practical proximity – philosophically realized through sympathetic resemblance as
a crucial imaginary for securing political vitality, fellow feeling and ongoing

relational exchange: a good correspondence.[28] According to eighteenth-century usage, a 'correspondence' indicates a 'relation of agreement, similarity, or analogy', and, perhaps most tellingly, 'the … *answering to each other in fitness or mutual adaptation*; congruity, harmony, agreement'.[29] While much has been said of the significance of eighteenth-century epistolary exchange in correspondence history, with fine attention being paid to the dissemination of political thought in print, my discussion prioritizes the *philosophical* attributes of correspondence that informed British-colonial exchange.[30] 'Correspondence' here entails a gradual progress of consensus that has, over time, generated what many now see as the prevailing Anglo-American myth. Although there is a rich history of correspondence theory, dating back to Aristotle, it is not my intention to unpick the nuances of ancient or early modern thought; rather, I will explore this singular progress of sympathetic agreement – or 'answering to each other' – that characterizes Anglo-American exchange. If we extrapolate from Charles Griswold's work on Adam Smith, then an idea of 'correspondence' in this sense reveals a deep transatlantic 'history of accommodations and claims to understanding, claims that come to be trustworthy only after standing up to repeated challenge in various contexts'.[31] Possessing both relational and dialogical qualities, a so-called 'good correspondence' is textured by a wide field of 'concordant responses', overlaying areas of potential strife with strategic norms of unity. Such an overlap secures a social and political alliance through real and imagined assurances of sound intelligence, mutual security and common progress through societal change.[32] All of this is seen in Irving's sketch. Weaving folklore into history, Irving's early American account is strangely shaped around a simple notion of a shared Anglo-American self-conception – a 'relation of similarity' being mysteriously held and secured within Rip's split constitutional frame.[33]

As we follow Rip's trail 'homeward' from the mountain – marking his transformation from a loyal subject of the crown to a free citizen of the state – we follow the path of natural man, as it were, journeying towards self-possession.[34] Rip is literally 'brought to a stand' at the foot of a powerful waterfall, searching the old familiar terrain for a now illusive stage of being.[35] When he finds that the old 'amphitheater' is gone and its mythical company dispersed, his constitutional advances him towards civilization, where he discovers his rightful place in political autonomy.[36] It is perhaps unsurprising that Rip's first act of self-representation is one of highly staged sympathetic mimicry, delivered from the outermost edge of a new American political order ('the skirts of the village'): '[the villagers] cast their eyes upon him [and] invariably stroked their chins. The constant recurrence of this gesture induced Rip, involuntarily, to do the same.'[37] Undergoing a then rapid stadial adaptation, Rip is drawn forth from the wilderness and propelled towards democratic freedom.[38] Yet even as he finds his 'precise counterpart' among near political neighbours (and security in their household commerce), his identity remains torn and allied to pre-war affections: 'Young Rip Van Winkle once – old Rip Van Winkle now!' he avers.[39] 'It is Rip Van Winkle – it is himself!' sounds the return.[40] As Rip strides towards self-determination, the illusion of an old-world continuity becomes increasingly apparent as a powerful and symptomatic doubling at the heart of his political transition.[41] And within his sensible form appears an intractable 'spirit of liberty' that takes its 'bias and direction' from England.[42]

In his 'Speech on the Conciliation with the American Colonies', delivered in 1775, political philosopher Edmund Burke makes some sense of this 'bias' by discerning common discursive ground in the revolutionary appeal to English passions, principles and appraisals.[43] The American 'love of liberty', Burke reminds Britons, has, 'as with you, fixed and attached on this specific point of taxing' and by 'jealous affection' has revealed a transatlantic fellowship with British political life.[44] 'The colonies draw from you, as with their life-blood', he asserts, 'these ideas and principles'.[45] Burke adds that such an ardent devotion to freedom coheres not around general liberties or abstract beliefs, but around specifically *English ideas* by right of *English descent* – and that from this heritage arises the public spirit that both fractures colonial governance (exposing imperial struggle as well as grassroots rebellion) and provokes long-lasting accord (inviting new Atlantic co-operation).[46] For 'your mode of governing them', he suggests, 'whether through lenity or indolence, through wisdom or mistake, *confirmed them in the imagination*, that they, as well as you, had an interest in these common principles'.[47] A lexicon of shared liberal values seeps through Burke's descant to bridge the political divide, conjoining Anglo-American interests in a review that recalls his earlier *Abridgment of English History* (1757). Grammars of jealousy, love and commonality here survey an 'ongoing process of [political] adjustment[s]', or alignments within British-colonial affairs – emplotting the search for 'mutual sympathy', or affective 'agreement', within long-running debates over political liberty and structural balance.[48] Steering the narrative towards shared ideological commitments, Burke's language of *'English descent'* strives towards principles of analogy in his struggle to decode the terms of revolutionary unrest, while at the same time refashioning the 'true temper of minds' towards future relational amity.[49]

To better understand Burke's art of political correspondence and to demonstrate how we might approach this eighteenth-century cultural and political discourse, it is worth turning our attention to the underpinning cult of sensibility, or the language of fellow feeling that then structured imperial bands.[50] For, by deploying an idea of heritable interests, Burke invites a relational concourse of emotional agreements and imaginative confirmations to create a 'stable structure of [political] concerns', to adopt Martha Nussbaum's phrase, between the centre and the periphery, thereby building a sense of imperial immediacy that would be conducive to transatlantic governance.[51] Political bonds of 'sentimental belonging' are used to define transatlantic political ideals. Moreover, they are artfully refigured to establish new relational proximities and to turn the remote Atlantic world into a governable space of 'civilizational' potential.[52] We see this not only in the political literature of Burke's day, but in a wide range of pre-independence pamphlets, educational texts and colonial writings. Such concerns are expressively drawn and tested, for instance, in a pair of little-known pre-independence sermons authored by two ministers in colonial British America. Produced in the winter of 1761, nearly fifteen years before Burke's speech, these were published together as a double eulogy, transmitting unifying ideals of transatlantic grief and imperial commitment.[53] As later seen in Burke's delivery, a strong rhetoric of English emotionalism – and 'jealous' consanguinity – likewise runs through these eulogia to contrive a felt unity in transatlantic political life.[54]

The publication opens with a memorial concerning the 'Life, Character and Death' of the Reverend Samuel Davies (a colonial minister and evangelist), as written by Presbyterian Minister David Bostwick.[55] In his heartfelt tribute, Bostwick uses strong emotive appeal to mourn the death of his friend and fellow Briton. 'As the following Discourse naturally calls the Tears of unfeigned Loyalty to flow from our Eyes', Bostwick laments, '... so the sudden unexpected DEATH of the worthy Author must add new Weight to our Affliction, and give a double Emphasis to all our Expressions of Grief'.[56] Bostwick's 'double Emphasis' then introduces Samuel Davies's final published work and turns out its character in the Reverend's own words, pronounced one month earlier to the student body at Princeton College: 'A Sermon Delivered at Nassau-Hall, January 14, 1761, On the Death of His Late Majesty King George II'.[57]

An eloquent exposition on King George II's life and reign, Davies's sermon critically reflects upon the virtues of modest rule. His meditation augments Bostwick's preface and through tearful expressions conveys deft rhetorical strategy, designed to arouse a practical political sympathy among congregants at the edge of empire.[58] Davies takes care to transport his audience, as it were, back to the beloved shores of England and once again into the triumph of an ardently felt and proximate political participation. Indulging in 'the swelling Tide of Grief', as Bostwick calls it, Davies pronounces a eulogy that is as much concerned with figures of the dead as it is with characters and characterizations of the living.[59] These figures are magnified as dual logics enlivening a uniform fiction – where the '*Hanover*-Family' shines forth as the locus of friendship and political trust.[60] Using sympathetic address, he 'confirms in the [colonial] imagination', à la Burke, a shared heritage of Anglo-American political accession.[61]

Functioning as a complex return to Davies's memorial, Bostwick's preface quickens a notion of cultural inter-permeation around colonial and British political ideals.[62] He emphasizes emotional acuity and moral judgement as co-dependent registers that together bind transatlantic fellows in a common sympathetic exchange. Commending Davies's talents, Bostwick uplifts his friend as a transatlantic ambassador of sound political sense:

> His Language was surpassingly beautiful and comprehensive, tending to make the most stupid Hearer sensibly feel, as well as clearly understand. Sublimity and Elegance, Plainness and Perspicuity, and all the Force and Energy that the Language of Mortals could convey, were the Ingredients of almost every Composition.[63]

In Davies's eulogy to King George II, this sensibility crafts its own imperial hermeneutics, where the sensible colonial subject is pictured as a loyal reflection of the Divine and characterized by habits of sincere reliance on the monarch. 'But notwithstanding this favourable and promising Posture of Affairs', Davies reflects, 'methinks we cannot make a Transition from Reign to Reign without some Suspence. We are passing into a new State of political Existence; entering a strange untried Period'.[64] While Davies admonishes his hearers to conform to an ongoing allegiance, it is telling that the practice of imperial submission still depends on an imaginary change of place with the person of the king himself – the adoption of his wishes and ways – and the continual imagining of oneself as a 'Fellow-Subject' with transatlantic brethren.[65] Such imagining secures the band of political subjugation. And in Davies's eulogy it likewise transmits a good correspondence – a sense of enduring cultural and political analogy – by interlacing 'felt' political sensibilities with otherwise 'disinterested' rights and claims. Transatlantic grief thus functions as a vehicle of 'Succession in the *Hanover*-Family'.[66] And through it, imperial sorrow is conveyed to English America as by means of a blood transfusion, where genealogical continuance is ensured by sheer force of sympathetic contagion: England mourns and so her colonies grieve.[67] Davies ultimately suggests that British colonials are predisposed to favour that which runs in their blood, conceiving them as long accustomed to practices of filial attachment and thus inclined – no matter 'Whatever Character [they] may hereafter sustain' – to behave in accordance with those affinities.[68]

As in Washington Irving's 'Rip Van Winkle', Davies too is playing with time in dramatizing his imperial resolve, here leveraging the power of a deep Anglo-Saxon sympathy to elicit a colonial change in political allegiance. By

eloquent sways his language manoeuvres loyal alignments and logical affections from the reign of King George II to the government of King George
III: 'While I invite you to drop your filial Tears over the sacred Dust of your
Common Father', Davies says, '... I cannot but congratulate you once more on
your being Coevals with George IIId'.[69] He urges fellow mourners to perform
the fitting friendship and stamps his tribute with concrete instructions for
demonstrating filial affection in practice: 'Civil society', he remarks, 'is [now]
to execute all [George III's] Patriot Designs'.[70] Engaging with this critically,
we find that a shared grammar of consanguinity performs its own tragedy
of mourning. It here rationalizes a strong kindred sense associated with the
transatlantic political imagining, whilst deriving legitimacy from 'a common
font of sentimental expression'.[71]

As Thomas Paine understands in his later political pamphlet, *Common Sense*
(1776), the trouble with such sentiment, however, is the mortality it conveys.
For there is an impassable gap between self and other (metropole and colony).
And over time, this weakens the sentimental exchange—yielding false imag-
inings, corrupted transmissions and failures in the sympathetic order. As was
understood in eighteenth-century philosophical and physiological discussions
of sympathetic consent, close bonds of proximity become the very channels
of mutual infirmity.[72] For Thomas Paine, the problem of distance signals this
reality.[73] Rather than inviting political stability, the transatlantic divide accen-
tuates tyranny, forecasting an increasingly ill correspondence and broken faith
in the unifying ideal.[74] Paine goes so far as to trace worsening British-colonial
symptoms through the time lag of real epistolary exchange, highlighting broken and delayed intelligence as clear proof of a failing 'common order'.[75] To
this end, the language of fellow feeling that once relayed imperial sorrow, as in
Davies's memorial, soon bears its own justifications for radical political severance. In his ideology of foreign relations, Paine invokes even the 'blood of the
slain' and 'the weeping voice of nature' to declare the fitting end of Britain's
political design: ''TIS TIME TO PART.'[76]

Indeed, it is at a revolutionary crossroads of ill-parting and severance that
Rip Van Winkle's own 'heart die[s] away' and where we find him politically
reborn only as he observes his kindred double – his corresponding self – as a
functioning post-war entity.[77] Behold! 'Rip looked and beheld a precise counterpart of himself as he went up the mountain', writes Irving.[78] Such was his
confusion that '[h]e doubted his own identity, and whether he was himself
or another man'.[79] At this point, he is confronted by local politicians and responds, somewhat trippingly, 'I'm not myself – I'm somebody else – that's me
yonder – no – that's somebody else got into my shoes', as self-representation
stumbles towards unity in a broken sympathetic exchange.[80] It is through the
eyes of this confused double agent that readers are left to ponder the fate of

Anglo-American securities. Irving's story rounds itself off with a simple scene of neighbourly repair, with the colonist-now-citizen Van Winkle left sitting 'once more on [a] bench', inhabiting the liminal space between constitutional interests.[81] Yet, as he takes his place in this duality his root character is left seemingly unchanged. Readers are again struck by the workings of an ancient sympathy taring the balance between liberty and authority, rights and toleration, freedom from the past and a longing for historical process.

In his critical *Reflections on Exile*, postcolonial scholar Edward Said offers a strikingly different lens through which to view Rip's seat on this political threshold.[82] While an eighteenth-century conjectural historian might take comfort in Rip's stadial path towards commerce, a postcolonialist today might wonder at the smooth nature of his post-war delivery. For this domestic picture of 'settled liminality', if we can call it that, contains the full vacuum of the war itself. Through this scene, Irving authors a sharp critique of any so-called authentic history that belies the ravages of wartime estrangement. His winsome end runs counter to the zeal of Thomas Paine or the impassioned rhetoric of his contemporaries, in whose work British-colonial life is staged as an active 'intelligence between hearts' or 'the call of blood' between metropole and colony: 'the colonies draw from you, as with their life-blood', declared Burke, and in governance they share your 'pulse'.[83] Such language registered the profound psychological and even corporeal damage done to the joined body politic and the injuries sustained through political separation: 'our affections [are] wounded', Paine writes, 'thro' a thousand pores'.[84] Although Rip carries such intelligence in his character (he is instinctively drawn homewards towards kin), he appears insensible to his own post-war displacement. In the end, the unity he conveys is a fiction that bears no wounds, no traumas and no costs, for 'the change of states and empires', as Irving writes, 'made but little impression on him'.[85] Balancing political severance and narrative continuity, Irving deploys the sympathetic imagination to conjecture a stable transatlantic history – an enduring correspondence – in the place of political fracture.

A Tenancy at Sufferance: 'Our Old Home'

So how does the theory of sympathy help us interpret this narrative progress? How does it help explain those confirmations of friendship that suggest lingering duty and dualism in the history of Anglo-American exchange? In short, it equips us to understand the role of the imagination in cultivating pre-independence and post-war political bonds. Read philosophically, the 'sympathetic imagination' offers a vital contribution to the Anglo-American political tradition.[86] It not only mediates, as it were, between British and American interests to transmit shared values (as seen in the rhetoric of Davies and Burke), but in so doing it conjures a common rationale for the pursuit of political liberty and good government.[87]

In 1863, New England novelist and short story writer Nathaniel Hawthorne would ponder these concerns in a series of transatlantic vignettes entitled *Our Old Home: A Series of English Sketches*.[88] Read as both personal memoir and diplomatic account, Hawthorne's *Our Old Home* exercises the familiar language of colonial fellow feeling to explore nineteenth-century transatlantic interactions.[89] In particular, Hawthorne's 'Consular' sketch, which follows his 1853 appointment to the Consul at Liverpool, captures the dynamic interactivity of the 'sympathetic imagination' operating as a core imperative of postcolonial diplomatic affairs.[90] From his interactions with fellow Americans at the Consul to his conversations with local Britons, sympathetic discourse opens the diplomatic 'gateway between the Old World and the New', providing not only a moderative and moderating impulse in communications (striving towards transatlantic harmony), but 'the means through which [political] emotions are conveyed and understood'.[91] Hawthorne's writing illustrates the manner in which the sympathetic imagination 'rushes in', as Charles Griswold suggests, to fill narrative gaps in diplomatic progress, supplying that vital concourse of sentiments that underpins Anglo-American security, political mirroring, cultural analogy and consent.[92] Moreover, it provides the narrative apparatus whereby 'hereditary sympathies' are explored and common values trafficked.[93] As with Davies a century before, Hawthorne uses sympathetic invention to explore the functional capacities of British-American ties, using creative analogy to foster a sense of coeval or heritable bonds.

Dedicating his work 'To A Friend', Hawthorne opens a diplomatic window into the ever-deepening 'progress of [Anglo-American] acquaintance'.[94] This he depicts through two maps hanging on the consulate walls: 'a large map of the United States (as they were twenty years ago but seem little likely to be twenty years hence), and a similar one of Great Britain'.[95] It is significant that these are seen to correspond by virtue of their former likeness (similarly cut and framed), but are differentiated and pulled apart, in Hawthorne's view, by the sheer force of growth and dissolution: America must expand, Britain contract. It is the sympathetic imagination, as he relates, that moderates this growing divide. The power of sympathy narrows an ever-increasing sense of cultural and political distance (and disinterest) by accomplishing deft patterns of psychological interchange and reversal, such that distant actors are able to imaginatively 'enter into' new transatlantic understandings. Arguably, a shared heritage of Enlightenment idea-making and constitutional values makes such returns possible. Despite the weakening arm of distance, neighbourly bonds of 'good-will' are seen to conserve near friendship.[96]

As if to model this accord, Hawthorne goes so far as to shuffle himself into his own sympathetic capacities, demonstrating the sympathetic art that arises through Anglo-American diplomacy. In reflecting on his work as Consul ('– that figure whom they called a Consul –'), he recalls having been 'but a sort of Double Gauger' measuring incoming and outgoing interests, all the while 'in a state of suspended animation'.[97] Not unlike the fictional Rip before him, his 'figure' is ever caught up in the project of Anglo-American peace – striving to reconcile differences between Great Britain and the new United States. Moreover, in becoming '– ... a Consul –', he is tasked with the arch work of sympathetic exchange. Hawthorne pictures himself bridging the oceanic divide and arbitrating across transatlantic identity channels. And what is the result of such diplomacy? His own doubled character in the crossover.[98] As with Rip Van Winkle, his sense of unity is accomplished 'through some mysterious medium of transmitted ideas, [with which he remains] intimately acquainted'.[99] This is perhaps Hawthorne's most sophisticated take on the role of transatlantic sympathy. For in mediating his own dual identity, he adopts the role of an impartial diplomatic observer, holding sympathy at its balance whilst superintending Anglo-American claims.[100]

Throughout his *Old Home* series, Hawthorne returns again and again to resonant themes of Anglo-American doublings, dual interests and relational proximity. Britons advertise for 'lost heirs', he writes, and Americans respond with a 'diseased appetite for English soil'.[101] False pedigrees, lost inheritances and estates are clear proof, he suggests, of a 'peculiar insanity that lies deep in the Anglo-American heart'.[102] In a series of colourful anecdotes, Hawthorne reveals a heritage of fraught liberal values that perhaps marks the 'special' (i.e. the different from what is usual) of lasting Anglo-American relations. Ultimately, as both Hawthorne and Burke suggest, it is by 'confirmations of imagination' that Britons and Americans have maintained their political and affective place in one another's lives and it is through lasting rhetorical and sympathetic channels that each holds some ground in the other.[103]

The idea of an *affective sufferance*, or an *affective 'tenancy at sufferance'*, seems apt. It is arrived at here through the legal concept of an 'estate at sufferance', which harkens back to Anglo-Norman etymology and appears in William Blackstone's mid-eighteenth-century *Commentaries on the Laws of England*: 'An estate at sufferance, is where one comes into possession of land by lawful title, but keeps it afterwards without any title at all.'[104] By derivation, a 'tenancy at sufferance', as it is now called in US law, is 'not a true tenancy', but is rather 'created by a tenant wrongfully retaining possession of property'.[105] This might occur when, for whatever reason, a life estate or other form of tenancy ends and the legal right to retain possession of that estate is dissolved. The idea of continuing in possession without the right to do so or cherishing a false holding of an expired estate (a Rip Van Winkle effect?) might be usefully extended to encompass a wide constellation of mutual claims. To characterize Anglo-Americans today as *affective tenants at sufferance* captures the highly complex and sympathetic inter-positioning of Americans and Britons since the time of revolution: transatlantic bedfellows maintaining co-tenancy in lost interests; co-tenants of a foreign past.[106]

Such conflicted terms of Anglo-American power have been transmitted from the pre-independence period to the present. As Christopher Hitchens relates in *Blood, Class and Empire*, liberty's call to symbiosis is ever entangled with the 'discordant intimacies' of prepossession: love and hate, rivalry and collusion, expansionism and restraint.[107] This has fuelled a strident tug-of-war in continuing Anglo-American affairs whilst conserving one long-running sentimental conversation as the transatlantic project of the two, to be taken up, ignored, lost, found or redirected at will, with all the fractured continuity of an eighteenth-century epistolary exchange.

Re-pair: 'The Good Correspondence'

If there is anything prophetic to be discerned in 'the good correspondence and friendship' pronounced in the 1783 Treaty of Peace (Paris), then it might be found in the fact that British and American resolve has ever since been inclined, if not towards 'special' friendship in exceptional terms, then certainly towards – albeit ever wrestling with – this fundamental principle of likeness: 'Homeless on a foreign shore', as Hawthorne has written, 'haunted' in mind, and ever scanning that two-way horizon in search of the lost estate.[108] The 'durable treaty' of 1783, as Richard Morris has called it, highlights these unsettled terms of dual interest. The treaty is its own testimony, as Morris suggests, to Anglo-American ingenuity and triumph, enabling by rhetorical design (and a fair dose of chance) the future course of American expansionism, whilst preserving intact and in composition the core conduits of a good old-fashioned covenant of trust.[109] That a productive amity remained resilient through the early years of American growth, and even more so during the long nineteenth century, speaks to the illusive power of Irving's 'kindred sympathies' manipulating the face of politics.[110] This is perhaps best signified, as Morris proposes, in the mutual disarmament of the US–Canadian border, developed through the Rush–Bagot Treaty and later concluded in the Treaty of Washington in 1871.[111]

But what has made it 'workable'? What vital repair was at work then, and has travelled down to us since, to sustain this sense of Anglo-American duality? Should perpetuity stand the measure for future political progress (is the 'special relationship' fated to endure)? Or 'Is all this to be at an end?', as Irving once wrote, this 'rare band' between nations?[112] To answer these questions, as with Ezra Pound on the edge of war, we might return again to documentary patterns of union and friendship, to the written transatlantic record as the ever-binding thing that has both opened and secured a shared heritage space between British and American interests. As Pound suggests in his fractured poetics, the very survival of shared values and the cultivation of political correspondence have depended invariably upon a sort of literary 'deep time' magic: the enduring tale of the tribe.[113]

While designations of 'reciprocal', 'sincere' and 'constant' friendship are employed liberally across the major Treaties of Peace signed by Great Britain in 1783 and 1784 (with France, Spain, America and Holland, gathered together in Charles Jenkinson's *Collection*), the use of the term 'correspondence' is uniquely foregrounded in the peace with America.[114] And while one might infer that this merely distinguishes a lasting bond between the colonizer and her colony, and to some degree that would be true, when interpreted contextually and dialogically relative to pre-independence wrongs and the terms upon which American liberty is declared, this 'good correspondence' wields singular sociopolitical power. It admits a set of hotly debated tropes associated with British-American unity and reaffirms (even if it cannot yet fully repair) joined transatlantic thinking around 'civilizational' progress and security.[115] The substance of the treaty itself, after all, rests upon 'It having pleased the Divine Providence to dispose *the hearts* of … George the Third … and the United States of America, to forget all past misunderstandings and differences that have unhappily interrupted the good correspondence and friendship which they mutually wish to restore'.[116] In this construction, the virtue of diplomatic forgetting appears most lenient in its rhetorical imagining and is thereby most instructive: for while the Treaty of Peace ratifies Anglo-American political severance, it likewise catches at shadows in striving to 'pick up where we left off' – progressing along a path of natural prepossession.

Nowhere is this more apparent than in the area of shared intelligence.[117] While it is true that a 'good correspondence' here denotes the intimate concord of sympathetic relations and political representation so ardently discussed in pre-independence political literature – the determination to 'answer each other in fitness or mutual adaptation' – it at the same time infers, and in compositional form here privileges, a stable intercourse of open communications and knowledge exchange.[118] Such phraseology appears frequently in early eighteenth-century British treaties, largely with a view to facilitating transnational information gathering or commercial traffic. There is, for example, the 'good correspondence' mentioned in the *Convention on the El Assiento de los Negroes*, signed with King Philip V of Spain in 1716; the 'good correspondence and security' discussed in the *Treaty between Ulrica Eleonora, Queen of Sweden and George, King of Great Britain* in 1720, which contracts to mutually 'discover and bring to light all dangers, conspiracies and machinations of the enemy, as soon as they come to their knowledge'; or the 'good correspondence and sincere amity' set out in the *Treaty of Defensive Alliance, betwixt France, Spain, and Great Britain*, signed at Madrid on 13 June 1721.[119] Likewise, the later 1783 Treaty of Versailles with Spain expresses a desire in Article VI for future 'good correspondence [to] reign between the two nations' relative to common navigation of 'the rivers Wallis or Bellize, and Rio Hondo', thereby mapping co-ordinates of trade and security in shared districts of the Spanish continent.[120]

Notably, by comparison, the formal 1783 Treaty of Peace between Britain and America presumes that such a vital and interactive concourse has always existed and that it might be steadily improved and advanced on new postcolonial terms – deftly eliding the unhappiness of the 'interrupting' period.[121] Consequently, the treaty marks the end of wartime grievances, whilst resetting Anglo-American channels for the 'rapid dissemination of information'.[122] Although a common seventeenth- and eighteenth-century rhetorical mechanism, then, the idea of a 'good correspondence' here signals a vital intention to build practical avenues of material congruity into the 'restored' friendship of the final accord.[123]

Importantly, by eliding a wide field of wartime grievances, this language of friendship has the added effect of subverting an emerging 'correspondence' newly established in the interim period: that of the competing wartime alliance between the Thirteen Colonies and France. Indeed, the entire determination of the 1778 *Treaty of Friendship and Commerce* between Louis XVI and the Thirteen Colonies had contracted to establish 'good understanding and *perfect* correspondence' between France and America, pronouncing a litany of transactional resolves and 'sensible proof[s] of affection'.[124] Drawn up at a decisive juncture in the war, this, too, was hard won. The Franco-American agreement was secured only after multiple appeals by American colonials for European assistance and after strategic interventions by the Committee of Secret Correspondence in 1775.[125] The 1778 *Treaty of Alliance* with France, which built upon the above *Treaty of Friendship and Commerce*, thus took care to redirect 'means of strengthening those connections' for fear Great Britain would become hostile in resenting 'the good correspondence which [was] the object' of that treaty.[126] And France was right to worry. After all, its so-called 'perfect' footing with the colonies led directly to the 1781 Siege of Yorktown and Britain's revolutionary defeat – opening new corridors for Franco-American alliance. That the 1783 Treaty of Peace takes care to author a 'good correspondence and friendship' between Britain and America is thus significant.[127]

Such language registers the Anglo-French wartime intervention whilst inter-posing a redoubled Anglo-American continuity.

Since the War for Independence, this 'durable' peace, as it has been called by historians, has preserved a crucial transatlantic fellowship in British-Ameri-can life.[128] And from the peace, in the immediate post-war period, Americans would deploy the hard lessons of colonial rule to redesign independent metrics of political amity and constitutional invention – seducing their old English passions (if we follow Burke) through a new democratic suite of 'cognitive ap-praisals'.[129] Despite political severance, the 1783 Treaty would rhetorically un-derwrite a legacy of 'good correspondence' – that is, transactional sympathies and capacities – into future relational goals with Britain, with both parties contracting to devise an overlapping heritage space, as it were, for outworking future transatlantic partnership and intelligence. I will go so far as to suggest that the language of correspondence that appears in the final Treaty of Peace is the strongest existing proof of any formalized mutual understanding, or 'spe-cial friendship', between Great Britain and the United States. Insofar as this language infers both 'sentimental belonging' and political accord, it conjures a resilient mythology of Anglo-American unity and alliance.[130]

Conclusion

In the throes of the Second World War, Winston Churchill would step into this heritage overlap to invite consensus around joint defence.[131] His language is remarkably full of Anglo-Saxon sentiment and decidedly demonstrates his deployment of the 'good correspondence' to achieve political ends. This is strikingly apparent in his continued efforts to nurture Anglo-American rela-tions at the start of the Cold War and most notably in his speech on 'The Sinews of Peace', delivered at Fulton, Missouri, in 1946.[132] In language ripe with imagery, Churchill activated 'a still workable dynamo' from early Ameri-can fragments of political literature.[133] He enjoined American co-operation on American terms and 'talk[ed] of friendship' in the good old revolutionary sense, by spelling out a new cause for joined action.[134] Invoking a long lega-cy of Anglo-American fellow feeling, his language stirred 'the little remains of kindred', as Paine once called them, that nearly two centuries before had seemed to spell only 'madness and folly'.[135] Grammars of sympathetic con-tinuity provided a rhetorical scaffolding upon which powers of imagination could secure new 'intimacies' of association.[136]

In a marvellous play on analogy, Churchill's speech reveals a wonderful consonance with early American works, including Paine's *Common Sense* from 1776. His language is characterized by familiar patterns of declaration and union, and seemingly reinvents Paine's eighteenth-century case for American political autonomy. This can be seen in Churchill's nimble transposition of Paine's exhortation to the colonists: 'To unite the sinews of commerce and defence is sound policy; for when our strength and our riches, play into each other's hand, we need fear no external enemy.'[137] As can be seen when comparing the two appeals, Churchill masterfully upends Paine's view of early American military and economic capacities, whilst refashioning his own case for twentieth-century wartime securities.[138] We gauge this best by reading the two in concert – the Anglo and the American together, as it were, Churchill's 'Sinews of Peace' and Paine's *Common Sense* (italicized, in square brackets):

> If the population of the English-speaking Commonwealths be added to that of the United States with all that such cooperation implies [*To unite the sinews*] in the air, on the sea, all over the globe and in science and in industry, and in moral force, [*of commerce and defence*] there will be no quivering precarious balance of power to offer its temptation to ambition or adventure [*is sound policy, for when our strength and our riches, play into each other's hand*]. On the contrary, there will be an overwhelming assurance of security [*we need fear no external enemy*].[139]

The importance of this synchrony between Churchill and Paine is found not in direct lines of influence or in perceived outcomes of the Fulton speech itself, which remain unclear and at the time were mixed, but in the simple overflow of corresponding values that have endured in diverse iterations down to the present. Since the close of the revolution, shared grammars of coeval friendship have reappeared in countless examples of linguistic overlay and reassemblage, conserving a shared heritage space for outworking liberal thought and consensus.

The political art of correspondence is an undervalued feature of this aspect of Anglo-American exchange. While transatlantic writers have long grappled with 'shared values' and 'special relations', philosophical ideals of 'likeness', 'analogy' or 'similitude' – here rooted in transatlantic Enlightenment thought – have not been understood for their importance in enduring rhetorical strategy. To that end, this chapter has sought to demonstrate the intricate workings of eighteenth-century correspondence as a vehicle of political ideation; has highlighted the role of the sympathetic imagination in Anglo-American cultural and diplomatic amity; and has thereby assigned new significance to the language of correspondence in the 1783 Treaty of Peace. Above all else, this chapter has approached the legacy of fellowship between Britons and Americans through the narrative lens of sympathetic interplay, showing how common political principles are frequently transmitted, transposed and stabilized through artful notions of shared identity and imaginative confirmation. A redoubled heritage is the cultural consequence of this conjectural progress – the 'answering to each other in fitness or mutual adaptation'.[140] Deftly formalized in the 1783 Treaty of Peace, the 'good correspondence' has preserved an overlapping arena for Anglo-American political debate.[141]

Kristin A. Cook is Visiting Research Fellow in Literature and Heritage at the University of Plymouth, England, and Senior Associate Tutor with the Centre for International Studies and Diplomacy, SOAS University of London. She has published on such topics as presidential legacy, American literary and legal history and the dissemination of Scottish Enlightenment thought in the early Atlantic world. She earned her PhD as a doctoral fellow with the Institute for Advanced Studies in the Humanities, University of Edinburgh, and currently serves as Vice-Chair of the Transatlantic Studies Association.

Notes

1. Ezra Pound, American expatriate writer, author of 'Adams Cantos' LXII–LXXI [62–71], in *Cantos* (New York: New Directions, 1972), 341–421. This chapter has benefitted from David Ten Eyck's careful insights into Pound's 'documentary method', collected in *Ezra Pound's Adams Cantos* (London: Bloomsbury, 2012), 39. The cultural weight of these cantos is critically overlooked, as Eyck suggests, due to controversy over their compositional value and Pound's fascist politics. See also M.A. Bernstein, *Tale of the Tribe: Ezra Pound and the Modern Verse Epic* (Princeton, NJ: Princeton University Press, 1980). Above quote 1: Letter from John Adams to Thomas McKean, Quincy, 31 August 1813, in J. Adams and C.F. Adams, *Life and Works of John Adams*, Vol. X (Boston, MA: Little, Brown and Company, 1856), 62. Above quote 2: W. Irving, 'English Writers on America', in *Sketch Book of Geoffrey Crayon, Gent.* (1820) (New York: Signet Classic, c.1961), 61–62.

2. In 1939, Pound travelled to the United States to persuade officials (hopefully Roosevelt) to avoid the war in Europe (see Eyck, *Adams Cantos*, 5 and notes). In many ways, Pound is seen in the *Cantos* to be working to create a correspondence between 'The Fascist Ideal', as he called it in 1936, and revolutionary America: see Eyck for a fine treatment of this complex documentary project. See also R. Bush, 'Late Cantos LXXII–CXVII', in I.B. Nadel (ed.), *Cambridge Companion to Ezra Pound* (Cambridge: Cambridge University Press, 2001), 109–38.

3. John Adams, American Founder from Massachusetts: generally conservative, he helped negotiate the final terms of peace with Great Britain and served his country as second President of the United States (1797–1801); Thomas Jefferson, American Founder from Virginia and author of the Declaration of Independence: he was lead negotiator of international treaties, Minister to France, Secretary of State and third President of the United States (1801–9); Edward Bancroft, born in Massachusetts, like Adams, but a double agent and spy for the United States and Britain during the American Revolution: he was tapped for information by the Committee of Secret Correspondence mentioned in 'Re-pair: "The Good Correspondence"' in this chapter; Sir Edward Coke, seventeenth-century English jurist whose ideas influenced revolutionary decision-making in law and constitutional invention.

4. Pound adapts excerpts from John Fiske's *American Revolution* (1891) and Albert Bushnell Hart's *Formation of the Union, 1750–1829* (1892). Both scholars 'adopted essentially Whiggish outlook[s]' that Pound used to unpack principles of historical progress: see Eyck, *Adams Cantos*, references to Fiske and Hart at 15. For more on Pound's sources, see F.K. Sanders, *John Adams Speaking: Pound's Sources for the Adams Cantos* (Orono: University of Maine Press, 1975).

5. Pound, 'Canto LXXI', in *Cantos*, 414–21 (417).

6. 'From John Adams to Thomas McKean, Quincy, 31 August 1813' and 'To John Adams from Thomas McKean, 20 August 1813', in *Life and Works*, 60–63. Thomas McKean, born in Pennsylvania and represented Delaware in the Stamp Tax Congress of 1765: a lawyer and a signer of the Declaration of Independence.

7. Eyck, *Adams Cantos*, 39, citing Pound, 'Jefferson–Adams Letters as a Shrine and a Monument' (1937), in W. Cookson (ed.), *Selected Prose, 1909–1965* (New York: New Directions, 1973), 147–58.

8. Ibid.

9. Ibid.

10. Ibid. Eyck refers explicitly to Pound's 1937 engagement with the Jefferson–Adams letters. See also J. Adams et al., *Jefferson–Adams Letters* (Chapel Hill: Published for the Institute of Early American History and Culture at Williamsburg, Virginia, by the University of North Carolina Press, Chapel Hill, 1988).

11. Irving, 'English Writers on America', in *Sketch Book*, 62.

12. 'Even during the late war [1812] …', wrote Irving, 'they still kept alive the sparks of future friendship': in 'English Writers on America', 61–62. For fine discussions on the 1783 Treaty, see R. Hoffman and P.J. Albert (eds), *Peace and the Peacemakers: The Treaty of 1783* (Charlottesville: University of Virginia Press, 1986). This chapter will address the 'diplomacy of trust' and related cultural implications for Anglo-American relations. In Hoffman and Albert (eds), see J.R. Dull, 'Vergennes, Rayneval, and the Diplomacy of Trust', 101–31 and M. Cunliffe, '"They Will *All* Speak English": Some Cultural Consequences of Independence', 132–59.

13. J. Rawls, *A Theory of Justice* (Cambridge, MA: Belknap Press of Harvard University Press, 1971, revised edn, 1999) and *Political Liberalism* (New York: Columbia University Press, 1993, expanded edn, 2005); M.C. Nussbaum, *Political Emotions: Why Love Matters for Justice* (Cambridge, MA: Belknap Press of Harvard University Press, 2013).

14. See A.P. Dobson and S. Marsh (eds), *Churchill and the Anglo-American Special Relationship* (Abingdon: Routledge, 2017).

15. From Scottish playwright J.M. Barrie's *Peter Pan and Wendy* (New York: Charles Scribner's Sons, 1911), chapter 3. See 'A Tenancy at Sufferance: "Our Old Home"' in this chapter on the role of the sympathetic imagination.

16. T. Paine, *Common Sense* (1776), in Paine, *Common Sense and Other Writings*, introduction and notes by J. Appleby (New York: Barnes & Noble Classics, 2005), 11–69, 45. W. Irving, 'Rip Van Winkle', first published 1819, in *Sketch Book of Geoffrey Crayon, Gent.*, published serially 1819–20 (New York: Signet Classic, 1961 edn), 37–55, 49.

17. Ibid.

18. Ibid.

19. This 'ancient inhabitant' is a descendant of an historian of the same name (ibid., 51).

20. Quoted in Bernstein, *Tale of the Tribe*, 8, from Kipling's address to the Royal Academy Dinner, 1906. Bernstein cites R. Kipling, 'Literature', from *A Book of Words*, Vol. XXXII of *Writings in Prose and Verse* (New York, 1928), 3–4.

21. À la Wittgenstein, where 'family resemblance' offers an analogy for understanding not only shared ancestry, but the linguistic 'overlapping and criss-crossing' of word uses that dem-

onstrate similarity of concept but not exactness: L. Wittgenstein, *Philosophical Investigations*, eds and trans. P.M.S. Hacker and J. Schulte, 4th edn (Oxford: Wiley-Blackwell, 2009), 66. On colonial identity, see R. Hoffman, M. Sobel, and F.J. Teute (eds), *Through a Glass Darkly: Reflections on Personal Identity in Early America* (Chapel Hill: University of North Carolina Press, 1997), especially K.A. Lockridge, 'Colonial Self-Fashioning: Paradoxes and Pathologies in the Construction of Genteel Identity in Eighteenth-Century America', 274–339.

22. Rip's long nap outlasting the war represents a sardonic commentary on George III's monarchical image during the first half of his reign. In a wonderful satire attributed to English caricaturist Thomas Rowlandson, we find the king (or possibly Lord North) fast asleep when he is supposed to be planning the 'reduction of America': see T. Rowlandson, 'The State Watchman discovered by the Genius of Britain studying plans for the Reduction of America' (London: J. Jones, 10 December 1781). That the etching follows the final defeat at Yorktown and includes the text 'Hello neighbour! What are you asleep' likewise resonates with Rip's desperate post-war search for missing British neighbours. On this and shifting British attitudes towards the monarchy more broadly, see L. Colley, *Britons: Forging the Nation 1707–1837* (London: Pimlico, 2003 edn), chapter 5, 195–236 (209).

23. In his wonderful use of time, place and plot, Irving seems to play upon the classical unities in structuring his narrative resolution to Rip's post-war crisis.

24. This quote from Locke's *Second Treatise of Government* is discussed by Jack P. Greene in his examination of the nature of the bond between Britain and her colonies: see J.P. Greene, *Understanding the American Revolution: Issues and Actors* (Charlottesville: University Press of Virginia, 1995), especially chapter 4, 'The American Revolution: An Explanation', 48–71 (50–52); citing J. Locke, *Two Treatises of Government*, ed. P. Laslett (Cambridge: University Press, 1960), 462–63.

25. Irving, 'Rip Van Winkle', in *Sketch Book*, 52.

26. Ibid.

27. On the Enlightenment in the Atlantic world, see S. Manning and F.D. Cogliano (eds), *Atlantic Enlightenment* (London: Routledge, 2016).

28. Sarah Knott unpacks issues of sensibility and political representation in her discussion of the post-war ratification debates, noting various departures from Britain. In S. Knott, *Sensibility and the American Revolution* (Chapel Hill: University of North Carolina Press, 2009), especially chapter 5 at 238–63 (243). See also A. Burstein, *Sentimental Democracy: The Evolution of America's Romantic Self-Image* (New York: Hill and Wang, 1999).

29. 'Correspondence, n.', *OED*; emphasis added by author.

30. See J. Daybell and A. Gordon (eds), *Cultures of Correspondence in Early Modern Britain* (Philadelphia: University of Pennsylvania Press, 2016), and on textual conversations in elite society, see D.S. Shields, *Civil Tongues and Polite Letters in British America* (Chapel Hill: University of North Carolina Press, 2012). The foremost study of power and political thought as disseminated through revolutionary pamphlets and texts remains B. Bailyn, *Ideological Origins of the American Revolution*, enl. edn (Cambridge, MA: Belknap Press of Harvard University Press, 1992).

31. C.L. Griswold Jr, 'Imagination: Morals, Science, and Arts', in K. Haakonssen (ed.), *Cambridge Companion to Adam Smith* (Cambridge: Cambridge University Press, 2006), 22–56 (35). Griswold identifies a similar process in the economics of buying and selling.

32. 'Correspondence, n.', *OED*. This accords with the eighteenth-century stadial theory of civilization being advanced by conjectural historians and philosophers of the Scottish Enlightenment, including Adam Ferguson, Adam Smith and Dugald Stewart.

33. 'Correspondence, n.', *OED*.

34. Irving, 'Rip Van Winkle', in *Sketch Book*, 47.

35. Irving's writing here transmits a soft echo of Paine's 'Thoughts on the Peace' in 1783. Following the war, Paine writes: '"The Times that Tried men's souls," are over – and the greatest and completest revolution the world ever knew, gloriously and happily accomplished. ... Even calmness has the power of stunning, when it opens too instantly upon us', in T. Paine, *The Crisis*., No. 13 [1783], 'Thoughts on the Peace, and the Probable Advantages Thereof.'

36. Irving, 'Rip Van Winkle', in *Sketch Book*, 46. A now dated definition of 'constitutional' suggests 'a walk for restoration of good health', which befits Rip's uncanny exercise; see *OED*, 'constitutional, n.'.

37. Irving, 'Rip Van Winkle', in *Sketch Book*, 47.

38. In his *Lectures on Jurisprudence (Report of 1762–3)*, Adam Smith identifies four 'states' of mankind relative to the acquisition of property. The four-stages theory is often used in conjunction with the Lockean theory of human progress and cognition. As Knud Haakonssen writes: 'Smith's stadial history is centrally concerned with the emergence of increasingly stronger government' to accommodate changes in ideas of personhood and to protect recognizable rights; K. Haakonssen (ed.), 'Introduction', *Cambridge Companion to Adam Smith* (Cambridge: Cambridge University Press, 2006), 18.

39. Irving, 'Rip Van Winkle', in *Sketch Book*, 51. 'As the door turneth upon his hinges, so doth the slothful upon his bed' (Prov. 26.14) accords with Rip's 'aversion to all kinds of profitable labor' and his son's 'lazy' disposition (39, 50). In the end, Rip rests happy, it would seem, between civilized 'friends' and 'former cronies' (52).

40. Ibid., 51. Rip's path towards naturalization is marked by a symbolic family reunion and declarative act: 'He caught his daughter and her child in his arms. I am your Father!' (51). On changes to the revolutionary family and the power of natural expression, see J. Fliegelman, *Prodigals and Pilgrims: The American Revolution Against Patriarchal Authority, 1750–1800* (Cambridge: Cambridge University Press, 1982) and *Declaring Independence: Jefferson, Natural Language & The Culture of Performance* (Stanford, CA: Stanford University Press, 1993).

41. Rip's Dutch-American identity is also visible here, splicing new American rights with English constitutional gains of the Revolution of 1688–89.

42. From Edmund Burke, 'Speech on the Conciliation with the American Colonies' (1775), in *Norton Anthology of English Literature*, 2846–49 (2847).

43. Ibid. On the topic of English identity, see D. Wahrman, 'The English Problem of Identity in the American Revolution', *AHR*, CVI (2001).

44. Burke, 'Speech on the Conciliation', 2847.

45. Ibid., 2846–47.

46. Ibid. For a provocative look at how this plays out among colonial gentry in the Anglo-Virginian context, see W. Holton, *Forced Founders: Indians, Debtors, Slaves, & the Making of the American Revolution in Virginia* (Chapel Hill: Published for the Omohundro Institute of Early American History and Culture, Williamsburg, Virginia, by the University of North Carolina Press, 1999).

47. Burke, 'Speech on the Conciliation', 2847, emphasis added by author. Burke builds his ideas upon his earlier work, *A Philosophical Enquiry into the Origin of our Ideas of the Sublime and the Beautiful* (1757), showing here that feelings of pleasure or pain are instinctual responses to liberty's concrete objects (i.e. the 'specific point of taxing').

48. See Griswold, 'Imagination: Morals, Science, and Arts', in Haakonssen (ed.), *Cambridge Companion to Adam Smith*, 35. 'Correspondence, n.', *OED*.

49. Ibid., 2846. Although Burke is known for his place in British imperial conservatism, the language of fellow feeling – read here as having 'an evaluative content' and thus the capacity to forge shared interests – necessarily opens pathways into determinedly liberal political values,

at times undercutting even Burke's professed animosity towards democratic government. This footnote draws on Nussbaum, *Political Emotions*, 5.

50. 'Sensibility, n.': consisting of 'emotion, feeling, affectivity', 'emotional awareness' or 'feelings associated with or arising from one's moral or aesthetic ideals or standards'; *OED*. See Knott, *Sensibility and the American Revolution*. On the eighteenth-century rhetoric of emotion, see N. Eustace, *Emotion, Power, and the Coming of the American Revolution* (Chapel Hill: University of North Carolina Press, 2008).

51. Nussbaum, *Political Emotions*, 145.

52. Knott, *Sensibility and the American Revolution*, 112. See R.M. Hendershot, 'Manipulating the Anglo-American Civilizational Identity in the Era of Churchill', in A.P. Dobson and S. Marsh (eds), *Churchill and the Anglo-American Special Relationship* (Abingdon: Routledge, 2017), 64–95.

53. S. Davies and D. Bostwick (Preface), 'Mr Davies's Sermon on the Death of King George II', 1761. Printed and sold by R. Draper, in Newbury-Street; and by Z. Fowle and S. Draper, at their printing-office in Marlborough-Street (Boston). Portions of the subsequent analysis are developed in a separate treatment by the author: see K.A. Cook, 'Executing Character: Of Sympathy, Self-Construction and Adam Smith, in Early America, 1716–1826' (unpublished PhD thesis: University of Edinburgh, 2012).

54. As Sam Edwards reflects elsewhere, 'the architecture of a myth' seems to rely upon those fora that 'call for, perform and *imagine* Anglo-American unity'. Nowhere is this more apparent than in eighteenth-century networks of pulpit, playhouse and print. See S. Edwards, 'The Architecture of a Myth: Constructing and Commemorating Churchill's Special Relationship, c. 1919–69', in Dobson and Marsh (eds), *Churchill*, 202–22 (203): for further consideration of Burke, see Bailey's contribution in this collection of essays.

55. Bostwick, 'Preface', 13 February 1761, New York, introducing Davies, 'Mr Davies's Sermon on the Death of King George II', v–xii. Bostwick was then Minister of the Presbyterian Congregation in New-York.

56. Ibid., v.

57. Davies, 'Sermon', 13–32.

58. 'Lament O ye Residents of Nassau-Hall! … Lament, O bereaved Congregation of Prince Town! … Lament with sympathizing Tears, ye Men of Learning, Genius, or Piety, and all ye noble Patrons of human Literature…', Bostwick, 'Preface', xi.

59. Ibid., xii.

60. Davies, 'Sermon', 32.

61. Burke, 'Speech on the Conciliation', 2847.

62. On the long eighteenth century, see K. Wilson (ed.), *A New Imperial History: Culture, Identity and Modernity in Britain and the Empire, 1660–1840* (Cambridge: Cambridge University Press, 2004).

63. Bostwick, 'Preface', vii–viii.

64. Davies, 'Sermon', 29.

65. Ibid., 15.

66. Ibid., 32.

67. As Enlightenment philosopher Adam Smith writes, between individuals 'The passions, upon some occasions, may seem to be transfused from one man to another, instantaneously, and antecedent to any knowledge of what excited them in the person principally concerned. Grief and joy, for example, strongly expressed in the look and gestures of any one, at once affect the spectator with some degree of a like painful or agreeable emotion', *TMS*, I.i.1.6. See *Theory of Moral Sentiments* [*TMS*], in D.D. Raphael and A.L. Macfie (eds), *Glasgow Edition of the Works*

and Correspondence of Adam Smith, series vol. I (Oxford University Press, 1976; as reprinted by Indianapolis: Liberty Fund, 1982).

68. Davies, 'Sermon', 31.

69. Ibid. 'Coeval, adj.', *OED*, 'Of equal antiquity, of contemporaneous origin, going back to the same date'.

70. Ibid., 32.

71. A. Dobson, 'Churchill, Fulton and the Cultural Underpinnings of the Anglo-American Special Relationship', Plenary Address, Transatlantic Studies Association Annual Conference, University College Cork, 10 July 2017. For 'a genealogical analysis of the career of sentiment in England and its colonies', see A.S. Rai, *Rule of Sympathy: Sentiment, Race, and Power, 1750–1850* (New York: Palgrave, 2002). Rai usefully problematizes ideas of civilizational progress and sentiment by grappling with much wider 'overlapping networks of practices, communities, institutions, and discourses' that cannot all be handled here, but which are vital to understanding British-colonial governance, ideas of otherness, Anglo-American political thought and analogical continuity (xvii).

72. For an eighteenth-century medical perspective on disease by sympathy/consent, see J. Crawford, 'Practical Remarks on the Sympathy of Parts of the Body...', article XV, in *Medical Essays and Observations of Medicine in the University of Edinburgh*, vol. 5, pt 2 (1744), as cited in A. Broadie, 'Sympathy and the Impartial Spectator', in Haakonssen (ed.), *Cambridge Companion to Adam Smith*, 158–88 (161).

73. Paine, 'Common Sense', 38, 45.

74. Ibid., 45: 'Every day wears out the little remains of kindred between us and them....'

75. Ibid., 38.

76. Ibid., 35. Paine speaks of European wars and laments the economic costs of America's ties with Britain.

77. Irving, 'Rip Van Winkle', in *Sketch Book*, 50.

78. Ibid.

79. Ibid. He is confused on seeing his son.

80. Ibid.

81. Ibid., 52.

82. E. Said, *Reflections on Exile* (London: Granta, 2001).

83. J.C. Hayes, 'The French Theater of Sympathy', in E. Schliesser (ed.), *Sympathy: A History* (Oxford: Oxford University Press, 2015), 199–207 (199). Burke, 'Speech on the Conciliation', 2846–47.

84. Paine, *Common Sense*, 45.

85. Irving, 'Rip Van Winkle', 52.

86. Griswold, 'Imagination', in Haakonssen (ed.), *Cambridge Companion to Adam Smith*.

87. D. Long, 'Adam Smith's Politics', in Haakonssen (ed.), *Cambridge Companion to Adam Smith*, 288–318 (290).

88. N. Hawthorne, *Our Old Home, A Series of English Sketches* (1863) (Boston, MA: James R. Osgood and Company, Late Ticknor & Fields, and Fields, Osgood & Co., 1876).

89. In colonial studies see Rai, *Rule of Sympathy*.

90. Griswold, 'Imagination', in Haakonssen (ed.), *Cambridge Companion to Adam Smith*.

91. Hawthorne, 'Consular Experiences', in *Our Old Home*, 19. Griswold, 'Imagination', 25.

92. Griswold, 'Imagination', in Haakonssen (ed.), *Cambridge Companion to Adam Smith*, 26, 47.

93. 'To A Friend.', Dedication to Franklin Pierce by Nathaniel Hawthorne, The Wayside, 2 July 1863, in *Our Old Home*, ix.

94. Hawthorne, Dedication, ix. To former US President Franklin Pierce.

95. Hawthorne, 'Consular Experiences', in *Our Old Home*, 14–15.

96. Smith, *Theory of Moral Sentiments*, VI.ii.2.5.

97. Hawthorne, 'Consular Experiences', in *Our Old Home*, 48.

98. For a compelling study of 'cultural time' in nineteenth-century English and American literature, see R. Weisbuch, *Atlantic Double-Cross: American Literature and British Influence in the Age of Emerson* (Chicago: University of Chicago Press, 1986).

99. Ibid.

100. The role of the 'impartial spectator' distinguishes Smith's theory.

101. Hawthorne, 'Consular Experiences', in *Our Old Home*, 28.

102. Ibid., 26.

103. Despite his consternation about 'men who have been in the habit of making playthings or tools of their imagination and sensibility', Hawthorne does both in his literary and consular professions. Shortly before taking up his appointment in Liverpool, for example, Hawthorne published a book of Greek myths for children, entitled *Tanglewood Tales for Girls and Boys* (1853).

104. 'Sufferance, n.', *OED*. Citing William Blackstone, *Commentaries on the Laws of England*, 1766, ii. 150; 'Tenancy at Sufferance', in Kenneth W. Clarkson et al., *West's Business Law: Text, Cases, Legal and Regulatory, Environment*, 5th edn (St Paul, MN: West Publishing Company, 1992), 1000.

105. 'Tenancy at Sufferance', *West's*.

106. See D. Lowenthal, *Past Is a Foreign Country* (Cambridge: Cambridge University Press, 1985).

107. Hitchens expands on his idea of 'discordant intimacy' in *Blood, Class and Empire: The Enduring Anglo-American Relationship* (New York: Nation Books, 2004), chapter 11.

108. *Definitive Treaty of Peace and Friendship between his Britannick Majesty, and the United States of America; signed at Paris, the 3d of September, 1783*, in Charles Jenkinson, *A Collection of all the Treaties of Peace, Alliance, and Commerce, between Great-Britain and other powers...* Vol. III (Piccadilly: Printed for J. Debrett, 1785), 410–16 (411). Hawthorne, 'Consular Experiences', in *Our Old Home*, 22.

109. See R.B. Morris, 'The Durable Significance of the Treaty of 1783', in Hoffman and Albert (eds), *Peace and the Peacemakers*, 230–50. Also, Morris, *The Peacemakers: The Great Powers and American Independence*, new edn (Boston, MA, 1983).

110. Irving, 'English Writers on America', in *Sketch Book*, 61.

111. Morris, 'Durable Significance', in Hoffman and Albert (eds), *Peace and the Peacemakers*, 250.

112. Irving, 'English Writers on America', in *Sketch Book*, 61.

113. W. Chi Dimock, 'Deep Time: American Literature and World History', *American Literary History* 13(4) (Winter 2001), 755–75. Bernstein, *Tale of the Tribe*.

114. Presumably such concord is understood to exist between Britain and France, as seen below.

115. Hendershot, 'Manipulating the Anglo-American Civilizational Identity in the Era of Churchill', in Dobson and Marsh (eds), *Churchill and the Anglo-American Special Relationship*, 64–95.

116. English translation; emphasis by the author. *Definitive Treaty of Peace and Friendship between his Britannick Majesty, and the United States of America; signed at Paris, the 3d of September, 1783*, in Jenkinson, *Collection*, Vol. III, 410–16 (411). Accessed at Hathitrust Digital Library: https://babel.hathitrust.org.

117. For a useful discussion concerning colonial intelligence sharing in the revolutionary era, see H.M. Ward, *War for Independence and the Transformation of American Society* (1938) (London:

University College London Press, 1999). Readers interested in post-1945 UK and US intelligence in the age of surveillance are referred to R. Jeffreys-Jones, *We Know All About You: The Story of Surveillance in Britain and America* (Oxford: Oxford University Press, 2017).

118. 'Correspondence, n.', *OED*. Ideas of 'fitness' and 'mutual adaptation' also point towards the heavily racialized discourses that would underpin twentieth-century debates and expansionist zeal regarding Anglo-Saxon 'stock', bloodlines and descent, recognized by Hitchens as the *Mayflower* complex: see Hitchens, *Blood, Class and Empire*, chapter 4.

119. 'Good' in the sense of advantageous or profitable. *Convention for explaining the articles of the Assiento, or contract for Negroes...* signed at Madrid, the 16/15 May 1716 [referring to the *El Assiento de los Negros, the Contract for Negroes*, 1715], in Jenkinson, *Collection*, Vol. II, 179–84 (181), *Treaty between Ulrica Eleonora...* in Vol. II, 251–64 (252–53); and *Treaty of Defensive Alliance...* in Vol. II, 268–72 (268). Accessed at Hathitrust Digital Library: https://babel.hathitrust.org.

120. Article VI contracts the rights of English labourers to settle in this district of the Spanish continent and to cut and sell logwood. The treaty safeguards the rights of British subjects to erect their own magazines for storing arms: *Definitive Treaty of Peace and Friendship between His Britannick Majesty and the King of Spain. Signed at Versailles the third day of September, 1783*, in Jenkinson, *Collection*, Vol. III, 392–99 (397).

121. 'Definitive Treaty of Peace', in Jenkinson, *Collection*.

122. F.D. Cogliano, *Revolutionary America, 1763–1815: A Political History*, 2nd edn (New York; London: Routledge, 2000), 69.

123. 'Definitive Treaty of Peace', in Jenkinson, *Collection*.

124. In Jenkinson, *Treaty of Alliance, eventual and defensive, between his Most Christian Majesty, Louis the Sixteenth, King of France and Navarre, and the Thirteen United States of America, concluded at Paris, 6th February, 1778*. Vol. III, 254–55 (255), emphasis added by author; with respect to the *Treaty of Friendship and Commerce, concluded between the French King and the United States of North America, February 6, 1778*. Vol. III, 242–54.

125. The committee was appointed by the Continental Congress in 1775 to solicit war supplies and foreign aid. See Herring, *From Colony to Superpower*, 151; see also Peter S. Onuf, 'The Declaration of Independence for Diplomatic Historians', *Diplomatic History* 22 (Winter 1998).

126. The Treaty of Peace was not definitive until Britain and France settled their post-war terms. See B. Perkins, 'The Peace of Paris: Patterns and Legacies', in R. Hoffman and P.J. Albert (eds), *Peace and the Peacemakers*, 190–229 (190). In Jenkinson, *Treaty of Alliance*, 256–59 (256).

127. 'Definitive Treaty of Peace', in Jenkinson, *Collection*.

128. Morris, in Hoffman and Albert (eds), *Peace and the Peacemakers*, 230–50.

129. Nussbaum, *Political Emotions*, 17. Nussbaum defends her view 'that emotions necessarily involve cognitive appraisals' in an earlier work, *Upheavals of Thought: The Intelligence of Emotions* (New York: Cambridge University Press, 2001).

130. Knott, *Sensibility and the American Revolution*, 112.

131. Here adapting John Rawls's notion of 'overlapping consensus' in political liberalism. See J. Rawls, *A Theory of Justice*, and *Political Liberalism*.

132. W. Churchill, 'The Sinews of Peace', delivered 5 March 1946, Westminster College, Fulton, Missouri, accessed through the National Churchill Museum: http://www.nationalchurchill-museum.org/sinews-of-peace-history.html.

133. Eyck, *Adams Cantos*, citing Pound, 39.

134. Paine, *Common Sense*, 45.

135. 'The last cord now is broken, the people of England are presenting addresses against us. There are injuries which nature cannot forgive; she would cease to be nature if she did' (*Common

Sense, 45). Paine disputes an idea that 'the government of America [might] return again into the hands of Britain' (45).

136. Ibid.: 'Fraternal association requires not only the growing friendship and mutual understanding between our two vast but kindred systems of society, but the continuance of the intimate relationship between our military advisers...'. On rhetoric, see W. Churchill, *Scaffolding of Rhetoric*, 1898: 'The direct, though not the admitted, object which the orator has in view is to allay the commonplace influences and critical faculties of his audience, by presenting to their imaginations a series of vivid impressions which are replaced before they can be too closely examined.'

137. Paine is here speaking of America's capacity to care for herself. He stridently opposes the prospect of returning to Britain, even on terms of peace, for a prolonged guardianship in the areas of naval security and defence. Paine, *Common Sense*, 46–55 (51).

138. Paine considers how America might rebuild her strength apart from Britain, addressing Continental disputes over trade and the naval force. Paine, *Common Sense*, 51.

139. Paine, *Common Sense*, 50: 'Wherefore if we must hereafter protect ourselves, why not do it for ourselves?' Churchill, 'Sinews of Peace'.

140. 'Correspondence, n.', *OED*.

141. 'Definitive Treaty', 411.

Bibliography

Adams, J., and C.F. Adams. *Life and Works of John Adams*. Boston, MA: Little, Brown and Company, Vol. X, 1856.

Adams, J., et al. *Jefferson–Adams Letters*. Chapel Hill: Published for the Institute of Early American History and Culture at Williamsburg, Virginia, by the University of North Carolina Press, Chapel Hill, 1988.

Bailyn, B. *Ideological Origins of the American Revolution*. Enl. edn. Cambridge, MA: Belknap Press of Harvard University Press, 1992.

Barrie, J.M. *Peter Pan and Wendy*. New York: Charles Scribner's Sons, 1911.

Bernstein, M.A. *Tale of the Tribe*. Princeton, NJ: Princeton University Press, 1980.

Blackstone, W. *Commentaries on the Laws of England*. Oxford: Clarendon Press, 1765–69.

Broadie, A. 'Sympathy and the Impartial Spectator', in K. Haakonssen (ed.), *Cambridge Companion to Adam Smith*. Cambridge: Cambridge University Press, 2006, 158–88.

Burke, E. 'Abridgement of English History' (1757), Project Gutenberg EBook of *Works of the Right Honourable Edmund Burke*, vol. VII. 14 King William Street, Strand, WC: John C. Nimmo, 1887, 159-488.

———. 'A Philosophical Enquiry into the Origin of Our Ideas of the Sublime and the Beautiful' (1757), in *Works of Edmund Burke*, vol. 1. London: George Bell & Sons, 1909, 49-181.

———. 'Speech on the Conciliation' (1775), in S. Greenblatt, L. Lipking and J. Noggle (eds), *Norton Anthology of English Literature, Restoration and Eighteenth Century*, Vol. C. 8th edn. New York: W.W. Norton & Company, 2846–49.

Burstein, A. *Sentimental Democracy*. New York: Hill and Wang, 1999.

Churchill, W. *Scaffolding of Rhetoric*. 1898. Accessed through the International Churchill Society: https://winstonchurchill.org.

_____. 'Sinews of Peace'. Delivered 5 March 1946. Westminster College, Fulton, Missouri. Accessed through the National Churchill Museum: https://www.nationalchurchillmuseum.org/sinews-of-peace-history.html.

Clarkson, K.W., et al. *West's Business Law*. 5th edn. St Paul, MN: West Publishing Company, 1992.

Cogliano, F.D. *Revolutionary America*. 2nd edn. New York: Routledge, 2000.

Colley, L. *Britons*. London: Pimlico, 2003.

Cook, K.A. 'Executing Character: Of Sympathy, Self-Construction and Adam Smith, in Early America, 1716–1826'. Unpublished PhD thesis. Edinburgh: University of Edinburgh, 2012.

Cunliffe, M. 'They Will *All* Speak English', in R. Hoffman and P.J. Albert (eds), *Peace and the Peacemakers*. Charlottesville: University of Virginia Press, 1986, 132–59.

Daybell, J., and A. Gordon (eds). *Cultures of Correspondence*. Philadelphia: University of Pennsylvania Press, 2016.

Davies, S., and D. Bostwick (Preface). 'Mr Davies's Sermon on the Death of King George II'. 1761. Printed and sold by R. Draper, in Newbury-Street; and by Z. Fowle and S. Draper, at their printing-office in Marlborough-Street (Boston).

Dimock, W.C. 'Deep Time: American Literature and World History', *American Literary History* 13(4) (Winter 2001), 755–75.

Dobson, A.P., and S. Marsh (eds). *Churchill and the Anglo-American Special Relationship*. Abingdon: Routledge, 2017.

Dull, J.R. 'Vergennes, Rayneval, and the Diplomacy of Trust', in R. Hoffman and P.J. Albert (eds), *Peace and the Peacemakers*. Charlottesville: University of Virginia Press, 1986, 101–31.

Edwards, S. 'Architecture of a Myth: Constructing and Commemorating Churchill's Special Relationship, c. 1919–69', in A.P. Dobson and S. Marsh (eds), *Churchill and the Anglo-American Special Relationship*. Abingdon: Routledge, 2017, 202–22.

Eustace, N. *Passion Is the Gale*. Chapel Hill: Published for the Omohundro Institute of Early American History and Culture, Williamsburg, Virginia, by University of North Carolina Press, 2008.

Eyck, D.T. *Ezra Pound's Adams Cantos*. London: Bloomsbury, 2012.

Fiske, J. *American Revolution*. Boston, MA: Houghton Mifflin and company, 1891.

Fliegelman, J. *Declaring Independence*. Stanford, CA: Stanford University Press, 1993.

_____. *Prodigals and Pilgrims*. Cambridge: Cambridge University Press, 1982.

Greene, J.P. *Understanding the American Revolution*. Charlottesville: University Press of Virginia, 1995.

Griswold, C.L., Jr. 'Imagination: Morals, Science, and Arts', in K. Haakonssen (ed.), *Cambridge Companion to Adam Smith*. Cambridge: Cambridge University Press, 2006, 22–56.

Haakonssen, K. (ed.). *Cambridge Companion to Adam Smith*. Cambridge: Cambridge University Press, 2006.

Hart, A.B. *Formation of the Union 1750–1829*. New York: Longmans, Green, 1892.

Hawthorne, N. *Our Old Home* (1863). Boston, MA: James R. Osgood and Company, Late Ticknor & Fields, and Fields, Osgood & Co., 1876.

_____. *Tanglewood Tales*. Boston, MA: Ticknor & Fields, 1853.

Hayes, J.C. 'French Theater of Sympathy', in E. Schliesser (ed.), *Sympathy*. Oxford: Oxford University Press, 2015, 199–207.

Hendershot, R.M. 'Manipulating the Anglo-American Civilizational Identity in the Era of Churchill', in A.P. Dobson and S. Marsh (eds), *Churchill and the Anglo-American Special Relationship*. Abingdon: Routledge, 2017, 64–95.

Herring, G.C. *From Colony to Superpower*. Oxford: Oxford University Press, 2011.

Hitchens, C. *Blood, Class and Empire*. New York: Nation Books, 2004.

Hoffman, R., M. Sobel and F.J. Teute (eds). *Through a Glass Darkly*. Chapel Hill: University of North Carolina Press, 1997.

Hoffman, R., and P.J. Albert (eds). *Peace and the Peacemakers*. Charlottesville: University of Virginia Press, 1986.

Holton, W. *Forced Founders*. Chapel Hill: Published for the Omohundro Institute of Early American History and Culture, Williamsburg, Virginia, by the University of North Carolina Press, 1999.

Irving, W. 'English Writers on America', in *Sketch Book of Geoffrey Crayon, Gent*. (1820) (New York: Signet Classic, c.1961), 56–64.

———. 'Rip Van Winkle', in *Sketch Book of Geoffrey Crayon, Gent*. (1820) (New York: Signet Classic, c.1961), 37–55.

Jeffreys-Jones, R. *We Know All About You: The Story of Surveillance in Britain and America*. Oxford: Oxford University Press, 2017.

Jenkinson, C. *A Collection of All the Treaties of Peace....* Piccadilly: Printed for J. Debrett, 1785. Accessed at Hathitrust Digital Library: https://babel.hathitrust.org.

Kipling, R. 'Literature', from *A Book of Words*, Vol. XXXII, in *Writings in Prose and Verse*. New York, 1928.

Knott, S. *Sensibility and the American Revolution*. Chapel Hill: Published for the Omohundro Institute of Early American History and Culture, Williamsburg, Virginia, by University of North Carolina Press, 2009.

Locke, J. *Two Treatises of Government*, ed. P. Laslett. Cambridge: Cambridge University Press, 1960.

Lockridge, K.A. 'Colonial Self-Fashioning: Paradoxes and Pathologies in the Construction of Genteel Identity in Eighteenth-Century America', in R. Hoffman, M. Sobel and F.J. Teute (eds), *Through a Glass Darkly*. Chapel Hill: University of North Carolina Press, 1997, 274–339.

Long, D. 'Adam Smith's Politics', in K. Haakonssen (ed.), *Cambridge Companion to Adam Smith*. Cambridge: Cambridge University Press, 2006, 288–318.

Lowenthal, D. *Past Is a Foreign Country*. Cambridge: Cambridge University Press, 1985.

Manning, S., and F.D. Cogliano (eds). *Atlantic Enlightenment*. London: Routledge, 2016.

Morris, R.B. 'The Durable Significance of the Treaty of 1853', in R. Hoffman and P.J. Albert (eds), *Peace and the Peacemakers*. Charlottesville: University of Virginia Press, 1986, 230–50.

Nadel, I.B. (ed.). *Cambridge Companion to Ezra Pound*. Cambridge: Cambridge University Press, 2001.

Nussbaum, M.C. *Political Emotions*. Cambridge, MA: Belknap Press of Harvard University Press, 2013.

———. *Upheavals of Thought*. New York: Cambridge University Press, 2001.

Onuf, P.S. 'Declaration of Independence for Diplomatic Historians', *Diplomatic History* 22(1) (Winter 1998), 71–83.

Paine, T. *Common Sense* (1776), in *Common Sense and Other Writings*, introduction and notes by J. Appleby. New York: Barnes & Noble Classics, 2005, 11–69.

———. *The Crisis.*, No. 13 (1783), in *Common Sense and Other Writings*, introduction and notes by J. Appleby. New York: Barnes & Noble Classics, 2005, 89–94.

Perkins, B. 'The Peace of Paris: Patterns and Legacies', in R. Hoffman and P.J. Albert (eds), *Peace and the Peacemakers*. Charlottesville: University of Virginia Press, 1986, 190–229.

Pound, E. *Cantos*. New York: New Directions, 1972.

———. 'Jefferson–Adams Letters as Shrine and Monument' (1937), in W. Cookson (ed.), *Selected Prose, 1909–1965*. New York: New Directions, 1973, 147–58.

Rai, A.S. *Rule of Sympathy*. New York: Palgrave, 2002.

Rawls, J. *Political Liberalism*. New York: Columbia University Press, 1993, expanded edn, 2005.

———. *A Theory of Justice*. Cambridge, MA: Belknap Press of Harvard University Press, 1971, revised edn, 1999.

Rowlandson, T. 'The State Watchman discovered…' (caricature). London: J. Jones, 10 December 1781.

Said, Edward. *Reflections on Exile*. London: Granta, 2001.

Sanders, F.K. *John Adams Speaking: Pound's Sources for the Adams Cantos*. Orono: University of Maine Press, 1975.

Shields, D.S. *Civil Tongues and Polite Letters*. Chapel Hill: Published for the Institute of Early American History and Culture, Williamsburg, Virginia by University of North Carolina Press, 1997.

Smith, A. *Lectures on Jurisprudence*, in R.L. Meek, D.D. Raphael and P.G. Stein (eds), *Glasgow Edition of the Works and Correspondence of Adam Smith*, series vol. V. Oxford University Press, 1978 edn, as reprinted by Indianapolis, IN: Liberty Fund, 1982.

———. *Theory of Moral Sentiments* (1759), in D.D. Raphael and A.L. Macfie (eds), *Glasgow Edition of the Works and Correspondence of Adam Smith*, series vol. I. Oxford University Press, 1976 edn, as reprinted by Indianapolis, IN: Liberty Fund, 1982.

'Tenancy at Sufferance', in Kenneth W. Clarkson et al., *West's Business Law: Text, Cases, Legal and Regulatory, Environment*, 5th edn (St Paul, MN: West Publishing Company, 1992), 1000.

Wahrman, D. 'English Problem of Identity in the American Revolution', *AHR* 106(4) (October 2001), 1236–62.

Ward, H. *War for Independence and the Transformation of American Society* (1938). London: University College London Press, 1999.

Weisbuch, R. *Atlantic Double-Cross*. Chicago: University of Chicago Press, 1986.

Wilson, K. (ed.). *A New Imperial History*. Cambridge: Cambridge University Press, 2004.

Wittgenstein, L. *Philosophical Investigations*, eds and trans. P.M.S. Hacker and J. Schulte. 4th edn. Oxford: Wiley-Blackwell, 2009.

Chapter 2

Burkean Peace Theory

Radicalism, Conservatism and the Constitutional Heritage of Britain and the United States in the Age of Revolutions

Gavin Bailey

Government founded on a moral theory, on a system of universal peace, on the indefeasible hereditary Rights of Man, is now revolving from west to east...

—Thomas Paine, *Rights of Man, Common Sense and Other Political Writings*

They have 'the rights of men'. Against these, there can be no prescription; against these no agreement is binding; these admit no temperament, and no compromise: Anything withheld from their full demand is so much of fraud and injustice.

—Edmund Burke, *Reflections on the Revolution in France*

Introduction

The United States (US) Declaration of Independence announced the secession of the thirteen American colonies from the British Empire on 4 July 1776 by the authority of the people. The US Federal Constitution of 1787 was proclaimed in the name of 'We, the people'. This clearly indicated the overthrow of the British constitutional settlement of 1688 based upon a mixed government of crown, aristocracy and elected legislature in favour of a new constitutional order based upon popular sovereignty, wider democratic representation and the natural rights of individuals. This was the view of the radical polemicist Thomas Paine, who saw all the new constitutions of the American Revolution, state and federal, as expressing the authority of the people. Paine believed the advent of the French Revolution, which followed in 1789, constituted the beginning of 'an age of revolutions', with the American precedent spreading internationally, giving rise to a new age of rational and pacific domestic and international politics.[1]

If Paine was the apostle of the new age of individual rights espoused by radicals in the age of revolutions, on the basis of his works *Common Sense* (1776) and the *Rights of Man* (1791–92), his counterpoint was Edmund Burke.[2] Burke's castigation of the French Revolution and the natural rights philosophy that propelled it in *Reflections on the Revolution in France* (1790) became a foundational text for modern conservatism. As a consequence, and despite his previous support of the American colonists in their struggle against Britain, Burke was swiftly identified as an apologist for monarchical government and aristocratic reaction against democratic republicanism. For Paine, the two revolutions were demonstrations of the same phenomenon: the overthrow of repressive monarchical tyranny in favour of enlightened democratic government. For Burke, they were dramatically different. For him, the American Revolution defended traditional liberties understood as integral components of the British constitutional order, while the radial cosmopolitan ideology of the French Revolution represented a dangerous threat to order and civilization.

Superficially, the divergence between Burke and Paine marked the divergence between the United States and Britain both in political terms as the United States became an independent nation and in terms of the respective developing constitutional political traditions of the two countries. Yet both men were products of the British eighteenth-century tradition of Whig liberalism. Paine came from humble working-class origins and had worked as a revenue inspector before emigrating to America on the recommendation of the great American Enlightenment thinker Benjamin Franklin. He became the voice of a newly socially mobile artisan class, largely excluded from the traditional body politic, and was attracted to the egalitarian republicanism of political radicals. Burke, an Irishman who entered British politics under the patronage of more privileged figures, rapidly became spokesman for the main opposition grouping of aristocratic Whig oligarchs in the Westminster Parliament. In the early twenty-first century, it seems apparent that Paine's vision of individual freedom achieved by democratic and secular liberalism emerged triumphant, at least in the United States and Britain, and arguably across the globe. By contrast, Burke's elitist conservatism, which aimed to preserve tradition by pragmatic and limited incremental change, appears to be the self-conscious voice of the past.

However, a re-examination of the developing constitutional traditions in both nations indicates that a congruent constitutional settlement developed that drew upon shared conservative and Burkean elements of the Whig tradition. Both nations grappled with the problems caused by reconciling their mutual sense of political liberty with the increasing demands for wider political participation in the early industrial age and the successful creation and operation of the fiscal-military nation-state in the international system. Both nations were influenced by, and reacted to, the aspirations of radicals to differing extents at differing moments. Nonetheless, despite their differing features, their constitutional development was marked by similar political principles and understandings of the canons of statecraft.

These reconciled the manifestation of centralized governmental power typified by the modern fiscal-military state with their common liberal heritage both internally and refracted into the diplomatic relationship between them. If the American Revolution (1775–83) represented a reiteration of Whig political philosophy in terms of the rejection of the extension of the powers of the metropolitan military-fiscal state into colonial government without representative consent, it also eventually generated a new American model of the centralized military-fiscal state based on parallel Whig precepts. A key end-product of this process of nation-state formation was, with the exception of the 1812 conflict, a growing tradition of peaceful coexistence between the now-separate entities of the British Atlantic Empire.

The growth of this tradition represented a self-conscious rejection of the ideological hostility between reactionary monarchy and democratic popular sovereignty predicted by Paine. Instead, their relationship was, in large part, defined by an intuitive and habitual pattern of behaviour by their respective political elites, a pattern that drew upon deep wellsprings in Anglo-American constitutional practice and political behaviour and that was characterized by the conservative liberalism of Burke.

The British Constitutional Model and the Fiscal-Military State

The starting point for both Paine and Burke was the British constitutional model, which had evolved as a consequence of the 'Glorious Revolution' of 1688. Three key elements were inextricably bound up in that revolution: a defence against the perceived encroachment of the royal prerogative upon asserted political liberties; protection of Protestant religious liberty; and a resolution to the Catholic Franco-Spanish national security threat through alliances with European Protestant powers such as Holland and Hanover. The Glorious Revolution reprised and resolved the political conflicts of the earlier Stuart monarchs. These had culminated in a final crisis over James II's attempts to modify the Protestant religious settlement by royal prerogative against political resistance, which coalesced around the Whig faction in Parliament. The

Whig position reflected the ideas of John Locke and his social contract theory expressed in his *Two Treatises on Government* (1690). Government authority should be legitimized by consent, legally secured through representative institutions such as Parliament, as typified by the Bill of Rights (1689). Without this consent, individuals retained a right of resistance against tyranny.

Politically, the Glorious Revolution led to a period of 'Whig Supremacy' between 1714 and 1760, headed by an oligarchy maintained by a patronage machine typified by the administration of Robert Walpole and his successors. Meanwhile, the Tory political opposition originally characterized by passive non-resistance to, and the restoration of, Stuart rule was re-absorbed into constitutional politics by a new synthesis of Whig and Tory ideology described by Henry St John, Viscount Bolingbroke. This accepted the Hanoverian succession and absorbed Tories into a 'Country' Whig faction, in opposition to the Walpolian 'Court' Whigs in government.[3] Bolingbroke's critique of the corruption of the Walpolian executive in *The Craftsman* mirrored that of the independent Whigs John Trenchard and Thomas Gordon in *Cato's Letters* and, along with Locke, provided the main ideological basis for political opposition, both in Britain and the colonies.[4]

The main focus for this opposition was the operation of the fiscal-military state under a growing national security bureaucracy. The 1688 settlement had produced a political establishment tied to a strategy of power projection in Europe and the state's capacities to sustain it. The defining characteristics of this model of the fiscal-military state were the financial and legislative machinery necessary to operate a funded national debt and the government bureaucracy necessary to support and maintain effective military forces.[5] Externally, the capabilities of the post-1688 fiscal-military state were predicated on involvement in entangling alliances and episodic preventive warfare demanded by balance of power politics.[6] Country Whig opposition ideology denounced not only this foreign policy, but also the corruptive influence of increasing executive patronage on the legislature made possible by the increased expenditures, military establishments and expanding bureaucracy of the fiscal-military state.

These two strains of Whig factionalism were eventually absorbed into an establishment consensus marked by the conduct and eventual settlement of the Seven Years War (1756–62). The war had originated in Anglo-French competition in the Ohio valley and then spread to become a global conflict culminating in decisive British victories, including the conquest and annexation of Canada. The conduct of the war had featured the successful projection of British military and naval power across the globe at great financial cost, made possible by the expanded operation of the British fiscal-military state. This had serious political consequences in Britain and America.

In Britain, the conclusion of the war had seen a new king, George III, impose policies that were perceived to threaten the existing political order. This began with the imposition of an unpopular peace settlement under the king's former tutor, Lord Bute, which ended nearly sixty years of Whig ministerial dominance over the executive. By appointing a series of successive ministries designed to unite around his approved policies, sustained in Parliament by government patronage, George III excluded from power while also entrenching a consistent Whig opposition faction. The division between Whig opposition and the new governmental establishment catalysed around policy in America, where the security costs associated with the military establishment necessary to defend the British colonies led to attempts to tax the colonists directly.[7] This brought on a new political crisis, pitching conservatives against radicals and exposing the limited application of the Bill of Rights to imperial possessions. The controversies involved led to a decade of increasingly polarized resistance to British policy affecting colonial legislative and property rights, escalating assertions of British legislative authority in response and finally the outbreak of rebellion in 1775.[8]

Burke, Paine and Whig Ideology

Burke's position in this crisis was essentially that of the leading establishment opposition spokesman. His objections to taxation policy in the colonies were conditioned by his Whig suspicions of executive abuse of power. In accordance with his views on the 1688 settlement, Burke accepted that the colonies were subject to parliamentary sovereignty but insisted that such sovereignty should be exercised wisely. It should not inflame colonial opposition by imposing legislation that violated long-standing customs and liberties, such as the near autonomy of the colonial assemblies. For Burke, British policy was at fault for attempting to impose taxation that violated colonial ideas of government by consent and overturned a prior tradition of 'wise and salutary neglect' by central government.[9]

This represented a critique made on grounds that were distinct from those of radicals, both in Britain and America. The issue for many of these radicals was taxation by representative bodies and the assertion of individual rights. While strongly critical of British policy, Burke rejected radical demands such as American representation in Parliament, the abandonment of mercantile restrictions on American trade or the instruction of representatives by their electors.[10] For him, consent involved decision-making by a representative elite and not popular delegation. Burke followed Montesquieu's veneration of the mixed-government model that the British constitution established after 1688, balancing monarchy, aristocracy and democratic representation in parliamentary sovereignty.[11] He saw the American Revolution as defending the balance of power involved in that model, with the abuses of an overreaching executive provoking an exceptional but justified defensive war.

In contrast, radical political demands sprang from a tradition of Whig ideology that was distinct from Burke's conservative liberalism. They followed the example of the 'Commonwealth men', Puritan and dissenting anti-monarchical republicans of the Stuart era. Their philosophy was drawn from the ideals of the Cromwellian Commonwealth represented by Algernon Sidney's *Discourses Concerning Government* (1698) and his martyrdom at the hands of the Stuarts in 1683. Although they had been marginalized by the Restoration and Hanoverian establishment, some of their objectives translated into Country Whig opposition, notably in the form of demands for more regular elections and above all more uniform representation in Parliament based upon expanded or universal suffrage.

Radical authors influenced by this tradition gained impetus in the imperial crisis as British liberty was perceived to be under threat. Jeremy Bentham's *Fragment on Government* (1776), Richard Price's *Observations on the Nature of Civil Liberty* (1776) and Joseph Priestley's *The Present State of Liberty in Great Britain and Her Colonies* (1769) all laid the foundations for the natural-rights model Paine developed in his *Rights of Man*.[12] Figures associated with these radicals enjoyed sympathetic relations with pre-revolutionary transatlantic American protagonists such as Benjamin Franklin. Radicals took the egalitarian nature of colonial society, which lacked a hereditary aristocracy or established church and featured more openly democratic colonial assemblies, as an idealized manifestation of radical English ideals.[13]

Within this context of radical thought, Paine's polemics in favour of American independence, laid out in *Common Sense* and *The American Crisis* (1776), seemed to capture the changing mood of the times and the spirit of the future. These appeared at precisely the right moment to catalyse popular support for independence and energize the colonists' struggle against Britain. This was not just a question of re-ordering domestic politics; a political philosophy of foreign policy as well as domestic government was central to Paine's constitutional thesis.[14] He outlined a future of pacific internal and international relations, which could be achieved by republican democracy as the political expression of human rationality. For Paine, American independence was an opportunity to overthrow a tyrannical monarchical regime and to recast government on a new basis of republican democracy as an expression of natural rights.

Where Paine and the radicals saw the American Revolution as an overthrow of the old order, Burke saw it as a defence of that established order. Initially convinced of the capacity of the British constitution to adapt and accommodate American demands, Burke had only slowly come to accept the inevitability of American independence. Burke's disagreement with the natural rights philosophy and the democratic radicalism that sprang from it only became clearly apparent in response to the French Revolution, which began in 1789. While the Whig opposition in Parliament welcomed this revolution as another iteration of the events of 1688, Burke was immediately and openly hostile, rejecting the parallel. His publication of *Reflections on the Revolution in France* specified these differences in detail and implicitly defined his understanding of the differences between the events of 1688 and 1776, on the one hand, and 1789 on the other.

Burke took a suspicious view of human nature and cautioned against the unleashing of popular forces that could overturn the stabilizing forces of government, social order and moral judgement to produce anarchy and autocracy. He recognized the necessity for change, but advocated slow, cautious and gradual reform to preserve the accumulated wisdom of the past embodied in existing institutions. Having previously advised the American colonists that the British Parliament was capable of 'renovating' and 'self-reformation', Burke denied that such legitimate reform was happening in France as republican democracy overthrew the competing institutions of mixed government, thereby annihilating the potential checks and balances against despotism.[15] Burke was immediately criticized by radicals and his former Whig allies as an anachronistic defender of the dead hand of repressive traditional authority. Characteristic of this response was Thomas Jefferson's reaction that that 'The Revolution in France does not astonish me so much as the revolution of Mr. Burke'.[16]

The radical philosophy of government based on popular sovereignty, rational cosmopolitanism and individual rights was expounded in Paine's response to Burke, *The Rights of Man*. Paine challenged Burke's understanding of the purpose of constitutional law and asserted that Britain had no constitution, as he defined it.[17] He rejected the determining role of the past as modern democracy apparently overthrew the *Ancien Régime* in Europe. Even the concept of revolution itself was reframed: it went from meaning a cyclical return to an original state to signifying an irreversible social and political change that led to something new.[18]

The crux of the disagreement between Burke and Paine lay in their differing understanding of liberty as something achieved by the exercise of individual natural rights or something mediated and secured by traditional institutions. In other words: the choice between revolution or reform. Central to this was their understanding of the American Revolution as a model for emulation, as an example of either conservative liberalism or radical democratic liberalism.

The Impact of the American Revolution and the Re-creation of the Fiscal-Military State

The first phase of the American Revolution seemed to mirror the convictions of the radicals. The organization of continent-wide protests against British policy and then the overthrow of British rule by mob violence, civil action and military force had all involved large-scale and successful popular engagement. Congress attempted to harness this popular engagement by encouraging the reconstitution of state governments with increased democratic input through wider electorates, annual elections, the use of secret ballots and weaker executives chosen by election. One example was Pennsylvania, where Paine was personally involved in the controversial imposition of a new and more democratic state constitution with a unicameral legislature.[19]

What began to reverse this apparent vindication of radical Whig ideology were the unfolding events of the War of Independence. Military success was determined by the capabilities of the fiscal-military state and, specifically, the capacity to generate and project force within the international system. The second phase of the conflict in 1776–78 involved significant setbacks for the colonies, attributable to the shortcomings of the colonial war effort, as the deployment of mobilized British military and naval power across the Atlantic led to the recapture of New York and Philadelphia. Only the intervention of French, Spanish and then Dutch forces in a global escalation of the war after the American victory at Saratoga changed this dynamic and drew the focus of British strategy and resources elsewhere. Even then, the Americans were never able to eject the British from New York and they were unable to defeat an offensive campaign in the southern states until the British force involved could be isolated and defeated by French naval power at Yorktown in 1781.

The significance of international politics to American success was well understood by the colonial leadership, as evidenced by the importance they attached to their efforts to secure diplomatic recognition and foreign financial and military support. A key factor constraining American diplomacy and military capability was the lack of an effective executive government. In this phase of the conflict, Congress struggled to reconcile the exercise of central authority necessary to maintain large military forces and conduct international diplomacy with a radical Whig ideology determined to resist the evils of centralized government.[20]

This problem came to a head with the Articles of Confederation, the first attempt to frame a constitution for national government. These had been drafted in 1777, but they were only ratified in 1781. In the interim, individual states had the power to delay or veto legislation by refusing ratification. The inability of the Confederation administration to pay and supply the Continental army led to mutinies in 1781 and 1783. As the war ended, states refused to comply with government financial requisitions and pursued independent revenue-raising activities and even foreign relations. State governments imperilled the peace terms through their refusal to accept litigation to recover loyalist losses leading to the continued British occupation of forts on the north-western border.[21] Trade income collapsed as a result of the exclusion of American ships from the British mercantile trading system, leaving ordinary Americans exposed to higher domestic tax rates than they had ever experienced under colonial rule.[22] Unrestricted state issuance of paper money risked resuming the inflationary spiral that had destroyed the value of Continental currency during the war. The outbreak of Shays' Rebellion in Massachusetts in 1786 highlighted the danger of popular insurrection against state governments that attempted to impose conservative tax policies in response to these problems.[23]

These experiences exposed the shortcomings of some of the popular radical notions of the day and led to a nationalist grouping, led by former military officers like Alexander Hamilton, financiers like Robert Morris, conservative politicians like John Jay and Gouverneur Morris and even republican legislators like James Madison, to push for a new and more effective federal constitution. In arguments rehearsed in *The Federalist Papers* (1787–88), Hamilton and his colleagues justified the ratification of a new constitution negotiated at Philadelphia in 1787–88, based on Madison's 'Virginia Plan'.[24] This subordinated state government to a new sovereign federal union. This was to be constructed with a system of checks and balances to forestall executive corruption, but it would also exert sovereignty over the state governments, which were vulnerable to the excesses of popular democracy. This led to the Constitution being defined as 'a conservative counterrevolution', representing a divergence between radical and conservative liberalism in American political history and an embodiment of English traditions.[25]

In reality, the Constitution is not a manifestation of reflexive reactionary counterrevolution. Rather, it reveals the deep wellspring of Burkean conservative liberalism that shaped American statecraft. This may seem perverse given the minimal acknowledgement of Burkeists in the American political tradition. Until the advent of the Cold War resurrected Burke's reputation in the cause of anti-communism, Burkeism was normally identified with figures that were firmly on the wrong side of history, such as Thomas Hutchinson, the last royal governor of Massachusetts, or marginal figures like Joseph Story, US Supreme Court justice.[26] A popular conservative president like Ronald Reagan would opt to cite Paine more frequently than Burke in his public speeches.[27] Yet an examination of the operation of key aspects of Burkean thinking, such as Hutchinson's belief in a living tradition of particular national historical experience or Story's advocation of the primacy of the US Constitution and common law, demonstrates that an essentially Burkean understanding of Anglo-American constitutional development was shared by lawmakers on both sides of the Atlantic.

A comparative examination of the constitutional provisions and Burke's criticism of French constitutional debates in *Reflections* indicates substantive anticipation of Burkean values. Like Burke, the Founders were well aware of the dangers of despotism arising from unrestricted democracy.[28] Burke and figures identified with his thinking, like John Adams, were frequently criticized for being apologists for aristocracy. In Burke's case, there was some truth to such criticism, but this reflected the particular social circumstances of Britain, where the aristocracy was a powerful and established constituency in the social order. Burke recognized that a British aristocratic political elite did not exist in America. In place of a hereditary aristocracy, Federalists like Adams or Hamilton wanted to ensure that the right sort of people – typically lawyers or landowners considered part of a natural colonial decision-making elite – served as legislative representatives. Madison might not have shared Burke's dim view of members of the French National Assembly as vexatious village lawyers dominated by a lynch mob.[29] But despite his denials that the Constitution involved representation by an aristocracy, his experience of the low quality of representatives in the Confederation Congress led him to echo Burkean thinking in his attempt to 'confine the choice to characters of general notoriety and so far be favourable to merit'.[30]

Although Madison sought a greater degree of democratic representation than Burke favoured, he argued for qualifications and constraints, including the 'filtering' of popular will through different forms of representation, as well as arguing for the necessity of a directly elected branch of the legislature to engender 'sympathy' between the people and their rulers.[31] Burke would have disputed the necessity of direct representation to establish popular will, but he accepted a degree of democratic representation as an essential social force and agreed with Madison's rejection of the radical Whig shibboleths of annual terms for representatives and instruction by their electorates.[32]

While Madison was successful in the House of Representatives in tying representation to taxable status and avoiding pocket boroughs, as experienced in Britain, aspects of the Constitution had clearly been designed to curb popular sovereignty in the separated branches of government. One such aspect was the composition of the Senate in the Connecticut compromise, whereby each state had equal representation, regardless of population. The role of the Senate was clear. Madison himself stated that it was required 'as a check on democracy', further strengthened against popular pressure by longer terms of office.[33] If the House was to be an openly representative body, the longer terms and less representative nature of the Senate would allow it to contest popular will in the House.

A second example was the role of the federal courts in enforcing federal law in the states and, more particularly, the innovation of a supreme court with the potential power of judicial review of legislation. This was successfully asserted in Marbury v. Madison in 1803, which has been described as 'an epoch-making settlement vindicating the power of judges to lay down the law to politicians in the name of the Constitution'.[34] The anti-populist role of the Supreme Court in upholding the constitution against repugnant state or even federal law would quickly be in evidence as Chief Justice John Marshall pursued a perceived Federalist, or pro-central government, brief against subsequent state governments and Republican presidents alike.[35] This effectively elevated the definitive interpretation of the Constitution to an unelected professional legal forum, steeped in the precedent traditions of British common law.

Finally, although the need for a strong executive necessitated a certain uneasy reference to the British model, the president would be elected for a fixed term by delegates from the state governments, rather than a popular vote, and subject to impeachment in Congress. Fears of the abuse of executive patronage were to be addressed by congressional confirmation of appointments.

The selection of delegates to the constitutional convention was left to the state governments, but ratification of the Constitution was taken directly to separate state conventions, largely to avoid predictable opposition to the expansion of federal government powers at the expense of the states. Acceptance of the scope and powers of the new constitution nonetheless demanded a compromise in the form of ten immediate amendments, presented as the Bill of Rights (1789).

If this was a self-conscious imitation of the checks and balances in a form of mixed government in the British constitution, then the Americans diverged over the role of religion in the state. Where the US Constitution prohibited religious tests, thereby confirming the Enlightenment ideal of freedom of conscience, the British constitution was openly sectarian, enforcing allegiance to the Church of England and only extending limited civic toleration of Catholics and dissenters outside the official sphere. In part, this can be explained by the differences in denominational composition and historical context. America had been settled by a range of diverse but distinct sects, ranging from Puritans and Congregationalists in New England, a range of European Protestant sects in the middle colonies and south, and small enclaves of Catholic settlement in Maryland and a non-denominational establishment in Rhode Island. Although the colonies included a substantial and politically significant Anglican/Episcopalian constituency, attempts to impose an Anglican

hierarchy appointed by the metropolitan government on the colonies provoked resistance.

The new Constitution sought to achieve a consensual social stability in
an official religious toleration that reflected a broad non-denominational
Protestant consensus in colonial political society. By contrast, Catholics and
dissenters in Britain were seen as threats to national security domestically and,
in the Catholic case, internationally. For the Founders, it was great power
competition in the international system by nation-states, rather than religion,
that represented the major security threat to the new nation. This was evident
in their defence of republican government in international affairs, which implicitly discounted the Painite view of pacific republican relations. Hamilton
made this explicit when dismissing 'visionary or designing men' advocating
'the paradox of perpetual peace' to be achieved by the 'pacific genius' of republics in place of monarchies. For him, the lesson of history was that republics
were as prone as other forms of government to wars driven by popular rage,
avarice and resentment, with little or no constraint from mutual commercial
interest.[36]

The success of the constitutional convention and the centrality of the constitution to the self-image and national identity of the United States led to the
constitution, and the Founding Fathers who created it, being swiftly elevated
to the Olympian plane. Burke understood and agreed with this veneration of
'canonized forefathers' tempering the spirit of freedom 'with an awful gravity'.[37] This soon assumed the appearance of deification, with the Constitution
being analogized to the Ark of the Covenant, produced 'on the holiest spot' in
America, visited by 'pilgrims' who came to worship before a shrine.[38] American conservatives, in particular, have been identified with such Constitutional
'fetishism'. In 1981, Barry Goldwater, a senator for three decades and the archetypal modern American conservative, confessed:

> Being a conservative in America traditionally has meant that one holds a deep,
> abiding respect for the Constitution. We conservatives believe sincerely in the in-
> tegrity of the Constitution. We treasure the freedoms that document protects.[39]

While Goldwater and his ilk were and remain clear believers in individual
rights, these rights were firmly anchored in a Burkean understanding of the
constitution as the referent object for the traditional expression of customary
rights, which would otherwise be lost in the abstract or speculative plane and
which transmitted them to future generations from the past.

This concept of prescriptive right, or legitimacy established by customary
practice, was central to Burke's writings and attracted considerable opposition from his critics. Yet even Paine himself, when arguing that the 1776

Pennsylvania constitution be given 'a fair trial' and accepted by a convention without a direct public vote, had effectively accepted the operation of prescriptive right.[40] To this day, Burkean echoes of prescription are hard to avoid in contemporary US politics, particularly when presidential appointments to the Supreme Court involve commentary on the requirement to follow established precedent, admitting a Burkean understanding of the prescriptive influence of both the Constitution and customary common law.[41]

This balanced appreciation of prescription was evident in the provisions in the Constitution regarding amendments. These represented a relatively high bar for reformers to clear and were designed to deter excessive change while allowing some change to be effected through due deliberation and lawful means. This acknowledged Burke's dicta that it was necessary to preserve the power to change, which should be codified in law rather than resting on the perpetual appeal to revolutionary force implied by Paine. Ultimately, there would only be two amendments between the adoption of the Bill of Rights and the 13th Amendment abolishing slavery in 1865.

Burke himself made little comment on the US Constitution at the time. Ironically, however, he did make one passing reference in response to a personal visit by Paine in 1788.[42] At that point, Paine had returned to Britain as a bridge-building entrepreneur after a period spent working as a Federalist propagandist promoting the new Constitutional settlement. Within a year, the outbreak of the French Revolution acrimoniously exposed their differences over the sources and embodiment of constitutional authority. Despite his initial doubt that the colonies could construct a viable constitution after the Declaration of Independence, it is clear that the record of the Founding Fathers, and in particular their capacity to restrain democratic excess while maintaining traditional liberties, would have met with Burkean approval. His dismissal of the French National Assembly as dominated by the mob waiting to execute their delegates 'if they should deviate into moderation' implied the clear difference between the two revolutions, as he saw it.[43]

Burke made his most definitive statement of this approval during a parliamentary debate on the Constitutional Act of 1791. The Act attempted to remedy the neglectful 'government by default' approach to colonial administration in Canada, which had largely persisted since the British conquest of 1760. This had been confirmed by the toleration of local civil law and religion mandated by the Quebec Act of 1774 and the subsequent abandonment of the parliamentary claim to colonial revenue powers in 1778.[44] Despite the acceptance of local representative assemblies in the 1791 Act, against the troubling background of the French Revolution, Burke both welcomed the Act and commented in passing that the American constitutional model (although unattractive to American loyalist refugees in Canada) embodied a republic 'as near to the principles of our Constitution as Republics could be'.[45]

The Republicans and the Federalist Tradition

Continuity between the American experience and the British model was implicit, but it was not a guarantee of future developments in America. Much would depend upon the direction taken by early political leadership. This leadership class, imbued with the populist Country Whig ideology of the American Revolution, soon split along factional lines defined by the radical/conservative divergence personified by Burke and Paine. Ultimately, early US governments would move away from the democratic radicalism of the tradition associated with Paine and demonstrate a partial but instinctual adherence to Burkean principles.

The ratification of the Constitution in 1789 inaugurated the Federalist era, a decade when government was dominated by figures associated with the need for a strong executive. Key Federalist figures included the first president George Washington (1789–97), who lent his considerable personal authority to establishing precedent in the role; John Adams, his vice-president and then the second president (1797–1801); and Hamilton, Washington's Secretary of the Treasury. As a party of government, the Federalists quickly came to be identified with a Burkean interpretation of Whig ideology. This involved the consolidation of executive power and defence of the established constitution against opposition demands couched in terms of popular sovereignty. It also featured a pragmatic and concessionary foreign policy that rejected the claims of radical ideology and accepted a substantial mutual interest in pacific Anglo-American relations.

What helped to perpetuate the identity of Federalism and a Federalist party was the growth of an oppositional party, the Republicans, which loosely coalesced around Thomas Jefferson and James Madison. The Republicans differed from the Federalists in domestic political terms, repeating the Country/Court Whig conflict of the pre-revolutionary era. These differences were evident in the controversial establishment of the First Bank of the United States, designed by Hamilton to perform the functions of a central bank like the Bank of England and representing a similar powerful nexus of the executive corruption implicit to the fiscal-military state to Republicans. Such ideological antagonisms were also evident in Republicans' sympathy for French Jacobin revolutionary ideology.

The French Revolution, the French Revolutionary War (1793–1803) and then the Napoleonic Wars (1803–15) elevated the ideological struggle between conservatism and revolutionary democracy to the world stage, in the process defining American politics far into the future. Jefferson gave significant rhetorical support to the cause of anti-monarchical democratic revolution in the name of universal natural rights, whereas Hamilton regarded the French Revolution with suspicion and as a threat to property and social order. A vitriolic factional dispute began, with Hamilton being accused of being a monarchist and British apologist as he attempted to conciliate the British government after the Anglo-French conflict began. In contrast, Jefferson deployed a selective Anglophobia to celebrate French successes at British expense while sympathizing with the Jacobins. For Jefferson and Republicans following his lead, the success of the French Revolution was essential to the security of American democracy.[46]

Republicans, who were soon joined by Madison, swiftly capitalized on anti-Federalism as an opposition constituency by mobilising dissent over the issue of states' rights against a Federal sovereignty that was exercised on disagreeable policy terms for many. Madison had already been forced to concede the Bill of Rights to facilitate ratification. Although the Bill of Rights was loosely modelled on the British Bill of Rights (1689), it contained explicit safeguards of individual rights. These highlighted the conceptual core of Republican opposition, which culminated in the Kentucky and Virginia Resolves (1798–99), made to defend those rights and restrict the exercise of federal power over the states in response to the Alien and Sedition Acts (1798).

The Alien and Sedition Acts restricted access to citizenship, permitted the expulsion of aliens on security grounds and restricted criticism of the Federal government. These provisions all reflected Federalist suspicions of democratic agitation inspired by the French Revolution. Taken together, they described the ultimate extent of Federalist rejection of radical Jacobinism, which followed a trajectory already described by Burke. The publication of Burke's *Reflections*, followed by the mass executions of the Reign of Terror of 1793 and the outbreak of Revolutionary warfare, led to a swift division between more conservative Whigs and radical sympathizers in both Britain and America. The American dimension of this division became quickly apparent after Jefferson identified himself with Paine's ideology by writing a dedication to the first edition of *The Rights of Man* published in America, resigning from Washington's administration and aligning himself with Madison's Republican opposition.

The international nature of the growing Federalist/Republican factional dispute was encapsulated in the Jay Treaty (1795), the keystone diplomatic achievement of the Washington administration. This negotiated a settlement of existing disputes with Britain, including the provocations caused by the enforcement of the British maritime blockade of France. The terms of the treaty, and the process of Senate ratification conducted in secret, inflamed Republican opposition. They saw the treaty and Washington's broader policy of neutrality in the Anglo-French conflict as abrogating the 1778 alliance with France and capitulating to the abuse of British naval power. The Republican reaction to Washington's Farewell Address (1797) was similar. Although its advocacy of non-intervention in European conflict faithfully echoed earlier Country Whig ideology and would subsequently become an article of faith for Jeffersonian Democrats in later US history, it was understood at the time to be a rejection of revolutionary ideological affinity with France.[47]

Worse was to follow for Francophile Republicans, as the corrupt conduct of French diplomacy with the United States triggered the 'XYZ' bribery scandal and the consequent 'quasi-war' with France in 1798. Although the administration of John Adams was able to reach a settlement in 1800, the brief conflict with France confirmed the gap between Republican hopes and Federalist policy. This gap would endure after Jefferson's apparent watershed victory in the 1800 presidential election. Jefferson's election eventually eclipsed Federalism as a viable political force and ushered in a Republican 'Virginia dynasty' of presidents, comprising Jefferson and his acolytes Madison and then James Monroe. However, the influence of Republican ideology on those administrations would prove to be less definitive and sometimes more tempered by Burkeism than might initially appear to be the case.

Jefferson's experience in government is indicative. Originally a champion of states' rights and strict construction of the constitution against the encroaching authority of the Federal government, the foreign-policy behaviour of his government soon followed the Federalist model. His accommodation with the Federalist practice of executive authority was evident in the tacit abandonment of his constitutional scruples about the powers of the executive during the process of the Louisiana Purchase from France (1803). With an almost Hamiltonian appreciation of the need for speed and secrecy in such high-order interstate diplomacy, Jefferson concluded the deal, funded the purchase using public credit and then established government in the annexed territory by presidential fiat. Internationally, Jefferson's conflict against Tripolitanian piracy in the Mediterranean (1801–5) involved sustained naval expeditionary warfare, a state capability previously decried by Republican opposition to Federalist naval rearmament policy.

Even the ideological antagonism central to the Republican view of Anglo-American relations declined as the nature of the French regime observably changed. By the time he entered office, even Jefferson saw little difference between the French emperor Napoleon and his previous bugbear, George III. By contrast, Jefferson became exceptionally cautious of the international dangers represented by French revolutionary principles after the slave revolt on Haiti (1791–1804) potentially threatened slave-owning states in the United States.

Even when dealing with Britain, the embodiment of political evil for Republicans, Jefferson adhered to cautious reason of state rather than ideological rigidity. The attack on the USS *Chesapeake* by a British warship in 1807 presented Jefferson with the clearest *casus belli* in more than a decade of fraught maritime relations with Britain. Yet he chose to de-escalate the issue and seek a diplomatic solution. This was concurrent with the implementation of the Embargo Act, which sought to impose sanctions on US maritime trade to force British concessions. Although this was a long-held Republican policy prescription for dealing with Britain, both issues indicated the extent to which Jefferson was prepared to employ cautious alternatives to the open conflict with Britain demanded by Republican ideologues.

Jefferson's ambiguity can be partially explained by the shortcomings of Country Whig ideology and by direct experience of the international system. On the ideological side, Republican hostility to executive corruption in a fiscal-military state proved to be as a malleable when in government as it had been for previous Whigs. During the Seven Years War, the Earl of Chatham had pursued a continental military commitment, the employment of unpopular Hessian mercenaries and an expensive series of overseas offensives. All of these policies conflicted with the Country Whig programme of isolationist retrenchment and militia service he had espoused in opposition.[48] When electoral process rather than revolution allowed Republicans to supplant the Federalists, they quickly reconciled themselves to the exercise of executive power in the fiscal-military state created by the Constitution. In international politics, they followed Chatham's example of balance of power policies informed by pragmatic interpretations of national interest, rather than the contrary demands of internationalist revolutionary ideology.

Republican ideology did achieve a final conflict with Britain (1812–15) during Madison's presidency. Provoked by an intensified British naval blockade of Europe initiated by a briefly hard-line British ministry, and a Republican position that combined belief in inviolable neutral rights in international trade, Country Whig prejudices against industrial trade as corrupting luxury and a mistaken estimation of the unique vulnerability of British commercial interests to American economic sanctions, the war was ended with a return to the status quo ante. The 1812 War did little other than expose the continuing shortcomings of an American war effort and foreign policy based on Republican ideology. The creation of an effective fiscal-military state by the Federalists proved to be less significant to American military capability than the continuing negative impact of Republican policies. Minimal taxation led to consequently minimal military preparedness. This was only compounded by Madison's mistaken evaluation of relative British power capabilities at the time of Napoleon's decisive defeat in Russia.

The post-war era was marked by continuing Republican dominance and the eclipse of the Federalist party. Republicans continued to debate 'strict construction' of the Constitution to limit governmental powers to those that were explicitly pronounced, but their acceptance of that Constitution without radical reform when in office indicated the obsolescence of the rigid ideological positions of the Federalist era.[49]

Indicative of this change was the decline into unpopularity and irrelevance of Burke's great rival. Paine's enthusiasm for the French Revolution expressed in *The Rights of Man* had led directly to his conviction for sedition in Britain and his flight to France. Initially welcomed by French radicals and elected as a representative in the National Convention, Paine had reversed his initial Federalism to enter the lists in defence of the pro-French Republican factionalism. Attempting to capitalize on both the international fame of the first president and the assumed commonality of the two revolutions, Paine dedicated *The Rights of Man* to Washington but was soon made aware of the gulf in sympathy between the Federalists and his fellow radicals. He quickly became a victim of French revolutionary politics, was imprisoned under the potential threat of execution and denounced Washington for his Burkean 'prudence' in failing to secure his prompt release. Paine finally returned to the United States in 1803 to find himself and his cause discredited by his denunciation of Washington, his open attack on religion in *The Age of Reason* (1794–1807) and his identification with the Jacobin security threat.[50]

After the decline of Francophile Republican revolutionary sympathy and the 1812 War, Britain and America groped their way back to the kind of prudence that had marked their previous relationship; diplomacy conducted by elite policymakers resulted in a series of limited concessional agreements to avoid war. Occasionally, this relationship was promoted by identifiably Burkean individuals, as exemplified by Richard Rush's involvement in the Rush–Bagot treaty, which disarmed naval forces on the Great Lakes (1818). More frequently, it was a product of habitual patterns of behaviour, evident even in the unlikely case of the populist Democrat president Andrew Jackson (1829–37).[51]

Jacksonian Democrats continued the Jeffersonian tradition of a rhetorical adherence to anti-elitism, individual rights and the primacy of popular sovereignty, which was certainly not Burkean. Nor was Jackson's approach to relations with Native Americans, whose treatment as conquered nations exhibited a racist imperialism and could be contrasted with Burke's rejection of historical British policy in Ireland or India.[52] Surprisingly, these positions did not guarantee that US foreign policy would be determined by the contemporary popular Anglophobia noted by Alexis de Tocqueville. Rather, Jackson pursued a pragmatic and conciliatory approach towards Britain.[53] The adversarial dynamic demanded by Jeffersonian ideology was instead expressed internally against opponents like Henry Clay, while behind the egalitarian rhetoric the dominance of the existing political elites continued.[54]

The Jacksonian era demonstrated that, despite the growing democratic populism of US politics, a limited but discernible Burkean qualification of Jeffersonian ideology could still be identified. This involved a traditional political elite upholding federal and executive authority at the expense of Jeffersonian strict construction. This was clearly apparent in the actions of Whig president John Tyler to help suppress the Dorr Rebellion in Rhode Island (1842) by prioritizing constitutional authority over efforts to convene a state constitutional convention to reduce the electoral property qualification.[55] The enduring influence of conservative instincts on both sides of the resumed Democrat–Whig party divide in US politics was evident in the reaction of the populist president Martin Van Buren when he briefly served as ambassador in London during the passage of the Great Reform Bill in 1832. Van Buren was more concerned with maintaining public order than celebrating the success of radical demands for increased democratic participation in government.[56]

Constitutional Development in Britain

This sense of priorities was analogous with the British experience. Although British radicals continued to adopt the United States as a democratic model to emulate, this did not determine the development of either constitutional reform or better relations with the United States. Rather, these flowed from the decisions of a governing elite, which prioritized national interests and defence of the established British constitutional settlement. This was evident in the evolution of concessionary policy on free trade, which threatened the accepted mercantile and naval basis of British power; religious toleration, which threatened to reignite religious conflict; and more representative democracy, which threatened political and social stability.

Ending the mercantilist trading policy exemplified by the restrictive Navigation Acts had long been an objective of radicals and became a particular focus of US trade policy, which sought commercial access to the British West Indies. An attempt to include a comprehensive commercial treaty was packaged into the terms of the peace in 1783, but this proved too much for a Parliament more concerned with restoring the status quo after an unsuccessful war. British policy remained wedded to the defence of economic nationalism and naval security interests implicit in the Navigation Acts for the next forty years.

Nonetheless, a series of limited concessions on US access to British West Indian trade were made in the closing decades of the eighteenth century. These met the pragmatic expectations of Federalists such as Adams and Hamilton, but failed to elicit reciprocal measures from the following Republican administrations. These administrations adhered to a narrow and legalistic interpretation of national commercial rights consistent with Jeffersonian policy, which sought to eliminate American trade with Britain on ideological grounds.[57] Substantial initiatives to broaden British trade relations were made under the ministry of William Pitt, not just in the form of the Jay Treaty, but also in the form of a commercial treaty with France in 1786. Despite the repeated provocations and difficulties involved in clashes between US neutral shipping and British wartime naval blockades of French-dominated Europe, Pitt and the Federalist administrations in the United States were able to manage the Anglo-American commercial relationship such that this period could be described as 'the first rapprochement' between the two countries.[58]

Pitt, who described himself as 'an independent Whig' in defiance of later characterizations as a reactionary Tory, took cautious reform beyond trade policy.[59] His initiatives to reform representation in the House of Commons in 1785 in consultation with moderate radicals, and to link the enfranchisement of Irish Catholics with the union of Britain and Ireland in 1800, ultimately failed.[60] But when considered in conjunction with his reform of government revenue and accounting administration and his covert adoption of Burkean economical reform to reduce crown patronage in Parliament, it is clear that there was considerable scope for liberal reform under what was classified as a Tory government. Ironically, this went further than Burke was comfortable with; he was deeply suspicious of parliamentary reform and the propensity for democracy to regress into tyranny.[61]

Pitt's approach to reform became uncompromising in response to the French Revolutionary War. This was demonstrated by a raft of openly repressive legislation designed to combat radical agitation, such as the Combination Acts (1799), which were concurrent with a series of wartime coalitions with reactionary continental powers. A series of subsequent ministries (including a brief Whig ministry in 1807) followed Pitt's model of defending national institutions against foreign and domestic Jacobinism as the Napoleonic Wars continued.

Representative of this continuity was Lord Castlereagh, who was foreign secretary for much of this period. Later admired by Henry Kissinger for his realism, he was less popular with contemporary radicals for similar reasons. His interpretation of balance of power politics as seeking an international

political equilibrium balancing rights, obligations and security within a framework of law, while avoiding action upon 'abstract and speculative principles',
was implicitly Burkean, as was his encouragement of a harmonious Anglo-
American relationship.[62] His support of Catholic toleration, his refusal to join
the reactionary Holy Alliance of European powers and his attempts to secure
an international antislavery treaty at the Congress of Vienna echoed much of
the platform of his Whig critic Henry Brougham, but could also be described
as Burkean.[63]

A more blustering style of nationalism featured in the foreign policy of
subsequent British governments. Castlereagh's rival and successor George
Canning indulged populist anti-Americanism. His ideological preference
for constitutional monarchy rather than republicanism in his policy on
emerging Latin American republics represented a symmetrical reflection of
the pro-republican Jeffersonianism of the contemporary US administration
of James Monroe.[64] But this did not prevent his recognition of mutual interests, most notably in his proposed Anglo-US initiative against European
involvement in Latin America, which prompted the unilateral US Monroe
Doctrine (1823).

This pragmatism was likewise evident in domestic British politics. The
ministry of Lord Liverpool, notorious for the agrarian protectionism of the
Corn Laws (1815) and the repression of radical political agitation typified
by the Peterloo Massacre (1819), would spend much of the 1820s engaged in
cautious reform. Liverpool gave his subordinates increasing scope to pursue
liberal ends, notably in Robert Peel's reform of the criminal law alongside
William Huskisson's repeal of the Combination Acts and progressive dismantling of the Navigation Acts. These were liberal policies pursued for pragmatic
ends, chiefly the preservation of the existing political establishment and the
maintenance of social harmony from a conservative perspective.[65] This approach was maintained by the Duke of Wellington, the closest thing to a
first-rank reactionary 'ultra' in British politics. Despite opposing almost every reform initiative proposed by the Whigs with prophesies of apocalyptic
disorder, when in power Wellington demonstrated a reluctant but pragmatic
approach to reform typified by the dismantling of the legal privileges of An-
glicanism in the repeal of the Test and Corporation Acts in 1828 and then
Catholic Emancipation in 1829.[66]

This approach culminated in the Great Reform Act of 1832 under the
Whig government of Lord Grey. This addressed several of the long-standing
demands of reformers: eliminating the worst of the rotten and pocket boroughs, redistributing seats to unrepresented industrial towns and imposing
uniform franchise qualifications. The Reform Act opened the way for the development of the aristocratic oligarchy of the Whigs into a socially broader

Liberal party, which influenced American reformers (notably in relation to slavery), but it was insufficient for the radicals.[67] They would return to the attack over the length of parliamentary terms, the payment of MPs and the lack of a secret ballot in the subsequent Chartist movement.[68] Grey's ultimate objective in the Act was explicitly Burkean rather than radical in sympathy: to preserve national institutions from revolutionary violence.[69] While Burke's ultimate attitude to reform had shifted to near hysteria in response to the degeneration of the French Revolution into autocracy, Grey's approach fulfilled Burke's original idealized view of the capacity of the British constitution to preserve and improve.[70]

Developments after the Reform Act followed this pattern of continuity. A combination of almost Jacksonian muscular populism and Burkean instincts of 'reform in order to conserve' was evident under Lord Palmerston.[71] His 'caustic and aggressive' approach to Anglo-American relations dominated the foreign policy of Liberal governments for the rest of the first half of the nineteenth century.[72] Despite his rhetoric, however, Palmerston's aggressive gunboat diplomacy was still remarkably restrained when it came to America and this was reflected on the American side. James Polk's preference for an expansionist war against Mexico rather than fulfilling his warlike electoral posturing against Britain at the time of the Oregon border dispute (1846) is one example; the reluctance of Abraham Lincoln and William Seward, his Anglophobe Secretary of State, to go to war over the *Trent* incident in 1861 (when Confederate emissaries were arrested on a British passenger ship) is another. Despite the influence of popular chauvinism on their rhetorical appeal to their electorates, the care both sides took to avoid conflict remains instructive.

The American domestic experience also indicated the influence of the preservation of traditional institutions characteristic of Burkean statecraft. Increasing waves of immigrants and a process of continual territorial expansion were absorbed by the 1789 Constitution with relatively little adaption until the great constitutional crisis of the 1861–65 Civil War. Although the fundamental driving issue behind the war was the maintenance of slavery, the dispute was expressed as a challenge to Federal sovereignty, drawing on Jeffersonian ideology of strict construction over states' rights. In a more definitive Burkean sense, Lincoln's avowed primary purpose in maintaining the Union by force echoed George III's response to the American Revolution and indicated the centrality of a prescriptive understanding of the Constitution and Federal authority.

The closest parallel with this experience for British statesmen was not slavery, which had been abolished in 1833, with the international slave trade being the target of an active interventionist foreign policy, but rather the

'Irish Question'. Generations of nineteenth-century politicians faced the challenge of reconciling legitimate governance with a lack of popular consent from an alienated Catholic majority through a series of constitutional initiatives: the granting of legislative autonomy as an expedient during the American War of Independence (1782), the Act of Union with Great Britain (1801), followed by various iterations of 'Home Rule' autonomy or civil concessions such as reform of land ownership to break up the absentee estates characteristic of the Protestant Ascendancy. Even here, despite hardline Tory resistance, Liberal measures made slow headway throughout the nineteenth century.

The final development that might be said to have moved Britain in tandem with the United States in terms of representative democracy was the further expansion of the suffrage involved in the 1867 Reform Act. This was not the product of the Liberal party, at that point led by William Gladstone, whose Burkean caution on the subject of parliamentary reform was such that his statements on the subject were greeted with ironical cheers.[73] Rather, it was a product of the Conservative party under Gladstone's great rival Benjamin Disraeli, whose 'Tory Democracy' was based upon a long-standing Burkean principle of protecting ancient institutions and safeguarding popular liberties.[74] Disraeli's success in securing popular support for Conservatism ushered in the long and successful political career of Lord Salisbury, a Tory peer who could be accurately described as fighting a life-long rearguard action in defence of the aristocratic order against democracy.[75]

Democratic Peace and the Liberal State

The most significant point about this process of concomitant constitutional development and Anglo-American relations is that it falsified the ideological assumptions of radicals in the Age of Revolution. Paine built upon Country Whig ideology and elements of Immanuel Kant's 'Perpetual Peace' thesis to determine the pacific nature of democratic relations and thereby justify democratic revolution. He assumed that modern interstate wars and the resultant fiscal-military state were an inescapable product of monarchical government in the international system and that domestic and international peace would automatically be promoted by republican government: 'Man is not the enemy of man, but through the medium of a false system of government.'[76] Burke took a diametrically opposed position in regard to the pacific nature of revolutionary republicanism: 'They are always at issue with governments, not on a question of abuse, but a question of competency, and a question of title.'[77]

Both anticipated later twentieth-century arguments outlined by Michael Doyle about the validity of democratic peace theory. Doyle described the inconsistent results of democratic liberal institutions spreading pacific state behaviour in the international system, basing his analysis upon the expansion of the number of liberal states and their peaceful relationships since the eighteenth century.[78] The United States and Britain represented a particular problem, having fought two wars against one another, but this problem could be avoided through the selective use of defining criteria. While the United States could be described as having the characteristics of a liberal state from its creation in 1776, Britain could be denied similar status until the passage of the Great Reform Act of 1832.

This distinction is no longer necessary or relevant. It can now be confirmed that Britain and the United States did experience a process of slow rapprochement throughout the nineteenth century, pioneered in the 1790s by Federalist administrations in a context defined by the 1789 Constitution. Recognizing the defects of the US government established by the American Revolution, they reformed and then governed a more Burkean model of an independent American fiscal-military state, which went against the Country Whig ideology and natural rights philosophy preferred by their Republican opposition. In both cases, their respective systems of government linked foreign and domestic policy so closely that the division between them became almost indistinguishable.[79]

Despite the apparent triumph of Jeffersonian Republicanism over the Federalist party, the policies pursued by Federalism would set the precedent both for subsequent US representative government under a strong executive and a bicameral democratic/quasi-aristocratic legislature, and also for the foreign-policy behaviour of that government.[80] As Max Edling has observed, understanding the behaviour of the early American republic demands consideration of the policies and utilization of political institutions, rather than partisan rhetoric.[81]

A key feature of that behaviour would be the rejection of the promotion of international republican revolution in favour of an interest-based realism that promoted pacific relations with Britain, the archetypal monarchical adversary of Republican ideology, at the same time as the United States gained the state capacity to conduct effective diplomacy and to expand and project power across the North American continent and eventually the international system. On the British side, the Great Rapprochement with the United States at the end of the nineteenth century can be seen to be the culmination of a longer-term established tradition of conciliation and preservation by an aristocratic order – Tory, Whig and Liberal – in order to accommodate itself to rising democratic power both at home and abroad.

Conclusion

In conclusion, it can be confirmed that the events of 1787–89 and the following period firmly established the United States as a state on the model of the British experience of 1688 rather than the French model of 1789. Both the United States and Britain rejected unrestricted democracy but were able to accommodate change and increasing democratic participation in government within existing constitutional traditions.

This accommodation also characterized their relationship with one another within the international system. Eliga Gould has asserted that the English-speaking empires on the North American continent replaced a competitive and war-ridden environment in the colonial era with a pacific international regime, animated by mutual beneficial trade and respect for the rule of law marked by binding treaties, reflecting but distinct from the European state system. If this is an accurate understanding of the particular environment created by the evolving Anglo-American relationship, it is now suggested that this was more a product of Burkean conservative liberal regimes than it was a product of internationalist revolutionary democracy.[82] It may be for this reason that Lord Ashburton, the British negotiator of the watershed Webster–Ashburton Treaty (1842), which represented the climactic Anglo-American diplomatic agreement of the period, voted against the Reform Act, while his counterpart Daniel Webster was a one-time Federalist.[83] If so, J.G.A. Pocock's comment that while Pitt the Younger resembled Hamilton, there was no British Jefferson, suggests the deeper and harmonizing influence of Burkean thinking on Britain and America.[84]

Despite the *de jure* separation of Britain and the United States, throughout the nineteenth century Anglo-American statesmen resolved tensions through concessions that rose above sectional and class interests and popular chauvinism to create a multi-dimensional rapprochement.[85] This proceeded from a fundamental ordering of constitutional liberty based on a conservative Burkean interpretation of Whig ideology, which advocated order, pragmatic reform and the value of historic traditions over revolutionary radicalism.[86] This conceptual basis for state formation and behaviour was projected into the international system, allowing the United States as an independent state to enter into a relationship with Britain that was generally calibrated by a nuanced and mutually sympathetic reading of balance of power politics rather than being determined by ideological hostility predicated on the antagonism between radical democracy and conservative reaction. This was an outcome defined by a Burkean understanding of their respective iterations of a Whig fiscal-military state rather than a Painite or even Jeffersonian one.[87]

This outcome represented a specific and particularly Anglo-American construct that operated to successfully manage the intense pressures promoting violent change generated in the revolutionary era on both sides of the Atlantic. It did not hinge upon the assertion of the philosophies of universal rights and democratic peace, but instead proceeded on a Burkean principle of the preservation of constitutional traditions of liberty under the centralized fiscal-military state and the concurrent promotion of harmony by government elites within the Anglo-American transatlantic polity.[88]

Gavin Bailey is a military and diplomatic historian of the Anglo-American relationship. He currently teaches Politics and International Relations at the University of Stirling, Scotland.

Notes

1. T. Paine, *Rights of Man, Common Sense and Other Political Writings* (Oxford: Oxford University Press, 2008), 197.

2. Y. Levin, *The Great Debate: Edmund Burke, Thomas Paine and the Birth of Right and Left* (New York: Basic Books, 2014), xix.

3. H.T. Dickinson, *Bolingbroke* (London: Constable, 1970), 182, 199–201.

4. B. Bailyn, *The Ideological Origins of the American Revolution* (London: The Belknap Press, 1992), 35–39.

5. B. Simms, *Three Victories and a Defeat: The Rise and Fall of the First British Empire* (London: Allen Lane, 2007), 38–42.

6. H.M. Scott, *British Foreign Policy in the Age of the American Revolution* (Oxford: Clarendon Press, 1990), 42–44.

7. J. Bullion, 'Securing the Peace: Lord Bute, the Plan for the Army, and the Origins of the American Revolution', in K.W. Schweitzer (ed.), *Lord Bute: Essays in Re-interpretation* (Leicester: Leicester University Press, 1988), 17–25.

8. J.P. Greene, *Peripheries and Center: Constitutional Development in the Extended Polities of the British Empire and the United States, 1607–1788* (Athens: The University of Georgia Press, 1986), 20.

9. E. Burke, 'Speech on Conciliation with America', in W.M. Elofson and J.A. Woods (eds), *The Writings and Speeches of Edmund Burke. Volume III. Party, Parliament, and the American War 1774–1780* (Oxford: Clarendon Press, 1996), 118.

10. R. Bourke, *Empire and Revolution: The Political Life of Edmund Burke* (Woodstock: Princeton University Press, 2015), 450–59.

11. Montesquieu's views were expressed in *The Spirit of the Laws* (1748).

12. C. Bonwick, *English Radicals and the American Revolution* (Chapel Hill: University of North Carolina Press, 1977), xiv, 14–15; J.R. Reich, *British Friends of the American Revolution* (London: Armok, 1998), 93–94.

13. E. Macleod, *British Visions of America, 1775–1820: Republican Realities* (London: Pickering and Chatto, 2013), 132–36.

14. G.C. Herring, *From Colony to Superpower: U.S. Foreign Relations Since 1776* (Oxford: Oxford University Press, 2008), 11.

15. E. Burke, 'Address to the Colonists', in Elofson and Woods, *The Writings and Speeches of Edmund Burke*, 31.

16. L.G. Mitchell (ed.), *The Writings and Speeches of Edmund Burke. Volume VIII. The French Revolution 1790–1794* (Oxford: Clarendon Press, 1989), 14.

17. Ibid., 4; Paine, *The Rights of Man*, 123–30.

18. E. Foner, *Tom Paine and Revolutionary America* (London: Oxford University Press, 1976), xv.

19. J. Keane, *Tom Paine: A Political Life* (London: Bloomsbury, 2009), 151–54.

20. E.W. Carp, *To Starve the Army at Pleasure: Continental Army Administration and American Political Culture 1775–1783* (Chapel Hill: University of North Carolina Press, 1984), 216–22.

21. M.J. Klarman, *The Framer's Coup: The Making of the United States Constitution* (New York: Oxford University Press, 2016), 45–46.

22. Ibid., 75–77.

23. Ibid., 88–93.

24. J. Madison, A. Hamilton and J. Jay, *The Federalist Papers* (London: Penguin, 1987), 15–27.

25. Klarman, *The Framer's Coup*, x; J.M. Rakove, 'Why American Constitutionalism Worked', in F.M. Turner (ed.), *Reflections on the Revolution in France* (London: Yale University Press, 2004), 250; S. Katz, 'The American Constitution: A Revolutionary Interpretation', in R. Beeman, S. Botein and E.C. Carter, *Beyond Confederation: Origins of the Constitution and American National Identity* (Chapel Hill: University of North Carolina Press, 1987), 31.

26. W. Pencak, *America's Burke: The Mind of Thomas Hutchinson* (London: University Press of America, 1982), 17. D. Maciag, *Edmund Burke in America: The Contested Career of the Father of Modern Conservatism* (Ithaca, NY: Cornell University Press, 2013), 93–96.

27. M.C. Henrie, 'Edmund Burke and Contemporary American Conservatism', in Ian Crowe (ed.), *Edmund Burke: His Life and Legacy* (Dublin: Four Courts Press, 1997), 200.

28. Klarman, *The Framer's Coup*, 74–75.

29. Burke, *Reflections*, 50.

30. Klarman, *The Framer's Coup*, 173. G. Wood, 'Interests and Disinterestedness in the Making of the Constitution', in Beeman et al., *Beyond Confederation*, 74–76.

31. Klarman, *The Framer's Coup*, 170. Madison expounded his views on filtration as 'Publius' in Federalist Numbers 10 and 63, Madison, Hamilton and Jay, *The Federalist Papers*, 126–28; 369–70. J.G.A. Pocock has identified that this 'leaned towards a Burkean position'. J.G.A. Pocock, *The Machiavellian Moment: Florentine Political Thought and the Atlantic Republican Tradition* (Princeton, NJ: Princeton University Press, 2016), 519–20.

32. Klarman, *The Framer's Coup*, 184, 194–95.

33. Ibid., 209.

34. B. Ackerman, *The Failure of the Founding Fathers: Jefferson, Marshall and the Rise of Presidential Democracy* (Cambridge: Harvard University Press, 2005), 8.

35. J.E. Smith, *John Marshall. Definer of a Nation* (New York: Henry Holt, 1996), 322–23.

36. Although Federalist Number 6 addressed the potential of domestic conflict between the component states of the United States, Hamilton's discussion was drawn from historical examples of foreign conflict between independent sovereign states. Alexander Hamilton as 'Publius', in Federalist Number 6, Madison, Hamilton and Jay, *The Federalist Papers*, 106–8.

37. Burke, *Reflections*, 34; B. Ackerman, *The Failure of the Founding Fathers*, 6.

38. Klarman, *The Framer's Coup*, 1–4; J. Murrin, 'A Roof Without Walls. The Dilemma of American National Identity', in Beeman et al., *Beyond Confederation*, 346.

39. R.D. Heffner, *A Documentary History of the United States* (New York: Penguin, 1991), 396.

40. Keane, *Tom Paine*, 151.

41. J. McCue, 'Edmund Burke and the British Constitution', in I. Crowe (ed.), *Edmund Burke. His Life and Legacy*, 175.

42. 'America looks as if she were taking something like a form'. Edmund Burke to Sir Gilbert Elliot, 3 September 1788, in H. Furber, *The Correspondence of Edmund Burke. Volume V July 1782 – June 1789* (London: Cambridge University Press, 1965), 415.

43. Burke, 'Address to the Colonists', in Elofson and Woods, *Party, Parliament and the American War*, 284; Burke to William Windham, 27 September 1789, in A. Cobban and R.A. Smith, *The Correspondence of Edmund Burke. Volume VI. July 1789 – December 1791* (London: Cambridge University Press, 1967), 24.

44. P. Marshall, 'British North America, 1760–1815', in P.J. Marshall (ed.), *The Oxford History of the British Empire. Volume II. The Eighteenth Century* (Oxford: Oxford University Press, 1998).

45. Speech on the Quebec Bill, 6 May 1791. P.J. Marshall, Donald C. Bryant and William B. Todd (eds), *The Writings and Speeches of Edmund Burke, Volume 4: Party, Parliament, and the Dividing of the Whigs: 1780–1794* (Oxford: Oxford University Press, 2016), 329–30.

46. R.W. Tucker and D.C. Henderson, *Empire of Liberty: The Statecraft of Thomas Jefferson* (Oxford: Oxford University Press, 1990), 37, 45.

47. J.T. Ellis, 'The Farewell: Washington's Wisdom at the End', in D. Higginbotham (ed.), *George Washington Reconsidered* (Charlottesville: University of Virginia Press, 2001), 233–36.

48. Simms, *Three Victories and a Defeat*, 417–26.

49. Ackerman, *The Failure of the Founding Fathers*, 93, 113.

50. S. Cotlar, *Tom Paine's America: The Rise and Fall of Transatlantic Radicalism in the Early Republic* (Charlottesville: University of Virginia Press, 2011), 207–11.

51. H.C. Allen, *Great Britain and the United States: A History of Anglo-American Relations 1783–1952* (London: Archon Books, 1969), 361.

52. D.W. Howe, *What Hath God Wrought: The Transformation of America, 1815–48* (New York: Oxford University Press, 2007), 421; Bourke, *Empire and Revolution*, 160–61.

53. A. de Tocqueville, *Democracy in America* (London: David Campbell, 1994), 428; Howe, *What Hath God Wrought*, 431.

54. Howe, *What Hath God Wrought*, 390. E. Pessen, *Jacksonian America: Society, Personality and Politics* (Chicago: University of Illinois Press, 1978), 81–2, 97, 192.

55. Ibid., 599–603.

56. Ibid., 438.

57. S. Elkins and E. McKitrick, *The Age of Federalism* (New York: Oxford University Press, 1993), 72–73.

58. Bradford Perkins, *The First Rappochement: England and the United States 1795–1805* (Berkeley: University of California Press, 1967).

59. W. Hague, *William Pitt the Younger* (London: Harper Collins, 2004), 56.

60. J. Cannon, *Parliamentary Reform 1640–1832* (London: Cambridge University Press, 1972), 85–97.

61. Burke in response to Henry Flood, 4 March 1790, in F.P. Lock, *Edmund Burke. Volume II, 1784–1797* (Oxford: Oxford University Press, 2006), 265.

62. John Bew, *Castlereagh: Enlightenment, War and Tyranny* (London: Quercus, 2011), 427, 445–46, 482; Trowbridge H. Ford, *Henry Brougham and His World: A Biography* (Chichester: Bary Rose, 1995), 79; John Clarke, *British Diplomacy and Foreign Policy 1782–1865* (London: Unwin Hyman, 1989), 16; K. Bourne, *Britain and the Balance of Power in North America 1815–1908* (London: Longmans, 1967), 7.

63. Bew, *Castlereagh*, 60, 295, 411.

64. Wendy Hinde, *George Canning* (London: Collins, 1973), 349–56.

65. J.E. Cookson, *Lord Liverpool's Administration: The Crucial Years 1815–22* (Edinburgh: Scottish Academic Press, 1975), 396–400.

66. J. Brooke and J. Gandy, *The Prime Minister's Papers: Wellington. Political Correspondence I: 1833-November 1834* (London: Her Majesty's Stationary Office, 1975), 5.

67. M. Gerlach, *British Liberalism and the United States: Political Thought in the Late Victorian Age* (Basingstoke: Palgrave, 2001), xvii.

68. Cannon, *Parliamentary Reform*, 204.

69. E. A Smith, *Lord Grey 1764–1845* (Stroud: Alan Sutton, 1996), 3, 262, 275; Cannon, *Parliamentary Reform*, 214.

70. 'A disposition to preserve, and an ability to improve, taken together, would be my standard of a statesman'. Burke, *Reflections*, 157–58.

71. J. Clarke, *British Diplomacy and Foreign Policy 1782–1865* (London: Unwin Hyman, 1989), 190.

72. J. Chambers, *Palmerston: The People's Darling* (London: John Murray, 2004), 198–99.

73. R. Shannon, *Gladstone. Volume 1 1809–1865* (London: Methuen, 1984), 30–31, 414.

74. T.A. Jenkins, *Disraeli and Victorian Conservatism* (Basingstoke: Macmillan, 1996), 23.

75. A. Roberts, *Salisbury: Victorian Titan* (London: Weidenfeld & Nicholson, 1999), 838.

76. T. Paine, *The Rights of Man. Part 1*, 196. Leading Republicans were strongly influenced by this approach, although it was usually expressed more cautiously, for example in Madison's essay 'Universal Peace' for the Republican *Federal Gazette*, January 1792. This attack on the Federalist state shared the perception that warfare was driven by monarchical reason of state, backed by the financial capacity of the military-fiscal state, and claimed republican exceptionalism in this respect. Ketcham, *James Madison*, 328–29; Tucker and Hendrickson, *Empire of Liberty*, 12–13, 44.

77. E. Burke, *Reflections*, 58.

78. M.W. Doyle, 'Kant, Liberal Legacies and Foreign Affairs, Part 1', *Philosophy and Public Affairs* 12(3) (1983)", 205–35.

79. Tucker and Henderson, *Empire of Liberty*, 39.

80. Herring, *From Colony to Superpower*, 56.

81. M.M. Edling, '"So Immense a Power in the Affairs of War": Alexander Hamilton and the Restoration of Public Credit', in *The William and Mary Quarterly, Third Series* 64(2) (2007), 326.

82. E.H. Gould, 'The Making of an Atlantic State System. Britain and the United States, 1795–1825', in J. Flavell and S. Conway (eds), *Britain and America Go to War: The Impact of War and Warfare in Anglo-America, 1754–1815* (Gainesville: University of Florida Press, 2004).

83. Cannon, *Parliamentary Reform*, 216.

84. Pocock, *The Machiavellian Moment*, 547.

85. P.E. Myers, *Dissolving Tensions: Rapprochement and Resolution in British–American–Canadian Relations in the Treaty of Washington Era, 1865–1914* (Kent, OH: Kent State University Press, 2015), 239.

86. There are clear parallels between Country Whigs John Trenchard and Thomas Gordon's advocacy of 'wise' and 'gentle and insensible methods' of policy and Burke's first *Speech on Conciliation with America*. No. 106 'Of Plantations and Colonies', in R. Hamowy, *Cato's Letters, or Essays on Liberty, Civil and Religious, and Other Important Subjects. Volume 2* (Indianapolis: Liberty Fund, 1995), 749–51; and Bourke, *Empire and Revolution*, 476–78.

87. Bourke, *Empire and Revolution*, 917, 923.

88. J. Israel, *The Expanding Blaze: How the American Revolution Ignited the World, 1775–1848* (Princeton, NJ: Princeton University Press, 2017), 601.

Bibliography

Ackerman, B. *The Failure of the Founding Fathers: Jefferson, Marshall and the Rise of Presidential Democracy*. Cambridge, MA: Harvard University Press, 2005.

Allen, H.C. *Great Britain and the United States: A History of Anglo-American Relations 1783–1952*. London: Archon Books, 1969.

Ayling, S. *Edmund Burke: His Life and Opinions*. London: John Murray, 1988.

Bailyn, B. *The Ideological Origins of the American Revolution*. London: The Belknap Press, 1992.

Beeman, R., S. Botein and E.C. Carter. *Beyond Confederation: Origins of the Constitution and American National Identity*. Chapel Hill: University of North Carolina Press, 1987.

Beer, S.H. *To Make a Nation: The Rediscovery of American Federalism*. Cambridge, MA: The Belknap Press, 1993.

Bew, J. *Castlereagh: Enlightenment, War and Tyranny*. London: Quercus, 2011.

Black, J. *George III: America's Last King*. London: Yale University Press, 2008.

Bonwick, C. *English Radicals and the American Revolution*. Chapel Hill: University of North Carolina Press, 1977.

Bourke, R. *Empire and Revolution: The Political Life of Edmund Burke*. Woodstock: Princeton University Press, 2015.

Bourne, K. *Britain and the Balance of Power in North America 1815–1908*. London: Longmans, 1967.

Brooke, J., and J. Gandy. *The Prime Minister's Papers: Wellington. Political Correspondence I: 1833–November 1834*. London: Her Majesty's Stationary Office, 1975.

Bullion, J. 'Securing the Peace: Lord Bute, the Plan for the Army, and the Origins of the American Revolution', in Karl W. Schweitzer (ed.), *Lord Bute: Essays in Re-interpretation*. Leicester: Leicester University Press, 1988, 17–39.

Burke, E. *Reflections on the Revolution in France*. Oxford: Oxford University Press, 1993.

Cannon, J. *Parliamentary Reform 1640–1832*. London: Cambridge University Press, 1972.

Carp, E.W. *To Starve the Army at Pleasure: Continental Army Administration and American Political Culture 1775–1783*. Chapel Hill: University of North Carolina Press, 1984.

Chambers, J. *Palmerston: The People's Darling*. London: John Murray, 2004.

Christie, I.R. *Myth and Reality in Late-Eighteenth-Century British Politics and Other Papers*. London: Macmillan, 1970.

Clarke, J. *British Diplomacy and Foreign Policy 1782–1865*. London: Unwin Hyman, 1989.

Cobban, A., and R.A. Smith. *The Correspondence of Edmund Burke. Volume VI. July 1789 – December 1791*. London: Cambridge University Press, 1967.

Cookson, J.E. *Lord Liverpool's Administration: The Crucial Years 1815–22*. Edinburgh: Scottish Academic Press, 1975.

Cotlar, S. *Tom Paine's America. The Rise and Fall of Transatlantic Radicalism in the Early Republic*. Charlottesville: University of Virginia Press, 2011.

Dickinson, H.T. *Bolingbroke*. London: Constable, 1970.

Doyle, M.W. 'Kant, Liberal Legacies and Foreign Affairs, Part 1', *Philosophy and Public Affairs* 12(3), 1983, 205–35.

Edling, M.M. '"So Immense a Power in the Affairs of War": Alexander Hamilton and the Restoration of Public Credit', in *The William and Mary Quarterly, Third Series* 64(2) (2007), 287–326.

Ellis, J.T. 'The Farewell: Washington's Wisdom at the End', in D. Higginbotham (ed.), *George Washington Reconsidered*. Charlottesville: University of Virginia Press, 2001, 212–49.

Foner, E. *Tom Paine and Revolutionary America*. London: Oxford University Press, 1976.

Ford, T.H. *Henry Brougham and His World: A Biography*. Chichester: Bary Rose, 1995.

Furber, H. *The Correspondence of Edmund Burke. Volume V July 1782 – June 1789*. London: Cambridge University Press, 1965.

Gerlach, M. *British Liberalism and the United States: Political Thought in the Late Victorian Age*. Basingstoke: Palgrave, 2001.

Gould, E.H. 'The Making of an Atlantic State System: Britain and the United States, 1795–1825', in J. Flavell and S. Conway (eds), *Britain and America Go to War: The Impact of War and Warfare in Anglo-America, 1754–1815*. Gainesville: University of Florida Press, 2004, 241–65.

Greene, J.P. *Peripheries and Center: Constitutional Development in the Extended Polities of the British Empire and the United States, 1607–1788*. Athens: The University of Georgia Press, 1986.

Hague, W. *William Pitt the Younger*. London: Harper Collins, 2004.

Hamowy, R. *Cato's Letters, or Essays on Liberty, Civil and Religious, and Other Important Subjects. Volume 2*. Indianapolis, IN: Liberty Fund, 1995.

Heffner, R.D. *A Documentary History of the United States*. New York: Penguin, 1991.

Henrie, M. 'Edmund Burke and Contemporary American Conservatism', in I. Crowe (ed.), *Edmund Burke: His Life and Legacy*. Dublin: Four Courts Press, 1997.

Herring, G.C. *From Colony to Superpower: U.S. Foreign Relations Since 1776*. Oxford: Oxford University Press, 2008.

Higginbotham, D. (ed.). *George Washington Reconsidered*. Charlottesville: University of Virginia Press, 2001.

Hinde, W. *George Canning*. London: Collins, 1973.

Howe, D.W. *What Hath God Wrought: The Transformation of America, 1815–48*. New York: Oxford University Press, 2007.

Israel, J. *The Expanding Blaze: How the American Revolution Ignited the World, 1775–1848*. Princeton, NJ: Princeton University Press, 2017.

Jenkins, T.A. *Disraeli and Victorian Conservatism*. Basingstoke: Macmillan, 1996.

Katz, S. 'The American Constitution: A Revolutionary Interpretation', in R. Beeman, S. Botein and E.C. Carter (eds), *Beyond Confederation: Origins of the Constitution and American National Identity*. Chapel Hill: University of North Carolina Press, 1987, 23–37.

Keane, J. *Tom Paine: A Political Life*. London: Bloomsbury, 2009.

Klarman, M.J. *The Framer's Coup: The Making of the United States Constitution*. New York: Oxford University Press, 2016.

Levin, Y. *The Great Debate: Edmund Burke, Thomas Paine and the Birth of Right and Left*. New York: Basic Books, 2014.

Lock, F.P. *Edmund Burke. Volume II, 1784–1797*. Oxford: Oxford University Press, 2006.

Maciag, D. *Edmund Burke in America: The Contested Career of the Father of Modern Conservatism*. Ithaca, NY: Cornell University Press, 2013.

Macleod, E. *British Visions of America, 1775–1820: Republican Realities*. London: Pickering and Chatto, 2013.

Madison, J., A. Hamilton and J. Jay. *The Federalist Papers*. London: Penguin, 1987.

Marshall, P.J. (ed.). *The Oxford History of the British Empire. Volume II. The Eighteenth Century*. Oxford: Oxford University Press, 1998.

Marshall, P.J., D.C. Bryant and William B. Todd (eds). *The Writings and Speeches of Edmund Burke, Volume 4: Party, Parliament, and the Dividing of the Whigs: 1780–1794*. Oxford: Oxford University Press, 2016.

McCue, J. 'Edmund Burke and the British Constitution', in Ian Crowe (ed.), *Edmund Burke. His Life and Legacy*. Dublin: Four Courts Press, 1997.

Mitchell, L.G. (ed.). *The Writings and Speeches of Edmund Burke. Volume VIII. The French Revolution 1790–94*. Oxford: Clarendon Press, 1989.

Myers, P.E. *Dissolving Tensions: Rapprochement and Resolution in British–American–Canadian Relations in the Treaty of Washington Era, 1865–1914*. Kent, OH: Kent State University Press, 2015.

Norris, J. *Shelburne and Reform*. London: Macmillan, 1963.

O'Neill, D. *Edmund Burke and the Conservative Logic of Empire*. Oakland: University of California Press, 2016.

Paine, T. *Rights of Man, Common Sense and Other Political Writings*. Oxford: Oxford University Press, 2008.

Pencak, W. *America's Burke: The Mind of Thomas Hutchinson*. London: University Press of America, 1982.

Perkins, B. *The First Rapprochement: England and the United States 1795–1805*. Berkeley: University of California Press, 1967.

Pessen, E. *Jacksonian America: Society, Personality and Politics*. Chicago: University of Illinois Press, 1978.

Pocock, J.G.A. *The Machiavellian Moment: Florentine Political Thought and the Atlantic Republican Tradition*. Princeton, NJ: Princeton University Press, 2016.

Rakove, J.M. 'Why American Constitutionalism Worked', in F.M. Turner (ed.), *Reflections on the Revolution in France*. London: Yale University Press, 2004, 248–67.

Reich, J.R. *British Friends of the American Revolution*. London: Armok, 1998.

Roberts, A. *Salisbury: Victorian Titan*. London: Weidenfeld & Nicholson, 1999.

Scott, H.M. *British Foreign Policy in the Age of the American Revolution*. Oxford: Clarendon Press, 1990.

Shannon, R. *Gladstone. Volume 1 1809–1865*. London: Methuen, 1984.

Simms, B. *Three Victories and a Defeat: The Rise and Fall of the First British Empire*. London: Allen Lane, 2007.

Smith, E.A. *Lord Grey 1764–1845*. Stroud: Alan Sutton, 1996.

Smith, J.E. *John Marshall: Definer of a Nation*. New York: Henry Holt, 1996.

Thomas, P.D.G. *John Wilkes: A Friend to Liberty*. Oxford: Clarendon Press, 1996.

Tocqueville, A. de. *Democracy in America*. London: David Campbell, 1994.

Tucker, R.W., and D.C. Henderson. *Empire of Liberty: The Statecraft of Thomas Jefferson*. Oxford: Oxford University Press, 1990.

Valentine, A. *Lord North. Volume 1*. Norman: University of Oklahoma Press, 1967.

Wood, G. 'Interests and Disinterestedness in the Making of the Constitution', in R, Beeman, S. Botein and E.C. Carter (eds), *Beyond Confederation: Origins of the Constitution and American National Identity*. Chapel Hill: University of North Carolina Press, 1987, 69–110.

Woods, J.A., and W.M. Elofson (eds). *The Writings of Edmund Burke. Volume III. Party, Parliament and the American War 1774–1780*. Oxford: Clarendon Press, 1996.

PART II

Ideological Philosophies

Chapter 3

Anglo-American Liberalism
The Tradition?
Alan P. Dobson

Introduction

The following quotations were written separately, in two different countries, about three hundred years apart.

> Man being born, as has been proved, with a title to perfect freedom, ... [has] an uncontrolled enjoyment of all the rights and privileges of the law of nature equally with any other man or number of men in the world ....[1]

> Individuals have rights, and there are things no person or group may do to them (without violating their rights). So strong and far-reaching are these rights that they raise the question of what, if anything, the state and its officials may do.[2]

The author of the first was English, John Locke, while the author of the second was American, Robert Nozick. Both saw major dangers in their respective societies and it is striking that they responded in similar ways, namely through the assertion of freedom and rights. How did two intellectuals three hundred years apart come to address their contemporary problems in such similar ways? The answer lies in the continuity and development of Liberal doctrine that spanned the Atlantic and helped to generate an Anglo-American political tradition with liberalism at its core. And that core emerged by dint of transatlantic exchange and mutual enrichment of often opposing ideas. This is a continuous dynamic that has repeatedly raised two key questions: what is the true condition of liberty? And what is the legitimate role and scope of government? These two questions in turn gave rise to the problem of how to reconcile liberty, equality and community. In the rest of this chapter these basic questions and how they have been answered are the focus of attention.

Before looking at what would later be understood as the Liberal substance of the Anglo-American political tradition, we need to address another question: what is meant here by liberalism?[3]

Liberalism and Sharing a Tradition

Liberalism is not a form of government; it is a way of life, but one that has much to say about what government should and should not do. Above all, liberalism celebrates the liberty of individuals defined in terms of equal rights to life, property, free speech, conscience and movement and, in its particular American iteration, the pursuit of happiness. Thomas Jefferson, author of the American Declaration of Independence and later president, asserted that rights were self-evident truths, but this was simply an attempt at persuasive rhetoric. Rights can more accurately be seen as moral claims. Cast in another way, individuals have the right to exercise their own rationality to decide on the kind of life that they wish to live in a secure environment provided by government. As one recent American commentator put it:

> Peace is good, to repeat, because it is the necessary condition of all private pursuits of happiness; and peace is a common good ... Mutual respect of individual rights, the political self-restraint of parties and sects, and a willingness to enlist the force of the community in support of this Liberal moderation: these are the core values of liberal politics.[4]

In a very real sense, Liberals have a clear definition of what it is to be human: rational, rights-carrying moral individuals valued as ends in themselves. Taking away someone's rights constitutes a failure to treat them with equal respect and is tantamount to an attack on their very humanity.[5] To secure such rights, people need government. John Locke argued that circumstances in which human beings found themselves without government, particularly the difficulty of securing property, would give rise to conflict and injustice because individuals could not be trusted to be judge and jury in their own cases. Thus, government was needed. A more fully fledged version of this problem was developed three hundred years later by American liberal theologian Rheinhold Niebuhr, who argued that human beings always have a stronger sense of their own interests than they do the interests of others.[6] The logical solution to this was the creation of government and the rule of law to order society impartially and protect individual rights. Sovereign powers were delegated by individuals to government in order that their interests could be promoted and their rights secured. And that was the rationale of government. If it did not carry out its obligations, then the people could ultimately recall what they had delegated, dissolve government and start again.

It is pertinent to note that three important features, one relating to government and two more broadly relating to society, seem to flow naturally from these foundational principles of liberalism.

Firstly, government should be self-limiting or limited because a *sine qua non* for its existence is that it secures individual rights and liberty, which are to be enjoyed in some degree of private space. However, the idea of limited government begs the question of exactly how limited. For example, while Locke advocated what are known as negative rights, that is, freedom from coercion, he also claimed that when individuals engaged their labour with the natural world and created property rights, they had an obligation to leave as much and as good for others. In a world of finite resources, that presumably implied government regulation to ensure that resources were available for all and also that 'freedoms from' might not deliver individual liberty to all without individuals being empowered in some way by positive action by government. As we shall see, all this mainly boiled down to the relationship between the individual and resources and came to dominate the Liberal debate about what it meant to enjoy liberty.

Secondly, while Liberals celebrate individualism, there is no necessary and fatal incompatibility between individualism and society. One of the purposes for which individuals create civil society under law is to be able to live together peacefully and pursue agreed common enterprises.

Thirdly, laissez-faire economics, though it often accompanies Liberal values, is not necessarily fundamental to liberalism. Much of the problem here is a failure to distinguish between liberty as licence and liberty as equal and independent citizenship. This was argued in England by Thomas Hill Green in the nineteenth century and more recently and pithily described by the American Ronald Dworkin: 'license ... is the degree to which a person is free from social or legal constraint to do what he might wish to do, and liberty as independence, that is the status of a person independent and equal rather than subservient.'[7] Under this Liberal understanding of liberty, contra Herbert Spencer, William G. Sumner, Friedrich Hayek, Milton Friedman and their popularizers (about whom, more shortly), laissez-faire economics is not a necessary component of Liberal freedom. Indeed, if it creates inequalities that compromise the idea of an equal and independent citizen, then it is the enemy of liberty.[8]

There has been continuous controversy within liberalism concerning whether liberty is tantamount simply to being free from external coercion (negative rights) or whether society needs to provide resources for individuals to fulfil themselves in order to truly enjoy liberty (positive rights). Within that debate, a tension arises between laissez-faire economics and levels of taxation to provide for a society that supports its less endowed and/or less industrious members. The latter is tantamount to slave labour for Nozick: that is, people are taxed against their will, their 'property' confiscated by government, for ends to which they may not subscribe. But in addition to this tension, there is another. While liberalism has waxed strongest within the Anglo-American political tradition, it inherited many of its central precepts from European philosophy and, in particular, Immanuel Kant and his idea of the essence of humanity being one's ability to make rational moral choices. It is in relation to this that some of the greatest controversy has arisen in contemporary liberalism. In latter-day iterations of liberalism, the freedom to exercise rights is deemed more important than whatever the exercise of such rights might produce. The only caveat is that in exercising one's rights one does not interfere with anyone else's freedom to do the same. These latter-day iterations call into question yet again the nature of freedom, the appropriate scope for government, how freely economic forces should be allowed to play and how one reconciles liberty, community and equality.

So, over time, as circumstances have changed, Liberals have engaged with a series of emerging political puzzles. Having created government, to secure rights and liberties, how can one ensure that individuals will remain free in the face of government power? Having a set of values that are seemingly compatible with capitalism (though perhaps not entirely so), should the individual be protected from the gross inequalities of material well-being that result from capitalism when, from one perspective, such conditions constitute an assault on the possibility of individual liberty itself? With industrialization having created a mass society, how can individualism be sustained in the face of the conformity of mass society and the coercion of popular opinion? And with the development of affluence, the decline of religion, albeit to a lesser extent in the United States than Britain, and the rise of scientific knowledge, all of which empowered the individual to embark upon new quests in search of individual autonomy and selfhood, how can such differences abide side by side and where is the sense of collective identity required for effective and efficient government to be found? Liberty from the state of nature brought problems relating to governmental powers. Liberty from material paucity and the arrival of the cornucopia of capitalism brought problems of debilitating inequality and a mass society with dangerous coercive potential. And, the liberation of the self raised the question of the extent of toleration of the other and posed a fundamental challenge to the viability of government itself through the corrosion of collective identity. These are the key issues with which the Anglo-American Liberal tradition has tussled.

Britain and the United States have different democratic traditions, institutions and practices, which means that a shared Liberal tradition must necessarily transcend such differences. A good starting point to demonstrate how it does so is to note that democracy is not tantamount to liberalism. Different forms of government, institutions and practices are all capable of manifesting Liberal values to one degree or another. (This was certainly Locke's view.) If one takes President Abraham Lincoln's classic definition of democracy – government of the people, by the people, for the people – then government might not necessarily embody liberal values. One of John Stuart Mill's fears was that conformism in modern society tended towards a majoritarianism that did not respect the principles of equality and independence, but instead sought conformism to a majority view of the good life.[9] Similarly, one can imagine a system of government that falls far short of Lincoln's democratic ideal while, in fact, embodying Liberal values to a considerable extent, namely British Victorian society. This is not to deny that there is often a link between democracy and Liberal values, simply that it is not a necessary one, or, as Isaiah Berlin put it, that there is no logical link between the two:

> Freedom in this sense is not, at any rate logically, connected with democracy or self-government. Self-government may, on the whole, provide a better guarantee of the preservation of civil liberties than other regimes, and has been defended as such by libertarians. But there is no necessary connection between individual liberty and democratic rule.[10]

Different forms of democracy and certain forms of non-democratic government can all confer upon their people and respect a degree of Liberal freedom. So, just because there are some very stark differences between government in the United States and Britain, that does not preclude the possibility of their sharing a Liberal tradition.

Much of the confusion that can be caused by those who only imperfectly understand liberalism arises from the assumption that it is tantamount to democracy and capitalism, and from a failure to distinguish between licence and liberty as equality and independence. At the same time, there are confusions or false precepts within liberalism, so, for example, following the American philosopher John Rawls, one might wish that government decisions could be made entirely on merit and in accordance with good reason, but unfortunately humankind argues about the nature of both merit and reason and in the public domain finds it difficult, nay perhaps impossible, to be impartial when encumbered, as it is, by values and preferences, which are far from being entirely a matter of rational choice.[11] The focus here is not broad enough to offer answers to or even engage with all these issues, but it does hone in on the development of Liberal ideas on either side of the Atlantic and how they have mutually interacted to produce a recognizable Anglo-American Liberal tradition.

The Origins of an Anglo-American Liberal Tradition

It seems likely that looking back on the time when the American colonies broke away from the mother country, most would imagine that liberalism was predominantly associated with the revolutionaries. However, a famous English contemporary, Samuel Johnson, considering the crisis that arose, rhetorically asked:

> How is it, that we always hear the loudest yelps for liberty among the drivers of negroes.[12]

Those 'drivers' included many of the Founding Fathers of the republic: George Washington, James Madison, Thomas Jefferson, Benjamin Franklin in his early life and even the man who uttered the aphorism 'Give me liberty or give me death!' – which clearly did not apply to his African slaves – Patrick Henry. Liberalism in Britain and the United States is a more complex story than one might first imagine.

To understand the dilemma that confronted the British and their American colonists at the end of the eighteenth century, it is necessary to grasp what had happened a hundred years earlier at the time of the constitutional crisis of the Glorious Revolution of 1688 and its aftermath. Limited space does not allow for the provision of much detail of this groundwork, which draws heavily on Lee Ward's hugely impressive study *The Politics of Liberty in England and Revolutionary America*.[13] The debates preceding the Glorious Revolution, about what to do with the latter-day Stuart monarchs, were anchored in deepseated concerns regarding a possible renewal of civil war and descent into anarchy, but nevertheless produced arguments across a broad spectrum, from moderate and conservative constitutional monarchism to radical republicanism: a journey between what are often referred to as moderate and radical Whigs.

Moderate Whigs, best epitomized by James Tyrrell, wanted to exclude the Stuart King James II and maintain traditional individual and parliamentary rights and privileges, but they did not want a dissolution of government, as they distrusted popular consent and were mindful of the possibility of renewed civil war. Walking this tightrope, with the threat of expansive royal authority on one side and anarchy and popular volatility on the other, the moderates drew on ideas of specific historical English developments. These embraced ideas of mixed government under fundamental laws that emerged through the mists of time as tensions between the monarch and the nobility were managed and given the imprimatur of limited popular consent, but popular consent that, once granted, could not be recalled. There would be no dissolution of government. The legitimate organs of government – in the context of the constitutional crisis James II posed, this meant Parliament – could and should determine succession of the crown. Sovereignty, once the people had consented, always rested with the king in Parliament. If the king acted outside his legitimate sphere, as James II was deemed to have done, then it was down to Parliament to correct matters. At the end of *Patriarcha non Monarcha*, invoking the German legal philosopher Samuel von Pufendorf, Tyrrell argued that fundamental law could and should limit the power of the monarch.[14] And so, there was a glorious but peaceful revolution, with continuity of government and the inheritance of rights and privileges running from the mists of Anglo-Saxon times of idealized democracy, through Magna Carta 1215, the Petition of Rights 1628 and the Bill of Rights 1689. This was not a democratic revolution. It was not even change based upon an appeal to popular consent. But it did much to uphold the Liberal values of the rule of law, constitutionalism and individual rights.

In contrast, the radical Whig take on things, argued pre-eminently by Algernon Sydney, emphasized the importance of popular consent mediated through the House of Commons, which should have regular elections based on a broad franchise. This would be where the delegated sovereignty of the people lay and the monarchy was surplus to requirements: a republic was what was needed. Sydney was scathingly critical of executive prerogative and the supposedly balanced and mixed British constitution that had evolved over time. He saw rights as inalienable and, like Locke, upheld the right of the people to revolution if the government acted contrary to the public interest. For Sydney, politics began and ended with the people.[15] Sydney was a radical and so was Locke in many respects, though the latter was much more tolerant of different forms of government, including the existing British mixed and balanced constitution with delegated sovereignty residing in the king in Parliament, provided such forms of government delivered on the protection of individual rights. This toleration of a variety of forms of government, including those that did not depend on direct popular consent, lent a more conservative hue to his ideas of government, ideas that were adopted in the United States.

During the crisis that eventually led to the creation of the United States of America, American debate mirrored arguments across the spectrum of thought that had developed in Britain during and after the crisis that resulted in the exclusion of the Stuarts. Moderate American colonials such as John Dickinson were reluctant to break from England and simply wanted readjustments that would protect the colonies from actions such as the imposition of domestic taxes for the British Treasury within the colonies.[16] Arguments like this fundamentally relied on the demand for the traditional rights of Englishmen to be fully applied in America. American moderates did not want dissolution of government and all the potential dangers that would come with it. They wanted the kind of continuity that reflected the moderate Whig arguments deployed in the Glorious Revolution. At the other end of the spectrum were much more radical arguments, which gained momentum as London proved recalcitrant to demands from America and found their most influential proponent in Tom Paine and his work *Common Sense*.[17] Paine, ploughing an intellectual furrow similar to that of Sydney, believed that the British constitution was unworkable, with its notion of mixed sovereignty, and fundamentally flawed because it did not rest on popular consent. Probably more than anyone, Paine shifted opinion in the colonies towards republicanism as the solution for government. Ironically, the author of the American Declaration of Independence, Thomas Jefferson, was initially less radical. He denied the authority of the English Parliament in the colonies, but not that of the monarch. He argued that the monarch should restrain the English Parliament in its policies and laws regarding the colonies, but unfortunately the monarch could only do that by more forcefully exercising prerogative powers in London, the very thing that the Glorious Revolution and *ex post facto* justifications of it in England had been so determined to rule out. If the monarch had acted as Jefferson advised, it would have overturned the constitutional settlement created by the Glorious Revolution and opened up Pandora's box of unrestrained monarchical power once again. In London, that could not be allowed. And so, the war in the colonies wended its tragic way onwards until the British defeat at Yorktown at the hands of the French and George Washington's Continental Army led to independence. But this independence reflected in many ways the liberalism of England.

What emerged in America was more representative, democratic and Liberal than government in London, but it was also very clearly based upon an integrated mixture of ideas that had originated primarily in England. John Adams's reflections on the representative assembly were that it 'should be in miniature an exact portrait of the people at large. It should think, reason and act like them.'[18] In the broad franchises (at least broad at the time: women were still entirely excluded) adopted by the individual states, Adams got his wish, a wish that would have been approved of by both Tyrrell and Sydney. But Adams also thought that a single body of government was dangerous and so argued for the separation of powers between the legislative, executive and judicial bodies. The Senate would thus balance the popular opinions of the House of Representatives and the three branches of government, which were institutionally separated but had overlapping powers, would check and balance each other. All this could have been designed by Locke, or perhaps more obviously by the French Enlightenment thinker Montesquieu, who had been much enamoured by the supposed checks and balances in the British political system. Like the moderates who had triumphed during the succession crisis in England, the victors in America, while more willing to call on popular consent, were also cautious of populism and inclined to adopt institutional checks and balances. Certain rights and liberties should simply be above and not subject to the whims of the people.

Unlike the 'revolutionaries' in England in 1688, however, the American colonists could not invoke the past to buttress their claim to rights and liberties because they were about to create a new political entity. Hence, and most significantly, to ensure the people of their rights in perpetuity, the constitution was to be regarded as fundamental law. Soon incorporated into this was a bill of universally applicable rights. And overseeing the integrity of both was the Supreme Court, which, in 1803, established the principle of judicial review in the case of Marbury versus Madison. There had been hints of similar developments in England, with Sir Edward Coke in Dr Bonham's legal case in 1610, but they had never progressed and the argument for, and soon the reality of, parliamentary supremacy ruled out the possibility of judicial review in Britain. Not so in the United States. The idea of fundamental law protected by judicial review became strongly established, which ensured the protection of individual rights. In a very strong sense, individual rights and the liberty that they secured seemed settled in the United States by the turn of the nineteenth century, at least for white males with a minimum of modest property means. The circle had been squared: rights were secured, but government was also restrained and limited institutionally. Furthermore, Jacksonian democracy in the 1830s, so called after President Andrew Jackson, emphasized states' rights, which buttressed restraints and limits on the Federal government and the legacy of this stretched down through the century to the Civil War. Things were less certain and clear in Britain. There, much was still to play for in the Liberal mind and so, perhaps not surprisingly, the development of Liberal thought was nurtured more consciously in Britain than in the United States as the nineteenth century unfolded. And no one did more to advance Liberal doctrine in their respective ways than John Stuart Mill and Herbert Spencer.

Mill and Spencer (and Sumner)

Much of what Mill had to say was compatible with the principles that governed in the United States. He inherited a lot from his father, James, and the great Utilitarian thinker Jeremy Bentham, and the driving Utilitarian moral principle of the greatest happiness of the greatest number for social and political arrangements strongly echoed the American Declaration of Independence's right to the pursuit of happiness.[19] Mill also started his most famous work *On Liberty* (1859) with the assertion that 'the sole end for which mankind are warranted, individually or collectively, in interfering with the liberty of action of any of their number, is self-protection'.[20] The idea of the primacy of individual liberty and limited government resonated strongly within American political culture. But Mill had more to say than just a traditional Liberal assertion of the primacy of the rights-carrying individual and limited government, particularly given the fact that effective constraints on the exercise of political power now existed in Britain and to an even greater extent in the United States. Government, for most, was not the threat it had been. Mill was much more concerned with the danger posed by mass society: 'That so few now dare to be eccentric, marks the chief danger of the time.'[21] This might sound trivial, but Mill was no intellectual *dilettante*. He was concerned that if individuals were to enjoy liberty, there had to be respect for difference; otherwise, the equal standing of individuals in society and hence a prerequisite for their liberty would be fatally compromised. His arguments were to be much debated in Britain, but in the United States such ideas had less of an impact. There were maybe four reasons why this was so: first, to many, the job seemed done by the constitution, the Bill of Rights and the Jacksonian emphasis on states' rights, and so individuals generally felt secure in their liberties; secondly, the freedom of frontier culture was pervasively influential in the United States and reinforced existing and widespread convictions about the happy condition of liberty and so there seemed little need to be concerned by Mill's thesis; thirdly, political debate in the United States was dominated by arguments between the North and the South, be they cast in terms of the '1828 tariff of abomination' that discriminated against the South's agricultural economy, the debate on slavery and freedom or the right to secede from the Union; and fourthly, the US still lagged well behind Britain in industrialization, which had created the undifferentiated masses in Britain and caused much of Mill's concern.

Mill was deeply disturbed by the impact of industrial capitalism on individuals and gradually edged his way towards a conviction that government intervention was more necessary than early Liberals, fearful of autocratic government, thought wise or necessary.[22] This change was also a function of the growth of wealth and its lopsided distribution. In some ways, this resurrected the idea that Locke had expressed about the need, when acquiring property, to leave as much and as good for others. If that implied government regulation, then the conditions spawned by industrialization seemed to do so as well. This intellectual shift among Liberals culminated in the nineteenth century in the ideas of Green and Leonard Trelawny Hobhouse and, as we shall see, in the late twentieth century, led to more contemporary ideas about rebalancing government intervention, regulating the economy and protecting individual freedoms formulated by American philosophers John Rawls and Ronald Dworkin. However, in the meantime, in the United States, concerns about government intervention and regulation were much more related to how to limit than empower government, at least regarding the economy.

As the United States industrialized, pushed along by the exigencies of Civil War, Americans also began to consider what liberty meant in the new social and economic environment spawned by large-scale manufacturing. They found answers in the work of someone who became an intellectual hero for them: the English Liberal philosopher Herbert Spencer. Between the Civil War and the end of the century, over one third of a million copies of his work were sold in the United States. His ideas were taken up with gusto by the American social philosopher and Yale professor William G. Sumner and had a widespread impact.[23]

Spencer thought that man must

> have liberty to go and come, to see, to feel, to speak, to work; to get food, raiment, shelter, and to provide for each and all needs of his nature ... He has a *right* to that liberty.[24]

And government should provide the context in which that right could be enjoyed, but this would not extend beyond defence of the country, maintaining internal order and the enforcement of contract. Spencer became the champion of laissez-faire because he believed that the laws of nature dictated it for the benefit of mankind. Unlike Mill and Green, who worried about the context of industrial society and its impact on individual liberty, the overriding concern for Spencer and Sumner was a rather different context, namely the laws of science in society and what they implied for humanity. This was a social science of the human condition derived from the ideas of Charles Darwin and metamorphosed into Social Darwinism. They feared not that social and economic conditions would undermine individual liberty, but that government would do so through ill-conceived notions of economic justice.

> Of man, as of all inferior creatures, the law by conformity to which the species is preserved, is that among adults the individuals best adapted to the conditions of their existence shall prosper most, and that individuals least adapted to the conditions of their existence shall prosper least – a law which, if un-interfered with, entails survival of the fittest...[25]

Spencer believed that progress could not be nurtured by helping those in need. Only the successful could succeed and they hindered the progress of society if they side-stepped their natural course of action to help those who were less successful in the race of life. Equally importantly, if government tried to interfere to help the failures in society, it would need to take resources from the successful to do so, which would not only be contrary to the laws of social evolution, but would also constitute coercion of the individual, thus depriving him/her of liberty. Spencer and Sumner thought that they had identified the natural realities of life: these amounted to self-help and survival of the fittest. Sumner, at one point, opined that the drunk in the gutter was where he should be. Speaking ironically, Sumner further observed that: 'Poverty is the best policy. If you get wealth you will have to support other people: if you do not get wealth, it will be the duty of other people to support you.' For Sumner, the contemporary thought of socialists or British reforming Liberals (such as Green) amounted to quackery. In contrast, he advocated the old doctrine of laissez-faire, which, translated into blunt English, meant: 'Mind your own business.'[26] This provided the intellectual underpinning in the United States of the Gospel of Wealth and the supremacy of banking and corporate wealth. Above anyone else, the Scottish-born American industrial giant Andrew Carnegie epitomized the worship of industrial wealth and progress untrammelled by government regulation. He declared that 'upon the sacredness of property civilization itself depends' and that 'Individualism, Private Property, the Law of Accumulation of Wealth, and the Law of Competition; ... these are the highest results of human experience'.[27] This could hardly have been put better by either Spencer or Sumner and such ideas, while challenged in the United States by populism and progressivism at the end of the nineteenth century and in the early twentieth century, were not to be fully, intellectually and effectively countered until American philosophical pragmatism and the New Deal in the 1930s and 1940s. In Britain, the story was a little different.

From Green to Dewey and the Mid-Twentieth-Century Consensus

While liberalism in the guise of Social Darwinism and the Gospel of Wealth buttressed industrial capitalism and its benefits and handicaps for the haves and have-nots respectively in the United States, it had a significant but lesser impact in Britain, where there developed on from Mill a new version of rights and liberties championed by Green and Hobhouse. Much of their thought, along with that of British socialist thinkers such as Sydney and Beatrice Webb and R.H. Tawney, would provide the intellectual underpinnings of what became known as social democracy or welfare liberalism.[28]

Welfare liberalism, like the broad doctrine of liberalism itself, was concerned with rights, liberty and the scope of government. The kind of liberalism that had largely gone before was best epitomized by what are commonly known as negative rights. If government could provide a safe framework within which men and later women could enjoy their rights in any way they desired, providing they did not interfere with anyone else's enjoyment of their rights to do the same, then all was well. The Canadian philosopher Charles Taylor equates such rights with what he calls an opportunity-concept. People have freedom that provides them with the opportunity to freely pursue what they wish.[29] What troubled men like Green was that this was all very well for the able and well-placed in society, but it let the hindmost be taken by the devil. He demanded positive rights to make equality of opportunity more of a reality: legal protection from exploitation and rights to health, education and welfare – what Taylor describes as an exercise-concept, whereby people have the ability to exercise control over their own lives. Furthermore, for Green, if individuals could not make the best of themselves in this way, then neither could society.

Green was a philosopher, not a policymaker, but his concerns and arguments in favour of government provision contributed to a change of attitudes that saw the introduction of a flurry of reforms, such as compulsory education in 1880, followed by the Balfour Education Act of 1902 and the provision of state pensions in 1908. Whereas Liberals once saw government as a potential threat to rights and liberty if not narrowly circumscribed, there now developed a view in favour of a more expansive role for government. Given the new industrial context of mass society, the Liberal view of rights and liberty changed, or rather the means for sustaining individual rights and liberty in that new context changed.

Just as America overtook Britain in the industrial sphere in the late nineteenth century, so in the twentieth century American Liberals began to catch up with their British counterparts in the nature of their concerns. Social Darwinism and laissez-faire economics were still central to many American Liberals' beliefs about individualism and liberty in the 1930s, but things were changing. In 1933, Adolf A. Berle and Gardiner C. Means published a ground-breaking work on corporations, which had a major impact not only in the United States, but also in Britain. Adam Smith's ideas of competition, balance, individual industry and the free market no longer captured the reality of corporate capitalism. The context had evolved and this raised questions regarding laissez-faire, individualism and liberty.

> As private enterprise disappears with increasing size, so also does individual initiative. The idea that an army operates on the basis of 'rugged individualism' would be ludicrous. Equally so is the same idea with respect to the modern corporation. Group activity, the coordinating of the different steps in production, the extreme division of labour in large scale enterprise necessarily imply not individualism but cooperation and the acceptance of authority almost to the point of autocracy. ... In modern industry, individual liberty is necessarily curbed.[30]

Three years earlier, in a similar vein, the leading pragmatist philosopher John Dewey, whose ideas were to be a major influence on President Franklin Roosevelt's great reforming New Deal in the 1930s, acerbically commented:

> One cannot imagine a bitterer comment on any professed individualism than that it subordinates the only creative individuality – that of mind – to the maintenance of a regime which gives the few an opportunity for being shrewd in the management of monetary business.[31]

Like Berle and Means, Dewey was concerned with the here and now:

> If one wants to know what the condition of liberty is at a given time, one has to examine what persons can do and what they cannot do. The moment one examines the question from the standpoint of effective action, it becomes evident that the demand for liberty is a demand for power, either for possession of powers of action not already possessed or for retention and expansion of powers already possessed.[32]

This was a clear departure from the strictures of minimalist or night-watchman government and laissez-faire, which defined the parameters of individualism and liberty for the Social Darwinists and the followers of the Gospel of Wealth. This view required government intervention. Like Green, Dewey was articulating the need for positive rights. In fact, the British were still ahead of the game. Much of what Dewey had to say had been argued previously by the likes of Green, albeit in a different form, in relation to the connection between individual empowerment and liberty, and John Maynard Keynes had been even more explicit in the early 1920s and 1930s about the false axioms of laissez-faire and advocated government intervention and regulation to manage economic activity.[33]

In the late 1930s and through the 1940s, there emerged a political drive for reform in both the United States and the United Kingdom on the basis of a consensus centred on a cluster of Liberal ideas that had merged in a process of mutual intellectual interaction. They resulted in forms of Keynesian macro-management of the economy, safeguards for employment and higher health, welfare and educational spending, partly aimed at reducing the impact of unequal wealth distribution. In the United States, Roosevelt's New Deal and President Harry Truman's Fair Deal implemented many, if not all, of these reforms: healthcare, unlike in Britain, was notably absent from government provision until President Lyndon B. Johnson's Great Society programme in the 1960s introduced Medicaid and Medicare. And this kind of Liberal reform even infected conservatives like President Dwight D.

Eisenhower, who, through the Federal Highway Act of 1956, set in motion the building of an interstate highway system that eventually cost over $500 billion of public expenditure in current prices. Similarly, but unsuccessfully, President Richard Nixon, in 1969, attempted to introduce a basic minimum family income of $1,600, well over $10,000 in current prices. In Britain, William Beveridge produced his famous report 'On Social Insurance and Allied Services' in 1942, which the Labour government of Clement Attlee used as the template for health and welfare reforms. And setting the example for American Conservatives, the governments of Winston Churchill, Anthony Eden and Harold Macmillan bought into welfare, health and education to such an extent that the term Butskellism was coined – an elision of the surnames of Rab Butler, sometime Conservative Chancellor of the Exchequer, among other things, and Hugh Gaitskill, leader of the Labour Party, 1955–63. The fact that these developments happened in both countries at more or less the same time and as the result of ideas emanating from both sides of the Atlantic illustrates the dynamism of an Anglo-American Liberal political tradition.

The Return of Laissez-faire, the Disavowal of Society and the Counterattack from Welfare Liberalism

This onward march of welfare liberalism ground to a halt, and then went into reverse, in the 1970s. Fuelling the change in political direction was a social conservative backlash against permissiveness towards divorce, promiscuous sexual behaviour, and gay and lesbian relationships, as well as more humane attitudes towards crime and punishment. This shift would pose new and long-term problems for liberalism, but the more immediate crisis was in economics. Keynesianism appeared to have no solution to the concurrent experience in the 1970s of rising prices and falling output, commonly known as stagflation. The economic stage was now returned to the alternative Liberal tradition derived from Spencer, Social Darwinism and the concept of the nightwatchman state. Largely reworked by Friedrich Hayek, ideas of laissez-faire and the minimalist state – sometimes directly from Hayek and sometimes via Milton Friedman and the Chicago School of Economics – had a huge, if rather varying, impact in the United States and Britain during the terms of office of Prime Minister Margaret Thatcher and President Ronald Reagan. And Thatcher, of course, declaimed that there was no such thing as society. Individualism and the minimalist state were rampant again, at least in political rhetoric, if not always in practice: Reagan's massive rearmament programme, for example, belied the principle of minimalist government.

Hayek was an Austrian-British economist and political thinker who had argued publicly against Keynes and his version of economic management in the 1930s. Hayek sounded a clarion call for the protection of individual freedom. By this, he meant that freedom is the protection of the individual from coercion by others. With such protection, individuals would flourish in pursuing their own conceptions of the good life and, in so doing, create a good and free society.[34] As Raymond Plant aptly put it: 'It is central to Hayek's theory of justice and law that the laws of a free society should be framed independently of a particular view of human purposes and goals.'[35] In trying to demonstrate the perniciousness of collectivism, Hayek wrote much about freedom and coercion and the free market. In *The Road to Serfdom* (1944) and his later work *The Constitution of Liberty* (1960), he tried to demonstrate an inextricable link between and interdependency of economic and political freedoms. This was one of the strongest articulations of the theory of negative rights to appear in the mid-twentieth century and, in the United States, was later widely and popularly disseminated by Milton Friedman and rehearsed with gusto by Robert Nozick. Such ideas were adopted to varying degrees as the mantra of contemporary British and American conservative parties during and long after the Reagan–Thatcher era.

When Reaganism and Thatcherism in turn ran into difficulties because of their inability to meet the needs of ordinary and disadvantaged people, and in light of increasing polarity between rich and poor, the pendulum swung again, with modernized versions of Green's social welfare-ism emerging in both the United States and Britain under Democrat President Bill Clinton and Labour Prime Minister Tony Blair respectively. But underlying all this was Liberal engagement with new challenges to the idea of liberty, which arose largely in the 1960s and developed momentum thereafter, though not in a straight, linear pattern. These issues related to women's rights to equality and, more controversially, control over their own bodies in the sense of a right to abortion; gay and transsexual rights; rights to same-sex marriage; rights to euthanasia; civil rights for all ethnic and racial groups; and the general challenge of rights in a multicultural society. At the same time, and running in parallel, renewed efforts were being made to square the circle of liberty and provide sufficient resources for individuals to be effectively empowered to fulfil themselves.

The contemporary focus for Liberals was a long and simmering problem, which had troubled thinkers throughout the development of Liberal doctrine, but which was now cast into a different context. The question had always been how to reconcile the idea of liberty with the necessity of government. But in the twentieth and twenty-first centuries, British and American Liberal thinkers were confronted with two vastly troubling developments that made this line of questioning even more poignant: could effective government actually be operationalized at all along the lines of Liberal values?

The first development was the widening gap between the rich and poor and a belief that for anyone to enjoy liberty they needed basic provisions of material comfort, health, education and welfare and legal safeguards against powerful forces in society. Those forces were primarily the danger to privacy arising from new media technology; dangers from inadequately controlled and hugely powerful economic structures; and dangers arising from terrorism, which prompted the major expansion of powers for government. All this challenged the long-held concern within the Liberal tradition that government must be severely restricted in its scope and reach. Ironically, the second problem was largely connected to the growth of affluence and widespread education, along with developments in science and the effects of mass migration. Affluence provided the wherewithal for the adoption of distinctive and alternative lifestyles; education expanded the horizons of what lifestyles might be possible; science gave rise to increasing possibilities regarding issues of life and death, especially abortion; and mass migration led to problems associated with living together in societies populated by people with radically different beliefs and cultures. At the very moment in time when new dangers were posed to minimalist state Liberals, there was a celebration of the potential for new selves through the acceptance of a wide range of ethnic and cultural diversity, more self-defined people – gay or transsexual – and all asserting more autonomy over their lives. Thus, Liberals had to tussle not only with whether or not society should respond to the need for greater equality of provision, but also with a profound question raised by some regarding the viability of government itself when based on Liberal values that nurtured such diversity and heterodoxy.

As a result, for their critics, Liberals depressingly seemed to pose more questions than they answered. Some Liberal thinkers shared this pessimism. For example, Isaiah Berlin was troubled by the idea that Liberal toleration extended to beliefs and practices that were severely at odds with core Liberal values and posed dangers to liberalism and its ability to provide for viable government. At best, there would always be difficult tensions to manage through debate and accommodation; at worst, multiculturalism might actually fatally undermine liberalism.[36] In the United States, in the aftermath of the Civil Rights Movement of the 1950s and 1960s, the success of the integrated melting pot seemed to belie Berlin's fears, but problems had been managed rather than fully solved and other issues troubled American and British society. As the British philosopher A.C. Grayling put it in 2010, the problem was broader than just multiculturalism for Berlin: 'The Liberal society is faced with a choice: require that everyone [including those from the same culture] sign up to shared values, which might well mean some major choices for some or all parties, or drift along with an increasingly problematic situation in the hope that tensions will not turn into conflicts, at least not too soon.'[37]

What Grayling is getting at here is the Liberal belief that rights and the liberty that they protect are so important that they create the concept of an autonomous individual who cannot be subject to authority contrary to their own will: in its extreme guise, this challenges the very viability of government. But Grayling places clear limits on what Liberals can tolerate as alternative lifestyles. For instance, 'girls undergoing female circumcision and forced marriages' do not fall within the toleration zone:

> I do not accept that a liberal society cannot be demanding – some would say illiberal – in a small number of vital, foundational respects: chiefly, in requiring that anyone who wishes to live in and benefit from membership of a liberal society should be prepared to live by its basic values even as – in conformity with them – he criticises them if he is so moved. This entails that when religious or cultural traditions come into sharp conflict with them, either they must accommodate themselves or yield, or if the espouser of them cannot do either, he must give up membership of the liberal society and seek a place where he can live according to his alternative values.[38]

This might be one way out for the Liberal. It deals with the problem of the limits of toleration posed by the illiberal practices of other cultures and it opens up the possibility of a more expansive type of government that can justify taxation for health, education, welfare and other provisions to help equalize the human condition to the point where equal opportunity and the ability to fulfil oneself become more realistically viable. But if it is a way out, then it has serious consequences for the limits of toleration and the rational universal claim of liberalism that everyone deserves equal respect and should be allowed to pursue their own notion of the good life providing that they do not interfere with others doing the same. In Locke's time, the idea of the rights of the autonomous individual also had radical, but, nevertheless, by comparison with modern times, limited implications. Society then might have been divided by religious differences, but religion and a rigid social structure also provided, at least in principle, an underlying common denominator around which society could rally. The problem for contemporary society is that there is no common glue to bind people together in collective endeavours. At least that is the view of communitarian critics of the Liberal agenda, a view also shared by republican critics, though the form of their critique is, in some ways, different. If no one can be coerced into embracing values to which they do not willingly subscribe, then that leaves the potentially corrosive effect of certain multicultural differences in place and childhood female circumcision, arranged marriages and so forth might continue. Edmund Fawcett, paraphrasing Alasdair McIntyre, a leading critic of liberalism, wrote: 'McIntyre pictured liberal society as a kindergarten of self-interested, isolated selves no longer even able to recognize the collective goods they were destroying.'[39] Similarly, the American philosopher Michael Sandel was fearful of prioritizing rights over any necessarily contested conceptions of the good life. By elevating the right to choose over whatever might be chosen resulted in what he dubbed *the procedural republic*. To his mind, this produces a morally desiccated terrain in which the state cannot sustain itself amidst moral scepticism, with the result that society finds it difficult, if not impossible, to say things such as that arranged marriages are wrong.[40] This foraging in the realm of Liberal critics has been conducted not only in order to demonstrate just how crucial these questions were and are for liberalism, but also to show that liberalism still tends to set the agenda of transatlantic political thought.

Rawls and Dworkin

To bring this short thesis on an Anglo-American Liberal political tradition to its close, first the ideas of Rawls will be explored to see how Liberals have tried to address the problem of freedom, positive rights and distributive justice and then, secondly, the ideas of Dworkin will be analysed to see how liberalism has tried to deal with controversial issues associated with freedom, such as gay rights and multiculturalism, and the way that they impacted on the viability of government itself driven by Liberal values. In looking at these thinkers, it is understood that they have inherited issues that have long been discussed by those who have gone before in the Anglo-American Liberal tradition and while the context continually changes, the two essential questions remain the same: what is the true condition of liberty? And what is the legitimate scope and role of government?

Most famously in his classic work *A Theory of Justice*, John Rawls set out to address problems that were afflicting the Liberal mind, namely how individuals could, through government, provide for their own health, education and welfare without compromising liberty considering people are required by government to pay taxes for such provision when they may not wish to do so. This task of striking a balance between taxation and social, health and education provision has been an enduring issue in elections in Britain and the United States – and, needless to say, elsewhere – for generations.

Rawls's starting point is akin to Locke's state of nature, but instead of an imaginary physical location, it consists of an imaginary state of mind.

It involves men and women making decisions about how to be governed without any knowledge of their own interests, abilities, sex, wealth, status, preferences and goals – that is, behind the veil of ignorance. Why does Rawls require this? The first thing we might observe is that it strips people down to their individual Kantian essence as human beings, namely rational decision-makers. Secondly, he wants to establish a scenario from which judgements that are issued are determined by *fairness*.[41] Under these conditions, Rawls believed that individuals would choose to enjoy fundamental rights to the utmost extent provided that they do not infringe on others' enjoyment of the same and within a regulated free-market economy that provides incentives and equal opportunity, but that is also moderated by the principle that inequality of condition is only tolerated so long as it benefits the least well off most. As Raymond Plant puts it: 'I will be protected whatever my conception of the good turns out to be and however disadvantaged I may be in terms of endowment and family background.'[42] Rawls set the stage for debate among Liberals and Conservatives alike in both Britain and the United States.

Ronald Dworkin in some ways epitomizes the amalgam of Anglo-American liberalism, not least because he split his career between New York and Yale universities, on the one hand, and Oxford and London universities on the other. After Rawls, he has probably been the greatest influence on the development of Anglo-American liberalism in the late twentieth and early twenty-first centuries. He shared Rawls' deep commitments to the individual and a form of social justice that demands a fairer distribution of resources. However, he argued that individuals in Rawls's original position were more than just rational decision-makers. They were, he believed, derived from a notion of society premised on the value of equality of concern and respect for all. While those behind the veil of ignorance might make rational decisions, the scenario behind the veil was predetermined by a moral choice, which set the parameters for what would count as a rational choice. Rawls's original scenario is then neither 'neutral' nor universally recognizable. It is permeated by liberal conceptions not shared by all. The question then becomes what justifies this principle?[43]

Dworkin believes that the state must exhibit equal respect and concern for all individuals because no one can ever achieve a position from which to demonstrate that their version of the good is superior to another. Dworkin sees this as a fundamental premise – so fundamental, in fact, that it does not lend itself to any kind of normal defence. However, as he points out: 'No self-respecting atheist can agree that a community in which religion is mandatory is for that reason finer, and no one who is homosexual that the eradication of homosexuality makes the community purer.'[44] It behoves government to acknowledge that 'equality justifies the traditional liberal principle that government should not enforce private morality of this sort'.[45]

The job of government is to provide a framework in which individuals are granted equal concern and respect and can respond to the challenges of life in whatever way they consider best. Dworkin believes in what he calls a life challenge model. By this, he means that a good society is one that will facilitate people living their lives to the full in whatever way they determine for themselves.[46] There are clear echoes of Thomas Hill Green here. Dworkin has his own version of the Rawlsian original position, but Dworkin's people, unlike Rawls's, know what their status and values are. However, Dworkin argues that even so and arguing on the basis of their own self-interest, they will agree that a form of government that practises neutrality in relation to its citizens' conceptions of the good life is the best form of government. There does not have to be discontinuity between personal morality and the creation of principles of justice for the state. So citizens must be provided with the space and opportunity to be moral persons. As much as possible, individuals should be allowed freedom to determine their own lives.[47] Justice is not about outcomes. It is about all individuals having the right to choose. That is the prerequisite both for any moral society and for the best society that can be achieved in the Liberal world of secular imperfection.

In Dworkin's view, many difficult issues, such as abortion and euthanasia, should remain within the private world, the world of individual autonomy. Not all, however, would agree that he has managed to fence off issues like abortion from the public domain.[48] But even apart from those 'private' issues, there are also those in the political domain and some of these are heavily contested: how does Dworkin's liberalism deal with these? Dworkin argues that issues in the public domain are dealt with by the exercise of good reason in a society imbued with Liberal values and this procedure gives authority to outcomes that all reasonable people can accord with. This position in the United States is based on two suppositions: first, that US constitutional principles are a reservoir of the consensus of values, rather similar to the idea of fundamental laws that has long characterized both US and British political traditions; and, secondly, that their interpretation and application by the Supreme Court is, or should be, acceptable to the citizenry because it is a process of public good reasoning. If legal judgements in hard cases can only be guided by, rather than definitively pronounced by, extant law, then law has to be applied through judgement.

Some defences of this Liberal form of judicial decision-making invoke sociological, pragmatic or utilitarian policy needs, but Dworkin rejects the charge of policymaking in those senses. Instead, he argues that judges have a duty to argue in harmony with the underlying political values of the system, namely, in the American case, the political morality spelt out in the theory of rights contained in the constitution, something rather akin to the English invoking of historical rights and privileges in the seventeenth century. Such rights are essentially moral claims that promulgate the notion that to be human is to be a rights carrier. Among other things, this line of thinking formulates for Dworkin a fundamental concept of human dignity and provides a grounding for collective action and a foil for allegations of Liberal moral scepticism. Judges have to take these fundamental principles and interpret and apply them through good argument, and it is this that keeps the constitution alive and at the heart of American democracy rather than a search for a mechanical application of the law, which is like chasing a mirage.[49] And Dworkin has his version of integrity to avoid the allegation of bias, the danger of which, one might recall, was the prime mover for Locke in the original shift from the state of nature into civil society overseen by government. Dworkin invokes the notion of judicial integrity to rescue public good reasoning from charges of politicization that might compromise the principle of governmental neutrality. Integrity, embodied in his fictional judge Hercules, means that the constitution must be interpreted according to its underlying principles and decisions must hold both vertically, in that they are in line or compatible with embedded Supreme Court precedent and other constitutional principles, and horizontally, in that if a judgement holds in one sphere, it holds in others.[50]

He acknowledges that 'not even the most scrupulous attention to integrity by all judges in all courts will produce uniform judicial decisions or guarantee decisions you approve, or protect you from those you hate'. We are governed 'not by an *ad hoc* list of detailed rules but by an ideal, and controversy is therefore at the heart of our story'.[51] And it is this procedure of public good reasoning that provides authority for government. Thus, Dworkin has two crucial moves in his argument. The first is the claim that the constitution is a reservoir of values upon which there is a widespread social consensus, so these values can be used to interpret hard cases; and the second is that these interpretations are applied by public good reasoning in the Supreme Court, which strives for impartiality (in Rawlsian terms, it does not invoke private comprehensive doctrines in hard cases), thus preserving the principle that government must be neutral in relation to competing value claims that depend upon a particular view of the good society.

However, it is not easy simultaneously to insist on state neutrality in relation to conceptions of the good life and to lay out the requirements for being able to live a good life. Some Liberals simply depart from these stipulations. The eminent Israeli political and legal philosopher Joseph Raz (interestingly a student of H.L.A. Hart at Oxford) argued: 'Autonomous life is valuable only if it is spent in the pursuit of acceptable and valuable projects and relationships.'[52]

As commentators Stephen Mulhall and Adam Swift opine: 'For Raz, a person's well-being does not depend upon her living the life that she believes to be of value, it depends upon her living a life that is valuable for reasons independent of her belief in its value.'[53]

The work of Rawls and Dworkin is an intellectual high point in the development of Anglo-American liberalism. In saying that, the intention is not to devalue the huge contributions made to liberalism in other countries or to suggest that Rawls and Dworkin were not majorly indebted to non-British and non-American thinkers. But their work stimulated debate in a way that no two other authors had done in the tradition for decades. And their work had practical consequences or intellectually reflected and helped justify social and political changes that have come about and still are coming about.

Dworkin, in particular, took on specific issues, such as abortion and euthanasia, and in Britain and America in the 1960s and 1970s, rights to abortion, with some restrictions, were passed into law. Interestingly, in the United States, the Supreme Court invoked the right of privacy in the Rowe versus Wade case as the main principle upon which to base abortion rights. Rights for gays, women, transsexuals and those of different races and creeds to those of their adopted country have all been improved and same-sex marriages have been approved. And while Isaiah Berlin might feel uneasy, if he were still with us, about the strains on Liberal values caused by modern multiculturalism, multicultural societies in Britain and the United States continue to flourish, though they are troubled. Even when Liberal values fail, such as with Anglo-American collusion on the rendition and torture of suspected terrorists, the political outcry has served to reign in and, in part, hold governments to account. At the very least such failures spawn works of outstanding philosophical polemic, such as A.C. Grayling's *Liberty in the Age of Terror*. The Liberal agenda is still alive and well and developing as it continues to ask the same questions but in a changing context as understanding of the different choices of selfhood expands and their needs are continuously revised: what is the true condition of liberty? And what is the legitimate role and scope of government?

Conclusion

Locke would have understood Nozick because he was a member of the political tradition of liberalism that Locke had done so much to further. The prime value of the individual has always been positioned at the heart of that tradition, though it has been conceived of in different ways. In particular, the dynamics of negative and positive rights caused controversy and contention, with British and American thinkers lined up shoulder to shoulder on each side of the debate: Spencer, Sumner, Hayek and Nozick versus Green, Dewey, Keynes, Berle and Rawls. And when the concerns shifted to problems of government posed by multiculturalism and tolerance, once again the debate straddled the Atlantic: Berlin, Dworkin and Grayling.

Currently, what was thought to be a form of Anglo-American consensus – often referred to as the third way – about the need for government to provide the kind of material wherewithal, health, education and welfare to meet the demands of Rawlsian justice as fairness or Dworkin's equality of concern and respect society back in the 1990s and the early new millennium has changed again, with a return to lower taxes and pared-back social provisions. Maybe history really is cyclical because we have been here before in the 1920s and 1930s and the 1980s. And Anglo-American liberalism is there at all stages of the cycle, irrespective of how context changes. The irony is that in trying to uphold the concept of the individual as an autonomous decision-maker able to choose whatever life s/he wants to live, that is, to enjoy liberty, there is no one clear route. Anglo-American liberalism has spent centuries tussling with the problems of how extensive rights should be and what the legitimate role of government might be and now it also tussles with the difficulty of reconciling government itself with such diversity that collective action is more and more difficult to achieve. These are the issues that have been at the heart of the transatlantic Liberal dialogue. It is still relevant and still challenging and being challenged. A.C. Grayling wrote the following in 2009:

> I wish to argue that the ideas which emerged in the eighteenth century about individual autonomy and rights, pluralism, a framework of impartial law impartially administered, privacy, freedom of thought and expression, democratic institutions, secularism, and the importance of education and equality of opportunity, are achievements of history that should be permanent because the principles and ideals they embody are universal and right.[54]

If one takes the substance of this quote and also bears in mind what was said about the contingent link between democracy and Liberal values, the importance of distributive justice in reflecting equality of concern and respect on the one hand and the belief in the 'watchman state' on the other, and the difficulty of governing in conditions of nurtured rich diversity, then what we have here is as good a summary of what liberalism promotes as we might wish to formulate. It encapsulates much of the Anglo-American Liberal tradition of values.

Alan P. Dobson, currently Honorary Professor at Swansea University, has held Chairs at Dundee University and at St Andrews (honorary) and fellowships at the Norwegian Nobel Institute, Saint Bonaventure University (Lenna), where he held a senior research fellowship, and Baylor University (Fulbright). He has written extensively on Anglo-American relations, international civil aviation and the Cold War strategic embargo. His most recent book is *A History of International Civil Aviation* (Routledge, 2017). He is currently working on a book about the United States, Britain and Canada at the Chicago International Civil Aviation Conference 1944. In 2014, he won the Virginia Military Institute's Adams Centre annual Cold War Essay prize. He founded the Transatlantic Studies Association in 2002 and chaired it until 2013 and is editor of both the *Journal of Transatlantic Studies*, which he founded in 2003, and the *International History Review*.

Notes

1. John Locke, *The Second Treatise of Government* (Oxford: Basil Blackwell, 1966), 43.

2. Robert Nozick, *Anarchy State and Utopia* (New York: Basic Books, 1974), ix.

3. Various takes on this may be found in Louis Hartz, *The Liberal Tradition in America* (New York: Harcourt, Brace & World, Inc., 1955); Kori Schake, *Safe Passage: The Transition from British to American Hegemony* (Cambridge, MA: Harvard University Press, 2017); Walter Russell Mead, *God and Gold: Britain, America, and the Making of the Modern World* (New York: Vintage Books, 2008).

4. Steven Kautz, *Liberalism and Community* (Ithaca, NY: Cornell University Press, 1995), 35.

5. Kautz is rather singular as a Liberal in that he denies the importance of equal respect and instead insists that Liberals only require a tolerance that keeps the peace and enables private space: see ibid.

6. Locke, *The Second Treatise of Government*, and Rheinhold Niebuhr, *Moral Man and Immoral Society* (New York: Charles Scribner's Sons, 1960).

7. T.H. Green, 'Liberal Legislation', in Paul Harris and John Morrow (eds), *T.H. Green Lectures: On the Principles of Political Obligation and Other Writings* (Cambridge: Cambridge University Press, 1986), 19; Ronald Dworkin, 'Liberty and Liberalism', in *Taking Rights Seriously* (London: Duckworth, 1977), 262.

8. Friedrich Hayek, *The Road to Serfdom* (London: George Routledge and Sons, 1944); Milton Friedman, *Free to Choose: A Personal Statement* (New York: Avon, 1980); Immanuel Kant, *The Metaphysics of Morals*, 1797, trans. and ed. Mary McGregor (Cambridge: Cambridge University Press, 1996), 30.

9. John Stuart Mill, 'On Liberty', extracts in Robert Eccleshall (ed.), *British Liberalism: Liberal Thought From the 1640s to the 1980s* (London: Longman, 1986), 157–63.

10. Isaiah Berlin, 'Two Concepts of Liberty', in David Miller (ed.), *Liberty* (Oxford: Oxford University Press, 1993), 42.

11. See John Rawls, *A Theory of Justice* (Oxford: Oxford University Press, 1980): to be fair to Rawls, he argued that he was writing about western politics and ideas of reason and not universally applicable ones. See also Michael Sandel, *Democracy's Discontent* (Cambridge, MA: Harvard University Press, 1998).

12. James Boswell, *Boswell Life of Johnson* (London: Oxford University Press, 1969), entry Tuesday, 29 September 1777, 876.

13. Lee Ward, *The Politics of Liberty in England and Revolutionary America* (Cambridge: Cambridge University Press), 2004.

14. James Tyrrell, *Patriarcha non Monarcha*, http://www.oll.libraryfund.org, retrieved 24 April 2018.

15. Algernon Sydney, *Discourses Concerning Government*, 1698, Section 44, http://www.oll.libraryfund.org, retrieved 26 March 2018.

16. John Dickinson, 'The Letters from a Farmer in Pennsylvania', in William E. Leuchtenberg and Bernard Wishy (eds), *Empire and Nation* (New York: Prentice-Hall, 1962), 3–85.

17. Tom Paine, *Common Sense* (New York, Dover Publications, 1997).

18. John Adams, 'Thoughts on Government Applicable to the Present State of the American Colonies 1776', in Andrew M. Scott (ed.), *Political Thought in America* (New York: Rinehart and Co., 1959), 103.

19. Little attention is paid here to Utilitarianism within the Liberal tradition; this is not solely by free choice, but partly dictated by trying to economize on space. However, like many others, the author sees considerable problems with Utilitarianism and its clash with the central Liberal idea of human beings as ends in themselves. As Rawls put it in *A Theory of Justice*: 'Each person possesses an inviolability founded on justice that even the welfare of society as a whole cannot override.' Rawls, *A Theory of Justice*, 3.

20. John Stuart Mill, *On Liberty* (London: Longmans, Green and Company, 1901), 6.

21. Ibid., see 37–40.

22. For consideration of Mill's views on government interventionism, see W.H. Greenleaf, *The British Political Tradition, Volume 2, The Ideological Heritage* (London: Methuen, 1983), 109–24.

23. John Kenneth Galbraith, *The Age of Uncertainty* (London: Book Club Associates, 1977), 45.

24. From Herbert Spencer, *Principles of Ethics, Volume 2, (1887)*, quoted by Greenleaf, *British Political Tradition*, 64.

25. Ibid.

26. W.G. Sumner, 'Liberty and Responsibility', in *Earth Hunger and Other Essays* (New Brunswick, NJ: Transaction Books, 1980), 169; and 'What Social Classes Owe to each Other', in Scott, *Political Thought*, 316–17.

27. For these and other remarks on wealth and the duty of the rich, see Andrew Carnegie, 'Wealth', in *North American Review* CXLVIII (June 1889). However, unlike Sumner, Carnegie believed that the rich had an obligation to engage in philanthropy.

28. For the essence of the socialist position, see R.H. Tawney, *Equality* (London: Unwin Books, 1964, first published 1931).

29. Charles Taylor, 'What's Wrong with Negative Liberty?', in Miller, *Liberty*, 143–44.

30. Adolf A. Berle and Gardiner C. Means, *The Modern Corporation and Private Property* (1933), extract in Scott, *Political Thought in America*, 588.

31. Joseph Ratner (ed.), *Intelligence in the Modern World: John Dewey's Philosophy* (New York: The Modern Library, 1939), 411, taken from the extract from 'Individualism Old and New', originally published 1930.

32. From John Dewey, 'Liberty and Social Control' (1935), in Scott, *Political Thought in America*, 568.

33. J.M. Keynes, *The General Theory of Employment, Interest and Money* (London: Palgrave Macmillan, 1936); and *The End of Laissez-Faire* (London: Hogarth Press, 1926), 39–40.

34. As we shall see below, Ronald Dworkin agreed entirely with this sentiment, but worked out its consequences in a way that would have been deeply uncongenial to Hayek. Dworkin's conception of equal rights entailed, for him, government action to prevent inequalities of condition challenging the principles of equal respect for and the equal value of all human beings.

35. Raymond Plant, *Modern Political Thought* (Oxford: Blackwell, 1995), 80.

36. Berlin, *Two Concepts of Liberty*, 33–57.

37. A.C. Grayling, *Liberty in the Age of Terror: A Defence of Civil Liberties and Enlightenment Values* (London: Bloomsbury, 2010), 166.

38. Grayling, *Liberty in the Age of Terror*, 167 and 166. The language often used here is of anti-perfectionist and perfectionist Liberals, that is, those who do not and those who do believe in substantive goods being promoted by government: Grayling falls into the latter category, as does Joseph Raz – see below.

39. Edmund Fawcett, *Liberalism: The Life of an Idea* (Princeton, NJ: Princeton University Press, 2014), 354.

40. Sandel, *Democracy's Discontent*, 4. The first successful UK prosecution for forced marriage occurred in June 2015 at Merthyr Crown Court.

41. Rawls abjures Utilitarian notions of justice because he fears that minorities can be treated as means to ends to which they do not subscribe under Utilitarianism's majoritarianism.

42. Plant, *Modern Political Thought*, 101.

43. Others have pointed out that Rawls has a particular view of rationality that, for example, does not take into account the fact that some behind the veil of ignorance may wish to gamble in the hope that they will be filthy rich in a society that does not have fairness as justice. One might also suggest that the choices behind the veil have little to do with morality and yet it seems strange or even unrealistic to organize a society divorced from moral choice.

44. Ibid., 206.

45. Ibid.

46. Ronald Dworkin, 'Can a Liberal State Support Art?', in his *A Matter of Principle* (Oxford: Clarendon Press 1996), 221–37.

47. Dworkin, *Taking Rights Seriously*.

48. For example, see Alan P. Dobson, 'Abortion and the Neutrality of the Liberal State', *Politics and Ethics Review* 2(ii) (2006), 178–201.

49. Antonin Scalia opposed Dworkin's position and put forward 'textualism' to establish that law not men govern. Dworkin responded by saying that there are two forms of textualism, a semantic originalism and an expectation originalism, and that Scalia wanted to be a semantic but slips into being an expectation originalist. Scalia spoke of the 8th Amendment's prohibition of 'cruel and unusual punishment' and stated that it could not be used to justify the abolition of the death penalty. However, if one were true to textual semantic originalism, then moral and philosophical reinterpretations would have to be exercised in the way Dworkin claims they should be exercised because if society now sees capital punishment as *meaning* a 'cruel and un-usual' punishment then it must be declared unconstitutional even though the people who drafted the 8th Amendment had no *expectation* that it would be used to prohibit capital punishment. Antonin Scalia, *A Matter of Interpretation· Federal Courts and the Law* (Princeton, NJ: Princeton University Press, 1997), 17, and Dworkin's *Comment*, 119–21.

50. Ronald Dworkin, *Law's Empire* (London: Fontana Press, 1991), chapters 6 and 7; and his *Life's Dominion* (London: Harper Collins, 1993), 145.

51. Ibid., 146–47.

52. Joseph Raz, *The Morality of Freedom* (Oxford: Oxford University Press, 1988), 417, quoted in Stephen Mulhall and Adam Swift, *Liberals and Communitarians* (Oxford: Blackwell, 1997), 312–13.

53. Ibid.

54. Grayling, *Age of Terrorism*.

Bibliography

Adams, John. 'Thoughts on Government Applicable to the Present State of the American Colonies 1776', in Andrew M. Scott (ed.), *Political Thought in America*. New York: Rinehart and Co., 1959, 102–6.

Berle, Adolf A., and Gardiner C. Means. 'The Modern Corporation and Private Property' (1933), extract in Andrew M. Scott (ed.), *Political Thought in America*. New York: Rinehart and Co., 1959, 581–89.

Berlin, Isaiah. 'Two Concepts of Liberty', in David Miller (ed.), *Liberty*. Oxford: Oxford University Press, 1993, 33–58.

Boswell, James. *Boswell Life of Johnson*. London: Oxford University Press, 1969.

Carnegie, Andrew. 'Wealth', *North American Review* CXLVIII (June 1889).

Dewey, John. 'Liberty and Social Control' (1935), in Andrew M. Scott (ed.), *Political Thought in America*. New York: Rinehart and Co., 1959, 568–70.

Dickinson, John. 'The Letters from a Farmer in Pennsylvania', in William E. Leuchtenberg and Bernard Wishy (eds), *Empire and Nation*. New York: Prentice-Hall, 1962, 3–85.

Dobson, Alan P. 'Abortion and the Neutrality of the Liberal State', *Politics and Ethics Review* 2(ii) (2006), 178–202.

Dworkin, Ronald. 'In Defence of Equality', *Social Philosophy and Policy* 1(i) (1983).

——. *Law's Empire*. London: Fontana Press, 1991.

——. 'Liberty and Liberalism', in *Taking Rights Seriously*. London: Duckworth, 1977, 259–66.

——. *Life's Dominion*. London: Harper Collins, 1993.

——. *A Matter of Principle*. Oxford: Clarendon, 1996.

Fawcett, Edmund. *Liberalism: The Life of an Idea*. Princeton, NJ: Princeton University Press, 2014.

Friedman, Milton. *Free to Choose: A Personal Statement*. New York: Avon, 1980.

Galbraith, John Kenneth. *The Age of Uncertainty*. London: Book Club Associates, 1977.

Grayling, A.C. *Liberty in the Age of Terror: A Defence of Civil Liberties and Enlightenment Values*. London: Bloomsbury, 2010.

Green, T.H. 'Liberal Legislation', in Paul Harris and John Morrow (eds), *T.H. Green Lectures: On the Principles of Political Obligation and Other Writings*. Cambridge: Cambridge University Press, 1986, chapter 2.

Greenleaf, W.H. *The British Political Tradition, Volume 2, The Ideological Heritage*. London: Methuen, 1983.

Hartz, Louis. *The Liberal Tradition in America*. New York: Harcourt, Brace & World, Inc., 1955.

Hayek, Friedrich. *The Road to Serfdom*. London: George Routledge and Sons, 1944.

Keynes, J.M. *The End of Laissez-Faire*. London: Hogarth Press, 1926.

Kant, Immanuel. *The Metaphysics of Morals* (1797), trans. and ed. Mary McGregor. Cambridge: Cambridge University Press, 1996.

Kautz, Steven. *Liberalism and Community*. Ithaca, NY: Cornell University Press, 1995.

Locke, John. *The Second Treatise of Government*. Oxford: Basil Blackwell, 1966.

Mead, Walter Russell. *God and Gold: Britain, America, and the Making of the Modern World*. New York: Vintage Books, 2008.

Mill, John Stuart. 'On Liberty', extracts in Robert Eccleshall (ed.), *British Liberalism: Liberal Thought from the 1640s to the 1980s*. London: Longman, 1986.

——. *On Liberty*. London: Longmans, Green and Company, 1901.

Mulhall, Stephen, and Adam Swift. *Liberals and Communitarians*. Oxford: Blackwell, 1997.

Niebuhr, Rheinhold. *Moral Man and Immoral Society*. New York: Charles Scribner's Sons, 1960.

Nozick, Robert. *Anarchy State and Utopia*. New York: Basic Books, 1974.

Paine, Tom. *Common Sense*. New York: Dover Publications, 1997.

Plant, Raymond. *Modern Political Thought*. Oxford: Blackwell, 1995.

Ramsay, Maureen. *What's Wrong with Liberalism: A Radical Critique of Liberal Political Philosophy*. London: Leicester University Press, 1997.

Ratner, Joseph (ed.). *Intelligence in the Modern World: John Dewey's Philosophy*. New York: The Modern Library, 1939.

Rawls, John. *A Theory of Justice*. Oxford: Oxford University Press, 1980.

Raz, Joseph. *The Morality of Freedom*. Oxford: Oxford University Press, 1988.

Sandel, Michael. *Democracy's Discontent*. Cambridge, MA: Harvard University Press, 1998.

Scalia, Antonin. *A Matter of Interpretation: Federal Courts and the Law*. Princeton, NJ: Princeton University Press, 1997.

Schake, Kori. *Safe Passage: The Transition from British to American Hegemony*. Cambridge, MA: Harvard University Press, 2017.

Sumner, W.G. 'Liberty and Responsibility', in *Earth Hunger and Other Essays*. New Brunswick, NJ: Transaction Books, 1980.

_____. 'What Social Classes Owe to Each Other', in Andrew M. Scott (ed.), *Political Thought in America*. New York: Rinehart and Co., 1959, 315–18.

Sydney, Algernon. *Discourses Concerning Government*, 1698, Section 44, http://www.oll.library-fund.org.

Tawney, R.H. *Equality*. London: Unwin Books, 1964.

Taylor, Charles. 'What's Wrong with Negative Liberty?', in David Miller (ed.), *Liberty*. Oxford: Oxford University Press, 1993.

Tyrrell, James. *Patriarcha non Monarcha*, http://www.oll.libraryfund.org.

Ward, Lee. *The Politics of Liberty in England and Revolutionary America*. Cambridge: Cambridge University Press, 2004.

Chapter 4

Of Friendships and Fissures

Anglo-American Conservatism

Reed Davis

Addressing the House of Commons in 1982, President Ronald Reagan briefly reminisced about an earlier visit to London with Prime Minister Margaret Thatcher. During a stopover at the British embassy in London, President Reagan told the assembled dignitaries, the prime minister had rather mischievously warned him not to be distressed by the sight of a portrait of King George III hanging on a wall at the embassy. 'She suggested that it was best to let bygones be bygones', Reagan quipped, 'and in view of our countries' remarkable friendship in succeeding years, she added that most Englishmen today would agree with Thomas Jefferson that a little rebellion now and then is a very good thing'. That Anglo-American conservatism may have finally evolved into a singular historical force embraced by both Americans and Englishmen should not be too surprising. After all, no less of an authority than Alexis de Tocqueville once declared that 'democratic peoples … in the end come to be alike in almost all matters'.[1] Accordingly, the spread of democracy means that 'the same ways of behaving, thinking and feeling are found in every corner of the world'.[2]

The Reagan–Thatcher partnership revived a moribund conservatism in both countries, unleashing a burst of conservative synergies whereby conservative ideas in one country inspired and were sometimes cross-fertilized by ideas from the other. Books were written, think tanks created and white papers exchanged, affording countless opportunities for one conservatism to leaven the other. After wandering in the wilderness for decades, conservatives were finally pouring into the promised lands of Pennsylvania Avenue and 10 Downing Street, eager to remake Anglo-American politics in their own rejuvenated image.

This essay plumbs the depths of Anglo-American conservatism in order to determine in what ways, if any, Anglo-American conservatisms have come to be alike. After establishing a working definition of conservatism, we begin by reviewing some of the key ideas of Edmund Burke, an eighteenth-century member of the British Parliament and a prolific man of letters who is considered by most scholars to be the father of conservatism. We then proceed from traditional British conservatism to its counterpart in the United States, the social conservatism of Russell Kirk and his fellow travellers. After a nod in the direction of libertarianism – a stalwart force in both post-war conservative movements – we review neoconservatism in the United States and Great Britain. Finally, we explore the recent burst of populism in both countries, as represented by President Donald Trump and the Brexit phenomenon, before drawing up something of a balance sheet.

What Is Conservatism?

Since it is predicated on a determination to, well, 'conserve', conservatism is notoriously difficult to define. As Jerry Muller points out, the list of institutions that conservatives have historically sought to protect is long and maddeningly diffuse. At one time or another, Muller observes, conservatives have defended royal absolutism, constitutional monarchy, constitutional liberalism, international trade, protectionism, the social hierarchy and individual liberty, among other things. Perhaps most problematically for those conservatives who believe in a uniquely Anglo-American conservatism, even a cursory look beyond their own national boundaries might force conservatives to admit that 'some of the institutions and practices they seek to conserve' in their own country are 'regarded as implausible or risible by their conservative counterparts' in others.[3] Noel O'Sullivan is reluctant to concede even the existence of a national tradition of conservatism, declaring that in no single individual does one see a pattern of thinking that fits neatly into a single tradition of conservative discourse.[4] For him, conservatism varies not just from country to country but also from thinker to thinker.

Conservatives find themselves in this predicament because all conservatives begin from the premise that each society has its own identity and will. From this, it follows that all reasonable people must, as Roger Scruton puts it, be open to the 'persuasions' of each and every social order.[5] It is for this reason that conservatives are reflexively suspicious of anything that smacks of social engineering. Indeed, Scruton goes so far as to say that 'a politician who seeks to impose upon [society] a given set of purposes, and seeks no understanding of the reason and values which the society proposes in return, acts in defiance of friendship'.[6] For the conservative, civic friendships and social personalities are complicated creations, forged in the fires of tradition, culture, history, language and prejudice. Consequently, political dogmas cannot do justice to the fullness of any given social personality. That is why conservatives struggle not only with sweeping social creeds and ideologies, but with definitions as well: they readily acknowledge that conservatism is plagued by a certain 'inarticulateness', unwilling as it is 'to translate itself into formulae or maxims, loathe to state its purpose or declare its view'.[7] Because conservatism lacks a single animating ideal, then, conservatism must necessarily assume a variety of forms. Consequently, the search for a universal, commonly accepted definition of conservatism is dismissed by some conservatives as the hobgoblin of little minds.

Nevertheless, the demand for a working definition of conservatism is not an unreasonable one. Some commentators believe that rather than combing through a set of common institutions, we should compile a list of shared dispositions in order to get a fix on conservatism. This was the tack taken by one of Great Britain's most prominent conservative thinkers, the philosopher Michael Oakeshott. 'To be conservative', Oakeshott insisted, 'is to be disposed to think and behave in certain manners; it is to prefer certain kinds of conduct and certain conditions of human circumstances to others; it is to be disposed to make certain kinds of choices'.[8] It is possible, to be sure, to mistake weaker characteristics of this disposition for better ones. Nevertheless, Oakeshott argued, conservatism revolves around

a propensity to use and to enjoy what is available rather than to wish for or to look for something else; to delight in what is present rather than what was or what may be. Reflection may bring to light an appropriate gratefulness for what is available, and consequently the acknowledgement of a gift or an inheritance from the past; but there is no mere idolizing what is past and gone. What is esteemed is the present; and it is esteemed not on account of its connections with a remote antiquity, nor because it is recognized to be more admirable than any possible alternative, but on account of its familiarity: not *Verweiledoch, du bist so schön*, but *Stay with me because I am attached to you.*[9]

Although Bruce Pilbeam's review of the many efforts to define conservatism is somewhat critical of Oakeshott's dispositional approach (Oakeshott's list of dispositions is a little too fuzzy for Pilbeam's liking), Pilbeam does pay tribute to Oakeshott's conviction that a definition of conservatism must include the notion that conservatism accepts the reality of limits, an acceptance that flows logically from the conviction that human beings are inherently imperfect.[10] According to this reading of history and human nature, humanity's ability to comprehend and mould the social order is sharply restricted. Human beings are simply made of too much 'crooked wood', to borrow C.S. Lewis's telling phrase, to serve as the raw material for a happy, healthy society. All conservatives, then, share a sense that there must be limits to human ambitions and lament the utopian hubris of those who loudly declare that nothing is forbidden because all things are possible. Thus, conservatism is best understood as a 'philosophy of imperfection',[11] a philosophy that rejects the belief that radical social reform is capable of straightening out the warped wood of human nature.

If we advance a definition of conservatism that stresses the recognition of limits, then we eventually end up with a rather loose, Aristotelian emphasis on *prudence* as a key ingredient of conservatism. To Aristotle's way of thinking, 'prudence is a truth-attaining rational quality, concerned with action in relation to the things that are good for human beings'.[12] As a guide to choice, prudence reckons not only with abstract ideals but also with specific facts, 'since it is concerned with action, and action deals with particular things'.[13] Virtue, then, guarantees that the ends of action are right and proper, while prudence attends to the means we adopt to achieve a given end in the context of a specific situation.

Prudence, in other words, pays close attention to the circumstances of action. As Burke explained, it is the power of circumstance to 'give in reality to every principle its distinguishing color and discriminating effect'.[14] For this reason, conservatives of all kinds are suspicious of abstract theories and metaphysical systems, at least as they pertain to the task of social reform. By its very nature, theory reaches beyond the contingencies of common experience in order to comprehend that which is timeless and universal. But given the vagaries of history and human action, theory is of very limited utility indeed in directing social action. And for some conservatives, as we will see – Burke comes readily to mind – theory is altogether useless as a guide to action. Given the failings of human nature and the power of circumstance, then, conservatives tend to rally around prudence as the chief feature of the conservative mind.

Early British Conservatism

In describing the various strands of Anglo-American conservatism, we begin with that which is historically antecedent to American conservatism, namely, with British 'Burkean' conservatism. Although histories of conservatism pay tribute to different 'founders' – Pilbeam, for example, begins with Edmund Burke, while Jerry Miller begins with David Hume – scholars generally agree that Burke exercised the most decisive influence over the development of British conservatism. For Burke, prudence begins with a respect for those customs and institutions sanctified by history. The fact that an institution or a practice boasts a lengthy record of survival is simple but powerful evidence that it serves some basic human need. Accordingly, we owe a 'natural and dutiful reverence to any institution that has existed through the ages and persists to the present day'.[15] This does not mean that the longevity of institutions is self-justifying. Bruce Frohnen explains Burke's position as follows:

> The conservative seeks to preserve institutions *because* they allow for and foster the practice of virtue. Institutions and indeed entire social systems (such as Communist states) that do not allow for the practice of conservative virtue are morally wrong and best abolished because they fit the nature of no man. Natural law dictates that history and circumstance take leading roles in forming the institutions that in turn perfect – or bring to proper fulfillment – human nature ... But if human nature is to be fulfilled, society must allow for the stable, familiar, and affectionate life that teaches men to love and serve their neighbors and thence their communities.[16]

Burkean conservatism, then, strives to preserve an attachment to a familiar way of living or to a way of life enjoyed by whole communities. For this reason, Burke viewed state and society in Britain as an organic whole. To Burke's way of thinking, statecraft should be animated by a pragmatic, prudential ethos, not by abstract or sweeping theoretical blueprints. The ongoing concern of responsible political leadership, then, should be 'that of deciding how much social and political reform could be accommodated within the mixed or balanced constitution'.[17] And in Burke's view, the answer to that question was almost always 'not much'.

This should not be taken to mean that Burke doggedly attached himself to tradition in a misguided effort to stave off social reform. Quite the contrary: Burke asserted that history and society were in constant motion and that managing change demanded a great deal more from statecraft than simply standing athwart history and yelling 'stop!' 'We must all obey the great law of change', Burke insisted, because 'it is the most powerful law of nature, and the means perhaps of its conservation. All that we can do, and that human wisdom can do, is to provide that the change shall proceed by insensible degrees. This has all the benefits which may be in change, without any of the inconveniences of mutation.'[18] Change by 'insensible degree' is a compressed definition of Burke's great doctrine of 'prescription'.

Prescription was, for Burke, the notion that change should be gradual or incremental; statesmen should always aim at improving or correcting existing practices and institutions, as opposed to sweeping them aside and beginning anew, as radicals like Thomas Paine believed. Burke's conservatism, then, readily acknowledged the need for change. In fact, Burke's conservatism was, ironically enough, more open to change than Paine's liberalism. As Yuval Levin has explained, Paine and his collaborators were attempting 'to establish the right permanent principles to guide the work of government'. Burke, however, believed that although the ends of government may be unchanging, 'the means to those ends must be altered as needed, and these sometimes must include even the details of the form of the government'.[19]

All of the inconveniences of 'mutation' guided by reason were, of course, fully evident in the French Revolution. Like all conservatives, Burke loathed the French Revolution (but supported the American one), pouring out his scorn for the Jacobins in what is perhaps his most widely celebrated work, *Reflections on the Revolution in France*.[20] Burke's belief in the complexity of history and human nature led him to doubt the efficacy of reason as a guiding light for political action, an outlook completely at odds with the cool confidence in rationality stoked by the *philosophes*. 'If there is one recurrent theme in Burke's letters speeches and writings', Harvey Mansfield has observed, 'it is his emphasis on the moral and practical evils that follow upon the intrusion of theory into political practice'.[21] In France, the violent zeal of the Jacobins, animated by the enlightened ideals of equality and liberty, unleashed unprecedented levels of chaos and terror, quickly degenerating into a living example of 'mob rule making its case in metaphysical abstractions'.[22]

Burkean conservatism rails against not only the radical egalitarianism set in motion by the Enlightenment but also all manner of libertarian, laissez-faire individualism. For British conservatives, society has something of a 'cellular' quality about it, which is to say that traditional conservatives view society not as a collection of 'lonely individuals' but as 'a grand union of functional groups'.[23] Indeed, we find our deepest fulfilment as human beings in groups; our families, churches and local communities give our lives meaning and purpose. These are the 'little platoons' that Burke celebrated and they create a vast, interlocking network that serves not only to unlock our potential for love and civic friendship, but also to resist the forward march of the all-powerful state. One must not push the cellular analogy too far, as conservatives insist on preserving the freedom and dignity of individuals. However, as Scruton has explained, 'the freedom that the British people esteem is not a special case of that freedom advocated by the American Republican Party, the freedom of pioneering dissenters struggling for community in a place without history, the freedom which is connected in some mysterious way with free enterprise and the market economy'.[24] Rather, freedom, as Burkean conservatives like Scruton understand it, is an 'ordered liberty', a freedom that balances liberty with social constraints.

American Conservatism

Burkean conservatism, then, constitutes the first of several strands of Anglo-American conservatism. In searching for the American counterpart to
Burkean conservatism, one must begin with the voluminous writings of Russell Kirk. Kirk was, by all accounts, the most influential American intellectual
labouring to preserve the Burkean legacy. And Kirk's intellectual contributions were substantial indeed. Kirk's first book, *The Conservative Mind*[25] –
which is ranked by some commentators alongside such iconic works as F.A.
Hayek's *The Road to Serfdom*[26] and Whittaker Chamber's *Witness*[27] – electri-
fied and galvanized American conservatives, eventually paving the way for
the so-called Reagan Revolution. Prior to that point, American conservatives
had few thinkers around whom they could rally or to whom they could look
for inspiration. Kirk's tome, however, changed all of that. As Clinton Rossiter put it, if Kirk's Burkean conservatism 'is not a doctrine to be followed,
it is certainly one to be understood and, if only for its eloquent obstinacy,
respected'.[28]

That Kirk was deeply influenced by Burke is undeniable. In fact, Kirk flatly
declared in the preface to *The Conservative Mind* that he was an unabashed
'Burkean conservative'. Declaring that the heart and soul of conservatism is
the preservation of the ancient moral customs of humankind, Kirk boiled
his understanding of conservatism down to six canons of thought: first, divine providence governs the social order as well as the individual conscience,
which means that political challenges are, at root, religious and moral; second, there is in social conservatism a profound affection for the variety
and mysteries of traditional ways of life, as distinguished from the dreary
monotony imposed by radicalism; third, a classless society is an affront to
decency, as civilized society requires orders and classes; fourth, there is a
close connection between freedom and private property; fifth, there must be
a belief in prescription and a profound distrust of any attempt to reconstruct
society according to a set of abstract principles; and sixth, statesmen must
at all times be guided by the virtue of prudence. Kirk claimed no originality
here – each of his six canons is suffused with the spirit of Burkean social
conservatism.

As the titular head of traditional conservatism, Kirk left behind a considerable intellectual legacy. A prolific writer, Kirk's conservatism influenced the
likes of M.E. Bradford, Richard Weaver, Patrick Buchanan and William F.
Buckley, among others. And searching as we are for examples of cross-fertilization, we note that Roger Scruton, the conservative English philosopher,
delivered an annual Heritage Foundation's Russell Kirk lecture. Indeed, Roger Scruton has become something of a staple at American universities and

conservative think tanks, having delivered public lectures at Princeton, the Wheatley Institution, the Heritage Foundation and the Hoover Institute.

But there is some irony here. On the one hand, Russel Kirk's conservatism did indeed ignite an intellectual and political firestorm: most commentators agree that there would have been no modern conservative movement had Kirk not written *The Conservative Mind.* On the other hand, his influence gradually shrank over time as other conservatisms such as libertarianism and neoconservatism emerged, species of conservatism whose core commitments grated on Kirk. However, the primary reason that Kirk's influence within American conservatism shrank over time is that Burkean conservatism is fundamentally at odds with American exceptionalism. Burke, we may recall, insisted that the rights of Englishmen were prescriptive rights. The Founders, however, grounded American government in the idea of natural rights. By this, the Founders meant to suggest that all that is politically proper can be discovered by human reason, a principle that Burke found profoundly unsettling and even dangerous. Or, as Alexander Hamilton put it, the Founders believed that human society was capable of establishing good government by 'reflection and choice' rather than 'accident and force'. Against Burke's particularism, then, the Founders made free use of certain universal ideas, such as the notion that all peoples possess the ability to create free governments. In doing so, they fractured the coherence of Anglo-American conservatism and exposed the limits of cross-fertilization and homogenization.

At this point, James Ceaser argues, conservatives could look at the American Revolution in one of two ways. On the one hand, conservatives could regard the American Revolution as an evil sibling of the French Revolution, with both revolutions threatening to undo western civilization. This, Ceaser avers, was the attitude of Joseph de Maistre, a Continental conservative whose conservatism far outstripped Burke's. (Unlike Burke, de Maistre insisted that religious faith serve as the foundation for social order.) Or, on the other hand, conservatives could separate the two revolutions and insist that the American Revolution was 'a special case inside a primarily conservative outlook'.[29] This was Burke's (and Kirk's) preferred solution: from their perspective, the foundation of the American Revolution lay not in natural rights but 'in the Americans' effort to vindicate their rights as Englishmen, which the English monarchs had not adequately respected'.[30] But the problem with the Anglo-American conservative solution, Ceaser maintains, is that virtually all of the Founders made the case for revolution in a rhetoric of natural rights that belies attempts to ground the purposes of government in historical or cultural norms. Even the great 'conservative' Hamilton accepted the existence of natural rights: 'The sacred rights of mankind are not to be rummaged for among old parchments, or musty records' but 'are written as with a sun beam in the whole volume of human nature, by the hand of the divinity itself'.[31]

It should be noted that there is an international or a foreign-policy dimension to Anglo-American conservatism as well as a domestic one. In foreign-policy matters, however, unlike domestic ones, American conservatives have been much more willing to follow the lead of the Founders; consequently, they pay close heed to George Washington's advice to avoid 'foreign entanglements' and are for that reason not only reflexively anti-war but downright hostile towards any manifestation of a politics of a pax Americana. President Richard Nixon's former speechwriter and recent candidate for the American presidency Pat Buchanan is perhaps most representative of this line of thinking. Buchanan warns American policymakers away from international commitments and the enduring temptation to destroy international 'monsters'. Indeed, conservatives like Buchanan warn of a day of reckoning when American foreign policy elites will discover that American military and political power has become dangerously overextended and will be unable to deliver on the war promises that they have handed out willy-nilly. And once awakened to what their statesmen have committed them to, Buchanan argues, the American people will rise up and refuse to shed the blood and expend the treasure that a politics of global hegemony demands of them.

Although most commentators accuse conservatives of isolationism, Buchanan vigorously rejects the charge, insisting that the term 'isolationism' is simply 'a dismissive slur on a tradition of U.S. independence in foreign policy and nonintervention in foreign wars that is forever associated with Washington's Farewell Address'.[32] As we pile one commitment on top of another in Eastern Europe, the Balkans, the Middle East and the Persian Gulf, Buchanan warns, 'American power continues to contract – a sure formula for foreign policy disaster'.[33]

As we will see in our discussion of neoconservatism, the conservative suspicion of abstract propositions fuels conservatives' distrust of the foreign policies of two of the other conservatisms: social conservatives disdain libertarianism, driven as it is, at least in part, by what social conservatives consider to be an unwavering commitment, grounded in theory, to free trade and open borders, and they distrust neoconservatism, grounded as they believe it is in a muscular determination to remake all societies the world over in a democratic image. Like all political realists, then, conservatives prefer to speak the language of national interest, arguing that the Founders were guided in their foreign-policy making by prudent regard for the national interest. Foreign policy, then, no less than domestic policy, must be guided by a spirit of incremental change informed by a clear assessment of the national interest.

Libertarianism

The second component of Anglo-American conservatism, like the first, also originated in Britain, to wit, in the London School of Economics. Libertarianism as a distinct school of thought began during the 1930s and 1940s, with the emergence of the Austrian school of economics as led by Ludwig von Mises and Friedrich Hayek, and then migrated to Great Britain. Not until Hayek sojourned at the University of Chicago in 1950 did libertarianism take root as an intellectual force in the United States.

Libertarianism teaches that a decentralized economic system predicated on the free choice of individuals is the most efficacious system available to human beings. That is, the most efficient economic systems are those that are free of central planning and government interference. Libertarians insist that no economic institution has produced and distributed scarce economic resources better than free and open markets. To libertarians, then, freedom works 'and the value of such efficient work, even if it could not be established objectively or philosophically, was apparent to any intelligent man who understood that scarcity was an inescapable fact of life'.[34]

Libertarians thus believe in the postulate of 'spontaneous order', or the notion that in both nature and human affairs, there is a tendency for all intelligent agents to discover coherent solutions to ongoing problems provided that their search for solutions is free from the interference of outside actors – such as a central planning agency – seeking to impose a comprehensive vision of the way things should be. The order preferred by libertarians, therefore, is one that is established to protect free, unencumbered interactions between and among individual agents, an order otherwise referred to as a 'system of natural liberty'. In economics, spontaneous order is created by Adam Smith's 'invisible hand', a creative force that works over our heads to transform the pursuit of self-interest into a common good that benefits all. As Smith explains it, the rich 'consume little more than the poor, and in spite of their natural selfishness and rapacity ... they divide with the poor the produce of all their improvements. They are led by an invisible hand to make nearly the same distribution of the necessaries of life, which would have been made, had the earth been divided in equal portions among all its inhabitants, and thus without intending it, without knowing it, advance the interest of the society, and afford means to the multiplication of the species.'[35] Economies are simply too complex to be managed by a single, centralized intelligence.

Given their commitment to spontaneous order, libertarians are dedicated to illuminating the irrationalities of planned economies, whether those economies be of the totalitarian or social democratic sort. But their animosity towards communism and planned economies of all types extends well beyond the economic folly of central planning: like social conservatives, libertarians also see a cruel, noxious hubris at work in radical politics like communism. This hubris manifests itself not only in the economic irrationalities of central planning, but also in the tyrannical attempt to impose a universal moral code dictated by the radical egalitarianism of socialism. As libertarians see it, the ideological morality of communism severely cramps human freedom, stripping human beings of the possibility of genuine moral decisions. For many libertarians, then, freedom is an end in itself because it makes moral life possible, while others see it primarily as an instrumental good, advancing the utilitarian principle of efficiency.

At first glance, libertarians seem to have much in common with social conservatives. Both are committed to the institutions of private property and limited government, and both abhor the crushing, levelling furies unleashed by radical egalitarianism. Both are anti-war. Both also cherish freedom, even though social conservatives prefer a more ordered liberty, while libertarians are far more socially permissive. Perhaps most importantly, both would agree that 'a nation is a kind of spontaneous social order emerging from historical experience and the unguided evolution of market and cultural forces'. Consequently, both traditions advance in their own way a rather Burkean understanding of political life 'as "grown" rather than "made"'.[36]

Nevertheless, libertarians and social conservatives tend to keep their distance from one another. Kirk, for example, consigned libertarians to the outer darkness of 'the terrible simplifiers' because they reduced all human beings to odourless, colourless atoms of self-interest whose interactions can be explained *in toto* by the laws of economics. Kirk also thought libertarians were 'metaphysically mad' because, in thrall to the laws of economics, they were indifferent to the significance of a transcendent moral order for human behaviour, an order that promised 'transcendent sanctions' on conduct when transgressed. Moreover, libertarians preach what Kirk considered to be an 'abstract' liberty. Because they promote an absolute liberty, or a liberty divorced from a prior constitutionally sanctioned order, libertarians threaten to undo the very liberty that they commend. Finally, Kirk was uncomfortable with the libertarians' single-minded focus on self-interest as a force for social order. To Kirk's way of thinking, society is a 'community of souls', one that joins the living and the dead into an organic whole. An Aristotelian notion of civic friendship, and not a naked cash nexus, should bind us together as citizens.

Libertarians, for their part, issued their own call to arms. Perhaps their most common objection to conservatism centred on the social conservatives' appreciation of government, an appreciation that libertarians worry does not sufficiently grasp the innate tendency of all governments to grow and threaten the liberty they were originally called on to protect. After all, von

Mises noted, it was conservatives who introduced socialism to Britain.[37] The freedom that libertarians demand, then, insists that individuals be accorded, above all else, the right to depart from traditional ways of thinking and being. More to the point, conservatives readily turn to the law to prop up those social institutions – the family, prayer in public schools – that they believe are conducive to human flourishing. Libertarians, for their part, do not deny the importance of moral sensibilities but refrain from appealing to political power to enforce them. This, they insist, eventually paves the way to a malignant, overweening state.

As for foreign policy, libertarians are as anti-war as social conservatives but tend to believe that free trade and (relatively) open borders, along with constant communication, are the best guarantors of peace and global prosperity. Most libertarians fret that the United States is overly dependent on its military to maintain peace in the far corners of the world. As Christopher Preble of the Cato Institute put it, war 'is the most far-reaching of all statist enterprises. It's an engine of collectivization that undermines private enterprise, raises taxes, destroys wealth, and subjects all aspects of the economy to regimentation and social planning.'[38] James Madison's maxim had it exactly right for libertarians: 'The loss of liberty at home', Madison wrote, 'is to be charged to the provisions against danger, real or pretended, from abroad'.[39]

Neoconservatism

With the emergence of neoconservatism during the 1970s, we encounter a conservatism that is uniquely American. Eventually migrating to Great Britain (although to somewhat lesser effect), neoconservatism is a species of conservatism that not only clearly contributes to the ongoing process of cross-fertilization, but – unlike classical conservatism or libertarianism – has also exercised a significant amount of political influence in the process, at least for a time.

However, in limning the critical features of neoconservatism, we are immediately confronted with a conundrum, namely, that the most influential strain of conservatism is virtually impossible to define. In fact, it has become so difficult to define neoconservatism that many commentators have come to believe that there is no such thing, maintaining that neoconservatism is so variable and amorphous that it exists only in the overheated imagination of an enthusiastic cabal of contemporary conservative thinkers. How is it possible, for example, to lump together individuals as different as Daniel Patrick Moynihan, Paul Wolfowitz, William Kristol and Mark Lilla? The problem is compounded by the fact that neoconservatism emerged from no electoral or economic base, never had a universally acknowledged leader and established no organization promoting its views. Too small and inchoate to be a political party, neoconservatism has been variously described by one of its leading lights as a 'persuasion' (albeit one that has unfolded 'erratically'), an 'intellectual undercurrent' and, a little more optimistically, 'a current of thought'. However, it has never been able to gather enough steam to be considered a 'movement' or even an 'ideology.'[40] As Justin Vaïsse explains,

> From the 1960s to the 2000s, neoconservatism transformed itself so thoroughly as to become unrecognizable. It moved from the left to the right side of the political chessboard. It shifted its focus from domestic issues to foreign affairs. In abandoning New York for Washington, it left the world of sociologists and intellectuals for that of influence and power. Born as a pure reaction to another intellectual and political movement – the protest of the 1960s, the counterculture, and the New Left – it survived the movement's demise. Yet this did not prevent Pohoretz, Kristol and other neoconservatives as well as outside observers from prematurely writing the movement's obituary at various points in history.[41]

Coming to grips with neoconservatism is no ivory-tower exercise: neoconservatism, after all, stands accused (by many conservatives to boot) of pushing the United States into another quagmire, namely the Gulf War. The United States' alleged failure in Iraq, then, is considered by some to be the failure of neoconservatism.

In order to get our bearings on neoconservatism, we turn out attention to its origins. As with our other conservatisms, there seems to be a 'founding father' of sorts for neoconservatism. Just as classical conservatism had its Burke and libertarianism had its Hayek and von Mises, so too does neoconservatism have its intellectual pioneer, namely, Irving Kristol. It is from Kristol, then, that we take our initial reading of what neoconservatism is. We make no effort to hammer neoconservatism into a coherent, self-evident whole. Instead, we rest content with simply sketching out some of its features and leave the task of hammering to others.

As Kristol makes clear, neoconservatism first originated in the dashed hopes of leftist intellectuals. More specifically, Kristol identifies three precipitating events that drove neoconservatism. First, there was the failure of President Lyndon Johnson's Great Society. When President Johnson's Great Society failed to live up to expectations, especially in programmes designed to end poverty, the consequent disappointment triggered quite a bit of soul-searching among erstwhile supporters. The fundamental problem of the war on poverty, Kristol believed, was its commitment to 'the sociological fantasy' that 'if one gave political power to the poor, by sponsoring "community action", they would then lift themselves out of poverty at the expense of the rich and powerful'.[42] Unlike the academics and intellectuals who had designed the anti-poverty programmes, Kristol and his circle of his friends, many of whom had been not only liberals but Trotskyites, had grown up in lower- or middle-class families and recognized that political militancy 'was no way for poor people to lift themselves out of poverty'.[43] Indeed, Kristol added, the whole American experiment to eradicate poverty was simply an echo of the old socialist canard that a great society could emerge only as the consequence of class struggle.

The fundamental problem with the welfare state, Kristol argued, is that it refuses to think realistically about human nature. Social reformers of the sort who designed or championed Johnson's Great Society believe that human nature is not only good but incorruptibly so. As a result, social reformers completely misread human motivation. When designing social programmes, there was thought to be no need to factor in incentives – rewards or punishments – because liberal social scientists believed with a blind, unshakeable faith that 'poor people only have good motivations'.[44] Such optimism need hardly concern itself with the outcomes of social reform, as all that is needed to design and run social programmes are good intentions. That is why, despite the disillusionment engendered by many Great Society programmes, there has been 'a lack of serious reflection on our experience with social policy', according to Kristol.[45]

This was the first hole that neoconservatives rushed in to plug. Consequently, neoconservatism gave rise to quite a bit of social science that was intended to gauge the effectiveness of public policy. The pre-eminent academic journal in this area was *Public Interest*, a quarterly journal founded by Irving Kristol and Daniel Bell. Readers were introduced to the likes of James Q. Wilson, Daniel Bell, Aaron Wildavsky, Seymour Martin Lipset and Nathan Glazer, among others, dealing with topics ranging from crime and criminality to the family. It is important to note that neoconservatives were not all that anxious to dismantle the welfare state, at least not completely; what neoconservatives intended to do was improve the efficiency and measure the cost of public programmes, not do away with them completely. Indeed, despite their relentless criticism of the Great Society, neoconservatives had in fact made their peace with the welfare state, unlike libertarians and traditional conservatives, who had been waging war on it since its inception. What bound neoconservatives together on this score, then, was an aversion to the ideological thinking championed by the left or to any social programme founded on a complete indifference to data, not necessarily an aversion to the programmes themselves.

Perhaps the chief mark of neoconservative public policy is its insistence on maximizing individual choice. Like libertarians, neoconservatives believe that free markets are good because they distribute goods and services rationally. Unlike libertarians, neoconservatives insist that the welfare state can coexist comfortably with free markets. Also unlike libertarians, neoconservatives give capitalism only 'two cheers', not three. What concerns neoconservatives is the potentially corrosive effect of unrestrained personal choice on culture. Like classical conservatives, then, neoconservatives worry a great deal about human character. 'In the end', Kristol declared, 'when all is said and done, the only authentic criterion for judging any economic or political system, or any set of social institutions, is this: what kind of people emerge from them?'[46] Since libertarians tend to wave off character concerns, neoconservatives and traditional conservatives have the potential to make common cause over the need to cultivate virtue and public spiritedness in democracy. However, traditional conservatives are just as put off as libertarians by neoconservatism's willing embrace of big government.

This emphasis on public spiritedness was triggered by the student rebellion of the 1960s and the rise of the counterculture, the second precipitating event of neoconservatism. Confronted by the libertinism unleashed by student leftists and bohemians, Kristol was a little surprised to discover just how culturally conservative he and his friends had become. They believed that liberal democracy required not just token acknowledgements of the need for public morality, but a serious, sustained effort at cultivating habits of self-restraint, habits that the counterculture attacked in favour of an ethos of self-expression, something neoconservatives could not abide any more than could traditional conservatives.

Neoconservatism's commitment to character formation compelled it to pay close attention to culture. Here, the arch-enemy, at least as many neoconservatives see it, is cultural relativism. 'Our Western failure to defend ourselves at home and stand up to our enemies', Douglas Murray has declared, 'is founded on our relativism'.[47] Cultural relativism is simply the idea that no one political regime, no way of life, no human desire is inherently any better than any other. This attitude, neoconservatives warn, will be the undoing of free governments everywhere, a conviction that drove many to the natural rights philosophy of Leo Strauss, the twentieth-century political philosopher who did more to revive classical natural rights philosophy than any other. The cardinal premise of natural rights philosophy is equality or the idea that human beings are born equal and are thus to be treated with dignity and respect. However, Kristol argued,

> it does not occur to us that, in a democracy, if the citizenry lack self-respect they will be incapable of any kind of respect – that to the degree we officially propound a mean and squalid view of humanity, there will emerge mean and squalid

human beings. All of us normally become what we are expected to become, and if our society thinks it normal for us to be enslaved to our appetites and our desires rather than to govern them, then we shall come to regard such enslavement as true liberty, and shall simultaneously regard any suggestion as an infraction of liberty.[48]

And how, exactly, does character come to be cultivated? Neoconservatives are not terribly clear on this point, other than agreeing that American republicanism demands more of civic virtue than any other form of governance. Nevertheless, it seems that Americans can nurture public spiritedness chiefly by keeping alive the habits of communication and co-operation fostered by local associations and churches, a prescription in keeping with Burke's teaching on 'little platoons' and Tocqueville's on civic and voluntary associations. Indeed, like Burke and Tocqueville, many neoconservatives evince a great deal of respect for religion. For example, Murray calls for a revival of faith-based education, insisting that an education explicitly grounded in the Judeo-Christian tradition is of great public benefit. 'Not only are children allowed to start off from the right moral place', Murray insists, 'but they are provided with the earliest – and for many of them, the only – opportunity to understand the basis of western art, history, and philosophy'. In fact, 'children ignorant of their nation's faith are most likely to feel alienated from the country they live in, precisely because, from the earliest age, they have been denied an opportunity to feel part of it'.[49]

Finally, the third precipitating event of neoconservatism was the Cold War. Here, Kristol's youthful Trotskyite background, which he shed during his undergraduate years, played a decisive role in shaping his understanding of world politics. Thanks to his immersion in leftist activism, Kristol wrote, 'I knew that if you took Marxist–Leninist doctrine as seriously as the Soviet leadership did, the broad outline of an appropriate American foreign policy almost designed itself'.[50] In other words, if decision-makers took a hard line against the Soviet Union or any other communist regime, Kristol insisted that they would be right more often than not. Contrary to what many on the left believed, neoconservatives like Kristol held that communism was to be both feared and resisted, as the Soviet Union was an 'evil empire' that was both morally abominable and relentlessly expansionist.

Neoconservatives, then, believed that American foreign policy should reckon as much with ideas as with interests. This ran contrary to much of what the Republican establishment believed, which was that the Soviet Union was simply another great power whose interests ran contrary to America's from time to time. From their perspective, deals could be struck, détente pursued and accommodations reached. Reagan's goal for American foreign policy towards the Soviets – 'we win, they lose' – was thus enthusiastically embraced by neo-conservatives as a more ethical and muscular alternative to the conciliatory approaches of Henry Kissinger and Richard Nixon.

After the Soviet Union collapsed and the Cold War came to its sudden end during the 1990s, the neoconservative approach to communism and the Cold War appeared to have been vindicated. By 1996, in fact, Norman Podhoretz, an editor of *Commentary* magazine, another leading neoconservative journal, declared that neoconservatism was now officially dead, having died 'not of failure, but of success'.[51] Joshua Muravchik, a consistent defender of neoconservatism, is not so sure. According to Muravchik, there is indeed a neoconservative way of thinking, at least in foreign affairs, one that is capable of guiding American decision-makers even after the collapse of the Soviet Union. In Muravchik's view, neoconservatives are, above all else, moralists; that is, they are quick to pass judgement on the international behaviour of states and leadership elites. The Soviet Union, of course, was judged in the harshest moral terms, as were leaders like Slobodan Milošević and Saddam Hussein. Conversely, neoconservatives believe that the United States has been a global force for good. Max Boot, for example, calls for a sustained American commitment to empire building because of America's determination to improve the living conditions of formerly war-torn or oppressed societies.[52]

Second, neoconservatives are internationalists, not isolationists, as war-averse libertarians and conservatives tend to be. 'Since America's security could be affected by events far from home', Muravchik writes, 'it was wiser to confront troubles early, even if afar than to wait for them to ripen and grow nearer'.[53] To this way of thinking, the world has been spared untold agony by smothering radical or corrupt insurgencies early and decisively.

Third, neoconservatives trust in the efficacy of military force to contain political wildfires, at least in comparison to United Nations pronouncements or economic weapons like sanctions. Beginning from the moralistic tendency to divide the world into friends and enemies rather than interests plain and simple, neoconservatives are quick not only to judge but also to act: trouble-makers need to be stopped and they need to be stopped sooner rather than later. And that usually requires the application of military force. Evildoers, almost by definition, respect little else.

Finally, neoconservatives believe in democracy. Democratic regimes, neoconservatives insist, echoing a theme of Immanuel Kant's and Woodrow Wilson's, tend to be more peaceful and prosperous than authoritarian or totalitarian regimes. Neoconservatism 'is indeed idealistic in its internationalism and its faith in democracy and freedom, but is hardheaded, not to say jaundiced, in its image of our adversaries and its assessment of international organizations'.[54] Neoconservatism's moralism, together with its appreciation for the use of military force, has prompted some commentators to label it the most diplomatically 'hot-headed' or hawkish of all the conservatisms, quick as it is to pass political judgement and act accordingly.

These four criteria do indeed make George Bush's war in Iraq a 'neocon' war, one that, despite setbacks and missteps during the transition to a democratic Iraq, most neoconservatives are happy to own. But such a statement must immediately be qualified, as we must once again note the difficulty of defining 'neoconservative'. Neoconservatism, we must remember, originated in a debate regarding domestic issues, not foreign-policy ones, which explains, at least in part, why Irving Kristol opposed the war in Iraq, whereas his son, William, supported it. It is for this reason that Vaïsse argues that perhaps the best way to define neoconservatism is to keep in mind when it is.

The war in Iraq marks the high-water mark of neoconservative influence, as the Bush administration had turned to neoconservative think tanks (such as the American Enterprise Institute) for foreign-policy advisors and administrators. Even Prime Minister Tony Blair was said to have fallen under the spell of neoconservatism (especially in foreign policy) cast by the defence intellectuals in the Bush administration.[55]

It is clear that American neoconservatism left its mark on British conservatism. Douglas Murray is among the most visible of the British neoconservative intellectuals. In his book, *Neoconservatism and Why We Need It*, he pleads with Americans, remarkably enough, not to abandon the neoconservative cause. Whether or not there is a direct line of influence here, at least one commentator finds it notable that so many of Murray's foreign-policy recommendations have been picked up by UKIP (United Kingdom Independence Party).[56] It may be that UKIP's own policy prescriptions have been derived from or reinforced by the presence of the Henry Jackson Society in London, an avowedly neoconservative think tank named in honour of Senator 'Scoop' Jackson, the United States senator who was perhaps the leading anti-communist in the United States Senate during the 1970s.

Nevertheless, despite the fact that many British intellectuals and commentators, ranging from Prof. Brendan Simms of Cambridge University to Melanie Phillips of *The Times* and *The Jerusalem Post*, have acknowledged the importance of the Henry Jackson Society to British politics and intellectual life, some argue that neoconservatism has yet to put down very deep roots in British public opinion. As Kristol noted, religious traditionalists – in other words, the religious right – make up a significant portion of American neoconservatives, as religious traditionalists share the neoconservative appreciation for traditional morality. However, because there really is nothing in Great Britain that corresponds to the American religious right and because

religious traditionalism is so feeble in Europe, as Kristol observed, the neoconservative potential there is weak.

As this section on neoconservatism draws to a close, we note in passing that
there is now something of an offshoot of neoconservatism, or perhaps conservatism more generally, emerging that some identify as 'national greatness
conservatism', a term we borrow from Vaïsse but deploy a little differently. By
his use of the phrase, Vaïsse sought to highlight the fact that many neoconservatives thought after the Soviet Union collapsed that the time was right to
construct something of a 'pax Americana', a form of international engagement
whereby America would acknowledge that it had 'a special responsibility, a
special vocation', and that it would betray its own universalist values if it did
not intervene, especially in the Balkans, 'to enforce respect for human rights,
defend democracy, and shape the world in its own image'.[57] Although we can
locate the earliest strains of the call to this sort of national greatness in the
pages of *The Weekly Standard*, the call to national greatness did not really seem
to gain much traction until President Donald Trump made a version of it
the cornerstone of his presidential campaign. Given the fact that President
Trump's policies, both at home and abroad, were not as yet fully formed before his defeat, we can only offer up the barest of summaries of his brand of
conservatism.

As Michael Anton notes, Donald Trump was one of the earliest political
presidential candidates not only to sense but to encourage a resurgence of
patriotism beginning to take hold in many parts of the world, particularly
in Europe and the United States. And putting one's own country first is a
good thing, in President Trump's view. Indeed, this seems to be the linchpin
of Trump's peculiar brand of conservatism. As Anton explains it, a Trump
Doctrine, for all its false starts and missteps, can be boiled down to this: 'Let's
all put our own countries first, and be candid about it, and recognize that it's
nothing to be ashamed of. Putting our interest first will make us all safer and
more prosperous.'[58]

Unlike the neoconservatives of the 1990s, however, Trump apparently has
no interest in creating either a pax Americana or a homogenized international
community created on the basis of some universalized political image. Moreover, he is quite obviously in favour of a strong military, but not for the sake of
spreading democracy to the far corners of the globe. In fact, Trump's neoconservatism was tailored to appeal to a war-weary nation, to those who believed
that the United States has spread itself militarily too thin across far too many
corners of the world and want to bring American troops home.

It seems that this is roughly the sort of nationalism that is spreading across
Europe, particularly in Great Britain, where both voters and elected officials
alike struggle with the apparent backlash against Britain's membership in the

European Union. What Britain is seeking to regain is not necessarily national greatness in the Trumpian mode but national independence, as many in Britain want to flee the grasp of the European Union. A return to sovereignty, then, not greatness, is what many conservatives aspire to. However, because national greatness conservatism is such a recent – but significant – phenomenon, settling on what it is or what people expect from it in either its British or American manifestation will probably necessitate awaiting at least one more election. Until then, we simply note its emergence.

Concluding Observations

As this brief overview reveals, the centripetal forces of democratic history that Tocqueville heralded do indeed seem to be pulling Anglo-American conservatisms into the same loose orbit, so long as it is understood that these are multifaceted conservatisms that are converging. In other words, with the exception of the religious right – a force conspicuously absent from British conservatism – American and British conservatism display almost identical cracks and fissures: both conservatisms are marked by strains of traditionalism, libertarianism, neoconservatism and populism. And cross-fertilization, it would appear, has only served to reinforce the differences within Anglo-American conservatism, not eliminate them.

At first glance, however, it seems that there may be limits to the homogenizing forces of history. After all, Britain is governed by a parliamentary system, while the United States is governed by a presidential one. In Britain, political battle is conducted by political parties far stronger than those in America. And given the fact that the winning party controls virtually all of the levers of power, losers there are bereft of almost all political responsibilities, except for those associated with the austere pleasures of membership in the loyal opposition. Augmenting the power of the winning party is the lack of a separation of powers in the British system: the parliamentary agenda is set by the prime minister (who is the head of the party), known well in advance, and need not contend with any form of political interference from the loyal opposition, save for suffering the indignities of whatever jeers and catcalls can be hurled from the backbenches.

In the American presidential system, marked chiefly by federalism, the separation of powers and a correspondingly weak party system, political power is much more diffuse. Not only are the different *branches* of government suspicious of one another, but so too are the different *levels* of government, as American federalism divides power along national, state and local lines, unlike Britain's unitary system, which is much more centralized.

Nevertheless, there are signs of convergence even here. Beginning with President Woodrow Wilson, the American left has long admired the institutional coherence of Britain's parliamentary system and sought to strengthen presidential leadership in the United States by insisting that the executive branch should attempt to assume as much power as it can in order to lead the country according to a rational, coherent national plan. To that end, Wilson declared that the administrative state would be a critical instrument of presidential leadership, an idea that has taken root in successive democratic administrations, especially those of Franklin Delano Roosevelt and Lyndon Johnson.[59] By expanding and strengthening the administrative state, American progressives hoped to overcome not only the separation of powers but American federalism as well, as empowering states and municipalities tends to diminish federal power, which is precisely what federalism was designed to do.

But as commentators have frequently noted, a vastly strengthened executive wielding enormous administrative power appeals not only to progressives but also to a good number of American conservatives. Many conservative congressional leaders find the administrative state rather convenient because, as Theodore Bromund explains, congressional leaders 'use it to avoid the actual trouble of responsibility'.[60] And neoconservatives, we may recall, simply regard the emergence of the administrative state as a normal manifestation of modern politics. Although congressional leaders of all stripes grumble about the transfer of power from the legislative branch to the executive, there have been few sustained efforts to redress the balance.[61]

Despite the somewhat bewildering condition of conservatism today, especially American conservatism,[62] some conservatives take heart from the very heterogeneity of the movement and believe that this heterogeneity augurs well for the future and the relevance of conservatism. According to James Ceaser, for example, it is important to recognize that what binds conservatism into a working whole is not a common set of ideas, but a common antipathy towards liberalism. ('It has been said in jest', Ceaser writes, 'that the conservative movement in America today is held together by two self-evident truths: Barack Obama and Nancy Pelosi'.)[63] Consequently, if by some strange dispensation liberalism 'were to cease to exist tomorrow', Ceaser maintains, 'conservatism would begin to break apart on the next day'. Ceaser believes that this common antipathy towards the liberal project has one great virtue, namely, it teaches conservatives the benefits of tolerance and civic friendship, qualities that he suggests sometimes elude those on the left. Because the left believes in the unifying power of general ideas, liberals are quick to cast out dissenters from among their ranks and label them as heretics. Conservatives, however, given their history, tend to be less schismatic than liberals because 'they have never operated under the illusion of ultimate agreement'.[64] This has the practical consequence of solidifying the conservative movement, albeit weakly, and inoculating it a little against the ferocity that marks so many of the left's internecine battles.

What, then, does the future hold for Anglo-American conservatism? It is difficult to know. Tocqueville prophesized that history would propel Anglo-American democracy – and by extension, Anglo-American conservatism – along a somewhat predictable path. No simple determinist, however, Tocqueville also believed that providence allows for a measure of human agency. This means that, as the election of Donald J. Trump and the rise of an Anglo-American populism illustrate, the evolution of Anglo-American conservatism may take some rather surprising twists and turns in the coming years. But rather than lament the course of human events, conservatives would do well to heed Thatcher and remember that a little rebellion now and then is a very good thing.

Reed Davis, emeritus professor, received his PhD from the University of Virginia in 1991 and taught political science at Seattle Pacific University from 1989 until his retirement in 2021. He served as department chair from 2006 to 2014 and created the Augustinian Fellowship, a study-abroad programme in France that he directed from 1994 until 2015. He is the author of *A Politics of Understanding: The International Thought of Raymond Aron* (LSU Press, 2010) and the editor of *Moral Reasoning and Statecraft: Essays Presented to Kenneth W. Thompson* (University Press of America, 1988). Before moving to Seattle Pacific University, he was Chief of Staff and Research Fellow at the Miller Center of Public Affairs at the University of Virginia.

Notes

1. A. de Tocqueville, *Democracy in America*, trans. G. Lawrence (New York: Anchor Books, 1968), 600.
2. Ibid., 615.
3. J. Muller (ed.), *Conservatism: An Anthology of Social and Political Thought from David Hume to the Present* (Princeton, NJ: Princeton University Press, 1997), 3.
4. N. O'Sullivan, *Conservatism* (New York: St Martin's Press, 1976), 28–29.
5. R. Scruton, *The Meaning of Conservatism* (South Bend, IN: St Augustine's Press, 2002), 14.
6. Ibid., 13.
7. Ibid., 9.

8. M. Oakeshott, *Rationalism in Politics and Other Essays* (Indianapolis, IN: Liberty Fund, 1962), 169.

9. Ibid., 168.

10. B. Pilbeam, *Conservatism in Crisis? Anglo-American Conservatism after the Cold War* (London: Palgrave-MacMillan, 2003), 6–10.

11. N. O'Sullivan, *Conservatism*, 11.

12. Aristotle, *Nichomachean Ethics*, ed. H. Rackham (Cambridge: Cambridge University Press, 1933), 339.

13. Ibid., 345–46.

14. E. Burke, *The Writings and Speeches of Edmund Burke*, ed. P. Marshall (Boston, MA: Little, Brown, 1901), II, 282.

15. I. Kramnick, *The Rage of Edmund Burke: Portrait of an Ambivalent Conservative* (New York: Basic Books, 1977), 25.

16. B. Frohnen, *Virtue and the Promise of Conservatism: The Legacy of Burke and Tocqueville* (Lawrenceville: The University of Kansas Press, 1973), 23–24.

17. N. O'Sullivan, *Conservatism*, 83.

18. E. Burke, *Writings and Speeches*, IX, 634.

19. Y. Levin, *The Great Debate: Edmund Burke, Thomas Paine and the Birth of Right and Left* (New York: Basic Books, 2014), 144.

20. E. Burke, *Reflections on the Revolution in France*, ed. Franklin Turner (New Haven, CT: Yale University Press, 2004).

21. H. Mansfield, 'Edmund Burke', in L. Strauss and J. Cropsey (eds), *History of Political Philosophy*, 3rd edn (Chicago: University of Chicago Press, 1963), 687–709.

22. Levin, *The Great Debate*, 27.

23. C. Rossiter, *Conservatism in America* (New York: Knopf, 1962), 27.

24. Scruton, *The Meaning of Conservatism*, 8.

25. R. Kirk, *The Conservative Mind* (Chicago: H. Regnery Co., 1953).

26. F. Hayek, *The Road to Serfdom* (Chicago: University of Chicago Press, 1944).

27. W. Chambers, *Witness* (New York: Random House, 1952).

28. Rossiter, *Conservatism in America*, 27.

29. J. Ceaser, *Reconstructing America: The Symbol of America in Modern Thought* (New Haven, CT: Yale University Press, 1997), 80.

30. Ibid., 83.

31. A. Hamilton, cited in ibid., 83–84.

32. P. Buchanan, *A Republic, Not an Empire: Reclaiming America's Destiny* (Washington, DC: Regnery, 1999), xii.

33. Ibid., xiii.

34. W.F. Buckley and C. Kesler (eds), *Keeping the Tablets: Modern American Conservative Thought* (New York City: HarperCollins, 1988), 7.

35. A. Smith, *The Theory of Moral Sentiments* (Indianapolis, IN: Liberty Fund, 1976), 184–85.

36. Buckley and Kesler, *Keeping the Tablets*, 12.

37. A. Young, 'The Real Churchill', *Mises Institute*, 27 February 2004, retrieved 29 February 2020 from http://www.mises.org/library/real-Churchill.

38. C. Preble, 'Toward a Libertarian Foreign Policy', *Cato Policy Report*, July/August 2015, retrieved 2 May 2019 from http://www.cato.org/policy-report/julyaugust-2015/toward-libertarian-foreign-policy.

39. Madison, *Writings of James Madison* (New York City: Library of America, 1999), 588.

40. I. Kristol, *Neoconservatism: The Autobiography of an Idea* (New York: The Free Press, 1995), 31–32.

41. J. Vaïsse, *Neoconservatism: The Biography of a Movement*, trans. A. Goldhammer (Cambridge, MA: Belknap Press, 2011), 4.

42. Kristol, *Neoconservatism*, 29.

43. Ibid., 30.

44. I. Kristol, *The Neoconservative Persuasion* (New York: Basic Books, 2013), 80.

45. Ibid., 77.

46. Ibid., 64

47. D. Murray, *Neoconservatism: Why We Need It* (New York: Encounter Books, 2006), 178.

48. Kristol, *The Neoconservative Persuasion*, 73.

49. Murray, *Neoconservatism*, 175–76.

50. Kristol, *Neoconservatism*, 34.

51. J. Muravchik, 'The Past, Present, and Future of Neoconservatism', *Commentary* 124(3) (2007), 21.

52. M. Boot, 'Neither New nor Nefarious: The Liberal Empire Strikes Back', *Current History* 667(102) (2003).

53. Muravchik, 'The Past, Present, and Future of Neoconservatism', 22.

54. Ibid.

55. For a discussion of Prime Minister Blair's neoconservative streak, see Geoffrey Wheatcroft, 'The Paradoxical Case of Tony Blair', *The Atlantic* 227(6), 22–40.

56. J. Conway, 'UKIP, Neoconservatism, and Douglas Murray', *The Commentator*, 7 May 2013, retrieved 15 June 2019 from http://www.thecommentator.com/article/3457/ukip-neoconservatism-and-dougleas-murray.

57. Vaïsse, *Neoconservatism*, 223–24.

58. M. Anton, 'The Trump Doctrine', *Foreign Policy*, Spring (232) (2019), 42.

59. J. Tulis, *The Rhetorical Presidency* (Princeton, NJ: Princeton University Press, 1988), 95–144.

60. T. Bromund, 'Conservatism Across the Atlantic', *The Heritage Foundation*, 18 October 2017, 1, retrieved 12 May 2019 from http://www.heritage.org/conservatism/commentary/conservatism-across-the-atlantic.

61. See J. Marini, *Unmasking the Administrative State: The Crisis of American Politics in the Twenty-First Century* (New York: Encounter Books, 2019).

62. See M. Continetti, 'Making Sense of the New American Right', *National Review*, 1 June 2019, retrieved 15 December 2019 from http://nationalreview.com/2019/06/new-american-right-schools-of-thought.

63. J. Ceaser, 'Four Heads and One Heart: The Modern Conservative Movement', a paper presented at the annual meeting of the American Political Science Association, Washington, DC, 2010, 1. Retrieved 7 January 2020 from https://ssrn.com/abstract=1643418.

64. Ibid.

Bibliography

Anton, M. 'The Trump Doctrine', *Foreign Policy*, Spring (232) (2019), 41–47.

Aristotle. *Nichomachean Ethics*, trans. H. Rackham. Cambridge: Cambridge University Press, 1933.

Boot, M. 'Neither New nor Nefarious: The Liberal Empire Strikes Back', *Current History* (667)102 (2003), 361–66.

Bromund, T. 'Conservatism Across the Atlantic', *The Heritage Foundation*, 18 October 2017. http://www.heritage.org/conservatism/commentary/conservatism-across-the-atlantic.

Buchanan, P. *A Republic Not an Empire: Reclaiming America's Destiny*. Washington, DC: Regnery, 1999.

Buckley, W., and Charles Kesler (eds). *Keeping the Tablets: Modern American Conservative Thought*. New York: HarperCollins, 1988.

Burke, E. *Reflections on the Revolution in France*, ed. Franklin Turner. New Haven, CT: Yale University Press, 2004.

———. *The Writings and Speeches of Edmund Burke*, ed. P. Marshall. Boston, MA: Little, Brown, 1901.

Ceaser, J. 'Four Heads and One Heart: The Modern Conservative Movement'. A paper presented at the annual meeting of the American Political Science Association, 2010.

———. *Liberal Democracy and Political Science*. Baltimore, MD: Johns Hopkins University Press, 1990.

———. *Reconstructing America: The Symbol of America in Modern Thought*. New Haven, CT: Yale University Press, 1997.

Chambers, W. *Witness*. New York: Random House, 1952.

Continetti, M. 'Making Sense of the New American Right', *National Review*, 1 June 2019. http://nationalreview.com/2019/06/new-american-right-schools-of-thought.

Conway, J. 'UKIP, Neoconservatism, and Douglas Murray', *The Commentator*, 7 May 2013.

Frohnen, B. *Virtue and the Promise of Conservatism: The Legacy of Burke and Tocqueville*. Lawrence: University of Kansas Press, 1993.

Hamilton, A. 'The Farmer Refuted', in Carson Holloway and Brad Wilson (eds), *The Political Writings of Alexander Hamilton*. Vol I. Cambridge: Cambridge University Press, 2017.

Hayek, F. *The Road to Serfdom*. Chicago: University of Chicago Press, 1944.

Kirk, R. *The Conservative Mind*. Chicago: H. Regnery Co., 1953.

Kramnick, I. *The Rage of Edmund Burke: Portrait of an Ambivalent Conservative*. New York: Basic Books, 1977.

Kristol, I. *Neoconservatism: The Autobiography of an Idea*. New York: The Free Press, 1995.

———. *The Neoconservative Persuasion*. New York: Basic Books, 2013.

Levin, Y. *The Great Debate: Edmund Burke, Thomas Paine and the Birth of Right and Left*. New York: Basic Books, 2014.

Madison, J. *Writings of James Madison*. New York: Library of America, 1999.

Marini, J. *Unmasking the Administrative State: The Crisis of American Politics in the Twenty-First Century*. New York: Encounter Books, 2019.

Muller, J. (ed.). *Conservatism: An Anthology of Social and Political Thought from David Hume to the Present*. Princeton, NJ: Princeton University Press, 1997.

Muravchik, J. 'The Past, Present, and Future of Neoconservatism', *Commentary* 124(3) (2007), 19–29.

Murray, D. *Neoconservatism: Why We Need It*. New York: Encounter Books, 2006.

Oakeshott, M. *Rationalism in Politics and Other Essays*. Indianapolis, IN: Liberty Fund, 1962.

O'Sullivan, N. *Conservatism*. New York: St Martin's Press, 1976.

Pilbeam, B. *Conservatism in Crisis? Anglo-American Conservative Ideology After the Cold War*. London: Palgrave MacMillan, 2003.

Preble, C. 'Toward a Libertarian Foreign Policy', *Cato Policy Report* (2005). http://www.cato.org/policy-report/julyaugust-2015/toward-libertarian-foreign-policy.

Rossiter, C. *Conservatism in America*. New York: Knopf, 1962.

Scruton, R. *The Meaning of Conservatism*. South Bend, IN: St Augustine's Press, 2002.

Smith, A. *The Theory of Moral Sentiments*. Indianapolis, IN: Liberty Fund, 1976.

Strauss, L., and J. Cropsey (eds). *History of Political Philosophy*. 3rd edn. Chicago: University of Chicago Press, 1963.

Tocqueville, A. de. *Democracy in America*, trans. G. Lawrence. New York: Anchor Books, 1968.

Tulis, J. *The Rhetorical Presidency*. Princeton, NJ: Princeton University Press, 1987.

Vaïsse, J. *Neoconservatism: The Biography of a Movement*, trans. A. Goldhammer. Cambridge, MA: Belknap Press, 2011.

PART III

Ideas and Institutions

Chapter 5

Rivalry and Reform

Abolition, Race and Anglo-American Relations in the Nineteenth Century

David Brown and Clive Webb

'In moral questions, I say, there are no nations.' So spoke the American social reformer Wendell Phillips, whose activism embraced numerous causes, the most important of which was the abolition of slavery.[1] Phillips railed against the current of nationalism that swept around the world during the nineteenth century. Freedom, he believed, was a human right that transcended the sovereign power of any nation-state. Other countries therefore had not only a right but also a responsibility to intercede in the domestic affairs of slave-owning nations. This chapter argues that the most important Anglo-American political connection of the nineteenth century was the common culture of reform activism fostered by the transatlantic abolitionist network that Phillips helped to establish. Inspired by evangelical religion and humanitarianism, British and American activists expanded the parameters of civil society and in turn fundamentally shaped the growth of liberal democracy in the Atlantic world. African Americans were the crucial link in the network, lecturing across the length and breadth of the British Isles not only to promote abolition but also to protest the spread of racist doctrines. Their efforts continued after the Civil War but without the support of white liberal allies, whose commitment to egalitarianism waned in the closing decades of the century.

The crusade against slavery established a transatlantic partnership, but this alliance was affected by the ebb and flow of political and nationalist rivalries between the two nations. Americans criticized the British for asserting global moral superiority in the wake of emancipation in the Caribbean while continuing to practise imperial dominance through empire. The British took the moral high ground by contrasting the supposed benevolence of empire with the barbarism of slavery in the American South. After the American Civil War, Britons continued to regard themselves as setting a superior moral example in their treatment of people of colour, contrasting 'enlightened' colonial rule with the violent oppression of southern blacks in the post-Reconstruction South. Each nation maintained that their political culture better embodied ideals of democracy and liberty, with regular accusations of hypocrisy on both sides. Co-operation was evident in many transatlantic initiatives, not just antislavery but also feminism, temperance, liberalism and free trade, although relations were also contentious at times as each country served as a critical foil for the other. Britain and the United States shared many commonalities – ideologically, socially, culturally and economically – but their connection was fractious, especially in the realm of diplomacy. Indeed, the volatility of political relations in the first century of US independence renders the attempt to depict a shared Anglo-American diplomatic liberalism before the twentieth century as a genuine political 'tradition' highly problematic. It is the men and women of the transatlantic reform movement and their pioneering lobbying tactics in pursuit of mutual goals and ideals that better exemplify Anglo-American political co-operation during the nineteenth century.

Building the Postcolonial Relationship

Diplomatic tensions between Britain and the United States following the American War of Independence made it seem unlikely that the two countries might cultivate a common political tradition. The Declaration of Independence compiled a long list of 'injuries and usurpations' abusing British authoritarianism, most especially its tyrannical form of government, which suggested difficult post-war relations. Revolutionary ideology drew inspiration from republican rhetoric and egalitarianism that grew organically – at least in part – from the colonial experience of self-government in the North American colonies, which was so different to British politics. Historians note the contradictory, conservative nature of the American Revolution and the limitations of its promise of universal freedom; nonetheless, the radical idea of natural rights distinguished the United States from the mother nation.[2] Other rebellions against privilege and monarchical rule followed on from the American example in the late 1780s in the Netherlands, Belgium and, most significantly, France. Republics, rather than monarchies, were seemingly the future and a powerful strain of 'conspiratorial Anglophobia' suffused early US politics, even if it was more imagined than real.[3]

On the British side, the acquisition of further West Indian colonies (Trinidad, Berbice and Demerara) in the late eighteenth century compensated for the embarrassment of losing the Revolutionary War and soon generated immense profits.[4] The subjugation of territories overseas, most notably India, which had a population of nearly 150 million, compared to just 4 million in the American colonies, reinforced Britain's position as a global force. The maintenance of thirteen North American colonies was an expensive business and British imperial power had probably become overstretched, not least because of Native American resistance to western encroachment. Moreover, the determination of the United States to remove the French and the Spanish from the North American interior proved strategically advantageous to Britain, checking the power of its European rivals. Anglo-American economic relations quickly recovered from the short-term disruption caused by the Revolutionary War. Transatlantic trade was essential to the growth of the American economy but also became more and more important across the ocean as southern cotton enabled a rapid expansion of the British textile industry.[5] Finally, more pacific Anglo-American relations helped to protect Canada. British governments worried greatly about their last remaining North American colony during the nineteenth century, although they probably exaggerated the threat of US annexation. Canada was unsuitable for plantation slavery and its acquisition would disrupt the political balance of slave and free states in the United States.[6]

A second transatlantic war that began in 1812 curtailed this early rapprochement. It was hardly conflict on the grand scale of the Napoleonic battles fought on European soil, though, and there was no outright winner at the war's conclusion in 1815. Diplomatic channels were restored successfully, in part because Britain and the United States shared a mutual interest in keeping rivals out of North America. President James Monroe's annual message to Congress on 2 December 1823, which came to be known as the 'Monroe Doctrine', constitutes a case in point. It is common knowledge that it took decades before 'doctrine' was applied to Monroe's pronouncement but less well known that the policy originated from an Anglo-American initiative proposed by George Canning, the British foreign secretary. Monroe's bold declaration was intended to curtail Russian designs in the Pacific Northwest and address fears that the French and the Spanish were about to reinforce their position in the Americas. However, the United States had no means of enforcement and therefore relied on British diplomatic clout and naval supremacy. Secretary of State John Quincy Adams persuaded James Monroe to reject British overtures to issue a unilateral statement but the success of the policy resided in Anglo-American partnership.[7]

The relationship between the US and British governments generally improved during the antebellum era, albeit with difficulties over slavery and abolition. The settlement of long-standing territorial issues reduced diplomatic friction and the lingering problem of Canada in Anglo-American relations has been overemphasized by some historians.[8] A rebellion in Upper Canada in November 1837 was quickly subdued and, although soliciting great sympathy in the United States, the reality was that 'the Americans did not, even in the heyday of Manifest Destiny, entertain thoughts of conquest'.[9] The border between Canada and Maine in the north-east was resolved by the Webster–Ashburton Treaty (1842), while the north-western border in Oregon was settled at the 49th parallel four years later. Just as important as the resolution of territorial disputes was the burgeoning Atlantic economy. The repeal of the Corn Laws in Britain in the 1840s signalled an unprecedented era of reciprocally beneficial free trade between the countries.[10]

Hostilities and mutual suspicion lingered, however, between politicians such as Andrew Jackson and Viscount Palmerston, to name but two. Southern enslavers worried about the precedent set by British emancipation in the Caribbean and feared further antislavery incursion within North America, especially when Texas broke from Mexico in 1836. Edward B. Rugemer's examination of the ways in which Caribbean emancipation impacted the United States provides a fresh transatlantic perspective on the coming of the Civil War. Robert Monroe Harrison, the American consul to Jamaica from 1831 to 1858, penned a series of reports on the supposedly disastrous results of British emancipation that stirred deep-seated fears of slave rebellion and stoked US Anglophobia.[11] There is no evidence to suggest that the British government wanted to interfere with domestic slavery in the United States. Undeniably, though, Her Majesty's Government built an antislavery network of allies and treaties to suppress the international slave trade and the Royal Navy searched vessels suspected of slave trading under foreign flags. The American government rejected repeated overtures to join the international antislavery crusade and provided staunch support to the southern slaveholding regime.[12]

How best to characterize Anglo-American relations in the first half of the nineteenth century? Was there a sense of shared goals and mutual interests? Traditional diplomatic history charts the development of US foreign policy, shaped to a great extent by relations with Great Britain. Historians no longer treat the first half of the nineteenth century as the 'great American Desert' or little more than the prelude to the Civil War, instead emphasizing the quest for territorial sovereignty over the North American continent.[13] This story reveals that the consolidation of American geopolitical power, national unity and cultural hegemony gained strength and legitimacy from the providential notion of manifest destiny and hardening doctrines of white supremacy. It was a process of empire building more usually associated with European imperial nations. The growth of US power was undermined by internal sectionalism and was of limited strategic importance outside of the North American continent, however, although the consequences for indigenous peoples were devastating. The United States was far less significant to British foreign policy than were

its European rivals, as reflected in the fact that a minister, rather than an ambassador, headed the British legation in Washington, DC, as late as 1893.[14]

Traditions do not lie in diplomacy alone and can be forged in other ways.
America was, in numerous ways, not a 'foreign' country at all to Britons, so
obvious were the ties of kith and kin and notions of 'the mother country' or
the idea that relations between the two countries were like that between a
parent and child. A strong Anglo-Saxon core and British values provided an
enduring foundation of the new republic.[15] Emigrants from the British Isles
came in their tens of thousands in the antebellum era to reinforce and reinfuse
Anglo culture. Eighty per cent of the 2,760,360 British immigrants who arrived in the United States between 1820 and 1910 were English.[16] Americans
celebrated Queen Victoria's coronation in 1838 and the Prince of Wales's thir-
ty-day tour in 1860 covered nearly 2,600 miles in total and was met with huge
popular enthusiasm, including an estimated audience of between 250,000 and
500,000 in New York alone.[17]

It is important not to present an overly rosy picture of reconciliation.
There was a persistent undercurrent of Anglophobia within American politics and popular culture. Regardless of political affiliation, it became routine
to complain of British plots and English arrogance in the decades following
the War of 1812.[18] In turn, British visitors regularly deprecated the antebellum United States. In the pantheon of those who thumbed their nose
at American society, in particular its lack of deference and its cult of individualism, Frances Trollope's *Domestic Manners of the Americans* (1832)
looms large. Charles Dickens was similarly dismissive on his trip to the
United States in the winter of 1842. Negative memories lingered. A *Harper's
Weekly* editorial welcoming the Prince of Wales's visit did not forget that his
country had 'waged unjust wars against us twice and ... employed Hessians
and Indians to commit barbarous atrocities upon our forefathers'.[19] Despite
the vitriol, Dickens's novels were wildly popular in the United States and
Americans identified with his characters. Southerners eagerly read Dickens
even though he was a harsh critic of slavery.[20] Literature served to reinforce connections, even if they were not of the happiest kind, in a way that
distinguished the Anglo-American relationship. Paul Giles suggests that a
'transatlantic imaginary' bridged the gap between the two nations, a thesis
supported by Ralph Waldo Emerson's 1857 observation that 'the American
is only the continuation of the English genius into new conditions, more
or less propitious'.[21] Commentators likened these critical spats to family
squabbles.[22]

A.G. Hopkins's argument that 'the history of the United States between
1783 and 1861 can be recast as an anticipation of what became the classic postcolonial dilemma: how to make formal independence effective' is

persuasive and captures the thrust of much recent scholarship.[23] The cult of
the Founding Fathers, the spread of evangelical Christianity, the rapid advance of democracy and liberal capitalism, with the associated philosophy of
individualism, pushed the United States along a distinct path. But American
uncertainty, in everything from literature to manners to national purpose, was
magnified by comparison with Britain. American identity emerged slowly in
the first half of the nineteenth century. Even Alexis de Tocqueville, the French
commentator whose writings did much to characterize the antebellum republic as a new, unique entity, referred to 'the English race in America'. Fierce
rivalries existed and squabbles were frequent, but, as an editorial in *The Times*
put it, to 'all practical purposes the United States are far more closely united
with this kingdom than any one of our colonies'.[24] It was arguably not until
the Civil War that the United States broke out of the ideological and cultural
British mould.

The Origins of Anglo-American Abolition

To locate an Anglo-American political tradition in the first half of the nineteenth century, then, we must look towards the exercise of politics of a different kind. C.A. Bayly's seminal *The Birth of the Modern World* argues that the
nineteenth century was the heyday of the nation-state, but also an era in which
politicians and governments were not the only political agents. The growth of
'international civil society' was nurtured by 'a set of networks of information
and political advocacy which, though less obvious than the rising national and
imperial state, was no less important'.[25] From this perspective, the strongest
transatlantic link was the British and American antislavery movement, which
worked 'together so closely that it is impossible to discuss the organizations of
one country without some reference to the societies of the other', and became
not only 'a touchstone of Anglo-American friendship' but also an exemplar of
radical political change being brought about by pressure groups.[26] Its leaders
were charismatic individuals of both sexes who replicated the role of elected
politicians and co-ordinated thousands of individuals in complicated organizational networks.[27]

The origins of Anglo-American antislavery lie in the 'deep-seated moral and theological dislike of slavery' of transatlantic Quaker networks that
influenced Protestant non-conformism in the eighteenth and early nineteenth centuries and fostered powerful revivals in the Atlantic world.[28] This
reflected changing intellectual currents as Enlightenment creeds of compas-
sionate humanitarianism and free labour served to isolate slavery as backwards
and anachronistic in the modern world.[29] The spiritual egalitarianism of the

Second Great Awakening nurtured the growth of a biracial antislavery movement in the United States, although the concomitant growth of plantation slavery in the opening decades of the nineteenth century ensured that abolition would not be secured without a momentous struggle. Nonetheless, Antislavery zeal was keenly felt by many Americans, such as the Connecticut minister Theodore Dwight Weld, who 'personally symbolized the fusion of American revivalism with the British antislavery movement'. Inspired by the Anglo-Canadian abolitionist Captain Charles Stuart, Weld converted to immediate abolitionism and Black civil rights in the 1830s.[30]

The abolitionist movement developed independently in Britain and the United States. The Pennsylvania Quakers issued the first antislavery resolution in 1688. From the mid-eighteenth century, Philadelphian Quaker John Woolman criticized slavery and refused to handle goods produced by the enslaved and, in 1784, the Pennsylvania Abolition Society was established. The (British) Society for Effecting the Abolition of the Slave Trade – formed in a London printing shop on 22 May 1787 – was the first national antislavery organization. Dedicated to ending the international slave trade, it grew quickly and pioneered tactics that became staple tools of Anglo-American antislavery: petitions, pamphlets, lectures, images and assorted paraphernalia that tugged at the moral heartstrings of the public. Particularly effective was the iconic 'Am I not a Man and a Brother?' image of a kneeling slave designed by English potter Josiah Wedgwood. This logo was disseminated in a myriad of forms from the late eighteenth century. The organizational framework of the society was impressive. Thomas Clarkson was the conduit between the headquarters in London and provincial branches around the country. Clarkson won a prize at Cambridge University for his dissertation, eventually published as 'An Essay on the Slavery and Commerce of the Human Species' (1786). He was an Anglican, as was Granville Sharpe, as the movement's membership expanded from its Quaker roots.

Two nationwide antislavery campaigns were co-ordinated in 1788 and 1792. The latter presented the largest number of petitions to Parliament in a single sitting (519) – four hundred thousand signatures in total, amounting to approximately 13 per cent of the adult male population in 1791. Parliament narrowly voted against ending the trade in 1792; subsequently, the Napoleonic Wars focused attention elsewhere until 1804.[31] This delay encouraged a British antislavery revival on the grounds of patriotism as Napoleon, who detested abolitionism and suppressed antislavery dissent, recovered from the Saint-Domingue debacle to stabilize plantation slavery and the slave trade in the French Caribbean.[32] To support antislavery was, in effect, to oppose Napoleon. The British Parliament approved a ban on the slave trade in conquered territories in 1805, a decision justified on humanitarian grounds but also to strengthen Britain's strategic position in its campaign against the French. Two years later, Parliament approved measures to end the British Atlantic slave trade completely.[33]

It was expected that the ban on international slave trading that came into effect on 1 January 1808 would mark the beginning of the end for British slavery. However, the West Indian enslaved population decreased at a negligible rate (just a 14 per cent decline between 1807 and 1834, while numbers rose in Barbados) and sugar production increased perennially.[34] The antislavery movement stirred again in response to the 1823 slave revolt in the British colony of Demerara, when the enslaved rose up to demand freedom and citizenship but avoided excessive bloodshed. A new campaign was planned to take on the West Indian Committee, the formidable lobby group defending the interests of Caribbean slaveholders that emerged from the Society of West Indian Planters and Merchants.[35] Veterans such as William Wilberforce, Thomas Clarkson and former governor of Sierra Leone Zachary McCaulay formed the Society for the Mitigation and Gradual Abolition of Slavery Throughout the British Dominions in 1823, although its parliamentary champion was Thomas Fowell Buxton. Commonly known as the Anti-Slavery Society, its objective was gradual emancipation with improved conditions for enslaved people in the Caribbean.

In 1824, the pamphlet *Immediate, Not Gradual Abolition* advocated immediate emancipation on the grounds of natural rights, proposing a grassroots campaign boycotting slave-produced goods, and sympathized with slave revolts as acts of self-defence. It presented a radical alternative to gradualism that proved crucial in accelerating the pace of change and highlighted the powerful role of women in the transatlantic movement. The author was Elizabeth Heyrick, a convert to Quakerism from Leicester inspired by events in Demerara, who had written many previous pamphlets which, like *Immediate, Not Gradual Abolition*, were published anonymously.[36] British campaigning began again with a new spirit of urgency. The contentious issues were whether to offer compensation to slaveholders and whether abolition should be immediate or gradual. Slow progress in Parliament, due to the strength of the West Indian lobby and the conservative tactics of Anti-Slavery Society leaders, encouraged a younger, radical element insistent on immediate abolition (the Agency Committee) to break away in 1832.

Two crucial developments in the early 1830s favoured the immediatists. First, the 1832 Reform Act doubled the size of the British electorate and placed a renewed emphasis on Parliament being responsive to public opinion. Second, the largest slave rebellion in the British Caribbean (the Baptist War in Jamaica, 1831–32) was perfectly timed to remind the public that slavery was far from moribund. White ministers fleeing from the confrontation scolded cruel Caribbean planters and praised the restraint and Christian behaviour of the enslaved. Approximately 1.5 million signatures were collected on five thousand public petitions sent to Parliament and a decision to approve the Slavery Abolition Act was agreed on 29 August 1833.[37] The act took effect on 1 August the following year on a gradual basis, with enslaved people having to serve apprenticeships of either four years (domestic) or six years (field hands). Parliament eventually responded to criticisms of the apprenticeship system, orchestrated by the British antislavery lobby, by implementing full emancipation in 1838. The impact of these measures powerfully reverberated across the Atlantic.

The bill to end apprenticeship marked the culmination of a busy period of antislavery activism and vindicated abolitionist tactics, but the work was far from finished. The British and Foreign Anti-Slavery Society (BFASS) was founded in 1839 to build on the movement's success and confront global slavery. Support came from a few surviving veterans of the first generation, most notably Clarkson, as well as Thomas Buxton, who had emerged as a national figure in the 1820s, but the driving forces were the members of the Agency Committee: John Scoble, G.W. Alexander and, most importantly, the Birmingham Quaker Joseph Sturge.[38] Based in London, the BFASS built a network of auxiliary societies in towns and cities throughout the country, drawing on long-standing antislavery support, particularly among Quaker families. The organization was dedicated to immediate, universal emancipation and resolved to correspond 'with the abolitionists in America, France and elsewhere, and to encourage them by every means in our power'.[39]

Building a Transatlantic Antislavery Movement

US abolitionists watched events across the Atlantic with much interest but did not play an instrumental part in the British campaign. Transatlantic links were built instead in joint opposition to the American Colonization Society (ACS). Founded in 1816 in Washington, DC, the ACS claimed to serve the interests of both races, justifying mass colonization of African Americans on the grounds that racism would never allow the peaceful coexistence of Black and white. African American abolitionists immediately responded, warning white antislavery activists of racist designs to remove Blacks against their will.[40] The British had prior experience of colonization, although of a very different kind, in the founding of Sierra Leone in the late eighteenth century. The intention of this *voluntary* settlement of a small number of Blacks in Africa was to have a civilizing effect – with those going acting like missionaries – rather than being a means of relocating millions of Blacks.[41] This was a crucial difference, but it did not prevent the ACS's Elliot Cresson crossing the Atlantic in 1830, intent on winning British support and funding.

Cresson met with initial success, presenting what seemed to be progressive plans that appealed to the British missionary principle of uplift. He claimed that the ACS stood for 'the final and entire abolition of slavery providing for the best interest of the Blacks, by establishing them in independence upon the coast of Africa … to spread the lights of civilization and Christianity among fifty millions who inhabited the dark regions'.[42] William Wilberforce, Thomas Clarkson and even George Thompson were impressed, but James Cropper in Liverpool and Charles Stuart, who had returned to Britain in 1829, were more sceptical.[43] The most important US abolitionist, William Lloyd Garrison, was also in Britain at this time. The Bostonian flirted with colonization in the 1820s, but decisively changed his position in *Thoughts on African Colonization* (1832). Garrison supported the British anti-coloniszation response and challenged Cresson to a public debate, which Cresson declined. This combined opposition, helped immeasurably by African American minister Reverend Nathaniel Paul, turned the tide and, in August 1833, leading British abolitionists signed a document, or 'Protest', rejecting the ACS. The British African Colonization Society, founded in July 1833, was essentially defunct by the summer of 1834. The combined efforts of British and American abolitionists 'laid the foundations for future Anglo-American contacts' and a viable transatlantic abolition movement took shape.[44]

The Anglo-American alliance flourished and was marked by racial and gender inclusiveness. Garrison formed the New England Anti-Slavery Society in 1832 and the American Anti-Slavery Society (AASS) in 1833, bringing together whites, free Blacks and escaped slaves, an eclectic group of men and women from different backgrounds inspired by evangelicalism. The AASS's Declaration of Sentiments, modified by the prominent abolitionist Lucretia Mott, established an astonishingly radical agenda that rejected colonization, demanded immediate emancipation and affirmed racial equality. George Thompson's trip to the United States in 1834 solidified transatlantic connections and his friendship with Garrison was pivotal to the success of the antislavery alliance. It was a friendship forged under duress as abolitionism was dangerous in the United States. In September 1835, a mob constructed a gallows outside Garrison's home in Boston with two nooses, one for Garrison, one for Thompson, and abolitionist meetings were regularly disrupted by violence.[45] Thompson became Garrison's stalwart ally and main British counterpart.

Like the British and Foreign Anti-Slavery Society, American abolitionists took an international perspective in the fight against injustice wherever and in whatever form it existed.[46] That said, their primary goal was to end US slavery and, to this end, British abolitionists were the key partners. Thus,

Garrison's famous *Liberator* newspaper, first published in 1831, had a transatlantic focus from the outset in its regular 'Foreign Items' section. The *Liberator* was read on both sides of the Atlantic, and the other major US abolitionist publication, the *Anti-Slavery Standard*, also had many British subscribers. In turn, readership of the British antislavery journals the *Anti-Slavery Advocate* (published by British Garrisonians) and the *Anti-Slavery Reporter* (published by the BFASS) also transcended the national divide. These journals bridged the Atlantic, providing an invaluable up-to-date summary of activities in both countries, which were a regular topic of conversation in the many letters exchanged by British and American abolitionists.[47]

The American movement replicated British tactics but was engaged in a struggle of a very different character. The British public was accepting of antislavery, whereas abolitionism was regarded with scepticism, if not hostility, in the United States. The cause was not helped by Garrison's abrasive, outspoken demeanour, which alienated those in his movement, as well as the mainstream. The New York brothers Arthur and Lewis Tappan led a break-away group that included James Gillespie Birney, Henry Stanton and Theodore Weld to found the American and Foreign Anti-Slavery Society in 1840. Garrison pushed 'the rights of women to the utmost extent', but the Tappans argued that the movement should focus on slavery alone. Garrison's tactic of 'moral suasion', which placed the onus on individuals to repent rather than attacking the system which sustained slavery as an institution, was also controversial. Another splinter group took an overtly political strategy when Gerrit Smith and Salmon P. Chase founded the abolitionist Liberty Party in 1840. The short-lived Free Soil Party replaced that organization, attracting antislavery Whigs and Democrats, as well as abolitionists, in contesting the 1848 and 1852 presidential elections on a simple platform of the non-extension of slavery. Its supporters were instrumental in the formation of the Republican Party in the mid-1850s. These splits in the American movement reflected the problem of achieving change in the complicated US political system.

The 1840 World Anti-Slavery Convention, hosted by the British and Foreign Anti-Slavery Society, gathered the Anglo-American antislavery community in London. It reinforced the message that slavery was morally repugnant and free labour the hallmark of civilized society, but also revealed significant factional divisions. Five hundred delegates (and large numbers of curious visitors) were present at the London Convention, which became notorious for not admitting nine female US abolitionists. This was essentially an American conflict that traversed the Atlantic, but British support for the women's inclusion was lukewarm at best. The AFASS had sent a letter to the BFASS protesting against admitting female delegates before the meeting began. Garrison, as well as other Americans such as the Black abolitionist

Charles Remond, chose to sit in the gallery with their excluded female colleagues, who included Lydia Maria Child and Maria Weston Chapman.
This was an inauspicious beginning and to the proceedings in which British
speakers celebrated the end of Caribbean slavery and somewhat condescend-
ingly counselled others on the best way forwards. Much of the discussion
centred on organized religion and its moral obligations, a difficult and highly
sensitive issue for Americans. While generally regarded as a success and the
literal beginnings of joint co-operation, some Americans at the 1840 Convention, as well as the later 1843 Convention in London, found the British
exceedingly critical of the United States and overly triumphal in claiming
antislavery as their own.[48]

This set the tone for a transatlantic relationship dogged by division. The
BFASS favoured the AFASS over the AASS. The supporters of Garrison
therefore courted other British antislavery constituencies over the next two
decades. Provincial antislavery societies in the major British cities were the
primary receptacles of Garrisonianism, although national rivals to the BFASS
emerged, and faded, periodically. In August 1846, for example, George
Thompson became the first president of the Anti-Slavery League, set up by
Thompson and his antislavery colleagues John Estlin and James Haughton, as
well as William Lovett and Henry Vincent of the London Workingmen's Association. This group built on the momentum generated by the British visit of
Garrison and Frederick Douglass in the summer of 1846 and both Americans
took part in the group's founding meetings. The Anti-Slavery League hoped
to replicate the success of the Anti-Corn Law League (ACLL), formed in
Manchester in 1838. The ACLL was held in high regard as a model pressure
group on both sides of the Atlantic, as were its primary figureheads Richard
Cobden and John Bright. Emphasizing the overlapping and fluid nature of
Anglo-American reform, Bright's sister was a Garrisonian and his brother
Jacob Bright corresponded with the Garrisonians.[49]

The Anti-Slavery League, and others like the short-lived Anglo-American
Anti-Slavery Association formed by Thompson and Bristolian John Estlin
in 1852, struggled to maintain momentum. In spite of several attempts at
reconciliation, the divide between the British Garrisonians and the BFASS
in London seemed intractable. British antislavery was not only troubled by
factionalism, but also by problems associated with Chartism (which had an
uneasy relationship with abolition), Irish repeal and the furore over the Free
Church of Scotland's acceptance of southern enslavers' funds.[50] The BFASS
controlled organized abolition in Britain at the national level up to the
American Civil War, but provincial societies in cities including Bristol, Dublin, Newcastle and Edinburgh were affiliated with Garrison and the AASS.
National rivalries intruded periodically. Americans regularly complained that

their British counterparts did not understand the limitations of the US political system or the violence faced by American abolitionists on a daily basis.

That said, problems of factional divisions have perhaps been overemphasized. As Betty Fladeland wisely noted, the net effect 'was to involve the British deeper and deeper in the American antislavery movement'.[51] Anglo-American abolitionism, strongly connected to feminism, religion and temperance, exerted a sustained influence in the public sphere.[52] A joint effort put pressure on the British government to oppose American annexation of Texas. Although ultimately defeated on this issue, Anglo-American abolitionists achieved victory in ensuring that Article X of the 1842 Webster–Ashburton Treaty, which enabled extradition of persons charged with a crime, was not used to return fugitive slaves to the United States from Canada. The British government was further urged to step up its antislavery efforts. The November 1841 rebellion on the US slave brig *Creole*, transporting 135 enslaved people from Richmond to New Orleans, is a good example. Enslaved captives overpowered the crew and sailed to the Bahamas, where they claimed their freedom. Black Bahamians, recently freed by the British, foiled the American consul's attempt to round up the escapees and commandeer a ship to sail them back to American shores. The United States demanded the return of the vessel and its cargo but, pressurized by a BFASS deputation including John Scoble and John Beaumont, Her Majesty's Government refused. In the House of Representatives, Joshua Giddings from Ohio, advised by the American abolitionist attorney James Birney, defended the decision not to return the *Creole* captives to their enslavers.[53] There is every reason to agree with historian David Turley's contention that the decade following the mid-1830s represented 'the high point of transatlantic abolitionism as a functioning international enterprise'.[54]

Broadening the Parameters of Civil Society

The antislavery movement's disregard for racial and gender barriers allowed marginalized groups to emerge as political agents. The experience of mobilization was enthralling and underpinned numerous reform causes during the nineteenth century. Antebellum abolitionism held particular appeal for middle-class women, regardless of race, as the parameters of femininity expanded to make women the primary guardians of morality. This shift was most pronounced in the United States. African Americans in Salem, Massachusetts, founded a female abolition society in 1832, followed a year later by the Boston Female Antislavery Society. It was the interracial Philadelphia Female Anti-Slavery Society (PFASS) that was the longest-lasting US female abolition society. Founded in December 1833, the PFASS was inspired by the example of the AASS and included key figures such as Lucretia Mott and the Horton sisters. Fittingly, their inaugural gathering was chaired by African American James McCrummell, one of the signatories of the Declaration of the AASS. Women were likely a majority in mid-nineteenth-century antislavery societies in Britain as well. They had participated previously, of course, but the antislavery campaigns of 1807 and 1833 targeted men – because, as voters, they were the most important constituency influencing Parliament. Even so, nearly 300,000 women signed antislavery petitions presented in 1833 alone, a quarter of the total number that year.[55]

Gender was no impediment to opposing US slavery and British women engaged in public speaking and other forms of direct action. It was middle-class women, typically Unitarians or Quakers, that formed the backbone of antislavery societies in London, Sheffield, Manchester, Edinburgh, Bristol and elsewhere. Their labour contributed a range of goods to American fund-raising events like the annual Anti-Slavery Bazaars that generated funds for the publication of print literature. Slavery violated cherished ideas of family and gender and undermined emerging notions of civility and the domestic sphere. British women were not as quick to link antislavery to feminism, nor were they as vocal as their American counterparts in pushing for equality.[56] Nonetheless, the widespread popularity of female antislavery was underlined by the 'mania' caused by Harriet Beecher Stowe's *Uncle Tom's Cabin* (1852). Historian David Reynolds uses the phrase 'Uncle Tomitudes' to capture the profound influence of the novel, which Britons read in their tens of thousands and which inspired multiple stage and musical adaptations. (In the United States, by contrast, the novel was far more controversial.) Stowe was presented with the antislavery 'Address to the Christian Women of America' during her triumphant 1853 tour of Great Britain, signed by 562,448 British women, in twenty-six bound volumes.[57]

Last, but far from least, Black abolitionists were the crucial link in the Anglo-American movement in the mid-nineteenth century. They regularly visited the British Isles – and some had a pressing need to leave the United States as a result of the strengthening of the US Fugitive Slave Act in 1850. It is hard to overstate the importance of these Black activists, who exerted a huge influence, far in excess of their numbers.[58] They received a rapturous welcome as the public packed into town halls and churches across the whole of the British Isles to hear about American slavery first-hand. Frederick Douglass, Henry Brown, Samuel Ward, Ellen and William Craft, William Wells Brown and many others captivated British audiences with their personal experiences of slavery, which gave them an unrivalled authenticity.[59] Sarah Parker Remond, who arrived in 1859 and was one of few female speakers, was perhaps the most prominent of the forty or so Black abolitionists who toured Britain during the Civil War (1861–65). Like her colleagues, Remond skilfully played on gender issues of emotional and sexual abuse. There was great interest in the literature of self-emancipated slaves and slave autobiographies were widely circulated in Britain.

African Americans were vital in sustaining British support for abolition during the 1850s. This was a decade in which Britons debated the supposed failure of Caribbean emancipation, which some blamed on the lackadaisical work habits of freed people. Racist propaganda became more prominent as pro-slavery writers responded to abolitionist attacks by focusing on race. One historian asserts that 'the rise of racism and the decline of abolitionism were thoroughly intertwined' and, in spite of anti-racist counter-narratives, 'racism clearly grew more powerful in Britain throughout the 1850s'.[60] According to this view, minstrelsy – a form of popular entertainment that consisted of songs and sketches by actors in blackface – and racial ethnology – a pseudoscience that stressed the natural hierarchy of race – traversed the Atlantic to overturn the dominant antislavery discourse rooted in the British civilizing mission and Christian brotherhood. This interpretation goes too far. Undeniably, the popularity of minstrelsy widely disseminated plantation stereotypes within the British public imagination. Yet minstrelsy's racial politics, and those of novels like *Uncle Tom's Cabin*, are difficult to pin down.[61] Racial ideology was contested and subverted by African American speakers who attacked slavery *and* prejudice in powerful performances that served as a crucial rebuttal of scientific doctrines of Black inferiority. Their lectures not only provided white audiences with an intimate view of American slavery, but also challenged racial stereotyping.[62] British antislavery activists also contested racial prejudice, although this is overlooked in recent historiography.[63]

The American Civil War was perhaps the crowning moment of transatlantic abolition and vindicated the movement's continued influence. It began badly for the antislavery cause, however, as the British failed to understand why their American counterparts rallied to the Union instead of welcoming secession as the best way to be rid of plantation slavery. Garrison had long advocated separation from the slave states but changed his stance. Abraham Lincoln's reluctance to make emancipation a war aim did not make the situation any easier and bitter recriminations reverberated back and forth across the Atlantic.[64] This internecine conflict emphasized how susceptible the movement was to quarrelling. However, the unpalatable prospect of British recognition of the Confederacy, with slavery as its cornerstone – as Union and Confederate propagandists in Britain sought to influence public opinion – eventually compelled a decisive response.[65]

In late 1862, the preliminary Emancipation Proclamation and rumours of Anglo-French mediation heightened by William Gladstone's 7 October 1862 speech at Newcastle, which hinted at Confederate recognition, prompted a nationwide antislavery revival. Organized by George Thompson and his son-in-law Frederick Chesson, the Emancipation Society was founded in London in November 1862, while the Manchester Union and Emancipation Society followed in January 1863, with auxiliary branches formed across the British Isles. They carried out a highly effective campaign of meetings and a mass dispersal of antislavery literature that has gone largely unnoticed to date.[66] In late December 1862, Thompson wrote Garrison that *the heart of the people is sound*. It would be impossible to carry a proslavery resolution in any packed assembly in the Kingdom'. Two months later, the Emancipation Society chairman celebrated 'the response that we have had from the various parts of the country' demonstrating 'that the old hatred of that colossal wrong is as intense in the hearts of the people as it was in' 1833.[67] He was not alone in comparing the mobilization of public support to that of prior campaigns. On both sides of the Atlantic, the joint efforts of thousands of men and women did much to shape the political response to US emancipation in a powerful affirmation of the influence of ordinary citizens.

Racial Anglo-Saxonism and Post-war Rapprochement

How the post-war reform of the southern states, particularly US policy towards the newly emancipated Black population, affected Anglo-American relations has received little attention from scholars. Historians refer to the late nineteenth and early twentieth centuries as the time of a 'Great Rapprochement'.[68] The antipathies that had fuelled economic rivalry, diplomatic tension and military conflict eased in the last third of the nineteenth century, succeeded by a new era of mutual co-operation. One of the most secure adhesives that bound the two countries together was a belief in a common destiny determined by the shared ancestry of their peoples. The concept of racial Anglo-Saxonism that gained cultural and intellectual currency on both sides of the Atlantic postulated that Britons and Americans were a superior race preordained to dominate the world. According to this doctrine, members of the Anglo-Saxon race shared certain characteristics that set them above other peoples, including their intelligence, enterprise and unique capacity for self-government. This white supremacist credo had, by the 1890s, all but entirely supplanted the biracial egalitarianism of the transatlantic abolitionist movement.[69]

The emerging entente between Britain and the United States resulted in mutual affirmation of one another in international affairs. Unlike other European countries, for instance, Britain supported the American imperialist appropriation of Cuba and the Philippines in the 1890s. To many British observers, American overseas expansion legitimized their own people's racial superiority. The seed first planted in American soil not only spread across that continent, but also started to take root farther afield. Through their common ideals, ingenuity and institutions, Britons and Americans were together engaged in a civilizing mission targeting the lesser races of the world. Theirs, in the words of a poem by Rudyard Kipling exhorting the United States to take control of the Philippines, was 'The White Man's Burden'.

The romanticism of this racial mythology was often far from consistent with lived reality. Mass immigration to the United States meant an increasingly diverse population that did not conform to the Anglo-Saxon paradigm.[70] Moreover, while historians have shown how Britain and the United States came to share a sense of common purpose in civilizing other races, no scholar has fully assessed how public debate about the people of colour already living within American borders pertained to that mission. The one exception is Christine Bolt, who studied British responses to race relations in the post-Civil War South. Bolt, however, took the story only to the end of Reconstruction in 1877. Furthermore, in the half-century since the publication of her pioneering study, no other historian has attempted to extend the chronology into the Jim Crow era.[71]

A belief in Anglo-Saxon supremacy undoubtedly brought Britons and Americans closer together in the late nineteenth century. In contemplating the fate of former slaves in the American South, however, some Britons concluded that certain Anglo-Saxons were superior to others. The brutal repression of African Americans demonstrated to British commentators that white southerners failed to respect their superior status as Anglo-Saxons, dishonouring the ideal of the white man's burden by forcing down, rather than raising up, a lesser race. It therefore became imperative for Britain to show through the example of its own supposedly paternalistic colonial rule how to govern people of colour. Thus, British responses to American racism demonstrate the persistent tension between the two nations even at a time of supposed rapprochement. The oppression of southern Blacks provided a perfect foil for Britons to moralize about the more enlightened leadership they bestowed on the benighted races of the world.

Reconstruction and the Rise of Jim Crow

British popular support for the Union cause during the American Civil War was withheld until President Lincoln unequivocally identified emancipation as one of its aims. Concern regarding the fate of African Americans continued long after the war was over and the newly free Black population looked uncertainly towards the future. Throughout Britain, Freedmen's Aid Societies – founded in some cases by the same activists who had earlier campaigned for the abolition of slavery – raised funds for the immediate material support of southern Blacks. Publications such as the *Anti-Slavery Reporter* continued to provide readers with regular commentary on events across the Atlantic. The tone of these periodicals was optimistic about the capability of African Americans to establish themselves as citizens in a free but fiercely competitive society. It was also clear, though, on the need for federal protection and support in the face of resistance from their former masters.[72]

One of the more hopeful forecasts for the future of African Americans came from Liberal MP Charles Wentworth Dilke, who, as part of a larger tour, visited the United States in the aftermath of the Civil War. In a written account of that experience entitled *Greater Britain* (1869), Dilke caricatured African Americans as guileless infants forever grinning and laughing. Rather than regarding this as their innate condition, however, he attributed it to the environment in which they had been forced to live and labour. 'That the negro slaves were lazy, thriftless, unchaste and thieves is true', Dilke pronounced, 'but it is as slaves, and not as negroes, that they were all these things; and, after all, the effects of slavery upon the slave are less terrible than its effects upon the master'. Now that they were liberated from their bondage, Dilke believed that the freed people would 'justify the hopes of their friends' by taking full advantage of their newfound opportunities.[73]

Britons who sent charitable donations overseas and wrote or read campaigning publications were not, however, representative of broader public opinion. From the outset, a more powerful strain of British public opinion perceived African Americans' capacity for progress within narrow parameters. Whether nature or, as Dilke claimed, nurture was the cause of Black inferiority, few Britons believed that African Americans could, in their current condition, exercise the full rights of citizenship. Several factors account for British aversion to the political agenda of Radical Republicans – including the confiscation and redistribution of land to former slaves and granting Black adult males the right to vote – who seized control of the Reconstruction process in 1867. The British press sided with Lincoln's successor, Andrew Johnson, who deemed that sectional reconciliation must be the political priority. They did so as much in their own national interest as in that of the United States. The restoration of the South to the Union would, it was supposed, strengthen congressional opposition to Fenians in the United States, whose plans to overthrow British rule in Ireland included the threat of an invasion of Canada. Britons further believed that the reinstatement of southern representatives to Congress would frustrate Washington's demand that London pay financial compensation for attacks on Union merchant vessels by Confederate naval raiders built in British shipyards during the Civil War.[74]

Growing racism also informed British attitudes towards the prospect of the South becoming an interracial democracy. The economic collapse of Jamaica after emancipation was a prominent topic in the 1850s and it was now used by some as prima facie evidence that Black people were woefully unprepared for the full rights of citizenship. The Morant Bay rebellion of October 1865, which led to the exclusion of free people of colour from the Jamaican House of Assembly, had a critical influence on British thinking, coinciding as it did with debate in the US Congress about Black suffrage.[75] Christine Bolt further suggests that federal government intervention in the southern states, particularly the proposed confiscation and redistribution of plantations for the benefit of former slaves, offended some Britons' ideas about the sanctity of property rights and the importance of self-help.[76] In this context, it is unsurprising that the British press saw the re-establishment of the Union as far more important than what British minister Sir Frederick Bruce deemed 'an artificial sympathy for the Negro' fuelled by northerners' desire for vengeance against the South.[77] 'Just as the immediate object of the war was the vindication of the Union, not the abolition of slavery', opined the *Daily Telegraph*, 'so the question of reconstruction will turn more on practical calculations as to the best means of restoring the integrity of the Republic, than on any abstract desire to promote the well-being of the Black'.[78]

The prospect of the enfranchisement of freedmen was heavily criticized in the British press. This censure must be understood in the context of British domestic politics. Congressional ratification of the 15th Amendment to the US Constitution, which extended the suffrage to Black adult males, came only three years after Parliament had passed a Reform Act (1867) that enlarged the electorate in England and Wales but still left two thirds of the adult male population unable to vote.[79] Writing in the Liberal *Fortnightly Review*, Scottish author Charles Mackay agreed with President Johnson that state legislatures, and not the federal government, should determine who had the right to vote, the outcome of which could be inferred from his own assessment of African Americans as being too 'ignorant' to exercise such a responsibility.[80] The more conservative *Saturday Review* opposed Black voting rights on the same grounds: 'It is probable that the PRESIDENT has exercised a sound judgment; for a demand that negroes should vote on equal terms with the higher race would have been criminally absurd.'[81] The possibility of African Americans assuming political power where they outnumbered whites affronted British sensibilities. According to the *Manchester Guardian*, 'The direct steps which are being taken for the purpose, and with the result, of placing the white population in actual subjugation to the ignorant masses so recently raised from a condition little above that of beasts of labour, constitute a monstrosity of injustice and folly.'[82]

In February 1868, Johnson's feud with Congress led to his impeachment. The British press was steadfast in its defence of the President. Criticism of Radical Republicans for what was seen as their vindictiveness towards former Confederates and their unfounded faith in African Americans was prominent in British reporting throughout Reconstruction. Although the role of fraud, intimidation and violence in the restoration of white rule was recognized, there was also a consensus of opinion that the South had returned to a more natural racial order. The British press consistently supported congressional moderates over radicals. The end of Reconstruction in 1877 and the sectional reconciliation that followed thereafter facilitated the emergence of a greater transatlantic consensus on the place of former slaves in American society.

That unanimity of mind on matters of race corresponded with and was fortified by the broader reconciliation of the two nations in the late nineteenth century. Numerous factors facilitated what came to be known as the 'Grand Rapprochement'. The rise of the United States as an industrial giant made it an important ally at a time when Germany and Russia threatened the global balance of power. Massive British investment in American railroads, estimated at over \$2 billion in 1910, also reinforced the economically interdependent relationship.[83] The growth of American imperial power and the struggle to maintain control of colonized peoples further created a sense of common purpose.[84] Buttressing this accord between Britain and the United States was a belief in the shared status of their peoples as members of a superior Anglo-Saxon race. Scientific and sociological theories such as eugenics and Social Darwinism gained increasing cultural and intellectual support on both sides of the Atlantic.

A leading exponent of the doctrine of racial Anglo-Saxonism was Oxford historian Edward A. Freeman. In *Some Impressions of the United States* (1883), Freeman articulated the common ancestral bond shared by Britons and Americans: 'My contention throughout my whole argument is that the great land of which I am speaking is still essentially an English land. It is no small witness to the toughness of fibre in the English folk wherever it settles that it is so.' The imperial expansion of the United States therefore represented to Freeman a further step on the route towards world domination first embarked on by his own nation. The African American had no place in this divine plan. Freeman found Black people 'repulsive'. On the prospect of the United States becoming an interracial democracy, he concluded that, 'The eternal laws of nature, the eternal distinction of colour, forbid the assimilation of the negro.' For this reason, Freeman supported the disfranchisement of African Americans and, indeed, of the Irish, too. 'Very many approved', he smirked, 'when

I suggested that the best remedy for whatever was amiss would be if every Irishman should kill a negro and be hanged for it'.[85]

Freeman was not alone among British commentators in his opinion that former slaves were incapable of taking their place as free citizens. In November and December 1890, *The Times* ran a ten-part series written by journalist William Laird Clowes on 'The Negro Question in the United States'. Clowes anticipated by more than a decade the school of thought on Reconstruction associated with the American historian William Dunning. His articles, later published in book form as *Black America: A Study of the Ex-Slave and His Late Master*, reflected and fortified the mythology of the Confederate Lost Cause, which gained increasing intellectual currency during the late nineteenth and early twentieth centuries. Clowes lauded the nobility of Confederates who had gone to war and died in defence of their homeland and damned the federal government for imposing punitive justice. 'They had fought, and had poured forth blood and treasure;' he wrote sentimentally, 'they had been beaten, and they had submitted, but they were not forgiven. They had enslaved the black. Henceforth, for a season, the black, ignorant, unscrupulous, dissolute, and corrupt, was to enslave them.' Far from descending into bitter recrimination, white southerners had, in redeeming the region from federal rule, established a paternalistic social order that steered the 'mental, physical and moral advancement' of African Americans within more carefully prescribed constraints. 'As a rule', Clowes pontificated, 'the grown negro, even if he has received a better education than the majority of his fellows, is in mind always a child'.[86]

Clowes's study illustrates the transatlantic dissemination of white supremacist narratives of southern race relations. Other British authors contributed to this consensual account of Anglo-Saxon racial supremacy, none more so than the Liberal politician, jurist and future British Ambassador to the United States, James Bryce, whose monumental study *The American Commonwealth* (1888) became a standard text on US race relations on both sides of the Atlantic. Bryce, whose racial beliefs hardened with time, believed that African Americans were developmentally three to four thousand years behind whites. They were, he wrote, 'a good-natured and easy-going race' who were 'content with the position of an inferior caste, doing the hard work, and especially the field work of the country'. Only a few exceptional African Americans, Bryce believed, possessed any capacity for self-improvement. While Bryce recognized that Black schools were seriously underfunded, he believed that most African American parents had little interest in improving the education of their children. After years of turbulence, the southern states had finally reached a renewed equilibrium. In the post-Reconstruction South, the African American 'is not now ill-treated and has little in the way of positive injustice or oppression to resent'.[87]

While Freeman, Clowes and Bryce wrote in their capacity as private citizens, their racial opinions were consistent with those of the highest levels of British government. In March 1899, Julian Pauncefote, the British Ambassador to Washington, sent a confidential memorandum to Prime Minister Robert Gascoyne-Cecil. It included a report by British diplomat Charles Eliot on race relations in the American South. While Eliot recognized the progress made by a small minority of African Americans, he concluded that most of them 'seem to be entirely wanting in foresight and continuity of purpose, their volition and intelligence are alike fragmentary'. Observing how 'the animal side of their nature prevails', Eliot stated that 'Ethically the American negroes do not appear to have made any great advance on the African savage'. As evidence of this, he pointed to the 'very common' acts of sexual assault committed by Black men on white women, which provoked the retaliatory actions of lynch mobs.[88]

Enduring Rivalry

The apparent convergence of opinion between Britons and Americans on the issue of race does not, however, tell the entire story. James Bryce had deemed the fortunes of African Americans favourable compared to those of former slaves in other societies, specifically the Caribbean. The notion that the American South served as a model of benevolent white rule, implicitly an endorsement of Britons' idealized image of their own empire, nevertheless suffered a serious blow during the last decade of the nineteenth century. Britain and the United States might have become diplomatically reconciled, but differences in their respective publics' opinions on racial politics revealed the persistence of a cultural transatlantic divide.

In 1893 and 1894, African American activist Ida B. Wells toured Britain at the invitation of the recently formed Society for the Recognition of the Brotherhood of Man. Wells followed in the footsteps of the Black abolitionists who, half a century earlier, had mobilized transatlantic opposition to American slavery. Her lectures on the brutalities of southern racism exposed the fallacies of a paternalistic social order espoused by authors such as Bryce and Clowes. Britons had historically accepted lynching in the United States as a necessary function of frontier justice. Wells, however, emphasized that mob violence occurred in communities where there was a fully operational criminal justice system. Her graphic accounts of the ferocity with which white mobs tortured and mutilated their Black victims also made clear to British audiences that lynching was far from a responsible measure in the maintenance of community law and order.[89]

Britons responded not only with moral condemnation of American racism, but also with sanctimonious assertions of their own superior treatment of other races.[90] Whereas before the American Civil War criticism of slavery was based on the universalist idea of the equality of all races, by the late nineteenth century even the most liberal Britons tended to believe in the superiority of their own race. The violent oppression of African Americans nonetheless offended the sense of 'fair play' that was a defining feature of nineteenth-century liberalism since it denied Black people the opportunity to develop.[91] British critics therefore came, by the turn of the century, to contrast the cruelty of the Jim Crow South with what they proudly believed to be the more benign rule of their nation's empire. J. Nelson Fraser, a member of the Indian Education Service, piously claimed in a published account of his American travels that, in the West Indian colonies, 'We hear neither of rape nor lynching there, but perhaps we have given the negro a position which America is not prepared to give him.'[92] Physician Theophilus Scholes similarly contrasted the barbarism of white southerners with the sense of paternal duty that shaped British colonial policy towards people of colour: 'Coming to the British Empire, we may say, that in no part of this vast dominion does the fever of "colour prejudice" show the *same* virulence as in the Southern States.' Taking the temperature of racial attitudes in the American South and the British Empire, he concluded that, while in the former it had reached feverish levels of 'hyper-pyrexia', in the latter such symptoms were 'comparatively mild, never rising more than one or two degrees above the normal'.[93]

While some commentators championed US imperialism as an affirmation of Anglo-Saxon supremacy, others saw the oppression of people of colour as evidence that the United States was unfit to share the world stage with Britain. 'Do the Americans desire to take their glorious share of "The White Man's Burden" by uplifting a degraded and down-trodden race?' historian Goldwin Smith asked in the *Contemporary Review*. 'They have a noble field within their own borders, where there are nine millions of negroes about as down-trodden and degraded as any race can be.'[94] Britons used Jim Crow as a means to cast their own colonial practices in a more advantageous light throughout and beyond the supposed Great Rapprochement. 'Now we Britons have various policies in regard to the black problem in our Empire', affirmed Liberal politician Harold Spender in his 1921 book *A Briton in America*. 'South Africa has one and India another. I do not say that these are perfect policies, but they are policies. America has no policy in regard to the black man.'[95] Such reasoning was still prevalent among British commentators during the later American civil rights revolution.

Transatlantic discourse on American race relations in the late nineteenth century did not therefore fully cohere into a common political culture. British opinion on the issue moved in and out of alignment with prevailing attitudes and practices in the United States. The rise of racial Anglo-Saxonism resulted in a greater degree of convergence from the late 1870s. However, the increasingly violent oppression of African Americans undermined any consensus. Some British commentators believed that criticism of US race relations threatened to undermine the new diplomatic accord. The *Pall Mall Gazette* decried the creation of an English Anti-Lynching Committee inspired by Ida B. Wells as an act of 'impertinent meddling with other people's business' by foolhardy 'busy-bodies'. Britain, the newspaper concluded, should refrain from interfering in the domestic affairs of the United States in the hope that this would encourage Americans to demonstrate similar restraint on the issue of Irish home rule.[96]

Britons, however, did not speak with a collective voice on the fate of former slaves in the American South. Authors and activists condemned Jim Crow while extolling the virtues of their own country's colonial policies. This criticism of southern racism was, moreover, only one front in a broader assault on the mistreatment of racial minorities in the United States. As Kate Flint has shown, Britons also favourably contrasted the treatment of First Nations people in Canada with their oppression on poorly administered reservations in the United States.[97] This sanctimonious attitude revealed how, despite rapprochement, many Britons regarded Americans as allies but not equals. When it came to bearing the White man's burden, there was much that Americans needed to learn from their example. The pride that Britons took in their own colonial policies fuelled rivalry with the United States, providing a means to claim superiority over a nation that threatened, especially in economic terms, to eclipse them.

Conclusion

The search for a common transatlantic political 'tradition' in the nineteenth century is problematic for a number of reasons. First, there were acute ideological differences not only between but also within the two countries. In the United States, slavery was the cause of internal friction that flamed into civil war. Even within the free states, there was violent division over slavery, with reactionary mobs assaulting and murdering abolitionists. Among the British public, there was greater accord about the evils of slavery, but disillusionment with the results of emancipation and intellectual rationalizations for imperial rule contributed to growing racism.[98] Second, diplomatic friction fostered by ideological differences over slavery and race, as well as a host of other geopolitical issues, contributed to persistent tensions between Britain and the United States. It was not until the twentieth century, with the scramble for empire largely resolved, that the threat posed by totalitarian regimes forced the two nations into a partnership on the basis of shared liberal goals of individual freedom and democracy. In focusing on non-state actors, this chapter reveals a more complicated story of Anglo-American convergence and divergence than has been conveyed by a historiography predicated on the concept of diplomatic rapprochement.

The mobilization of British and American reformers in common cause against the enforced servitude of Black people represents the pinnacle of a transnational liberal reforming tradition. A longer view of the nineteenth century that includes the decades following emancipation nonetheless shows how progressive reformers failed to sustain their humanitarian concern for African Americans. The generation of liberal intellectuals and activists who came to prominence on either side of the Atlantic during the late nineteenth century had their political roots in the abolitionist movement but remained conspicuously indifferent to the fate of former slaves as they became subordinated by a new system of white supremacist rule in the American South.[99] Although the threads of humanitarian reform became increasingly frayed, they did not unravel altogether. The role of African Americans in establishing and sustaining both of these movements reveals their critical importance to transatlantic reform and progressivism. Black activists' mobilization of British opposition to slavery and, later, lynching points to a culture of transatlantic political dissent that did have an enduring impact beyond the nineteenth century.

David Brown is Senior Lecturer in American Studies at the University of Manchester. He is the author of *Southern Outcast: Hinton Rowan Helper and the Impending Crisis of the South* (Louisiana State University Press, 2006) and co-author of *Race in the American South* (Edinburgh University Press, 2007) and *A Concise American History* (Taylor & Francis, 2020). His current research examines the Manchester Union and Emancipation Society and the London Emancipation Society that led an antislavery revival in Britain during the American Civil War.

Clive Webb is Professor of Modern American History at the University of Sussex. He has written numerous books and articles on the United States and United Kingdom and the relationship between them.

Notes

1. Frank Thistlethwaite, *America and the Atlantic Community: Anglo-American Aspects, 1790–1850* (New York: Harper & Row, 1959), 109.

2. Gordon S. Wood, *The Radicalism of the American Revolution* (New York: Alfred A. Knopf, 1992) is now dated. See Alan Taylor, *American Revolutions: A Continental History, 1750–1804* (New York: W.W. Norton, 2016).

3. Lawrence A. Peskin, 'Conspiratorial Anglophobia and the War of 1812', *Journal of American History* 98(3) (2011), 647–69.

4. Seymour *Drescher, Econocide: British Slavery in the Era of Abolition* (Chapel Hill: University of North Carolina Press, 2010 [1977]).

5. British sources accounted for over 75 per cent of long-term foreign investment in the United States up to 1853. Robert Lipsey, 'US Foreign Trade and the Balance of Payments, 1800–1913', in S. Engerman and R. Gallman (eds), *The Cambridge Economic History of the United States* (Cambridge: Cambridge University Press, 2000), 685–732.

6. Richard W. Maass, '"Difficult to Relinquish Territory Which Had Been Conquered": Expansionism in the War of 1812', *Diplomatic History* 39(1) (2015), 70–97.

7. Kinley J. Brauer, 'The United States and British Imperial Expansion, 1815–60', *Diplomatic History* 12(1) (1988), 19–37. Jay Sexton, *The Monroe Doctrine: Empire and Nation in Nineteenth-Century America* (New York: Hill and Wang, 2011) is the standard text.

8. See, for example, Kathleen Burk, *Old World, New World: Great Britain and America from the Beginning* (London: Little, Brown, 2007), 260.

9. Bradford Perkins, *The Cambridge History of American Foreign Relations. Volume 1: The Creation of a Republican Empire, 1776–1865* (Cambridge: Cambridge University Press, 1993), 207.

10. Although Marc-William Palen, *The Conspiracy of Free Trade: The Anglo-American Struggle over Empire and Economic Globalization, 1846–1896* (Cambridge: Cambridge University Press, 2017) complicates the thesis that protectionism was eradicated.

11. Edward B. Rugemer, *The Problem of Emancipation: The Caribbean Roots of the American Civil War* (Baton Rouge: Louisiana State University Press, 2008).

12. On the British antislavery state, see *Richard Huzzey, Freedom Burning: Anti-Slavery and Empire in Victorian Britain* (Ithaca, NY: Cornell University Press, 2012). The federal government protected slavery 'on the high seas, in relations with foreign governments, in the District of Columbia, in the federal territories, and to some extent even in the free states'. Don E. Fehrenbacher, *The Slaveholding Republic: An Account of the United States Government's Relations to Slavery*, completed and edited by Ward M. McAfee (New York: Oxford University Press, 2001), 296–97.

13. Kinley Brauer, 'The Great American Desert Revisited: Recent Literature and Prospects for the Study of American Foreign Relations, 1815–61', *Diplomatic History* 13(3) (1989), 395–417. For more recent interpretations, see the essays in Michael J. Hogan (ed.), *Paths to Power: The Historiography of American Foreign Relations to 1941* (Cambridge: Cambridge University Press, 2000) and Jay Sexton, 'Towards a Synthesis of Foreign Relations in the Civil War Era, 1848–77', *American Nineteenth Century History* 5(3) (2004), 50–73.

14. William Earl Weeks, *The New Cambridge History of American Foreign Relations, Volume 1. Dimensions of the Early American Empire, 1754–1865* (Cambridge: Cambridge University Press, 2013) provides an overview.

15. Eric Kaufman, *The Rise and Fall of Anglo-America* (Cambridge, MA: Harvard University Press, 2004).

16. David T. Gleeson (ed.), *English Ethnicity and Culture in North America* (Columbia: University of South Carolina Press, 2017), 3.

17. Eliza Tamarkin, *Anglophilia: Deference, Devotion, and Antebellum America* (Chicago: University of Chicago Press, 2008), 30; Skye Montgomery, 'Reannealing of the Heart Ties: The Rhetoric of Anglo-American Kinship and the Politics of Reconciliation in the Prince of Wales's 1860 Tour', *Journal of the Civil War Era* 6(2) (2016), 193–219.

18. Sam W. Haynes, *Unfinished Revolution: The Early American Republic in a British World* (Charlottesville: University of Virginia Press, 2010).

19. *Harper's Weekly*, 20 October 1860, in Montgomery, 'Reannealing', 200.

20. Jonathan Daniel Wells, 'Charles Dickens, the American South, and the Transatlantic Debate over Slavery', *Slavery & Abolition* 36(1) (2015), 1–25.

21. Paul Giles, *Virtual Americas: Transatlantic Fictions and the Transatlantic Imaginary* (Durham, NC: Duke University Press, 2002); F.K. Prochaska. *Eminent Victorians on American Democracy: The View from Albion* (Oxford: Oxford University Press, 2012), 35.

22. Kevin Phillips, *The Cousins' Wars: Religion, Politics, and the Triumph of Anglo-America* (New York: Basic Books, 1999) provides a 700-page exploration of this theme.

23. A.G. Hopkins, *American Empire: A Global History* (Princeton, NJ: Princeton University Press, 2018), 187. Hopkins draws from Haynes, *Unfinished Revolution*; Frank Prochaska, *The Eagle and the Crown: Americans and the British Monarchy* (New Haven, CT: Yale University Press, 2008); Sexton, *Monroe Doctrine*; Kariann Yokota, *Unbecoming British: How Revolutionary America Became a Postcolonial Nation* (Oxford: Oxford University Press, 2011). For a more sceptical view, see Duncan Andrew Campbell, *Unlikely Allies: Britain, America and the Origins of the Special Relationship* (London: Hambledon Continuum, 2007).

24. *The Times*, 4 July 1841, in Temperley, *Britain and American*, 35. For a contrasting view, see Lloyd S. Kramer, *Nationalism: Political Cultures in Europe and America, 1775–1865* (Chapel Hill: University of North Carolina Press, 2011).

25. C.A. Bayly, *The Birth of the Modern World, 1780–1914* (Oxford: Blackwell, 2004), 118.

26. Clare Taylor, *British and American Abolitionists: An Episode in Transatlantic Understanding* (Edinburgh: Edinburgh University Press, 1974), 1–2.

27. Simon Morgan, 'The Political as Personal: Transatlantic Abolitionism c. 1833–67', in William Mulligan and Maurice Bric (eds), *A Global History of Anti-Slavery Politics in the Nineteenth Century* (London: Palgrave, 2013), 78–96.

28. James Walvin, *Making the Black Atlantic: Britain and the African Diaspora* (London: Cassell, 2000), 141.

29. Antebellum economists were actually not as certain of slavery's unprofitability as Adam Smith had been before them. Nonetheless, the connection between free labour and civilized society was widely perceived to be axiomatic outside the American South. Seymour Drescher, *The Mighty Experiment: Free Labor versus Slavery in the British Emancipation* (New York: Oxford University Press, 2002); Seymour Drescher, 'Free Labor vs Slave Labor: The British and Caribbean Cases', in Stanley L. Engerman (ed.), *Terms of Labor: Slavery, Serfdom, and Free Labor* (Stanford, CA: Stanford University Press, 1999), 50–86.

30. David Brion Davis, *Inhuman Bondage: The Rise and Fall of Slavery in the New World* (New York: Oxford University Press, 2006), 252. See also Robert H. Abzug, *Passionate Liberator: Theodore Dwight Weld and the Dilemma of Reform* (New York: Oxford University Press, 1980).

31. Robin Blackburn, *The Overthrow of Colonial Slavery, 1776–1848* (London: Verso, 1988), 144; J.R. Oldfield, *Popular Politics and British Anti-Slavery* (Manchester: Manchester University Press, 1995), 96–119.

32. Lawrence C. Jennings, *French Anti-Slavery: The Movement for the Abolition of Slavery in France, 1802–1848* (Cambridge: Cambridge University Press, 2000).

33. Roger Anstey, *The Atlantic Slave Trade in British Abolition, 1760–1810* (London: Macmillan, 1975).

34. Blackburn, *Overthrow*, 423–24; David Eltis, *Economic Growth and the Ending of the Transatlantic Slave Trade* (New York: Oxford University Press, 1987).

35. The West Indian Committee could count on more MPs than had been previously thought: as many as eighty in 1830. Nicholas Draper, 'The Rise of a New Planter Class? Some Countercurrents from British Guiana and Trinidad, 1807–33', *Atlantic Studies* 9(1) (2012), 75–76; B.W. Higman, 'The West India "Interest" in Parliament, 1807–1833', *Historical Studies* 13 (1967), 1–19.

36. Clare Midgley, 'The Dissenting Voice of Elizabeth Heyrick: An Exploration of the Links between Gender, Religious Dissent, and Anti-Slavery Radicalism', in Elizabeth J. Clapp and Julie Roy Jeffrey (eds), *Women, Dissent, and Anti-Slavery in Britain and America, 1790–1865* (Oxford: Oxford University Press, 2011), 88–110.

37. Blackburn, *Overthrow*, 455.

38. James Heartfield, *The British and Foreign Anti-Slavery Society, 1838–1956: A History* (London: Hurst & Company, 2016), 26.

39. BFASS minutes, cited in Betty Fladeland, *Men and Brothers: Anglo-American Antislavery Cooperation* (Urbana: University of Illinois Press, 1972), 260.

40. Eric Burin, *Slavery and the Peculiar Solution: A History of the American Colonization Society* (Gainesville: University Press of Florida, 2005).

41. David Turley, *The Culture of English Antislavery, 1770–1860* (London: Routledge, 1991), 206–9.

42. Cited in Richard J.M. Blackett, '"And there Shall Be No More Sea": William Lloyd Garrison and the Transatlantic Abolitionist Movement', in James Brewer Stewart (ed.), *William Lloyd Garrison at Two Hundred: History, Legacy, and Memory* (New Haven, CT: Yale University Press, 2008), 15.

43. Charles Stuart, *American Colonization Society* (n.p., 1831); idem, *Remarks on the Colony of Liberia and the American Colonization Society* (London, 1832); idem, *The American Colonization Scheme Further Unravelled* (Bath, 1833); idem, *Facts Designed to Exhibit the Real Character and Tendency of the American Colonization Society* (Liverpool, 1833). See Anthony J. Barker, *Captain Charles Stuart, Anglo-American Abolitionist* (Baton Rouge: Louisiana State University Press, 1983).

44. R.J.M. Blackett, *Building an Antislavery Wall: Black Americans in the Atlantic Abolitionist Movement, 1830–1860* (Ithaca, NY: Cornell University Press, 1983), 69; R.J.M. Blackett, 'Anglo-American Opposition to Liberian Colonization, 1831–1833', *Historian* 41(2) (1979), 276–94.

45. C. Duncan Rice, 'The Anti-Slavery Mission of George Thompson to the United States, 1834–1835', *Journal of American Studies* 2(1) (1968), 13–31.

46. Manisha Sinha, *The Slave's Cause: A History of Abolition* (New Haven, CT: Yale University Press, 2016), esp. 339–80.

47. Correspondence that has been collated in Taylor, *British and American Abolitionists*.

48. Maurice Bric, 'Debating Slavery and Empire', in Mulligan and Bric (eds), *Global History of Anti-Slavery Politics*, 59–77.

49. W. Caleb McDaniel, *The Problem of Democracy in the Age of Slavery: Garrison Abolitionists and Transatlantic Reform* (Baton Rouge: Louisiana State University Press, 2013), 164. For a detailed assessment of the relationship between the ACLL and abolition in both Britain and

the United States, see Simon Morgan, 'The Anti-Corn Law League and British Anti-Slavery in Transatlantic Perspective, 1838–1846', *The Historical Journal* 52(1) (2009), 87–107.

50. Betty Fladeland, *Abolitionists and Working-Class Problems in the Age of Industrialization* (Baton Rouge: Louisiana State University Press, 1984); Alasdair Pettinger, 'Send Back the Money: Douglas and the Free Church of Scotland', in Alan J. Rice and Martin Crawford (eds), *Liberating Sojourn: Frederick Douglass and Transatlantic Reform* (Athens: University of Georgia Press, 1999), 31–55.

51. Ibid, 301.

52. Kathryn Kish Sklar and James Brewer Stewart (eds), *Women's Rights and Transatlantic Antislavery in the Era of Emancipation* (New Haven, CT: Yale University Press, 2007); Clapp and Roy, *Women, Dissent, and Anti-Slavery*.

53. Jeffrey R. Kerr-Ritchie, *Rebellious Passage: The Creole Revolt and America's Coastal Slave Trade* (Cambridge: Cambridge University Press, 2019).

54. Turley, *Culture of English Antislavery*, 197, 211–17.

55. Susan Zaeske, *Signatures of Citizenship: Petitioning, Antislavery, and Women's Political Identity* (Chapel Hill: University of North Carolina Press, 2003), 44.

56. Clare Midgley, *Women against Slavery: The British Campaigns, 1780–1870* (London: Routledge, 1995).

57. Sarah Meer, *Uncle Tom Mania: Slavery, Minstrelsy, and Transatlantic Culture in the 1850s* (Athens: University of Georgia Press, 2005) takes the phrase 'Tom Mania' from *The Spectator*; David S. Reynolds, *Mightier Than the Sword: Uncle Tom's Cabin and the Battle for America* (New York: W.W. Norton, 2011), 117–28.

58. For a pioneering attempt to assess the scale of black abolitionist lectures, see Hannah-Rose Murray, '"With Almost Electric Speed": Mapping African American Abolitionists in Britain and Ireland, 1838–1847', *Slavery & Abolition* 40(3) (2019), 522–42.

59. The work of Richard Blackett is the starting point for consideration of African American abolitionists in Britain and all others follow in his footsteps. See also essays in Rice and Crawford, *Liberating Sojourn*, and 'African Americans and Transatlantic Abolition, 1845–1865', a special edition of *Slavery & Abolition* 33(2) (2012).

60. Hugh Dubrulle, *Ambivalent Nation: How Britain Imagined the American Civil War* (Baton Rouge: Louisiana State University Press, 2018), 88–89.

61. Sarah Meer, 'Competing Representations: Douglass, the Ethiopian Serenaders, and Ethnic Exhibition in London', in *Liberating Sojourn*; Meer, *Uncle Tom Mania*; Audrey Fisch, *American Slaves in Victorian England: Abolitionist Politics in Popular Literature and Culture* (Cambridge: Cambridge University Press, 2000).

62. Sinha, *The Slave's Cause*, 344; Britt Rusert, *Fugitive Science: Empiricism and Freedom in Early African American Culture* (New York: New York University Press, 2017), 113–48. Hazel Watero emphasizes the difficulty of reaching decisive conclusions in *Racism on the Victorian Stage: Representations of Slavery and the Black Character* (Cambridge: Cambridge University Press, 2007).

63. David Turley, 'British Unitarian Abolitionists, Frederick Douglass, and Racial Equality', in *Liberating Sojourn*, 56–70.

64. On the Anglo-American abolitionist 'rupture', see McDaniel, *The Problem of Democracy*, 210–32. But Matthew Griffin, 'George Thompson, Transatlantic Abolitionism, and Britain in the American Civil War', *Slavery & Abolition* 40(3) (2019), 563–82, contests the extent of the split.

65. R.J.M. Blackett, *Divided Hearts: Britain and the American Civil War* (Baton Rouge, LA: Louisiana State University Press, 2001).

66. The Union and Emancipation Society's final report (1866) recorded that the organization alone held a minimum of five hundred meetings and distributed four hundred thousand antislavery books and pamphlets. Brian Jenkins, *Britain and the War for the Union. Volume 2* (Montreal: McGill-Queen's University Press, 1980), 209–34, provides the fullest discussion.

67. George Thompson to William Lloyd Garrison, 25 December 1862, in W.P. Garrison and F.J. Garrison, *William Lloyd Garrison* (London, 1899), IV, 67; William Evans, *The Liberator*, 27 March 1863.

68. Bradford Perkins, *The Great Rapprochement: England and the United States, 1895–1914* (New York: Atheneum, 1968).

69. The influence of racial ideology on Anglo-American relations is assessed in Stuart Anderson, *Race and Rapprochement: Anglo-Saxonism and Anglo-American Relations, 1895–1904* (Rutherford, NJ: Fairleigh Dickinson University Press, 1981); Reginald Horsman, *Race and Manifest Destiny: The Origins of Racial Anglo-Saxonism* (Cambridge, MA: Harvard University Press, 1981); and Paul A. Kramer, 'Empires, Exceptions, and Anglo-Saxons: Race and Rule between the British and United States Empires, 1880–1910', *Journal of American History* 88(4) (2002), 1315–53.

70. Stephen Tufnell, '"Uncle Sam Is to Be Sacrificed": Anglophobia in Late Nineteenth-Century Politics and Culture', *American Nineteenth Century History* 12(1) (2011), 81–83.

71. Christine Bolt, *The Anti-Slavery Movement and Reconstruction: A Study of Anglo-American Co-operation 1833–1877* (London: Institute of Race Relations/Oxford University Press, 1969).

72. 'The Freed Negroes in America', *The Leisure Hour* 699 (20 May 1865), 320. For a detailed account of British philanthropic support for newly emancipated slaves, see Bolt, *Anti-Slavery Movement and Reconstruction*, 54–140.

73. Charles Wentworth Dilke, *Greater Britain: A Record of Travel in English-Speaking Countries during 1866–7* (Philadelphia, PA: J.B. Lippincott, 1869), 17, 20. For a similarly positive appraisal of African Americans' potential, see Charles Beadle, *A Trip to the United States in 1887* (London: J.S. Virtue, 1887), 69.

74. Eric Foner, 'Andrew Johnson and Reconstruction: A British View', *Journal of Southern History* 41(3) (1975), 381–90.

75. Morant Bay was 'the major turning point in English racial attitudes'. Duncan Andrew Campbell, *English Public Opinion and the American Civil War* (Woodbridge: The Boydell Press, 2003), 126.

76. Bolt, *The Anti-Slavery Movement and Reconstruction*, 161–62.

77. Foner, 'Andrew Johnson and Reconstruction', 388.

78. Untitled editorial, *Daily Telegraph*, 4 January 1866, 4. For further examples of British press support for Johnson, see the untitled editorials in *The Times*, 28 June 1865, 11 and 2 March 1866, 7.

79. Marilyn Lake and Henry Reynolds, *Drawing the Global Colour Line: White Men's Countries and the International Challenge of Racial Equality* (Cambridge: Cambridge University Press, 2008), 65.

80. Charles MacKay, 'President Johnson and the Reconstruction of the Union', *Fortnightly Review* 4(22) (1 April 1866), 487.

81. 'Negro Suffrage and Reconstruction', *Saturday Review* 20(522) (28 October 1865), 537.

82. Editorial, *Manchester Guardian*, 24 August 1867, 4. See also 'Negro Suffrage', *Pall Mall Gazette*, 12 June 1865, for a viciously racist criticism of extending the vote.

83. Wilkins, *History of Foreign Investment in the United States*, 728, n. 35.

84. Lake and Reynolds, *Drawing the Global Colour Line*, 63–64, 71–72, 74.

85. Edward A. Freeman, *Some Impressions of the United States* (New York: Henry Holt, 1883), 138, 148, 143–44, 139.

86. William Laird Clowes, 'The Negro Question in the United States', *The Times*, 27 November 1890, 3, and 26 December 1890, 10.

87. James Bryce, *American Commonwealth*, II (London: Macmillan, Second Revised Edition, 1889), 724, 306, 307. See also Lake and Reynolds, *Drawing the Global Colour Line*, 49–50, 61, 64.

88. Julian Paucefote to Lord Salisbury, confidential memorandum, 3 March 1899, FO 881/7148, National Archives, Kew, London.

89. Sarah L. Silkey, *Black Woman Reformer: Ida B. Wells Lynching, and Transatlantic Activism* (Athens: University of Georgia Press, 2015).

90. For examples of British writers' censure of southern lynch mobs, see the Right Hon. the Earl and the Countess of Meath, *Thoughts on Imperial and Social Subjects* (London: Wells Gardner, Darton & Co., 1906), 160; Sydney Olivier, *White Capital and Coloured Labour* (London: Independent Labour Party, 1906), 48–50; William Archer, *Through Afro-America: An English Reading of the Race Problem* (London: Chapman and Hall, 1910), 24–28; Sir Harry H. Johnston, *The Negro in the New World* (London: Methuen, 1910), 466.

91. Leslie Butler, *Critical Americans: Victorian Intellectuals and Transatlantic Liberal Reform* (Chapel Hill: University of North Carolina Press, 2007), 87–117.

92. J. Nelson Fraser, *America, Old and New: Impressions of Six Months in the States* (London: John Ouseley, 1912), 278.

93. Theophilus E.S. Scholes, *The British Empire and Alliances; or, Britain's Duty to Her Colonies and Subject Races* (London: Elliot Stock, 1899), 395.

94. Goldwin Smith, 'Imperialism in the United States', *Contemporary Review* 75 (May 1899), 623.

95. Harold Spender, *A Briton in America* (London: William Heinemann, 1921), 248.

96. 'The Alabama Coon', *Pall Mall Gazette*, 6 October 1894, 1.

97. Kate Flint, *The Transatlantic Indian, 1776–1930* (Princeton, NJ: Princeton University Press, 2009).

98. Pinpointing differences of opinion between Britons is a difficult challenge, but particularly in the last third of the nineteenth century. While the mass meetings during the American Civil War provide an insight into working-class attitudes, the decades that follow are evidenced primarily by a print culture reflective of middle- and upper-class opinion.

99. For more on these reformers, see Butler, *Critical Victorians*, and, on their failure to focus on racial issues, see the review of this book by Van Gosse in *American Historical Review* 113(2) (2008), 520–21.

Bibliography

Abzug, Robert H. *Passionate Liberator: Theodore Dwight Weld and the Dilemma of Reform*. New York: Oxford University Press, 1980.

Anderson, Stuart. *Race and Rapprochement: Anglo-Saxonism and Anglo-American Relations, 1895–1904*. Rutherford, NJ: Fairleigh Dickinson University Press, 1981.

Anstey, Roger. *The Atlantic Slave Trade in British Abolition, 1760–1810*. London: Macmillan, 1975.

Archer, William. *Through Afro-America: An English Reading of the Race Problem*. London: Chapman and Hall, 1910.

Barker, Anthony J. *Captain Charles Stuart, Anglo-American Abolitionist*. Baton Rouge: Louisiana State University Press, 1983.

Bayly, C.A. *The Birth of the Modern World, 1780–1914*. Oxford: Blackwell, 2004.

Beadle, Charles. *A Trip to the United States in 1887*. London: J.S. Virtue, 1887.

Blackburn, Robin. *The Overthrow of Colonial Slavery, 1776–1848*. London: Verso, 1988.

Blackett, Richard J.M. '"And There Shall Be No More Sea": William Lloyd Garrison and the Transatlantic Abolitionist Movement', in James Brewer Stewart (ed.), *William Lloyd Garrison at Two Hundred: History, Legacy, and Memory*. New Haven, CT: Yale University Press, 2008, 113–41.

_____. 'Anglo-American Opposition to Liberian Colonization, 1831–1833', *Historian* 41(2) (1979), 276–94.

_____. *Building an Antislavery Wall: Black Americans in the Atlantic Abolitionist Movement, 1830–1860*. Ithaca, NY: Cornell University Press, 1983.

_____. *Divided Hearts: Britain and the American Civil War*. Baton Rouge: Louisiana State University Press, 2001.

Bolt, Christine. *The Anti-Slavery Movement and Reconstruction: A Study of Anglo-American Co-operation 1833–1877*. London: Institute of Race Relations/Oxford University Press, 1969.

Brauer, Kinley. 'The Great American Desert Revisited: Recent Literature and Prospects for the Study of American Foreign Relations, 1815–61', *Diplomatic History* 13(3) (1989), 395–417.

_____. 'The United States and British Imperial Expansion, 1815–60', *Diplomatic History* 12(1) (1988), 19–37.

Bric, Maurice. 'Debating Slavery and Empire', in William Mulligan and Maurice Bric (eds), *A Global History of Anti-Slavery Politics in the Nineteenth Century*. London: Palgrave, 2013, 59–77.

Bryce, James. *American Commonwealth*, II. London: Macmillan, Second Revised Edition, 1889.

Burin, Eric. *Slavery and the Peculiar Solution: A History of the American Colonization Society*. Gainesville: University Press of Florida, 2005.

Burk, Kathleen. *Old World, New World: Great Britain and America from the Beginning*. London: Little, Brown, 2007.

Butler, Leslie. *Critical Americans: Victorian Intellectuals and Transatlantic Liberal Reform*. Chapel Hill: University of North Carolina Press, 2007.

Campbell, Duncan Andrew. *English Public Opinion and the American Civil War*. Woodbridge: The Boydell Press, 2003.

_____. *Unlikely Allies: Britain, America and the Origins of the Special Relationship*. London: Hambledon Continuum, 2007.

Clowes, William Laird. 'The Negro Question in the United States', *The Times*, 27 November 1890, 3, and 26 December 1890, 10.

Davis, David Brion. *Inhuman Bondage: The Rise and Fall of Slavery in the New World*. New York: Oxford University Press, 2006.

Dilke, Charles Wentworth. *Greater Britain: A Record of Travel in English-Speaking Countries during 1866–7*. Philadelphia, PA: J.B. Lippincott, 1869.

Draper, Nicholas. 'The Rise of a New Planter Class? Some Countercurrents from British Guiana and Trinidad, 1807–33', *Atlantic Studies* 9(1) (2012), 65–83.

Drescher, Seymour. *Econocide: British Slavery in the Era of Abolition*. Chapel Hill: University of North Carolina Press, 2010 [1977].

_____. 'Free Labor vs Slave Labor: The British and Caribbean Cases', in Stanley L. Engerman (ed.), *Terms of Labor: Slavery, Serfdom, and Free Labor*. Stanford, CA: Stanford University Press, 1999, 50–86.

_____. *The Mighty Experiment: Free Labor versus Slavery in the British Emancipation*. New York: Oxford University Press, 2002.

Dubrulle, Hugh. *Ambivalent Nation: How Britain Imagined the American Civil War*. Baton Rouge: Louisiana State University Press, 2018.

Eltis, David. *Economic Growth and the Ending of the Transatlantic Slave Trade*. New York: Oxford University Press, 1987.

Fehrenbacher, Don E. *The Slaveholding Republic: An Account of the United States Government's Relations to Slavery*, completed and edited by Ward M. McAfee. New York: Oxford University Press, 2001.

Fisch, Audrey. *American Slaves in Victorian England: Abolitionist Politics in Popular Literature and Culture*. Cambridge: Cambridge University Press, 2000.

Fladeland, Betty. *Abolitionists and Working-Class Problems in the Age of Industrialization*. Baton Rouge: Louisiana State University Press, 1984.

_____. *Men and Brothers: Anglo-American Antislavery Cooperation*. Urbana: University of Illinois Press, 1972.

Flint, Kate. *The Transatlantic Indian, 1776–1930*. Princeton, NJ: Princeton University Press, 2009.

Foner, Eric. 'Andrew Johnson and Reconstruction: A British View', *Journal of Southern History* 41(3) (1975), 381–90.

Fraser, Nelson. *America, Old and New: Impressions of Six Months in the States*. London: John Ouseley, 1912.

Freeman, Edward A. *Some Impressions of the United States*. New York: Henry Holt, 1883.

Giles, Paul. *Virtual Americas: Transatlantic Fictions and the Transatlantic Imaginary*. Durham, NC: Duke University Press, 2002.

Gleeson, David T. (ed.). *English Ethnicity and Culture in North America*. Columbia: University of South Carolina Press, 2017.

Griffin, Matthew. 'George Thompson, Transatlantic Abolitionism, and Britain in the American Civil War', *Slavery & Abolition* 40(3) (2019), 563–82.

Haynes, Sam W. *Unfinished Revolution: The Early American Republic in a British World*. Charlottesville: University of Virginia Press, 2010.

Heartfield, James. *The British and Foreign Anti-Slavery Society, 1838–1956: A History*. London: Hurst & Company, 2016.

Higman, B.W. 'The West India "Interest" in Parliament, 1807–1833', *Historical Studies* 13 (1967), 1–19.

Hogan, Michael J. (ed.). *Paths to Power: The Historiography of American Foreign Relations to 1941*. Cambridge: Cambridge University Press, 2000.

Hopkins, A.G. *American Empire: A Global History*. Princeton, NJ: Princeton University Press, 2018.

Horsman, Reginald. *Race and Manifest Destiny: The Origins of Racial Anglo-Saxonism*. Cambridge, MA: Harvard University Press, 1981.

Huzzey, Richard. *Freedom Burning: Anti-Slavery and Empire in Victorian Britain*. Ithaca, NY: Cornell University Press, 2012.

Jenkins, Brian. *Britain and the War for the Union. Volume 2*. Montreal: McGill-Queen's University Press, 1980.

Jennings, Lawrence C. *French Anti-Slavery: The Movement for the Abolition of Slavery in France, 1802–1848*. Cambridge: Cambridge University Press, 2000.

Johnston, Sir Harry H. *The Negro in the New World*. London: Methuen, 1910.

Kaufman, Eric. *The Rise and Fall of Anglo-America*. Cambridge, MA: Harvard University Press, 2004.

Kerr-Richie, Jeffrey R. *Rebellious Passage: The Creole Revolt and America's Coastal Slave Trade*. Cambridge: Cambridge University Press, 2019.

Kramer, Lloyd S., *Nationalism: Political Cultures in Europe and America, 1775–1865*. Chapel Hill: University of North Carolina Press, 2011.

Kramer, Paul A. 'Empires, Exceptions, and Anglo-Saxons: Race and Rule between the British and United States Empires, 1880–1910', *Journal of American History* 88(4) (2002), 1315–53.

Lake, Marilyn, and Henry Reynolds. *Drawing the Global Colour Line: White Men's Countries and the International Challenge of Racial Equality*. Cambridge: Cambridge University Press, 2008.

Lipsey, Robert. 'US Foreign Trade and the Balance of Payments, 1800–1913', in S. Engerman and R. Gallman (eds), *The Cambridge Economic History of the United States*. Cambridge: Cambridge University Press, 2000, 685–732.

Maass, Richard W. '"Difficult to Relinquish Territory Which Had Been Conquered": Expansionism in the War of 1812', *Diplomatic History* 39(1) (2015), 70–97.

MacKay, Charles. 'President Johnson and the Reconstruction of the Union', *Fortnightly Review* 4(22) (1 April 1866, 477–90.

McDaniel, W. Caleb. *The Problem of Democracy in the Age of Slavery: Garrison Abolitionists and Transatlantic Reform*. Baton Rouge: Louisiana State University Press, 2013.

Meer, Sarah. *Uncle Tom Mania: Slavery, Minstrelsy, and Transatlantic Culture in the 1850s*. Athens: University of Georgia Press, 2005.

Midgley, Clare. 'The Dissenting Voice of Elizabeth Heyrick: An Exploration of the Links between Gender, Religious Dissent, and Anti-Slavery Radicalism', in Elizabeth J. Clapp and Julie Roy Jeffrey (eds), *Women, Dissent, and Anti-Slavery in Britain and America, 1790–1865*. Oxford: Oxford University Press, 2011, 88–110.

_____. *Women against Slavery: The British Campaigns, 1780–1870*. London: Routledge, 1995.

Montgomery, Skye. 'Reannealing of the Heart Ties: The Rhetoric of Anglo-American Kinship and the Politics of Reconciliation in the Prince of Wales's 1860 Tour', *Journal of the Civil War Era* 6(2) (2016), 193–219.

Morgan, Simon. 'The Anti-Corn Law League and British Anti-Slavery in Transatlantic Perspective, 1838–1846', *The Historical Journal* 52(1) (2009), 87–107.

_____. 'The Political as Personal: Transatlantic Abolitionism c. 1833–67', in William Mulligan and Maurice Bric (eds), *A Global History of Anti-Slavery Politics in the Nineteenth Century*. London: Palgrave, 2013, 78–96.

Murray, Hannah-Rose. '"With Almost Electric Speed": Mapping African American Abolitionists in Britain and Ireland, 1838–1847', *Slavery & Abolition* 40(3) (2019), 522–42.

Oldfield, J.R. *Popular Politics and British Anti-Slavery*. Manchester: Manchester University Press, 1995.

Olivier, Sydney. *White Capital and Coloured Labour*. London: Independent Labour Party, 1906.

Palen, Marc-William. *The Conspiracy of Free Trade: The Anglo-American Struggle over Empire and Economic Globalization, 1846–1896*. Cambridge: Cambridge University Press, 2017.

Perkins, Bradford. *The Cambridge History of American Foreign Relations, Volume 1: The Creation of a Republican Empire, 1776–1865*. Cambridge: Cambridge University Press, 1993.

_____. *The Great Rapprochement: England and the United States, 1895–1914*. New York: Atheneum, 1968.

Peskin, Lawrence A. 'Conspiratorial Anglophobia and the War of 1812', *Journal of American History* 98(3) (2011), 647–69.

Phillips, Kevin. *The Cousins' Wars: Religion, Politics, and the Triumph of Anglo-America*. New York: Basic Books, 1999.

Prochaska, Frank. *The Eagle and the Crown: Americans and the British Monarchy*. New Haven, CT: Yale University Press, 2008.

_____. *Eminent Victorians on American Democracy: The View from Albion*. Oxford: Oxford University Press, 2012.

Reynolds, David S. *Mightier Than the Sword: Uncle Tom's Cabin and the Battle for America*. New York: W.W. Norton, 2011.

Rice, Alan J., and Martin Crawford (eds). *Liberating Sojourn: Frederick Douglass and Transatlantic Reform*. Athens: University of Georgia Press, 1999.

Rice, C. Duncan. 'The Anti-Slavery Mission of George Thompson to the United States, 1834–1835', *Journal of American Studies* 2(1) (1968), 13–31.

The Right Hon. the Earl and the Countess of Meath. *Thoughts on Imperial and Social Subjects*. London: Wells Gardner, Darton & Co., 1906.

Rugemer, Edward B. *The Problem of Emancipation: The Caribbean Roots of the American Civil War*. Baton Rouge: Louisiana State University Press, 2008.

Rusert, Britt. *Fugitive Science: Empiricism and Freedom in Early African American Culture*. New York: New York University Press, 2017.

Scholes, Theophilus E.S. *The British Empire and Alliances; or, Britain's Duty to Her Colonies and Subject Races*. London: Elliot Stock, 1899.

Sexton, Jay. *The Monroe Doctrine: Empire and Nation in Nineteenth-Century America*. New York: Hill and Wang, 2011.

_____. 'Towards a Synthesis of Foreign Relations in the Civil War Era, 1848–77', *American Nineteenth Century History* 5(3) (2004), 50–73.

Silkey, Sarah L. *Black Woman Reformer: Ida B. Wells Lynching, and Transatlantic Activism*. Athens: University of Georgia Press, 2015.

Sinha, Manisha. *The Slave's Cause: A History of Abolition*. New Haven, CT: Yale University Press, 2016.

Sklar, Kathryn Kish, and James Brewer Stewart (eds). *Women's Rights and Transatlantic Antislavery in the Era of Emancipation*. New Haven, CT: Yale University Press, 2007.

Smith, Goldwin. 'Imperialism in the United States', *Contemporary Review* 75 (May 1899), 620–28.

Spender, Harold. *A Briton in America*. London: William Heinemann, 1921.

Tamarkin, Eliza. *Anglophilia: Deference, Devotion, and Antebellum America*. Chicago: University of Chicago Press, 2008.

Taylor, Alan. *American Revolutions: A Continental History, 1750–1804*. New York: W.W. Norton, 2016.

Taylor, Clare. *British and American Abolitionists: An Episode in Transatlantic Understanding*. Edinburgh: Edinburgh University Press, 1974.

Thistlethwaite, Frank. *America and the Atlantic Community: Anglo-American Aspects, 1790–1850*. New York: Harper & Row, 1959.

Tufnell, Stephen. '"Uncle Sam Is to Be Sacrificed": Anglophobia in Late Nineteenth-Century Politics and Culture', *American Nineteenth Century History* 12(1) (2011), 77–99.

Turley, David. *The Culture of English Antislavery, 1770–1860*. London: Routledge, 1991.

Walvin, James. *Making the Black Atlantic: Britain and the African Diaspora*. London: Cassell, 2000.

Waters, Hazel. *Racism on the Victorian Stage: Representations of Slavery and the Black Character*. Cambridge: Cambridge University Press, 2007.

Weeks, William Earl. *The New Cambridge History of American Foreign Relations, Volume 1: Dimensions of the Early American Empire, 1754–1865*. Cambridge: Cambridge University Press, 2013.

Wells, Jonathan Daniel. 'Charles Dickens, the American South, and the Transatlantic Debate over Slavery', *Slavery & Abolition* 36(1) (2015), 1–25.

Wood, Gordon S. *The Radicalism of the American Revolution*. New York: Alfred A. Knopf, 1992.

Yokota, Kariann. *Unbecoming British: How Revolutionary America Became a Postcolonial Nation*. Oxford: Oxford University Press, 2011.

Zaeske, Susan. *Signatures of Citizenship: Petitioning, Antislavery, and Women's Political Identity*. Chapel Hill: University of North Carolina Press, 2003.

Chapter 6

The US Postcolonial e/Empire
The Case of the Missing Upper Case
David Ryan

Introduction

The United States is a postcolonial empire. Its hybrid identity facilitated opportunity. It moved from colonial liberation to border colonization. Later, it colonized territory overseas and simultaneously advanced ideologies of self-determination, famously captured in keystone documents that hold a traditional narrative arc together: the Declaration of Independence, the Monroe Doctrine, Woodrow Wilson's Fourteen Points, the Atlantic Charter. It abjured colonialism but maintains overseas colonies. The July 2019 edition of the influential journal *Foreign Affairs* contains an article on 'America's Forgotten Colony: Ending Puerto Rico's Perpetual Crisis'.[1] *Expansionism*, as a descriptor, satisfied both US imperialists and anti-imperialists in their struggle over the Philippines. Howard Zinn characterized the term as 'a more sophisticated approach to imperialism than the traditional empire building of Europe'; it accrued the benefits while avoiding the stigma and the costs.[2] The Open Door notes, economic integration and, ultimately, globalization also facilitated US opportunity. Washington occupied Nicaragua, Santo Domingo and Haiti for years without declaring their colonial status; Cuba also had an ambivalent status from 1902 to 1934. At one level, the United States can be considered an 'incoherent'[3] empire. At another level, its experience parallels that of the British. Empires 'build on the structures and policies of their predecessors', Maya Jasanoff argues; many of its doctrinal and institutional traditions derive from the British.[4] The British practised informal empire associated with 'free' trade; London engaged in formal empire, upon which the sun never set. It exercised hegemony and dominated sea routes and markets. Like the flow tide, its political, economic and cultural reach extended to various 'blank spaces'. In the nineteenth century, both empires flowed in different regions; the British tide began to ebb in the twentieth century and the United States began to ebb more obviously in the twenty-first.

The United States is 'post-colonial' with a hyphen to signify its emergence out of a colonial system, freed from the British with Thomas Jefferson's magnanimous gestures at independence, on life, liberty and the pursuit of happiness. Governments were only just if based on the consent of the governed. The American War of Independence separated the colonies from the metropole; yet, like many post-colonial nations, the US economy remained dependent on Britain, with which its culture and language maintained an affiliation.

The United States is postcolonial without a hyphen to signify that it spent a lot of its discursive energies talking back to the British. Its 1776 identity pivoted on its famous declaration, which required a break from the past, a new history and a factitious past, stressing continuity with older ideals and 'invented traditions'[5] that informed a disparate population of who they were. They 'monumentalised' the revolution and the Founding Fathers,[6] reducing the meta-narrative of US history to a benign story of US exceptionalism.

History produces a multitude of narratives. Yet the reductive process of historiography privileges accounts that speaks to us, 'while ignoring or marginalizing … the greater number of' stories[7] that eventually produce more varied histories from below and elsewhere, social and cultural histories, oral and 'people's' histories. National histories practise exclusion and exception.[8] Like most empires, US history occluded the voices of others: Native Americans, African-Americans, women, Central Americans, Cubans, Filipinos, Vietnamese and others until comparatively recently – just as the traditional British histories largely ignored postcolonial narratives before the 1970s.

Such practices were essential to their respective identities, the probity of their authority, their parochial legitimacy. Initially, US identity was constructed against the British and European 'other', yet eventually its strategic interests and alliances fused them together in the benign language of the 'special relationship',[9] the West[10] and empires 'by invitation' or 'integration'.[11] The depth of collaborative thinking is depicted well in Or Rosenboim's *The Emergence of Globalism: Visions of World Order in Britain and The United States, 1939–1950*,[12] which also considers the intersection of the ebb and flow of empires.

Even my laptop is in on the act: when I type 'the American empire' (lower case), I am allowed to proceed unimpeded by distraction or correction. When I type 'the British empire', the grammar check immediately suggests I capitalize the word 'Empire'. The assumption, presumably in the programming and replicated in much historiography, is that one is a formal proper noun, the other informal, less definite, fluid, – unworthy of being a 'proper' noun.

The question of American empire is a recurrent debate, rising with and retracting after periods of colonization and military intervention, particularly in the 1890s, 1920s, 1960s and after 2003. Proponents and opponents square off with pens, typewriters and laptops, to advocate or deny; too often, US identity and its exceptional history are contrasted with a stable set of assumptions regarding the British Empire. The possession of direct formal colonies is contrasted with the loose 'informal' traits of empire, as though the British had not also engaged in such economic practices.

So this chapter deals with the traditions and definitions of empire, without attempting to fix it in a 'formulated phrase', but rather arguing that the perspective from which the case is made is crucial to understanding the representation of e/Empire, and the identity of the United States and Britain as empires. It considers representation, practice, identity and historiography, stressing the variety of empire that both have engaged. My argument is that despite the differences advanced in the historiography and various other forms of knowledge production, there are also a multitude of similarities that are frequently elided in the two empires' identity struggles and the stories they tell about themselves. The variety of interpretation is crucial and when the two e/Empires are provincialized, the contrast is less stark. As Dominique Eddé writes of Edward Said's method, 'What is the knowledge that "authorises" domination or the power of one people over another, one vision over another? What other knowledge can be used to dismantle the conclusions of the first?'[13]

The intrepid reporter Tintin travels through a critique of imperialism in one of his adventures set in 1930s Shanghai. The Japanese have invaded, the secondary protagonists are the British, the Americans; the scene illustrates an evolving relationship. The cartoonist Hergé, who later became controversial, depicted all nationalities in stereotypes, essential signs of national identities. There is a sequence in *The Blue Lotus* soon after Tintin arrives in Shanghai after having travelled through India, where he was the guest of the Maharaja of Gaipajama. Tintin's rickshaw puller runs into a larger-than-life American: Gibbons. Gibbons assaults the rickshaw runner in front of a poster in vernacular script that reads 'Down with Imperialism'. After Tintin intervenes, Gibbons retreats to the Occidental Private Club, where he is greeted by two old English hands: 'You look peeved old chap!' states the elderly, white-haired gentleman from behind a bucket of ice and a soda fountain. Gibbons relates his outrage at a European boy trying to stop him 'beating a native ... Intolerable!' In conspiratorial fury, he asks: 'What's the world coming to? ... It's up to us to civilise the savages! We soon won't have any control at all ... and look what we've done for them, all the benefits ... [next frame] of our superb western civilisation ... [next frame, in which he smashes the oncoming waiter's tray before releasing his rage], Yes, our superb western civilization.'[14] Here, in a few frames, are the discourses on imperialism and resistance, on domestic dissent, on civilization and savagery, on orientalism and occidentalism and, at least in this context, the shared experiences of 'the West'. Paul A. Kramer argues that American officials circulated widely 'in the British colonial world', watching closely, following developments and learning.[15] There is an implication of continuity in British and American objectives and outlooks, if not formal ideologies, which is reflected in early twenty-first-century historiography.[16]

As time and tide wore on, the definition of empire not only broadened; no longer territorial or political, empires also operated in the economic, cultural, ideological and intellectual domains. Postcolonial authors admonished others to 'decolonise' their minds.[17] Empire existed in diverse and various forms,[18] from colonies to plantations, from settlements to trading ports, strategic nodes and military forts. The US and British empires assumed different forms at different times and in different places. This variety problematized exceptional histories and complicated the certitude of the lines of inquiry and argument pursued by historians bent on discovering the patterns of the past.

In 1988, when Lloyd Gardner delivered his presidential address to the Society for Historians of American Foreign Relations, he observed that the 'past is unpredictable'. Americans were having it out over the decline of an empire they had 'never previously acknowledged'. Citing Thomas Flanagan's *The Tenants of Time*, he likened the past to a kaleidoscope; a simple turn can upset the beautiful arrangement of colours. One character explains: 'What matters is that there can never not be a pattern. Kaleidoscopes and historians are patternmakers.'[19] Narrative arcs were delineated in texts, reduced and reproduced in historiography, yet variety was essential to the longevity and endurance of empire, which assumed one form here but not there, now but not then. Adaptability in the 'search for opportunity'[20] is one of several common features of the US and British experiences.

The 1776–83 British loss of America 'was the prelude to a colossal expansion of [British] scale and ambition'. It pushed London to rethink empire on a global scale, sometimes with lower defence costs. Maritime primacy, a Pacific power, Australian settlement and opportunities in China were vigorously established. Variety persisted as a result of conquest, as in India; the dominions, as in Canada and Australia; and the empire of free trade. In 1985, when Rajiv Gandhi, the late Indian prime minister, addressed the US Congress, he made the link between the American Revolution and the Indian colonial experience: British Army General, Charles Cornwallis moved from Yorktown to Bengal, and later Ireland. When Gandhi alluded to the Boston Tea Party, he got it wrong; that tea was from China not India.[21] For John Darwin, the versatility of the British empire is its hallmark; versatility in 'method, outlook and object'.[22]

It is not just a case of apples and oranges. If the British and American empires are to be considered, the metaphor needs to be elaborated upon to capture the two empires' variety in time and space. Grapes and bananas might be added to the fruit baskets. Some small, others large; some ripening, others blossoming; some rotting, others just plain rotten. 'Provincial' narratives add to the mix. Walter LaFeber writes that the United States competed with Europeans, that they were vulnerable to similar demands and corruptions; 'that they appeared, with good reason, to Filipinos, Cubans, Chinese, and Central Americans as little different than other imperialists was true as well'.[23] The hand that turns the kaleidoscope determines the pattern.

Traditions, Definitions, Paradigms

Ernest Gellner, modifying Thomas Hobbes, observed that the life of ideas is nasty, brutish and short, unless saved by a paradigm.[24] In turn, paradigms risk becoming 'regimes of truth' that constrain interpretation. Postcolonialism took aim at traditional paradigms of empire to recover from the past what had not been written.[25] Even though dissent was always present, Said, following Nietzsche and Foucault, argued that knowledge was a product of power and authors like Ranajit Guha and Partha Chatterjee argued that extant history was a product of imperialism.[26]

Exploration 'is a knowledge-producing enterprise'. It is undertaken for a variety of different reasons: to search for resources, to acquire territory, to advance trade, to secure missionary conversions and so forth. In Dane Kennedy's *The Last Blank Spaces* (2013), he notes the 'irreconcilable tension between exploration as experience and exploration as epistemology'.[27] The struggle over definitions is a struggle over interpretation and identity, attempts to consolidate positions in the historiography. Empire 'is a term so variable in its meanings that its value as a conceptual category is contingent on the adoption of a comparative frame of reference'.[28] Decentred narratives augment comparison by challenging previous exceptional arguments. Yet, at times, postcolonial narratives also essential-*ized* empire and the 'West'.[29]

The problems of location are accentuated by scope. In US historiography, 'those most reluctant to acknowledge the existence of an American empire have defined imperialism narrowly'. They have equated it with colonialism; it is limited to a few places and times. 'By contrast', Joseph A. Fry contends, 'those historians most disturbed by US actions abroad have defined imperialism more broadly'.[30] John Gallagher and Ronald Robinson famously described the methodological problem in 1953:

> The imperial historian … is very much at the mercy of his own particular concept of empire. By that, he decides what facts are of 'imperial' significance; his data are

limited in the same way as his concept, and his final interpretation itself depends largely upon the scope of his hypothesis. Different hypotheses have led to conflicting conclusions. Since imperial historians are writing about different empires and since they are generalizing from eccentric or isolated aspects of them, it is hardly surprising that these historians sometimes contradict each other.[31]

The paradigm is intended to provide ideational longevity; it is itself set within a temporal and spatial context, just as concepts such as empire, imperialism and colonialism are understood in time and vary according to cultural expectations and intellectual objectives. Historiography changes as the relationships between *place, procedure* (discipline or methodology) and *text* develop.[32] Temporal context is vital. The impact of postcolonialism, 'with its strange language and theoretical promiscuity',[33] has forced traditionalists to reconsider and sometimes revise.

Definitions are important, but our cultural and academic understandings of the term 'empire' and its cousins 'imperialism', 'colonialism', 'hegemony', 'conquest' and 'globalization' evolve. Crucially, the changing world order provides different opportunities, which give rise to 'semantic differences' and sometimes fixed assertions: 'Britain built an empire; the United States sought hegemony.'[34] US ideologies of self-determination precluded admissions of empire. The United States decentred the narrative and then rowed against the tide of its imperialism in the context of decolonization.

The crucial point is that the British and American empires varied across time and space; thus, broad conceptions of the term 'empire' capture the wide-ranging experiences it encompasses. The discourses on empire relate to where and by whom they are produced. They cannot be reduced to stable characteristics that remain fixed over time. The United States and Britain were not the same, but both practised similar conceptual forms of empire. Like many other empires, both the United States and Britain had justificatory ideologies, pursued their own sectoral interests, pursued opportunity, extended some benefits, imposed brutal repression, invited resistance, revolution and the search for independence, and would ultimately face a range of narratives 'from below' and revisionist histories from within. Both still measure distances in miles.

Definitions abound. Michael Doyle's *Empires* (1986) and Herfried Münkler's *Empires* (2007) are influential.[35] Doyle sees empire as 'a relationship, formal or informal, in which one state controls the effective political sovereignty of another political society. It can be achieved by force, by political collaboration, by economic, social, or cultural dependence. Imperialism is simply the process or policy of establishing or maintaining an empire.'[36] Though we might fix the term 'in a formulated phrase', it would still be 'sprawling on a pin' and 'wriggling on the wall', like T.S. Eliot's struggle with definition, character, purpose and identity.[37] Empire, as a term, 'frays at the edges', A.G. Hopkins writes, because empires 'have changed their structure and their function'.[38] Historicists insist that 'extra-temporal metaphysical principles' are tempered by the particular and the local.[39]

Paradigms aside, we also need safety nets for the life of ideas, historical experience and the particular. Darwin writes that to 'follow the action, we must see it in slow motion: breaking it down into components and phases; digging out the ideas that made empire seem "reasonable"; tracing the methods on which empire rulers relied; explaining the grievances that led to revolt; tracking the means by which revolt was usually suppressed'.[40] Sensitivity to historiographical evolution and an understanding of why and how our knowledge changed over time, from metropolitan perspectives to the *World Histories from Below*, are essential.[41]

If there must be an overarching definition, Charles S. Maier proposes: 'Empires are contests for the control of human resources that are fought out on the micro and macro levels simultaneously.'[42] Such scope facilitates wide understanding. Hopkins suggests that 'in the most general terms, an empire is a species of the genus expansion'. States might expand without being imperial; he argues that 'imperialism … expresses an intention to dominate other states or peoples'.[43]

After September 2001 and the 2003 US invasion of Iraq, Maier revisited the question of US empire. In the polarized debate, he avoided a definitive label; some traits were there, 'but not all'.[44] Maier writes: 'An empire … is not just a state that subjugates other peoples or states. It is not just a "superstate" or a large component of the state system. It is a system of rule that transforms society at home even as it stabilizes inequality transnationally by replicating it geographically, in the core and on the periphery.' It is believed to 'expand its control by conquest or coercion, and, second, to control the political loyalty of the territories it subjugates'. These lands may be ruled directly or through 'compliant native leaders'. And so the United States is not a complete empire because it does not fulfil the criterion of 'expansion by conquest – so long as the history of continental expansion is whited out from the record'. The facile separation of contiguous and overseas empire frequently rescues US identity. Maier recounts that the Native American was repeatedly dispossessed, but writes that Americans 'do not usually envisage the absorption of North American territory as part of an imperial program'.[45] Even if US Founders conceived a US empire,[46] characterized benignly, it is not a common feature of traditional textbooks.

The relationship between power and knowledge, between feeling and impression, is important. In recent decades, revisionist histories have been joined by more admiring studies; after 9/11, both strands have advanced their theses.

Revisionists, including William Appleman Williams, LaFeber and Lloyd C. Gardner, advanced arguments regarding US empire from the 1950s.[47] More recently, admiring studies of empire include Niall Ferguson's *Empire* (2003) and *Colossus* (2004), which urges the United States to come to terms with its identity and its 'responsibilities'.[48] Others have seen empire in the discourse on 'humanitarian intervention' and in the 'war on terror'.[49] Certainly the Iraq war rejuvenated the empire debate[50] *and* also revived interest in the British Empire.[51]

Britain and the United States have practised many forms of empire. Amongst other places, the British colonized the eastern seaboard of the Americas; the United States expanded through border colonization across the continent.[52] Formal empire was practised in India and the Philippines. Informal empire preceded the formal with the East India Tea Company, while informal empire post-dated the US decolonization of the Philippines. When the Philippines was decolonized in 1946, it was 'the *only* colony of all America's unincorporated territories to receive independence'.[53] 'Dollar Diplomacy' was more effective. Republicans and Democrats considered empire a political liability; Washington ended the occupation of the Dominican Republic in 1924, Nicaragua in 1933 and Haiti in 1934. Congress was uninterested in 'populations that could not vote'; US racism and fear of competition contributed to the momentum.[54] The Depression prompted President Franklin D. Roosevelt to 'liberate' the Philippines, thereby jettisoning agricultural competition. FDR was blunt: 'Let's get rid of the Philippines; that's the most important thing. Let's be frank about it.' One historian observed that Washington wanted 'independence *from* the Philippines'.[55]

Informal empire was practised by Britain and the United States in Latin America at different times.[56] Hegemony and the ability to shape the world order and write the 'rules of the game' were common objectives.[57] Economic integration with unequal terms of trade was practised after decolonization.[58] The Bush doctrine echoes that of Theodore Roosevelt, which in turn parallels the Blair doctrine. Breaking from Westphalia, all insisted that governments could be held responsible for conditions within their borders; sovereignty was conditional: 'governments that fail to act like respectable, law-abiding states will lose their sovereignty'.[59] Theodore Roosevelt wanted stability, order and prosperity: 'if a nation shows that it knows how to act with reasonable efficiency and decency in social and political matters, if it keeps order and pays its obligations, it need fear no interference from the United States.' But the United States might 'reluctantly, in flagrant cases of wrongdoing or impotence, [resort] to the exercise of an international police power'.[60]

Such evolution is obvious in Kennedy's *The Imperial History Wars* (2018),[61] Julian Go's *Patterns of Empire* (2011)[62] and Ray Kiely's *Rethinking Imperialism*

(2010).[63] There are still exceptionalists who insist on the unique attributes of the British Empire and its enduring qualities. There are exceptionalists in the United States who insist that their version of empire is quite unique. There are the traditional US exceptionalists who deny empire. The debate will persist.

Representation

US postcolonialism and historical disruption are central to US identity. The Declaration of Independence and the Monroe Doctrine, a 'diplomatic declaration of independence', assisted conceptual separation and US exceptionalism.[64] Both contributed to a reductive narrative. Kennedy observes that the 'enduring belief among Americans that their country's heritage and ambitions are inimical to empire and imperialism has sustained an exceptionalist view of American history that resists comparative considerations of the consequences of global power'.[65] Bernard Porter adds that 'America was at least *as* imperialist as Britain throughout her history as a nation – from the very time, ... when they split apart – despite her obstinate insistence for much of that period that she was not imperialist at all, by *contrast* with Britain'. Comparatively speaking, the United States was quite ordinary.[66]

Differences are sustained by three factors. First, the persistent depth of US exceptionalism. Second, a fundamental misunderstanding of British imperialism. The third factor relates to semantics, between formal and informal, contiguous and overseas territories. Such views, Porter argues, are not logical or historical: why should a stretch of water make a difference? The Roman Empire was contiguous. In the 1940s, the distinction was known as the 'salt water fallacy'. The United States is only different 'if you insist you have to get there by boat'.[67] A map of an empire with distributed territories looks like what one might expect an empire to look like; the US landmass looks like a nation. Its informal empire is not shaded on a map.[68]

US commentators sometimes described the United States as a benevolent empire; the imputation was that the British did not hold this view of their empire. Such US views are postcolonial and share, at least in terms of theme and target, some attributes of contemporary postcolonial discourse. But mostly US discourse denied claims to empire. It is problematic, as Kramer argues, to adopt the 'historical actors' categories as his [the historian's] own'.[69] Yet Marilyn B. Young also contends that 'policy-makers and, in large measure, the American public, live deeply inside an exceptionalist ideology that has retroactively shaped the material world the historians interpret'.[70] Their isolated histories define their own terms of debate and, as Said observes, 'the rhetoric of power all too easily produces an illusion of benevolence when deployed in an imperial setting'.[71] There is little doubt that US imperialists believed in their own good works, but that does not mean they were justified.[72] Terrible atrocities have been committed throughout US history, culminating in Iraq and other wars, but regrets and apology are rare. US denial of empire persisted even as it deepened its engagement. Denial advanced in the twentieth century, after the 'aberration' of the post-1898 years, especially as Wilsonian, Leninist and other rhetoric promised world orders based on self-determination. Empire acquired a pejorative status as independence movements advanced their cause against the British. Native American resistance lost power in the nineteenth century.[73]

The United States expanded rapidly, acquiring territory from a variety of Native American nations and from Spain, France, Mexico and Russia, after settling with the British. The process is comparable to the 'settler expansion' and 'border colonization' of South Africa, Canada, Australia and New Zealand or Russia and China.[74] The Northwest Ordinance of 1787 set out stages leading to statehood: governors were appointed, legislatures created after white populations reached five thousand, constitutions written and approved by Congress. California and New Mexico were run by military governors. Go concludes, 'In sum, the territorial system entailed a colonial structure very much akin to Britain's overseas empire.'[75] The United States fought much weaker forces in the south: the Mexicans in the middle of the nineteenth century, the Spanish at the end.[76] In the north, the British contained the United States at the 49th parallel, the Canadian border. There was violent resistance from the outset; for a time, inhabitants remained 'subjects' of US sovereignty. When citizenship was conferred, it was to the white population, not African or Native Americans.[77]

Woodrow Wilson and Franklin D. Roosevelt, in seminal US documents on self-determination and the stated purpose of US foreign policy, such as the Fourteen Points and Atlantic Charter, which cultivated separate identities to distance European empires, advanced strategic intent based on sentiment and selective history. Such identity, even as 'the Western alliance' was solidified, was indispensable given the Soviet challenge and struggles for national self-determination. The documents signalled the promotion of free trade and opposition to empire.[78] The United States offered inspiration for some and legacies of disappointment for others as it compromised on self-determination. Even as the United States set out its anti-imperial stall, there was considerable accommodation with the British Empire and British socialism after the Second World War.

Despite ideological differences, a shared imperial experience played a role in the Great Rapprochement of the early twentieth century. The US–Spanish–Cuban–Filipino and the Boer wars had an impact. The wider understanding of imperialism and informal empires in China and Latin America also signalled shared objectives. Bradford Perkins writes: 'Looming over all these things lay doctrines which very often suggested the superior virtue of the Anglo-Saxon and in other ways indicated the similarity and common interests of the two peoples.' Imperialism was in fashion in metropolitan centres, augmented by narratives of civilization.[79] Later still, the transatlantic Anglophone relationship and deepening levels of strategic co-operation led to the relationship being referred to as the 'special relationship'.[80] The Blair–Bush relationship and operations from Kosovo to Iraq exhibit similar yet distinct inclinations.[81]

Until recently, the historiographies of empire spoke of difference and exceptionalism; history contributes to the assertion of sovereignty as nation-states materialize.[82] Obviously national histories developed in powerful milieus of cultural production.[83] Said observes: 'The power to narrate, or to block other narratives from forming and emerging, is very important to culture and imperialism, and constitutes one of the main connections between them.'[84] Joyce Appleby, Jill Lepore and David Thelen emphasize the relationship between history and national identity. Lepore writes that 'often, histories of nation-states are little more than myths that hide the seams that stitch the nation to the state'. Born in contradiction, Americans 'will forever fight over the meaning of its history'. She recalls that the big histories of George Bancroft, who also served as US Secretary of War, were closely associated with 'manifest destinies'.[85] The processes of territorial colonization and epistemology intermingled.

The 'Empire of Liberty', in early American discourse, was a self-referential contrast to the British Empire, which, according to the US Declaration of Independence, operated a 'tyranny over these States'.[86] The frame remains pertinent in contemporary history in David Reynolds's *America, Empire of Liberty* (2009).[87] In the foreword to *The United States and Decolonization* (2000), Warren Kimball wrote: '*Colonialism*. The word brings an automatic frown and shake of the head among Americans. Historical memory is part of what nations are all about, and a visceral dislike of colonialism is part of the American self-image.'[88] Kimball identified a popular US belief regarding its identity and a popular propensity to elide aspects of US history.

Despite significant undercurrents of dissent from Jonathan Swift to J.A. Hobson and Richard Cobden, from Charles Beard to William Appleman Williams and the Wisconsin School, British imperial history was closely associated with the Foreign and Commonwealth Office. In the United States, Hopkins writes, 'much of this literature remains consistent with the national epic in emphasizing the need to defend and then spread the benefits of political and economic freedom. When the demands of the Cold War called, academia responded by demonstrating that it was not lacking in patriotism.'[89] Nationalism informed 'basic working premises'.[90] Both in academia and popular culture, there has been 'a tendency to remove the United States from the domain of the international'. American history is landlocked and 'here', as opposed to the international, which is 'over there'. American history has been provincialized rather than integrated; it has been isolated rather than internationalized.[91] Kramer connected the history of US empire with that of its European rivals and exemplars. The links were 'dense and complex', he writes in relation to naval rivalry, economic competition and wresting 'geopolitical spheres of influence. At the same time, Americans continued to turn to European precedents for guidance and inspiration.'[92] Senator Albert Beveridge drew the lines between the United States and British directly. Kramer cites him: 'The American cause was nothing less than that of the "English-speaking and Teutonic peoples" whom God had prepared for "a thousand years" to become "the master organizers of the world," possessors of what he had called, in the 1898 address, "the blood of government".'[93]

Later, policymakers emphasized difference, especially on the eve of decolonization in the 1950s. President Dwight D. Eisenhower's National Security Council considered the US dilemma. The resulting policy document (NSC 5719) illustrated the conundrum:

> Premature independence would be as harmful to our interests in Africa as would be a continuation of nineteenth century colonialism, and we must tailor our policies to the capabilities and needs of each particular area as well as to our over-all relations with the metropolitan power concerned. It should be noted that all the metropolitan powers are associated with us in the NATO alliance or in military base agreements.

In the policy guidance section, the document suggested that Washington support the principle of self-determination, but stressed 'responsibilities'. Moreover, it stated that care should be taken to 'avoid U.S. identification with those policies of the metropolitan powers, which are stagnant or repressive, and, to the extent practicable, seek effective means of influencing the metropolitan powers to abandon or modify such policies'. And, for good measure, it was recommended that Washington 'emphasize through all appropriate media the colonial policies of the Soviet Union and particularly the fact that the Soviet colonial empire has continued to expand throughout the period when Western colonialism has been contracting'.[94]

The rhetorical distancing not only relied on collective memory and the 'imagined community', but was also imperative to US Cold War strategy. Set against Moscow, the West offered coherence; viewed from 'the South', the 'West' was ambiguous, 'not quite one thing, not quite the other'.[95] At the higher orders of alterity, the West stood for freedom, in contrast to the Soviets. At another level, the West encompassed imperialism, both British and US.[96] For David Gress, narratives of Western cohesion can only be sustained at the highest levels of abstraction, given that empire and self-determination are conceptually conflicted.[97] FDR liked to loathe empire, yet his affinity with Winston Churchill, who famously indicated, 'I have not become the King's First Minister in order to preside over the liquidation of the British Empire', complicated his position.[98]

The post-war colonial world was vital to the United States even as it advanced narratives of freedom and self-determination. Robert E. Wood argues that 'the European Recovery Program was not simply about either Europe or recovery; it was much more ambitious than that'.[99] It was about a vision of an integrated world that saw a cohesion in the transatlantic relationship, integrated with the economies and materials from around the colonial world, both formal and informal.[100] Decolonization facilitated the preservation of economic ties and the ability to maintain military bases and intelligence assets. Local forces were trained, order was fought for and the informal ties kept the former colony 'in the system'. But there were no flags, no formal control, no assertions of power through symbolic parades. Kimball concludes: 'As Vietnam and Iran demonstrated, that path had its dangers. As the collapse of the Cold War demonstrated, that path had its successes.'[101] Earlier British free traders 'believed, the empire of rule, on display in India, was wasteful and violent, a saga of futile belligerence as an obsolete aristocracy clung to power'.[102] But when 'free trade liberalism' went awry, the British stepped up the process of formal colonization, whereas Washington resorted to frequent military intervention. In both cases, the prospect of withdrawal implied the abandonment of a significant investment that they had already made and 'none of the powers ... seriously considered such a response to the first signs of resistance or instability'.[103]

Echoing Gallagher and Robinson's intervention, which complicated the discourse on empire, in recent decades concepts such as 'globalization', 'humanitarian intervention' and 'soft power' have also complicated the debate.[104] Jackson Lears suggests that 'Apologists for empire acknowledged the importance of foreign investment opportunities, raw materials, and markets, but more commonly they traded in euphemisms masquerading as concepts – destiny, responsibility, civilization, progress – the ancestors of such contemporary banalities as "globalization"'. Such thinking arose from the providentially decreed belief that America should regenerate the world and that the world wanted such regeneration.[105]

Mapping and Identity

Visual depiction enhances differences in identity. Gallagher and Robinson noted that for 'purposes of economic analysis it would clearly be unreal to define imperial history exclusively as the history of those colonies coloured red on the map'.[106] In comparative terms, the contrast is stark. A small island, Britain, and all the red spaces, set against a blue United States, with the Philippines and a few other dots. Besides, the continental United States elides imperial identity. It is coloured blue, but it is axiomatically assumed to be a natural state, not a representation of border colonization, conquest, repression and removal. The uniform shading is filled with histories of 'manifest destiny'.

The British Empire, starting in London, crossed the Atlantic to encompass Canada, even if it lost the thirteen colonies on the eastern shore of what we now call the United States. The shading did not cover the informal empire the British had established in large swathes of Latin America. From Vancouver, it took off again, extending to Hong Kong, Malaya, Singapore, up into the subcontinent of India and across that ocean to vast swathes of East Africa and other spaces. Though formally subject to the League of Nations, after the First World War Britain effectively ruled Tanganyika, Palestine and Iraq. And the Anglo-Persian agreement of 1919 undermined Iranian sovereignty, which deeply upset the nationalist and future prime minister of Iran, Mohammad Mossadegh, then sequestered in Switzerland.[107] The romance of empire remains in literature; territorial remnants are represented in books like Tristram Hunt's *Ten Cities that Made an Empire* (2014), spanning vignette histories of Boston, Bridgetown, Dublin, Cape Town, Calcutta, Hong Kong, Bombay, Melbourne, New Delhi and Liverpool.[108]

Comparatively speaking, the map of the US empire was limited: the continental empire had disappeared in the narratives of 'manifest destiny'; there was Cuba, Guam, Samoa, the Philippines and Hawaii, but some of these had been returned, some incorporated, some considered so insignificant that they did not merit sustained attention. The Philippines was explained away by reference to a 'psychic crisis' and the Teller Amendment (1898) prohibited the acquisition of further territory; Cuban sugar competed with that of Colorado, from where Henry Teller originated. As Benedict Anderson has so influentially demonstrated, the icon of the nation was captured in a variety of forms, the logo map being amongst the most important.[109] Our visual knowledge reinforces limited conceptions of US empire set against the cartographic swathes of British red.

'Maps have been the weapons of imperialism' as much as warships or guns, J.B. Harley maintains. They were used for colonial promotion; they staked out and claimed territory on paper before the ground was settled; and the 'blank spaces' reinforced notions of 'terra nullius' – 'maps anticipated empire'. They reinforced narratives of territorial status and legitimacy and buttressed official rhetoric, histories and popular songs in defence of empire. They affirmed understanding. For Harley, 'Maps may be read as texts of power-knowledge no less than other fabricated systems of signs.'[110] The map-maker approached a complex reality and produced an 'artificially simplified world. The images which made the esoteric exoteric carried the potential to constrain the way people thought and acted.'[111] When Said's 'imaginative geographies' are combined with binary categories, the West and the Orient, us and them, the Other, the shaded areas are 'imbued with contrasting cultural meanings and political significance, making them discursive repositories of imperial efforts to exert power'.[112] Such images advance forgetting by enhancing a stable identity on the basis of a disparate history.[113]

Visually, the British Empire was clearly just that: an empire. Famously, George Macartney's observation became a celebration of its reach: 'A vast empire on which the sun never sets.'[114] In 1898, as the United States acquired the Philippines, the *World* carried a graphic: 'The Sun This Day Does Not Set on Uncle Sam's Domain'; the subheading read: 'Before his sunset, light, fails, the Philippines; Maine glories in the dawn.'[115] Yet the inclination to depict the United States as such disappeared over the twentieth century as US identity was stiffened with Cold War resolve and unbroken narratives from 1776 to 1989. Moreover, Spanish America and the consciousness of the part it played in making the United States disappeared. In his address to the American Historical Association in 1932, Herbert Bolton implored the audience to think in terms of hemispheric history and recognize the role of the Spanish, but his plea fell on deaf ears. The narrative of Puritan settlers not only diminished the Jamestown settlement, but 'left little space' for Spanish settlement in California, Florida, New Mexico, much of which was colonized after the Mexican–American War of 1846–48, and extensions north into what is now Washington, Oregon, Colorado, Utah and Arizona. The Hispanic populations of these areas, by 2015 some fifty-seven million, which accounted for some 54 per cent of total US population growth from 2000 to 2014, will in due course 'need to be better acquainted with the realities of that story'.[116]

Beyond the unity of the logo map, there was, for a half-century, the Philippines and a few dots around the Pacific, strategically necessary, beyond explanation, unresolved. Described by Daniel Immerwahr as the pointillism empire, by 1945, 'the United States had the fifth-largest colonial empire in the world, containing nearly twenty million people'.[117] Puerto Rico's status bedevils its identity. In terms of territoriality, Go argues that 'the United States is probably the *only* colonial empire that has *not* decolonized'.[118]

Practice and Perception

On the question of empire, identity rarely accords with other perceptions. In 1927, Walter Lippmann advanced an ironic observation in his *Men of Destiny*:

> All the world thinks of the United States today as an empire, except the people of the United States. We shrink from the word 'empire', and insist that it should not be used to describe the domination we exercise from Alaska to the Philippines, from Cuba to Panama, and beyond. We feel that there ought to be some other name for the civilizing work which we do so reluctantly in these backward countries ... We have learned to think of empires as troublesome and as immoral, and to admit that we have an empire still seems to most Americans like admitting that they have gone out into a wicked world and there lost their political chastity.

*   *   *

> Foreigners pay little attention to what we say. They observe what we do. We on the other hand think of what we feel. And the result is that we go on creating what mankind calls an empire while we continue to believe quite sincerely that it is not an empire because it does not feel to us the way we imagine an empire ought to feel.[119]

Recent comparative historiography limits US claims to exceptionalism and casts lines of continuity between the empires. Porter's *Empire and Superempire* (2006) stresses similarities.[120] Go's *Patterns of Empire* (2011) focuses on the repetition of forms, practices, policies and ideologies.[121] Hopkins's *American Empire* (2018) situates the US experience in a 'global perspective', concentrating on shared trajectories in different temporal frames. His aim is not to 'put the United States down, but rather to put it in – to the mainstream of Western history'.[122] Kennedy's *Imperial History Wars* (2018) delineates the schools of thought on the British Empire, drawing the United States into the evolving story, endorsing Go, albeit departing on US decline.[123] When the variation in the British experience is considered, from Ireland, America, Australia, Canada, India, Jamaica, Egypt, South and East Africa, and the Falklands to Hong Kong, it becomes difficult to contrive a fixed understanding of empire.[124] In any case study, interpretive difference remains; contrast Darwin's *Unfinished Empire* (2012) with Shashi Tharoor's *Inglorious Empire* (2017).[125]

Conceptually, both the United States and Britain engaged in various forms of empire; they exhibited forms of colonialism, imperialism, conquest and hegemony and advanced ideologies and 'visions' of greatness. Yet no single vision lay behind the idea of empire. For Britain, Darwin writes, 'there was agreement on one thing: that the point of expansion was to make England richer'.[126] Both believed in hierarchies of race; Americans were deeply influenced by Anglo-Saxonism, believing that they were a 'people united by uncommon qualities and common interests'. The United States moved in the nineteenth century to 'claim their pride of place in a trans-Atlantic community of English speaking people'. The memories of the 'fratricidal' War of Independence was dimmed. School textbooks celebrated transatlantic ties, as captured in the poem 'America and Britons' from the 1830s: 'The voice of blood shall reach, / More audibly than speech, / We are one.' Both feared instability, rebellion and revolution.[127]

When the UN Charter rejected colonialism in favour of sovereign states, Darwin writes, 'colonial rule had lost what remained of its moral legitimacy as a form of enlightened trusteeship'.[128] Even if there were conceptions of benevolence, what Williams labelled 'the imperialism of idealism', such benevolent constructions of US foreign policy and Woodrow Wilson in particular neglect Wilson's advocacy of overseas expansion and military intervention.[129] Wilson was quite racist in his application of self-determination, which evoked bitter reactions in Ireland, India and Indochina. Mao likened Wilson in Paris to 'an ant on a hot skillet' conceding to imperial return and retention.[130]

The informal phases of the British empire are lost in US conceptions of empire that rest on geographical imagination. Darwin argues: 'It helps to remind us that staring at maps can sometimes delude. For the invisible empire was functionally inseparable from its visible counterpart.' Informal colonies like Argentina and Egypt were often commercially or strategically more valuable. Such imperialism obviated the costs and efforts of direct rule; 'it was a compromise that depended on the cooperation of locals and the absence of rivals.'[131]

Globalization has rejuvenated an interest in economic analysis,[132] but it has done so in a period of seismic intellectual change, advanced by postmodernism and postcolonialism. 'Late capitalism', the term Jameson used to describe the post-war economy that rose with the decline of formal empire, facilitated postmodern dispositions. Beyond the intellectual shift[133] and despite efforts to establish the New International Economic Order in the 1970s, there has been extensive debate regarding whether decolonized nations benefitted from economic integration.[134]

Notwithstanding the US revisionists' contribution, the recent 'revival' has spurred interest in informal empire.[135] Both Britain and the United States operated informal empires. For the British, the unshaded areas included China and Latin America during the nineteenth and the early twentieth centuries. For the United States, they included Central America, Latin America and China. Go argues that if there was an 'overarching ideology' for Britain, 'it was not about empire but economics: specifically, free trade. This is a feature of British foreign policy that exceptionalist thought has run the risk of occluding by treating free trade as somehow America's special provenance. ... Britain articulated the free trade ideal long before presumably anti-imperial Americans did.'[136] Darwin concurs that commercial success underpinned Britain's 'world-spanning' power and thus 'the great advantage of an industrial empire lay in its ability to *integrate* a wide range of regions, however remote, into a single system of wealth and power'.[137] When they could, the British bypassed colonization; Viscount and British Prime Minister Henry Palmerston, who dominated issues of British foreign policy, refused the acquisition of Abyssinia and Egypt in the mid-nineteenth century. He stated: 'We want to trade with Egypt and to travel through Egypt but we do not want the burden of governing Egypt. Let us try to improve all those countries by the general influence of our commerce.'[138] The rationale is not far removed from US arguments on the benefits of free trade, prosperity and democratic peace, stretching from the rhetoric of Theodore Roosevelt to that of Bill Clinton. The British expanded exponentially, but also rejected many colonial opportunities.[139] The US preference for free trade, the Open Door or fair field and no favour ultimately found varied expression in modernization theory, neoliberalism and globalization, which attracted resistance and protest, as well as consensual engagement.

Territoriality

Territory is important to comparison. The expanse of US territorial possessions provided the foundations for its power. Manifest destiny and maps might obscure empire, but, like Canada, New Zealand, Australia and other settler colonies, these land masses remain empires, dispossessing earlier settlers. Even if they no longer engage in imperialism; they did once.

The United States was created by imperialism, colonialism and empire. That the states were ultimately incorporated and acquired equal rights in a federal system cannot explain away the process of acquisition and the habitual violence that attended settlement.[140] Hopkins argues the 'conviction that the United States had, and has, a unique providential mission has helped to form the character of American nationalism and the content of its history'. Most imperial powers have reached for some ideological perfume.[141] The vision of empire was originally clear. Founding Father and Secretary to the US Treasury Alexander Hamilton spoke of the 'Hercules in the cradle'. Not just the exemplar 'city on the hill', but the 'unchained embodiment of aggressive masculine power'. George Washington spoke of the 'rising American empire'; Thomas Jefferson softened it in his 'empire of liberty'.[142] Jefferson's vision eyed the entire continent, including the Southern Hemisphere, which should not accept any 'blot or mixture on that surface'. The form was uncertain, but there was no doubt 'about libertarian expansion'.[143] Soon afterwards, Secretary of State, later President, John Quincy Adams corresponded with Stratford Canning, the British Minister to the United States. Adams assured him that they would not encroach on British territory, 'but leave the rest of this continent to us'. Adams also envisaged a transcontinental empire; to pretend otherwise, he argued, would only 'add to our ambition hypocrisy'.[144] Later, Theodore Roosevelt turned the tables on the Anti-Imperialists by insinuating that withdrawal from the Philippines would betray Jefferson's legacy; and if they should give up the islands, where should they stop? California, New Mexico, Oregon? The Anti-Imperialist arguments rested on exceptional narratives. Overseas colonization betrayed US history, ideologies and republican inclinations.[145] Salt water apparently did make the difference. When FDR told Oliver Stanley, the British Colonial Secretary, that he did not intend to be rude, but that the British had not acquired Hong Kong by purchase, 'Stanley retorted: "Let me see, Mr President, that was about the time of the Mexican War"'.[146] At least until the Civil War, empire was frequently used in US discourse.[147]

While the traditional US exceptionalists simply deny empire or at least repress the descriptor, the revived exceptionalism asserts the unique quality of US empire. The Philippines and islands elsewhere were ultimately subject to a much more liberal experience and even if the United States is charged with acquisition, it 'ended up democratizing them, teaching other peoples the ways of self-government, and spreading American doctrines of freedom and liberty'.[148]

Go questions the disposition. He avoids the discourse of comparative malevolence or benevolence and some of the easier postcolonial assertions, that the experiences in the Philippines or India, in Malaya or California did not differ. Go breaks down some of the paradigmatic contrasts in the historiography. Just as US politicians, media and historians claimed liberal exceptionalism, so too did the British. Where Go sees areas of comparative liberalism in various forms of local governance, he also sees comparative forms of violence. Moreover, fixation on the Philippines and India, the prime examples, obscures the diversity of empire and the diversity of engagement, experience and resistance. 'One of the underlying assumptions of liberal exceptionalism', he writes, 'is that there is indeed such a thing as a single national style of colonial governance; a singular rule for all of America's colonial rules. To say that the U.S. empire is special or unique for its colonial governance is to assume that there is a uniformity to colonial practice and forms across the U.S. empire – a unique type.'[149]

Denis Judd's premise departs from the idea that 'far from the sum of the Empire being greater than its parts, generally the opposite was true'. The identity of individuals, except perhaps the colonial elite, was not linked to the whole, the empire, but to their diverse situations and conditions. Within the British empire, identity was disparate.[150]

The Provincial West

In the early 1990s, Amy Kaplan noted that in much of the critique of empire in postcolonial analysis, the United States is notable for its absence – it is simply not there as part of the discourse. Extending Williams's observation that 'one of the central themes of American historiography' is that 'there is no American Empire', she and Donald E. Pease set out to address three further absences: 'the absence of culture from the history of U.S. imperialism; the absence of empire from the study of American culture; and the absence of the United States from the postcolonial study of imperialism.'[151] Said concurred: 'Curiously ... so influential has been the discourse insisting on American specialness, altruism, and opportunity that "imperialism" as a word or ideology has turned up only rarely and recently in accounts of United States culture, politics, history.'[152] His *Culture and Imperialism* (1993) attempts to fill the 'blank spaces'. He situated US imperial culture after chapters on empire, geography and culture, Joseph Conrad, Jane Austen, Giuseppe Verdi and Egypt, Albert Camus and Algeria. In *Visualizing American Empire* (2010), David Brody added a deep reading of US culture in the Philippines.[153] This bibliography has expanded rapidly in recent years.[154]

'A truly post-colonial history would allow us to see the imperial past for what it was: a shameful record of economic exploitation, cultural aggression, physical brutality (and periodic atrocity) and decisive misrule.' As Darwin describes this approach to this history, the assumptions are of evil and abnormality; yet he argues that empire 'has been the political rule of the road over much of the world and over most of world history'.[155]

Though it is tempting to generalize in narratives of unified opposition and the 'vision of the vanquished', the multitude of colonial experience and resistance was particular and different. The trauma of occupation struck peoples throughout the colonial world and those subject to empire, but the forms of occupation, intervention and the impacts of empire or imperialism are different everywhere and felt in different ways.[156] There are two things to note in relation to the disparate practices of postcolonialism. First, that the disciplinary practice arose out of the collapse of the European empires, especially from the 1970s; they engaged in the project of talking back to the European metropolitan centres – not, initially, to the United States. Theorists sought to deconstruct the knowledge and the 'truth regimes' of the European discourses, writing themselves back into 'a history others have written'.[157] Moreover, as

Kennedy wryly noted, 'Decolonization robbed imperial history of most of its practical incentives', having previously been closely aligned to the 'official mind' in London.[158] The objective of postcolonial theory was to dismantle 'Western modes of domination [which] requires the deconstruction of Western structures of knowledge'.[159]

These decentred narratives sometimes essential-*ized* images of the empire.[160] At times, resistance to empire adopted 'western' paradigms for political effect; *they* had betrayed *their* own ideology. If history could serve as 'an agent of liberation', tradition and romantic notions of Indian nationalism had to 'accommodate the Indian experiences of the West at their most positive', using such concepts of freedom and self-determination to 'act as a counter-historiography to the colonialist one, which was becoming more strident in the face of nationalist agitation'. Rabindranath Tagore regarded Mohandas Karamchand (Mahatma) Gandhi's use of history as 'nothing more than the imitation of a Western idea', which ultimately created the 'unnatural nation' to use Ramachandra Guha's frame.[161] Ranajit Guha took it further, contending that the very discipline of history was itself imperial.[162] Thus, historians like Bankim Chandra Chatterjee and G.K. Gokhale, while both critical of the British in India, differed on whether to use the British frame of a unified India as a point of departure for understanding 'Indian' nationalism.[163] While Gandhi liked to hold the European mirror up to the British, at least for tactical purposes, Tagore thought 'Europe has completely lost her former moral prestige in Asia'.[164]

Frequently, the histories of anti-colonial movements focus entirely on nationalist movements that have explicitly accepted the European constructed unit of *the* nation as the point of reference.[165] Reactions to that given frame gave rise to observations that 'We have become strangers in our own country', whether it was Indians in post-1947 India, Vietnamese after 1954, or Mexicans after 1848.

Such psychological, cultural and historical analysis lingered long after the British, French, Dutch or American flags were lowered. It was not just neo-colonialism and economic dependency; persisting cultural and intellectual perspectives were a 'kind of neo-colonialism of the mind'.[166] In that sense, Ngũgĩ wa Thiong'O stressed the imperative to 'decolonize the mind', long after Kenyan political independence.[167]

Ironically, after Wilson delivered his Fourteen Points in January 1918 and subsequent speeches in Paris, he inspired nationalist leaders throughout the world with his messages on self-determination, but not in Central America or the Caribbean. John Maynard Keynes observed that US 'prestige and a moral influence throughout the world [was] unequalled in history'.[168] Yet, ironically, US history has not resonated abroad.[169] Dependency theorists and those influenced by them were similarly talking back to the US empire, especially the informal US empire.[170]

The irony of the impact of postcolonial discourse has been that it has not only provided the critique of the British and other empires, but it has also rejuvenated the interest in imperial and commonwealth history, stretching the methodological boundaries of the field, 'taking it in directions that the conventional historiography of the British Empire has hardly begun to consider'.[171]

A pivotal contribution centred on 'Western constructions of the Other', contrasted with exceptional metropolitan histories.[172] It is a short leap from the West assessing the impact of colonialism through Western prisms to the construction of benign narratives that attended their justifications. Yet, more recently, the reaction against 'imperial whiggism' is also under revision.[173] A further irony, of course, is that the backlash has fuelled the revival of the exceptionalist arguments about the British Empire, the school of what Fergal Keane calls 'It Wasn't So Bad after All'.[174]

For some, it was bad enough that the British lost their empire, but that the knowledge base, the curricula, the truth 'regimes' should come under attack was more difficult. Now, after the phases of guilt and apology, there are renewed efforts to restore traditional narratives. The statues of the British Raj may have been removed to Coronation Park north of Old Delhi;[175] the revision of British curricula would meet with further resistance.

When one adopts Dipesh Chakrabarty's method of provincializing interpretation, which examines the experience of empire at the point of application as opposed to examining it from the perspective of intent or 'national style', the stories are quite different: Guam and Samoa might stand in contrast to the Philippines.[176] One of Chakrabarty's objectives was to 'provincialise Europe'; he argued that many of the universal claims and much of the narrative authority were products of particular areas and are not universal.[177]

Conclusion

As a postcolonial empire, it was imperative for Washington to define its identity in contrast to that of the British. At that relatively superficial rhetorical level, which is also reflected in its formal ideologies, the US traditions of foreign policy and empire are different. Many of the differences of US exceptionalism are captured in its traditional histories, which have, in themselves, remained isolated from international engagement until comparatively recently. US exceptionalism remains a strong but rapidly diminishing influence in US culture. The 'American dream' is sundered; the impact of the culture wars, the financial downturn and the costs of recent wars have eroded US confidence;

external macro-economic challenges and loss in three out of its four last major wars have taken their toll on exceptionalism.

But its informal ideologies and its colonial, economic, military and cultural practices, at least at a conceptual level, reflect many of the traditions in which the British engaged. US visions of itself, its certainty, its arrogance regarding its power, its formal and informal empires, its economic penetration of global markets and its military reach speak to practices in which the British also engaged. On maps, we do not see the world divided into five US 'regional commands', with well over seven hundred military bases in more than one hundred and fifty countries.[178] The historiographical discussion gives rise to points of comparison, yet the variety of forms and practices of empire and imperialism that underlie the superstructure needs to be remembered.

The conceptual postcolonial criticisms of the West, with the 'special re-lationship' at the heart of its security arrangements, at times also elide the particularities and diverse range of experience that empire imposed on lives and regions, which were left with countries that were very much creations of exogenous forces. The United States was sometimes absent from postcolonial discourse because this was primarily aimed at European empires and the US hybrid identity facilitated the initial disregard. Ultimately, despite the denial in some US historiography, despite the concession to the lower-case empire, but unease with the upper-case Empire, there are deep lines of continuity, of shared values and practices, of engagement in a full variety of forms of empire and imperial practice. Those lines of shared experience were often articulat-ed by US imperialists, especially in the late nineteenth century. References to 'Anglo-Saxon' heritage was a frequent refrain used to legitimate colonial rule. Kramer writes that 'the United States was merely fulfilling Anglo-Sax-on responsibilities dictated by its racial-historical character'. It was, for US imperialists, responding to Kipling's injunction to take up 'the White Man's Burden'.[179] Yet, as the anti-imperial formal ideologies took hold, the sense of shared experience and 'duty' was augmented by the US postcolonial vision of itself and its history. Certainly, Lippmann had a point when he observed that when US historiography and practice are provincialized, foreigners watch US intervention and pay little heed to US rhetoric. And so, 'we go on creating what mankind calls an empire while we continue to believe quite sincerely that it is not an empire because it does not feel to us the way we imagine an empire ought to feel'.[180]

David Ryan is Professor of Modern History at University College Cork, Ireland and Honorary Researcher at the Centre for War and Diplomacy, Lancaster University. He has published extensively on contemporary history and US foreign policy, concentrating on interventions in the post-Vietnam era. His books include *Not Even Past: How the United States Ends Wars*, edited with David Fitzgerald and John M. Thompson (Berghahn, 2020); *Obama, US Foreign Policy and the Dilemmas of Intervention*, co-authored with David Fitzgerald (Palgrave, 2014); *US Foreign Policy and the Other*, edited with Michael Cullinane (Berghahn, 2015); *Frustrated Empire: US Foreign Policy from 9/11 to Iraq* (Pluto and University of Michigan, 2007); *Vietnam in Iraq: Tactics, Lessons, Legacies and Ghosts*, edited with John Dumbrell (Routledge, 2007); *The United States and Europe in the Twentieth Century* (Longman, 2003); *US Foreign Policy in World History* (Routledge, 2000); and *US–Sandinista Diplomatic Relations: Voice of Intolerance* (MacMillan, 1995). He is also the author of numerous articles.

Notes

1. Antonio Weiss and Brad Setser, 'America's Forgotten Colony: Ending Puerto Rico's Perpetual Crisis', *Foreign Affairs* 98(4) (July 2019), 158–68.

2. David Ryan, *US Foreign Policy in World History* (London: Routledge, 2000), 66; Michael Patrick Cullinane, *Liberty and American Anti-Imperialism, 1898–1909* (New York: Palgrave Macmillan, 2012); Howard Zinn, *A People's History of the United States* (London: Longman, 1980), 294.

3. Michael Mann, *Incoherent Empire* (London: Verso, 2003).

4. Maya Jasanoff, 'What New Empires Inherit from Old Ones', *History News Network*, 12 December 2005, https://historynewsnetwork.org/article/18853; Dane Kennedy, *The Imperial History Wars: Debating the British Empire* (London: Bloomsbury, 2018), 107.

5. Eric Hobsbawm and Terence Ranger (eds), *The Invention of Tradition* (Cambridge: Cambridge University Press, 1983), 2.

6. Anders Stephanson, *Manifest Destiny: American Expansion and the Empire of Right* (New York: Hill and Wang, 1995), 20.

7. Thomas Bender, 'Historians, the Nation, and the Plentitude of Narratives', in Thomas Bender (ed.), *Rethinking American History in a Global Age* (Berkeley: University of California Press, 2002), 1.

8. Joyce Appleby, Lynn Hunt and Margaret Jacob, *Telling the Truth about History* (New York: W.W. Norton & Company, 1994); David Thelen, 'Making History and Making the United States', *Journal of American Studies* 32(3) (December 1998), 373–97; Ian Tyrrell, 'Making Nations/Making States: American Historians in the Context of Empire', *Journal of American History* 86(3) (December 1999), 1015–44.

9. Alan Dobson, *Anglo-American Relations in the Twentieth Century: Of Friendship, Conflict and the Rise and Decline of Superpowers* (London: Routledge, 1995); Alan Dobson and Steve Marsh, 'Anglo-American Relations: End of a Special Relationship?', *The International History Review* 36(4) (2014), 673–97; John Dumbrell, *A Special Relationship: Anglo-American Relations in the Cold War and After* (London: Macmillan, 2001); David Reynolds, 'The Special Relationship: Rethinking Anglo-American Relations', *International Affairs* 65(1) (1989), 89–111.

10. David Gress, *From Plato to NATO: The Idea of the West and Its Opponents* (New York: The Free Press, 1998).

11. Geir Lundestad, '"Empire by Invitation" in the American Century', *Diplomatic History* 23(2) (Spring 1999); Geir Lundestad, *'Empire' by Integration: The United States and European Integration, 1945–1997* (Oxford: Oxford University Press, 1998).

12. Or Rosenboim, *The Emergence of Globalism: Visions of World Order in Britain and the United States, 1939–1950* (Princeton, NJ: Princeton University Press, 2017).

13. Dominique Edde, *Edward Said: His Thought as a Novel* (London: Verso, 2019), 9.

14. Hergé, *The Blue Lotus. The Adventures of Tintin* (London: Mammoth, 1990), 6–7; Michael Farr, *Tintin: The Complete Companion* (Brussels: Editions Moulinsart, 2001), 52.

15. Paul A. Kramer, *The Blood of Government: Race, Empire, the United States, & the Philippines* (Chapel Hill: University of North Carolina Press, 2006), 11.

16. Kennedy, *Imperial History Wars*; Julian Go, *Patterns of Empire: The British and American Empires, 1688 to the Present* (Cambridge: Cambridge University Press, 2011); A.G. Hopkins, *American Empire: A Global History* (Princeton, NJ: Princeton University Press, 2018).

17. Martin J. Wiener, 'The Idea of "Colonial Legacy" and the Historiography of Empire', *Journal of the Historical Society* 13(1) (March 2013), 1–32; Ngũgĩ wa Thiong'o, *Moving the Centre: The Struggle for Cultural Freedoms* (London: James Currey, 1993).

18. Bernard Porter, *Empire and Superempire: Britain, America and the World* (New Haven, CT: Yale University Press, 2006), 17–22.

19. Lloyd C. Gardner, 'Lost Empires', *Diplomatic History* 13(1) (Winter 1989), 1.

20. Walter LaFeber, *The American Search for Opportunity, 1865–1913* (Cambridge: Cambridge University Press, 1993).

21. Shashi Tharoor, *Inglorious Empire: What the British Did to India* (London: Penguin, 2017), 203.

22. John Darwin, *Unfinished Empire: The Global Expansion of Britain* (London: Penguin, 2012), 24–29, 388.

23. LaFeber, *Opportunity*, 237.

24. Ernest Gellner, *Reason and Culture: The Historic Role of Rationality and Rationalism* (Oxford: Blackwell, 1992), 113.

25. Citing Hofmannsthal, Gabrielle M. Spiegel, 'Revising the Past / Revisiting the Present: How Change Happens in Historiography', *History and Theory* 46, Theme Issue (December 2007): 4.

26. Georg G. Iggers and Q. Edward Wang, *A Global History of Modern Historiography* (Harlow: Longman, 2008), 283–89.

27. Dane Kennedy, *The Last Blank Spaces: Exploring Africa and Australia* (Cambridge, MA: Harvard University Press, 2013), 1–2.

28. Kennedy, *Imperial History Wars*, 102.

29. Iggers and Wang, *Global History*, 229–32.

30. Joseph A. Fry, 'Imperialism, American Style, 1890–1916', in Gordon Martel (ed.), *American Foreign Relations Reconsidered 1890–1993* (London: Routledge, 1994), 53.

31. John Gallagher and Ronald Robinson, 'The Imperialism of Free Trade', *The Economic History Review* 6(1) (1953): 1.

32. Citing Michel de Certeau, Spiegel, 'Revising the Past', 6.

33. Kennedy, *Imperial History Wars*, 39.

34. Hopkins, *American Empire*, 32.

35. Michael Doyle, *Empires* (Ithaca: Cornell University Press, 1986); Herfried Munkler, *Empires: The Logic of World Domination from Ancient Rome to the United States* (Cambridge: Polity Press, 2007).

36. Ibid., 45.

37. T.S. Eliot, 'The Love Song of J. Alfred Prufrock', in *Selected Poems* (London: Faber and Faber, 1954), 13.

38. Hopkins, *American Empire*, 25–26; Munkler, *Empires*.

39. Spiegel, 'Revising the Past', 2; Paul Hamilton, *Historicism* (London: Routledge, 1996).

40. Darwin, *Unfinished Empire*, 13.

41. Antoinette Burton and Tony Ballantyne (eds), *World Histories from Below: Disruption and Dissent, 1750 to the Present* (London: Bloomsbury, 2016).

42. Charles S. Maier, *Among Empires: American Ascendancy and Its Predecessors* (Cambridge, MA: Harvard University Press, 2006), 59.

43. Hopkins, *American Empire*, 26–27.

44. Maier, *Among Empires*, 3.

45. Ibid., 14–15, 20–21, 24–26.

46. Richard H. Immerman, *Empire for Liberty: A History of American Imperialism from Benjamin Franklin to Paul Wolfowitz* (Princeton, NJ: Princeton University Press, 2010), 20–58.

47. William Appleman Williams, *The Tragedy of American Diplomacy* (New York: Delta, 1962); William Appleman Williams, *Empire as a Way of Life* (New York: Oxford University Press, 1980); William Appleman Williams, *The Roots of the Modern American Empire: A Study of the Growth and Shaping of Social Consciousness in a Market Place Society* (London: Anthony Blond, 1969); Walter LaFeber, *The New Empire: An Interpretation of American Expansion 1860–1898* (Ithaca, NY: Cornell University Press, 1963); LaFeber, *Opportunity*; Lloyd C. Gardner, 'Lost Empires', *Diplomatic History* 13(1) (Winter 1989), 1–13.

48. Niall Ferguson, *Empire: How Britain Made the Modern World* (London: Allen Lane, 2003); Niall Ferguson, *Colossus: The Price of America's Empire* (London: Allen Lane, 2004).

49. Munkler, *Empires*, 148.

50. Lloyd C. Gardner and Marilyn B. Young (eds), *The New American Empire: A 21st Century Teach-In on U.S. Foreign Policy* (New York: The New Press, 2005); Anne Norton, *Leo Strauss and the Politics of American Empire* (New Haven, CT: Yale University Press, 2004); Greg Grandin, *Empire's Workshop: Latin America, the United States, and the Rise of the New Imperialism* (New York: Henry Holt, 2006); David Ryan, *Frustrated Empire: US Foreign Policy, 9/11 to Iraq* (London: Pluto, 2007); Michael H. Hunt and Steven I. Levine, *Arc of Empire: America's Wars in Asia from the Philippines to Vietnam* (Chapel Hill: University of North Carolina Press, 2012); Mann, *Incoherent Empire*; Eric Hobsbawm, *On Empire: America, War, and Global Supremacy* (New York: Pantheon Books, 2008); Immerman, *Empire for Liberty*; Andrew J. Bacevich, *American Empire: The Realities and Consequences of U.S. Diplomacy* (Cambridge, MA: Harvard University Press, 2002); Chalmers Johnson, *The Sorrows of Empire: Militarism, Secrecy, and the End of the Republic* (New York: Henry Holt, 2004); Derek Gregory, *The Colonial Present: Afghanistan, Palestine, Iraq* (Cambridge: Blackwell, 2004).2005

51. Kennedy, *Imperial History Wars*, 3.

52. Jürgen Osterhammel, *Colonialism: A Theoretical Overview* (Princeton, NJ: Markus Wiener, 1997).

53. Go, *Patterns of Empire*, 65.

54. Moore, *American Imperialism*, 4–5.

55. Ibid., 269–70, citing Theodore Friend's 1965 *Between Two Empires*.

56. Victor Bulmer-Thomas, *The Economic History of Latin America since Independence* (Cambridge: Cambridge University Press, 1994); Walter LaFeber, *Inevitable Revolutions: The United States in Central America* (New York: W.W. Norton & Company, 1983).

57. Jeremy Black, *Great Powers and the Quest for Hegemony: The World Order since 1500* (London: Routledge, 2008).

58. D.K. Fieldhouse, *The West and the Third World: Trade, Colonialism, Dependence and Development* (Cambridge: Blackwell, 1999).

59. G. John Ikenberry, *Liberal Order & Imperial Ambition: Essays on American Power and World Politics* (Cambridge: Polity Press, 2006), 221.

60. Ryan, *US Foreign Policy in World History*, 78.

61. Kennedy, *Imperial History Wars*.

62. Go, *Patterns of Empire*.

63. Ray Kiely, *Rethinking Imperialism* (London: Palgrave Macmillan, 2010).

64. Bradford Perkins, *The Creation of a Republican Empire, 1776–1865* (Cambridge: Cambridge University Press, 1993), 169, 155–56; Ryan, *US Foreign Policy in World History*, 43.

65. Kennedy, *Imperial History Wars*, 102.

66. Porter, *Empire and Superempire*, 7.

67. Ibid., 64, 67.

68. Munkler, *Empires*, 10.

69. Paul A. Kramer, 'How Not to Write the History of U.S. Empire', *Diplomatic History* 42(5) (November 2018), 916.

70. Marilyn B. Young, 'The Age of Global Power', in Thomas Bender (ed.), *Rethinking American History in a Global Age* (Berkeley: University of California Press, 2002), 275.

71. Edward W. Said, *Culture and Imperialism* (London: Chatto & Windus, 1993), xix.

72. Colin D. Moore, *American Imperialism and the State, 1893–1921* (Cambridge: Cambridge University Press, 2017), 29.

73. Gregory H. Nobles, *American Frontiers: Cultural Encounters and Continental Conquest* (London: Penguin, 1997); Walter L. Hixon, '"No Savage Shall Inherit the Land": The Indian Enemy Other, Indiscriminate Warfare, and American National Identity, 1607–1783', in Michael Patrick Cullinane and David Ryan (eds), *U.S. Foreign Policy and the Other* (New York: Berghahn, 2017).

74. Kennedy, *Imperial History Wars*, 110; Jürgen Osterhammel, *Colonialism: A Theoretical Overview* (Princeton, NJ: Markus Wiener, 1997), 5–6.

75. Go, *Patterns of Empire*, 46.

76. Munkler, *Empires*, 36.

77. Go, *Patterns of Empire*, 53–54.

78. David Ryan and Victor Pungong (eds), *The United States and Decolonization: Power and Freedom* (London: Macmillan, 2000), passim.

79. Bradford Perkins, *The Great Rapprochement: England and the United States, 1895–1914* (London: Victor Gollancz, 1969), 64–65.

80. Rosenboim, *Globalism*.

81. David Ryan, 'Culture and Re-Membering the Alliance in Kosovo and Iraq: Anglo-American Ironics under Clinton, Blair and Bush', in Robert Hendershot and Steve Marsh (eds), *Culture Matters: Anglo-American Relations and the Intangibles of 'Specialness'* (Manchester: Manchester University Press, 2020); Richard Toye, 'Why Is the British Empire Still so Controversial', *Empire: The Controversies of British Imperialism* [blog], 25 November 2017, https://about.futurelearn.com/blog/british-empire.

82. Prasenjit Duara, 'Transnationalism and the Challenge to National Histories', in Thomas Bender (ed.), *Rethinking American History in a Global Age* (Berkeley: University of California Press, 2002).

83. Pierre Bourdieu, *The Field of Cultural Production: Essays on Art and Literature* (Cambridge: Polity Press, 1993).

84. Said, *Culture and Imperialism*, xiii.

85. Jill Lepore, 'A New Americanism: Why a Nation Needs a National Story', *Foreign Affairs* 98(2) (April 2019), 12–13, 19; Jill Lepore, *These Truths: A History of the United States* (New York: W.W. Norton & Company, 2018); Thelen, 'Making History'; Appleby, Hunt, and Jacob, *Telling the Truth about History*.

86. Thomas Jefferson, 'The Declaration of Independence, 1776', in Henry Steele Commager (ed.), *Documents of American History* (New York: Appleton Century Crofts, 1963).

87. David Reynolds, *America, Empire of Liberty: A New History* (London: Allen Lane, 2009).

88. Warren Kimball, 'Foreword', in David Ryan and Victor Pungong (eds), *The United States and Decolonization: Power and Freedom* (London: Macmillan, 2000), xiii.

89. Darwin, *Unfinished Empire*, 30–32; Hopkins, *American Empire*, 18.

90. Thomas Bender, 'Historians, the Nation, and the Plentitude of Narratives', in Thomas Bender (ed.), *Rethinking American History in a Global Age* (Berkeley: University of California Press, 2002), 2.

91. Ibid., 5.

92. Kramer, *The Blood of Government*, 11.

93. Ibid., 2.

94. National Security Council, 'National Security Council, U.S. Policy Toward Africa South of the Sahara Prior to Calendar Year 1960, NSC 5719, Record Group 273', 31 July 1957, NARA.

95. Siri Hustvedt, *Living, Thinking, Looking* (London: Sceptre, 2012), 22.

96. Johannes Fabian, *Memory against Culture: Arguments and Reminders* (Durham, NC: Duke University Press, 2007), 27–29.

97. David Gress, *From Plato to NATO: The Idea of the West and Its Opponents* (New York: The Free Press, 1998), 411.

98. Warren Kimball, *The Juggler: Franklin Roosevelt as Wartime Statesman* (Princeton, NJ: Princeton University Press, 1991).

99. Robert E. Wood, 'From the Marshall Plan to the Third World', in Melvyn P. Leffler and David S. Painter (eds), *Origins of the Cold War: An International History* (London: Routledge, 1994), 202–5.

100. Melvyn P. Leffler, *A Preponderance of Power: National Security, the Truman Administration, and the Cold War* (Stanford, CA: Stanford University Press, 1992), 18–19.

101. Kimball, 'Foreword', xvi.

102. Darwin, *Unfinished Empire*, 29.

103. Munkler, *Empires*, 26–27.

104. Barrie Axford, *The Global System: Economics, Politics and Culture* (Cambridge: Polity Press, 1995); Ankie Hoogvelt, *Globalization and the Postcolonial World: The New Political Economy of Development* (London: Macmillan, 1997); Saskia Sassen, *Globalization and Its Discontents: Essays on the New Mobility of People and Money* (New York: The New Press, 1998); Andrew Hurrell and Ngaire Woods (eds), *Inequality, Globalization, and World Politics* (Oxford: Oxford University Press, 1999); Mark Rupert, *Ideologies of Globalization: Contending Visions of a New World Order* (London: Routledge, 2000); Joseph Stiglitz, *Globalization and Its Discontents* (London: Penguin, 2002); Alfred E. Eckes and Thomas W. Zeiler, *Globalization and the American Century* (Cambridge: Cambridge University Press, 2003); Neil Smith, *The Endgame of Globalization* (New York: Routledge, 2005), 1997.

105. Jackson Lears, 'How the US Began Its Empire', *New York Review of Books* 64(3) (23 February 2017), 37.

106. Gallagher and Robinson, 'The Imperialism of Free Trade', 1.

107. Pankaj Mishra, *From the Ruins of Empire: The Intellectuals Who Remade Asia* (New York: Farrar, Straus and Giroux, 2012), 202.

108. Tristram Hunt, *Ten Cities that Made an Empire* (London: Allen Lane, 2014).

109. Benedict Anderson, *Imagined Communities: Reflections on the Origins and Spread of Nationalism* (London: Verso, 1983), 170–78.

110. J.B. Harley, *The New Nature of Maps: Essays in the History of Cartography* (Baltimore, MD: Johns Hopkins Press, 2001), 57–59, 112–14.

111. Ibid., 113.

112. Kennedy, *Imperial History Wars*, 47; Said, *Culture and Imperialism*, 159.

113. Paul Connerton, *How Modernity Forgets* (Cambridge: Cambridge University Press, 2009), 10.

114. Hopkins, *American Empire*, 83.

115. Reproduced in Brody, *Visualizing American Empire*, 96.

116. J.H. Elliot, 'Spain's America', *New York Review of Books* 66(8) (22 May 2019): 44–45.

117. Daniel Immerwahr, 'Writing the History of the Greater United States: A Reply to Paul Kramer', *Diplomatic History* 42(2) (April 2019), 399, quoting W.E.B. Du Bois, *Color and Democracy: Colonies and Peace* (New York, 1945).

118. Go, *Patterns of Empire*, 118.

119. Walter Lippmann, *Men of Destiny* (New York: Macmillan, 1927); David Ryan and Victor Pungong (eds), *The United States and Decolonization: Power and Freedom* (London: Macmillan, 2000), 18–19.

120. Porter, *Empire and Superempire*.

121. Go, *Patterns of Empire*.

122. Hopkins, *American Empire*, 691.

123. Kennedy, *Imperial History Wars*.

124. Denis Judd, *Empire: The British Imperial Experience, from 1765 to the Present* (London: HarperCollins, 1996).

125. Darwin, *Unfinished Empire*; Tharoor, *Inglorious Empire*.

126. Darwin, *Unfinished Empire*, 20.

127. Michael H. Hunt, *Ideology and U.S. Foreign Policy* (New Haven, CT: Yale University Press, 1987), 77–78.

128. Darwin, *Unfinished Empire*, 3.

129. Williams, *The Tragedy of American Diplomacy*, 53, 64; Lloyd C. Gardner, *Safe for Democracy: The Anglo-American Response to Revolution, 1913–1923* (Oxford: Oxford University Press, 1987).

130. Pankaj Mishra, *From the Ruins of Empire: The Intellectuals Who Remade Asia* (New York: Farrar, Straus and Giroux, 2012), 199.

131. Darwin, *Unfinished Empire*, 392.

132. Hopkins, *American Empire*, 12.

133. Spiegel, 'Revising the Past', 14; Fredric Jameson, *Postmodernism, or, the Cultural Logic of Late Capitalism* (London: Verso, 1991), xx.

134. Fieldhouse, *West and the Third World*, 3; Adom Getachew, *Worldmaking after Empire: The Rise and Fall of Self-Determination* (Princeton, NJ: Princeton University Press, 2019).

135. Hopkins, *American Empire*, 12, 15.

136. Go, *Patterns of Empire*, 112.

137. Darwin, *Unfinished Empire*, 393–95.

138. Go, *Patterns of Empire*, 115.

139. Ibid., 111.

140. Hixon, 'No Savage Shall Inherit the Land', 16–41.

141. Hopkins, *American Empire*, 15–17.

142. Walter L. Hixon, *The Myth of American Diplomacy: National Identity and U.S. Foreign Policy* (New Haven, CT: Yale University Press, 2008), 43.

143. Stephanson, *Manifest Destiny*, 23.

144. Walter LaFeber (ed), *John Quincy Adams and American Continental Empire: Letters, Papers and Speeches* (Chicago: Quadrangle Books, 1965), 37.

145. Robert L. Beisner, 'The Anti-Imperialist Case and Failure', in Thomas G. Paterson and Stephen G. Rabe (eds), *Imperial Surge: The United States Abroad, the 1890s-Early 1900s* (Lexington: D.C. Heath, 1992), 111–26.

146. Go, *Patterns of Empire*, 38.

147. Ibid., 36.

148. Ibid., 68.

149. Ibid., 72–81.

150. Judd, *Empire*, 1, 3.

151. Amy Kaplan, '"Left Alone with America": The Absence of Empire in the Study of American Culture', in *Cultures of United States Imperialism* (Durham, NC: Duke University Press, 1993).

152. Said, *Culture and Imperialism*, 7.

153. Brody, *Visualizing Empire*.

154. Kramer, 'Not to Write'.

155. Darwin, *Unfinished Empire*, 6–7.

156. Marc Ferro, *Colonization: A Global History* (London: Routledge, 1997), 186.

157. Jonathan Culler, *Literary Theory* (Oxford: Oxford University Press, 1997), 130–31.

158. Kennedy, *Imperial History Wars*, 7.

159. Ibid., 10.

160. Iggers and Wang, *Global History*, 229–32.

161. Ibid., 229–32; Ramachandra Guha, *India after Gandhi: The History of the World's Largest Democracy* (New Delhi: Picador, 2017), ix–xxxiv.

162. Kennedy, *Imperial History Wars*, 53.

163. Ferro, *Colonization*, 208.

164. Mishra, *From the Ruins of Empire*, 186.

165. Heather Streets-Salter, 'International and Global Anti-Colonial Movements', in Antoinette Burton and Tony Ballantyne (eds), *World Histories from Below: Disruption and Dissent, 1750 to the Present* (London: Bloomsbury, 2016), 47.

166. Wiener, 'Colonial Legacy', 9.

167. Ngũgĩ, *Moving the Centre*.

168. Mishra, *From the Ruins of Empire*, 188.

169. Bender, 'Rethinking', 18; Francois Weil, 'Do American Historical Narratives Travel?', in Thomas Bender (ed.), *Rethinking American History in a Global Age* (Berkeley: University of California Press, 2002), 317–42.

170. Kiely, *Rethinking Imperialism*, 120–22; Maier, *Among Empires*, 48–59; Andre Gunder Frank, *Capitalism and Underdevelopment in Latin America: Historical Studies of Chile and Brazil* (London: Penguin, 1971).

171. Kennedy, *Imperial History Wars*, 18.

172. Ibid., 19.

173. Wiener, 'Colonial Legacy', 3.

174. Fergal Keane, 'On Colonial Violence', Speech, School of History, University College Cork, Ireland (2018).

175. Steve Coll, 'Things to Think About When Taking Down Statues', *The New Yorker*, 31 August 2017.

176. Go, *Patterns of Empire*, 84.

177. Kennedy, *Imperial History Wars*, 52.

178. Munkler, *Empires*, 150.

179. Kramer, *The Blood of Government*, 11.

180. Lippmann, *Men of Destiny*; Ryan and Pungong, *The United States and Decolonization*, 18–19.

Bibliography

Axford, Barrie. *The Global System: Economics, Politics and Culture*. Cambridge: Polity Press, 1995.

Bacevich, Andrew J. *American Empire: The Realities and Consequences of U.S. Diplomacy*. Cambridge, MA: Harvard University Press, 2002.

Beisner, Robert L. 'The Anti-Imperialist Case and Failure', in Thomas G. Paterson and Stephen G. Rabe (eds), *Imperial Surge: The United States Abroad, the 1890s-Early 1900s*. Lexington: D.C. Heath, 1992, 111–26.

Bello, Walden. *Dilemmas of Domination: The Unmaking of the American Empire*. New York: Metropolitan Books, 2005.

Bender, Thomas. 'Historians, the Nation, and the Plentitude of Narratives', in Thomas Bender (ed.), *Rethinking American History in a Global Age*. Berkeley: University of California Press, 2002, 1–21.

Betts, Raymond F. *Decolonization*. London: Routledge, 1998.

Black, Jeremy. *Great Powers and the Quest for Hegemony: The World Order since 1500*. London: Routledge, 2008.

Brody, David. *Visualizing American Empire: Orientalism and Imperialism in the Philippines*. Chicago: University of Chicago, 2010.

Bulmer-Thomas, Victor. *The Economic History of Latin America since Independence*. Cambridge: Cambridge University Press, 1994.

Burton, Antoinette, and Tony Ballantyne (eds). *World Histories from Below: Disruption and Dissent, 1750 to the Present*. London: Bloomsbury, 2016.

Cohen, Warren I. *America's Failing Empire: U.S. Foreign Policy since the Cold War*. Malden, MA: Blackwell, 2005.

Coll, Steve. 'Things to Think About When Taking Down Statues', *The New Yorker*, 31 August 2017.

Culler, Jonathan. *Literary Theory. A Very Short Introduction*. Oxford: Oxford University Press, 1997.

Cullinane, Michael Patrick. *Liberty and American Anti-Imperialism, 1898–1909*. New York: Palgrave Macmillan, 2012.

Cullinane, Michael Patrick, and David Ryan (eds). *U.S. Foreign Policy and the Other*. New York: Berghahn, 2015.

Darwin, John. *Unfinished Empire: The Global Expansion of Britain*. London: Penguin, 2012.

Davis, Richard. 'Perspectives on the End of Empire: The Historiographical Debate', *Cercles* 28 (2013), 3–25.

Doyle, Michael. *Empires*. Ithaca, NY: Cornell University Press, 1986.

Duara, Prasenjit. 'Transnationalism and the Challenge to National Histories', in Thomas Bender (ed.), *Rethinking American History in a Global Age*. Berkeley: University of California Press, 2002, 25–46.

Eckes, Alfred E., and Thomas W. Zeiler. *Globalization and the American Century*. Cambridge: Cambridge University Press, 2003.

Elliot, J.H. 'Spain's America', *New York Review of Books* 66(8) (22 May 2019), 44–45.

Fabian, Johannes. *Memory against Culture: Arguments and Reminders*. Durham, NC: Duke University Press, 2007.

Farr, Michael. *Tintin: The Complete Companion*. Brussels: Editions Moulinsart, 2001.

Ferguson, Niall. *Colossus: The Price of America's Empire*. London: Allen Lane, 2004.

———. *Empire: How Britain Made the Modern World*. London: Allen Lane, 2003.

———. 'Hegemony or Empire?', *Foreign Affairs* 82(5) (October 2003), 154–61.

Ferro, Marc. *Colonization: A Global History*. London: Routledge, 1997.

Fieldhouse, D.K. *The West and the Third World: Trade, Colonialism, Dependence and Development*. Cambridge: Blackwell, 1999.

Frank, Andre Gunder. *Capitalism and Underdevelopment in Latin America: Historical Studies of Chile and Brazil*. London: Penguin, 1971.

Fry, Joseph A. 'Imperialism, American Style, 1890–1916', in Gordon Martel (ed.), *American Foreign Relations Reconsidered 1890–1993*. London: Routledge, 1994, 52–67.

Gallagher, John, and Ronald Robinson. 'The Imperialism of Free Trade', *The Economic History Review* 6(1) (1953), 1–15.

Gardner, Lloyd C. 'Lost Empires', *Diplomatic History* 13(1) (Winter 1989), 1–13.

———. *Safe for Democracy: The Anglo-American Response to Revolution, 1913–1923*. Oxford: Oxford University Press, 1987.

Gardner, Lloyd C., and Marilyn B. Young (eds). *The New American Empire: A 21st Century Teach-In on U.S. Foreign Policy*. New York: The New Press, 2005.

Gellner, Ernest. *Reason and Culture: The Historic Role of Rationality and Rationalism*. Oxford: Blackwell, 1992.

Getachew, Adom. *Worldmaking after Empire: The Rise and Fall of Self-Determination*. Princeton, NJ: Princeton University Press, 2019.

Go, Julian. *Patterns of Empire: The British and American Empires, 1688 to the Present*. Cambridge: Cambridge University Press, 2011.

Grandin, Greg. *Empire's Workshop: Latin America, the United States, and the Rise of the New Imperialism*. New York: Henry Holt, 2006.

———. *The End of the Myth: From the Frontier to the Border Wall in the Mind of America*. New York: Metropolitan Books, 2019.

Gregory, Derek. *The Colonial Present: Afghanistan, Palestine, Iraq*. Cambridge: Blackwell, 2004.

Gress, David. *From Plato to NATO: The Idea of the West and Its Opponents*. New York: The Free Press, 1998.

Guha, Ramachandra. *India after Gandhi: The History of the World's Largest Democracy*. New Delhi: Picador, 2017.

Harley, J.B. *The New Nature of Maps: Essays in the History of Cartography*. Baltimore, MD: Johns Hopkins Press, 2001.

Hart, Jonathan. *Empires and Colonies*. Cambridge: Polity Press, 2008.

Hergé. *The Blue Lotus. The Adventures of Tintin*. London: Mammoth, 1990.

Hitchens, Christopher. *Blood, Class, and Nostalgia: Anglo-American Ironies*. London: Chatto & Windus, 1990.

Hixon, Walter L. "'No Savage Shall Inherit the Land'": The Indian Enemy Other, Indiscriminate Warfare, and American National Identity, 1607–1783', in Michael Patrick Cullinane and David Ryan (eds), *U.S. Foreign Policy and the Other*. New York: Berghahn, 2017, 16–41.

———. *The Myth of American Diplomacy: National Identity and U.S. Foreign Policy*. New Haven, CT: Yale University Press, 2008.

Hobsbawm, Eric. *The Age of Empire 1875–1914*. London: Weidenfeld & Nicolson, 1987.

———. *Age of Extremes: The Short Twentieth Century, 1914–1991*. London: Michael Joseph, 1994.

———. *On Empire: America, War, and Global Supremacy*. New York: Pantheon Books, 2008.

Hoogvelt, Ankie. *Globalization and the Postcolonial World: The New Political Economy of Development*. London: Macmillan, 1997.

Hopkins, A.G. *American Empire: A Global History*. Princeton, NJ: Princeton University Press, 2018.

Hunt, Michael H. *The American Ascendancy: How the United States Gained and Wielded Global Dominance*. Chapel Hill: University of North Carolina Press, 2007.

———. *Ideology and U.S. Foreign Policy*. New Haven, CT: Yale University Press, 1987.

Hunt, Michael H., and Steven I. Levine. *Arc of Empire: America's Wars in Asia from the Philippines to Vietnam*. Chapel Hill: University of North Carolina Press, 2012.

Hunt, Tristram. *Ten Cities that Made an Empire*. London: Allen Lane, 2014.

Hurrell, Andrew, and Ngaire Woods (eds). *Inequality, Globalization, and World Politics*. Oxford: Oxford University Press, 1999.

Hustvedt, Siri. *Living, Thinking, Looking*. London: Sceptre, 2012.

Iggers, Georg G., and Q. Edward Wang. *A Global History of Modern Historiography*. Harlow: Longman, 2008.

Ikenberry, G. John. *Liberal Order & Imperial Ambition: Essays on American Power and World Politics*. Cambridge: Polity Press, 2006.

Immerman, Richard H. *Empire for Liberty: A History of American Imperialism from Benjamin Franklin to Paul Wolfowitz*. Princeton, NJ: Princeton University Press, 2010.

Immerwahr, Daniel. 'A.G. Hopkins. American Empire: A Global History', *H-Diplo* 20(33) (22 April 2019), https://networks.h-net.org/node/28443/discussions/4033475/roundtable-xx-33-ag-hopkins-american-empire-global-history.

———. 'The Greater United States: Territory and Empire in U.S. History', *Diplomatic History* 40(3) (June 2016), 373–91.

———. *How to Hide an Empire: A Short History of the Greater United States*. London: Bodley Head, 2019.

———. 'Writing the History of the Greater United States: A Reply to Paul Kramer', *Diplomatic History* 42(2) (April 2019), 397–403.

Jasanoff, Maya. 'Power Is Shifting Eastwards … Travels in Central Asia Prompt a Breezy Analysis of How the World Will Be', Review, *The Guardian* (London), 11 May 2019, 14.

———. 'What New Empires Inherit from Old Ones', *History News Network*, 12 December 2005. https://historynewsnetwork.org/article/18853.

Jefferson, Thomas. 'The Declaration of Independence, 1776', in Henry Steele Commager (ed.), *Documents of American History*. New York: Appleton Century Crofts, 1963, 100–2.

Johnson, Chalmers. *The Sorrows of Empire: Militarism, Secrecy, and the End of the Republic*. New York: Henry Holt, 2004.

Judd, Denis. *Empire: The British Imperial Experience, from 1765 to the Present*. London: Harper-Collins, 1996.

Kaplan, Amy, and Donald E. Pease (eds). *Cultures of United States Imperialism*. Durham, NC: Duke University Press, 1993.

Keane, Fergal. 'On Colonial Violence'. Speech, School of History, University College Cork, Ireland (2018).

Kennedy, Dane. *The Imperial History Wars: Debating the British Empire*. London: Bloomsbury, 2018.

———. *The Last Blank Spaces: Exploring Africa and Australia*. Cambridge, MA: Harvard University Press, 2013.

Kiely, Ray. *Rethinking Imperialism*. London: Palgrave Macmillan, 2010.

Kiernan, V.G. *Imperialism and Its Contradictions*. New York: Routledge, 1995.

Kiernan, Victor. *The Lords of Human Kind: European Attitudes to Other Cultures in the Imperial Age*. London: Serif, 1969.

Kimball, Warren. 'Foreword', in David Ryan and Victor Pungong (eds), *The United States and Decolonization: Power and Freedom*. London: Macmillan, 2000, xiii–xvii.

———. *The Juggler: Franklin Roosevelt as Wartime Statesman*. Princeton, NJ: Princeton University Press, 1991.

Kramer, Paul A. *The Blood of Government: Race, Empire, the United States, & the Philippines*. Chapel Hill: University of North Carolina Press, 2006.

———. 'How Not to Write the History of U.S. Empire', *Diplomatic History* 42(5) (November 2018), 911–31.

LaFeber, Walter. *The American Search for Opportunity, 1865–1913*. The Cambridge History of American Foreign Relations. Cambridge: Cambridge University Press, 1993.

———. *Inevitable Revolutions: The United States in Central America*. New York: W.W. Norton & Company, 1983.

———. *The New Empire: An Interpretation of American Expansion 1860–1898*. Ithaca, NY: Cornell University Press, 1963.

———. 'The Post September 11 Debate over Empire, Globalization, and Fragmentation', *Political Science Quarterly* 117(1) (Spring 2002), 1–17.

——— (ed.). *John Quincy Adams and American Continental Empire: Letters, Papers and Speeches*. Chicago: Quadrangle Books, 1965.

Lears, Jackson. 'How the US Began Its Empire', *The New York Review of Books* 64(3) (23 February 2017), 37–40.

———. 'Imperial Exceptionalism', *The New York Review of Books* 66(2) (7 February 2019), 8–10.

Leffler, Melvyn P. *A Preponderance of Power: National Security, the Truman Administration, and the Cold War*. Stanford, CA: Stanford University Press, 1992.

Lepore, Jill. 'A New Americanism: Why a Nation Needs a National Story', *Foreign Affairs* 98(2) (April 2019), 10–19.

———. *These Truths: A History of the United States*. New York: W.W. Norton & Company, 2018.

Lippmann, Walter. *Men of Destiny*. New York: Macmillan, 1927.

Maier, Charles S. *Among Empires: American Ascendancy and Its Predecessors*. Cambridge, MA: Harvard University Press, 2006.

Mann, Michael. *Incoherent Empire*. London: Verso, 2003.

McCormick, Thomas J. *America's Half-Century: United States Foreign Policy in the Cold War*. Baltimore, MD: Johns Hopkins Press, 1989.

Mishra, Pankaj. *From the Ruins of Empire: The Intellectuals Who Remade Asia*. New York: Farrar, Straus and Giroux, 2012.

Moore, Colin D. *American Imperialism and the State, 1893–1921*. Cambridge: Cambridge University Press, 2017.

Munkler, Herfried. *Empires: The Logic of World Domination from Ancient Rome to the United States*. Cambridge: Polity Press, 2007.

Ngũgĩ, wa Thiong'o. *Moving the Centre: The Struggle for Cultural Freedoms*. London: James Currey, 1993.

Nobles, Gregory H. *American Frontiers: Cultural Encounters and Continental Conquest*. London: Penguin, 1997.

Norton, Anne. *Leo Strauss and the Politics of American Empire*. New Haven, CT: Yale University Press, 2004.

Osterhammel, Jürgen. *Colonialism: A Theoretical Overview*. Princeton, NJ: Markus Wiener, 1997.

Pagden, Anthony. *Lords of All the World: Ideologies of Empire in Spain, Britain and France, c.1500–c.1800*. New Haven, CT: Yale University Press, n.d.

Perkins, Bradford. *The Creation of a Republican Empire, 1776–1865*. Cambridge: Cambridge University Press, 1993.

———. *The Great Rapprochement: England and the United States, 1895–1914*. London: Victor Gollancz, 1969.

Pomper, Philip. 'The History and Theory of Empires', *History and Theory* 44(4) (December 2005), 1–27.

Porter, Bernard. *Empire and Superempire: Britain, America and the World*. New Haven, CT: Yale University Press, 2006.

Reynolds, David. *America, Empire of Liberty: A New History*. London: Allen Lane, 2009.

Rosenboim, Or. *The Emergence of Globalism: Visions of World Order in Britain and The United States, 1939–1950*. Princeton, NJ: Princeton University Press, 2017.

Rupert, Mark. *Ideologies of Globalization: Contending Visions of a New World Order*. London: Routledge, 2000.

Ryan, David. 'Culture and Re-Membering the Alliance in Kosovo and Iraq: Anglo-American Ironies under Clinton, Blair and Bush', in Robert Hendershot and Steve Marsh (eds), *Culture Matters: Anglo-American Relations and the Intangibles of 'Specialness'*. Manchester: Manchester University Press, 2020, 243–70.

———. *Frustrated Empire: US Foreign Policy, 9/11 to Iraq*. London: Pluto, 2007.

———. 'Tragedy after Tragedy: The Failure to Recognise Limits in US Foreign Policy'. Conference paper, Rutgers University, New Brunswick, NJ, 2009.

Ryan, David, and Victor Pungong (eds). *The United States and Decolonization: Power and Freedom*. London: Macmillan, 2000.

Said, Edward W. *Culture and Imperialism*. London: Chatto & Windus, 1993.

Sassen, Saskia. *Globalization and Its Discontents: Essays on the New Mobility of People and Money*. New York: The New Press, 1998.

Smith, Neil. *The Endgame of Globalization*. New York: Routledge, 2005.

Spiegel, Gabrielle M. 'Revising the Past / Revisiting the Present: How Change Happens in Historiography', *History and Theory* 46, Theme Issue (December 2007), 1–19.

Stephanson, Anders. *Manifest Destiny: American Expansion and the Empire of Right*. New York: Hill and Wang, 1995.

Stiglitz, Joseph. *Globalization and Its Discontents*. London: Penguin, 2002.

Streets-Salter, Heather. 'International and Global Anti-Colonial Movements', in Antoinette Burton and Tony Ballantyne (eds), *World Histories from Below: Disruption and Dissent, 1750 to the Present*. London: Bloomsbury, 2016.

Tharoor, Shashi. *Inglorious Empire: What the British Did to India*. London: Penguin, 2017.

Thelen, David. 'Making History and Making the United States', *Journal of American Studies* 32(3) (December 1998), 373–97.

Toye, Richard. 'Why Is the British Empire Still so Controversial', *Empire: The Controversies of British Imperialism* [blog], 25 November 2017. https://about.futurelearn.com/blog/british-empire.

Tyrrell, Ian. 'Making Nations/Making States: American Historians in the Context of Empire', *Journal of American History* 86(3) (December 1999), 1015–44.

———. *Transnational Nation: United States History in Global Perspective since 1789*. Basingstoke: Palgrave Macmillan, 2007.

Weil, Francois. 'Do American Historical Narratives Travel?', in Thomas Bender (ed.), *Rethinking American History in a Global Age*. Berkeley: University of California Press, 2002, 317–42.

Weiss, Antonio, and Brad Setser. 'America's Forgotten Colony: Ending Puerto Rico's Perpetual Crisis', *Foreign Affairs* 98(4) (July 2019), 158–68.

Wiener, Martin J. 'The Idea of "Colonial Legacy" and the Historiography of Empire', *Journal of the Historical Society* 13(1) (March 2013), 1–32.

Williams, William Appleman. *Empire as a Way of Life*. New York: Oxford University Press, 1980.

———. *The Roots of the Modern American Empire: A Study of the Growth and Shaping of Social Consciousness in a Market Place Society*. London: Anthony Blond, 1969.

———. *The Tragedy of American Diplomacy*. New York: Delta, 1962.

Wood, Robert E. 'From the Marshall Plan to the Third World', in Melvyn P. Leffler and David S. Painter (eds), *Origins of the Cold War: An International History*. London: Routledge, 1994, 239–50.

Young, Marilyn B. 'The Age of Global Power', in Thomas Bender (ed.), *Rethinking American History in a Global Age*. Berkeley: University of California Press, 2002, 274–94.

Zinn, Howard. *A People's History of the United States*. London: Longman, 1980.

Chapter 7

The Anglo-American Tradition in International Law

David Clinton

To discern and describe a tradition of thinking about the law of nations among publicists and practitioners in the United Kingdom and the United States is a challenging task. Certainly, it cannot be said that every writer on international law over four centuries in the English-speaking world has held one view of the nature, sources, content and evolution of international law. What Arnold Wolfers and Laurence Martin said of international relations thought in general – that it 'may be dangerous to lump together into [a] distinct [category] all Anglo-American theorists … as if agreement within [this] camp had been the rule', when 'on most points it has not' – could be said as well of international law.[1] Nor is it possible to assert that one way of conceiving of international law is exclusively characteristic of Anglo-American thinkers and no one in the non-Anglo-American world; rather, the same variety is found among scholars of international law in every country and language, and these authorities have regularly cited, borrowed from and contended with one another without regard to nationality.

What one can say is that certain broadly defined attitudes towards the subject have frequently appeared among Anglo-American writers and that these attitudes, while not unique to the United Kingdom and the United States, have seemed to form the main current of this branch of the mighty river system that is the international legal community. That is, not all British and American authors on international law have adopted the views that will be discussed in this chapter and not all authors outside the Anglo-American world have rejected them, but there is a general approach to international law that frequently underpins the scholarship and commentary on the subject in the two countries. This approach is recognizably Anglo-American, even if it is not monopolized by Anglo-American authorities, nor is it taken by all Anglo-American writers, among whom considerable diversity exists. It is a tendency and not an orthodoxy, a set of inclinations shared by some others in some different national traditions and not a fixed set of views bearing a UK-US copyright.

The origins of international law extend to the ancient world, well before anyone had conceived of a polity resembling the United Kingdom or any European peoples had reached North America. Yet conceptions of a set of standards embodying justice that transcended any single political community or could be found in recognizably similar forms in many separate political communities, which are evident especially in Roman and Thomistic thought, had their effect on later ages. It is the particular use that has been made of this shared inheritance by writers and political leaders in the Anglo-American world that is the concern of this chapter.

The Limitations of International Law

To begin with a consideration of what international law is not, one may consider Anglo-American conceptions of its origins, its destiny and its contemporary functions. In each case, the thinkers examined here, while appreciative of the many contributions of the law of nations, have propounded ideas that did not accord law too 'high' a place either in social interaction generally or in international life in particular. They have avoided disappointment by restraining expectations.

Although many writers have found the ultimate origin of international law in divine ordinance and the need for international law in human sin, few if any have asserted that international laws represent the unmediated commands of the deity. Nor have they generally contended that human reason is powerful enough to discern at a stroke the principles of rightful international conduct and reduce them to specific legal rules. Rather, they have most commonly found that many different public authorities, using their intellect and their moral intuition as best they can, have, through trial and error, independently arrived at their best approximation of what reason and morality demand; and their interactions have revealed an impressive degree of similarity among the precepts that they have developed separately. They have termed these precepts the law of nations and the validity of this system of law, they have claimed, is demonstrated by the common utility that has resulted in its universal acceptance and survival as a common code.

Alberico Gentili (1552–1608) fled religious persecution in his native Italy, travelling to England at the age of twenty-eight and pursuing careers in academia and the law there for the rest of his life; therefore, he may be considered a contributor to the Anglo-American tradition and perhaps even one of its founders. While for him 'the law of nations is that which is in use among all the nations of men, which native reason has established among all human beings, and which is equally observed by all mankind ... this statement ... must not be understood to mean that all nations actually came together at a given time, and that then the law of nations was established'. Rather, the fact that the law of nations was 'a natural law' was evident in that it was independently arrived at as a just rule within many realms and thus 'successively seemed acceptable to all men'. Not a formalized code, this law was unwritten and was 'like a custom and ... established in the same manner'. A mixture of what was naturally just and what had developed through practice as a common standard of right conduct, then, the law of nations reflected both natural reason and the wisdom of accumulated custom. Derived from 'Nature herself', it was authenticated by human practice and demonstrated by widespread, though separate, adoption.[2]

Nearly three centuries later, this same theme of variegated and mixed derivations of international law appeared in the volume on the laws of war published by Henry W. Halleck (soon to become general-in-chief of the United States army in the American Civil War). 'The rules which ought to regulate the conduct of nations in their mutual intercourse', Halleck declared, were 'undoubtedly deduced' in part 'from reason and justice' (or inherent standards of right and wrong), in part 'from the nature of society existing between independent states or bodies politic' (or the kind of relations that must exist among societies that have no common superior) and in part 'from usage, and the agreements or compacts entered into between different nations' (or the actions of states themselves in conventions and treaties they created or the practices they followed).[3]

This mention of 'the nature of society existing between independent states' constitutes an example of a frequently voiced description of the origin of international law – that it derives not, strictly speaking, simply from the consent of states expressed through their agreements or their conduct, nor does it derive from the principles of natural law transmuted to the circumstances of states; rather, that it arises from the inherent nature of the relations that must, by necessity, exist among entities that acknowledge no common superior but have enough to do with one another that they require some predictable rules for their interactions. 'It can be argued that "law" is the hallmark of any political community which exists for the common good. Law is necessary for the society to function and, because it is necessary, it is *ex hypothesi* binding', one contemporary British scholar of international law suggests. 'Therefore, because international society is a community of interacting and interdependent states, it also needs rules governing its life.'[4]

James Kent ('Chancellor Kent', an American legal scholar of the early nineteenth century) and other writers have dwelt on, and often begun with, the inescapable influence of living as a state, and a state among other states, on the conception of international law as a necessary and beneficial institution for carrying on the natural and inevitable commercial and political relations that must develop among a series of independent but neighbouring political communities, especially when those communities are marked by 'a common origin, and were governed by similar institutions, manners, laws, and religion', as Kent said.[5] John Westlake, the holder of the Whewell Chair in International Law at Cambridge in the late nineteenth century, similarly founded his analysis of 'the law of the society of states or nations' on the assumption of 'a state, which in its turn lives among states'.[6] The mid-nineteenth-century English jurist Robert Phillimore introduced a more theological element when he stated, 'The necessity of mutual intercourse is laid in the nature of States, as it is of Individuals, by God, who willed the State and created the Individual', but he drew a similar conclusion regarding the necessity of international law when he contended, 'The intercourse of Nations, therefore, gives rise to International Rights and Duties, and these require an International Law for their regulation and enforcement.'[7] The Scottish academician James Lorimer wrestled with 'the great [contending but ultimately reconcilable] facts that whilst, on the one hand, the object of legislation is to protect separate and independent life, and to vindicate unfettered activity, however feeble, – on the other hand, absolute isolation and indifference to each other's actions and each other's interests is inconsistent with that mutual dependence which God has established amongst the children of Adam, – that, if we are to be free at all, we can be free only by each other's aid'.[8] Complete isolation for a state being even more difficult to accomplish than life as a true hermit for an individual human being, states must practically always pursue their corporate existence among other states, leading to a kind of society among themselves, the mutual dealings of which demand some sort of law.

The twentieth-century British practitioner and student of international law James Brierly summarized this point about reason, practice and the social necessities of a society of states when he stated, 'The sources of international law are custom and reason' – to which he added, 'probably', treaties. Custom and treaties appear in their familiar guises of the rules that states accept in their repeated behaviour and those that states create in 'black-letter' law by signing written agreements containing obligatory codes of conduct. 'Reason', however, takes on a somewhat different cast, as Brierly transformed it from native and universal human reason meditating on the nature of things as God or Nature has created them into '"judicial" reason', or the kind of thinking employed by lawyers in respecting precedents, discerning analogies between apparently different sets of circumstances and unearthing from these circumstances the more fundamental principles that make them into rules of law.[9]

Gentili the scholar, Halleck the general and Brierly the advocate were at one and were also representative of the Anglo-American tradition more generally, in viewing international law as a unique admixture. It begins with natural law, a set of inherently right standards of justice discovered, not created, by human beings. It adds the reason that allows humans to discern these standards and put them into words. And it concludes with positivism, or the belief that law is indeed created by human beings, these enactments of humans themselves being recorded in their consistent practice or their deliberate authorship. Custom is elevated by its asserted derivation from divine or semi-divine sources, while the reliance on natural law is restrained by the need to find it endorsed by the practices shared but independently arrived at by many political communities over a long period of time. What this conception of the origins of international law may lack in blinding clarity and consistency of vision it gains back in the solidity it draws from relying on the strengths of both the naturalist and the positivist interpretations, without being fully captured by either. Over the four centuries of the existence of an Anglo-American tradition of international law, the balance has shifted, from a heavy reliance on natural law at the outset, through a period, in the seventeenth through the nineteenth centuries, in which positivism gained increasing ground and, in the twentieth century, a revival of interest in standards that are recognized or discovered by human reason and not created by it. But only rarely has one side or the other of this amalgam been lost.[10]

A similar modesty of conception may be found in the acceptance – or, indeed, the insistence – that this framework of law does not form a world state in embryo. Law in the Anglo-American tradition is usually a 'gentle civilizer' of the relations among independent political communities that have, through their formal actions in reducing it to written form in their treaties and conventions, as well as their regular reaffirmation in their customary behaviour, sustained it and regularly modified it as their well-being in evolving conditions has indicated. They have created international institutions to do in concert that which seems to them likely to be done less effectively by each of them acting alone. They have not, by and large, granted irrevocable powers to legal institutions that they cannot control, either through the fundamental charters of these institutions (charters that themselves have the character of international law) or through the power of the purse (that is, the dependence of such institutions on the monies granted to them by national governments). In his monumental study of international organization, for example, Inis

Claude relegates world government to the very end of the book and goes to pains to distinguish both the theory and practice of world government and international organizations.[11]

Halleck's identification of a particular kind of society that exists among entities that are themselves communities and may participate in a community among themselves but have no sovereign ruler over them all itself assumed that if a world government were to come into being, international law would be transformed into something fundamentally different from what it intrinsically is. In becoming domestic law, it would cease to be international law. Nor does the broad mainstream of thinking on international law hold it to be a mere way station on the way to world government.[12]

Thus, Richard Zouche (1590–1661), an English judge and parliamentarian, often described as the first systematic writer on international law, defined law between nations (or *jus inter gentes*, a usage that he did much to create) as 'the law which is recognized in the community of different princes or peoples who hold sovereign power' – the central fact being that each of these princes or peoples holds sovereign or ultimate power, rather than living under the sovereignty of a higher authority. The lack of such an authority did not prevent there from being a degree of community among them and Zouche was clear that peace is to be found in concord among multiple sovereigns that have accepted law among themselves and not in the medieval idealist hope for universal peace under a common authority.[13] Phillimore, in the nineteenth century, began his examination of international law by criticizing the German author Christian Wolff for accepting 'the false hypothesis that there existed *de facto* a great republic of which all nations were members'.[14] This rejection of the notion that international law is a building block of world government rests on a distinction between, on one hand, a state with a government capable of enacting laws and imposing penalties on violators of those laws and, on the other, a society of such states, in which neither an international legislature nor an international executive exists, but nevertheless the contact and similarity among these states is sufficient to render each willing to exercise self-restraint and all willing to consider at times restraining others who transgress too dangerously a consensus on proper behaviour. 'These things being so', Westlake suggested, 'states live together in the civilised world substantially as men live together in a state, the difference being one of machinery, and we are entitled to say that there is a society of states and a law of that society'.[15] It is that 'difference of machinery' that makes a society of states only 'substantially' (and not wholly) like a society that is coincident with a state and renders international law different in kind from the legislation of a hypothesized world government.[16]

The very utility that has helped states to make an informal norm into a positive or customary law also gives states a potent incentive to obey such a law, even in cases in which their immediate benefit might seem to lie in its violation. In that sense, the major weight of the Anglo-American tradition could be said to fall in the 'Grotian' scale.[17] That same utility can also induce states to act as enforcers of law, whether in the first instance through their expressions of disapproval of the actions taken by others that are generally considered to be inconsistent with international legal standards, in the second instance by their lessened willingness to co-operate diplomatically with a violator of international law, in the third instance by their individual or collective imposition of sanctions (often economic) on such an international bad citizen, or in the final analysis through the use of armed force to counter actions viewed as sufficiently dangerous to themselves and to international life as a whole to require a military response.

The mention of the use of power, whether diplomatic, economic or military, to counter violations of international law that are seen as hazardous to international society and its members recalls the fact that in a world of multiple independent states there are bound to exist disparities of power among these states. In a final example of modesty in eschewing high ambitions, Anglo-American thought has by and large accepted inequality as a fact of international life – not inequality in relation to certain basic legal rights held by all states, such as territorial integrity, but inequality in the conclusion that the great powers must take the lead in countering law-breaking states and in forming international coalitions to oppose such violations and these powers must possess the requisite rights and duties, recognized under international law, to enable them to carry out this leadership role. Indeed, Hedley Bull sees the category of 'great powers' as an institution of international life itself, which, alongside international law, can serve as an instrument of international order.[18] Whether acting informally to preserve or restore an international distribution of power that would restrain a state from gathering into its hands the capacity to 'give the law to nations' or acting in formal concert with other states in the operation of collective security as codified in the League of Nations Covenant and the United Nations Charter, states have found ways to curb the behaviour of other states.[19] In all these instances, however, the greatest role has been played by those possessing the greatest capabilities and the Anglo-American tradition has almost never included advocates of levelling international society so far as to abolish the inequalities of power that sustain the division of that society into leaders and followers. This way of treating international law has therefore had to confront the dilemma of how to concentrate power to the extent that it successfully counteracts attempts at aggression without allowing that power itself to become a danger to international society as a whole, but it has not by and large been attracted to an international form of anti-trust action that would break up all forms of concentrated power.

The Possibilities of International Law

This discussion of Anglo-American thinking on what international law cannot or should not do may lead to the conclusion that it relegates international law to a modest and confined role in international life, more constrained than the comparatively robust and expansive conceptions held in other countries. It is true that in his article on international relations as 'an American social science', Stanley Hoffmann contrasts the 'precepts of law and the realities of politics' and contends that a rich understanding of international relations helps one 'understand the fumblings and failures of international law'.[20] In these passages, Hoffmann, who accepted some doctrines of realism and heavily qualified others, appears to hew to the suspicion of E.H. Carr, a much more unqualified realist, that law is only a cover for the self-interest of dominant international players.[21] Likewise, C.A.W. Manning, who, like Hoffmann, grants greater weight to the shared interests and norms of an international society than does Carr, admits both that in the existing international order 'the highest authority' is not international law but 'the individual sovereign state' and that 'all too often, when [international law is] appealed to, its trumpet gives forth an uncertain sound'.[22] Yet such an inference of incapacity and impotence would have to contend with the fact that the development of thought and practice in the English-speaking world on the legal component of international life has held relatively high hopes for advancement and growth in international law in at least three respects: its fundamentally progressive nature, its concentration on an expanding liberty and its conviction that justice and advantage are ultimately compatible in the international dealings of states.

A striking characteristic of most Anglo-American treatments of international law is the confidence that, over a long period of maturation and despite occasional setbacks, the general trend has been the strengthening, expansion, clarification and focusing of humanity's understanding of the contribution that law can make to human happiness. Almost uniformly, accounts of the origins and development of international law begin with descriptions of a state of affairs that is only vaguely 'international' in the contemporary sense of the word and 'law-like' only in the most rudimentary understanding of that term. Chancellor Kent gave an account that is representative in his commentaries on international law: 'The most refined states among the ancients seem to have had no conception of the moral obligations of justice and humanity between nations, and there was no such thing in existence as the science of

International Law.' It was only after a long passage of time, including the advent of Christianity and the habituation of many states to living in a condition of independence but also of mutual society, that one could look back and see a pattern in 'the feeble beginnings, the slow and interrupted progress, and final and triumphant success, of the principles of public right'.[23] The common attitude may be seen in the confidence that success in this ascent had been both 'triumphant' and 'final'.

Likewise, Henry Wheaton, both a jurist and a diplomat in the United States in the first half of the nineteenth century, began his work *Elements of International Law* with the assertion that '"eternal war against the Barbarians," was the Shibboleth of the most civilized and enlightened peoples of antiquity'. Many events in world history, including the transformation of religion from a divisive to a unifying force in human relations, the influence of Roman law on succeeding generations, 'the establishment of the system of a balance of power among the European States' and the beneficent example of Grotius and his followers, had led to modern enlightenment and the rise of contemporary 'public jurists', whom Wheaton, quoting Patrick Henry, described as 'these illustrious authors – these friends of human nature – these kind instructors of human errors and frailties – these benevolent spirits who held up the torch of science to a benighted world'.[24]

Later in the nineteenth century and on the other side of the Atlantic, Lorimer, in an introductory lecture on public law in 1878, told his students that a 'reasoned system of international law' was in the process of development as the study of law adopted the dispassionate methods of the natural sciences. 'The laws of health and wealth are progressively revealed, and man becomes gradually acquainted with physics and physiology, hygiene and economics' and the same process could occur and was occurring in 'ethics, politics, and jurisprudence'. The physical sciences were marked by 'the unfaltering steps with which they march along from discovery to discovery' and in politics and jurisprudence a similar evolution could be seen as 'the philosophical point of view has tended to take the place of the theocratic'. Lorimer contrasted 'dogma' – the product of divine revelation, which, because of its origin, could not be touched and was therefore incapable of any progress – with 'doctrine' – the product of reason, which, through debate and evidence, would be progressively improved – and found that 'dogma is being rapidly superseded by doctrine even in theology'.[25]

'Looking back over the last couple of centuries, we see international law at the close of each fifty years in a more solid position than that which it occupied at the beginning of the period', the English lawyer William E. Hall assured readers of his *Treatise on International Law*, published in 1924. 'Progressively it has taken firmer hold, it has extended its sphere of operation, it has ceased to trouble itself about trivial formalities, it has more and more dared to grapple in detail with the fundamental facts in the relations of States.'[26] From its origins in disputes often relating to matters of precedence and honours, the realm of international law had come increasingly to encompass matters of security, prosperity and mutually beneficial co-operation. A quarter of a century after Hall penned his treatise, Philip Jessup, an American scholar of international law and future judge on the International Court of Justice, noted that this expression of confidence in the progress (and progressiveness) of international law had been 'quoted with approval by the Judicial Committee of the Privy Council' ten years after its publication, arguing that the receptiveness of international law to alteration and improvement could be seen in the realm of national policy as well as that of academic debate.[27]

Sometime naïve and triumphalist, sometimes sophisticated and cautious, this confidence in progress has been a frequent feature of Anglo-American attitudes towards international law. It has undoubtedly had its counterparts in other parts of the world and some of its sharpest critics have come from within the Anglo-American context itself – see George Kennan's trenchant critique of 'the legalistic-moralistic approach to international problems' – but that it has, again, in Kennan's words, 'run like a red skein' through discussions of international law on both sides of the Atlantic for a considerable period of time seems a reasonable conclusion.[28]

This progressivist attitude has served as a natural counterpart of an equally strong belief that just international action and the best interests of the states making up international society would ultimately coincide. Whether found in Wheaton's contention that 'Sound policy can never authorize a resort to such measures as are prohibited by the law of nations, founded on the principles of eternal justice; and, on the other hand, the law of nations ought not to prohibit that which sound policy dictates as necessary to the security of any State' or Lorimer's declaration that 'did I believe international relations to be governed by no permanent laws, either moral or social, … I should abandon the study of international jurisprudence in disgust, as an occupation that was unworthy of a rational being or an honest man', the language of Anglo-American international law brims with the faith that the just and the advantageous cannot in the long run, or as each should be truly understood, conflict.[29] Even Leo Gross – born in Austria and a student of Hans Kelsen, but with an Anglo-American educational background that included the London School of Economics, Columbia University and Harvard University, before he spent four decades teaching in the United States, serving as an adviser to the US Department of State and as publisher of *The American Journal of International Law* – agreed that, to his regret, no 'law of subordination' was coming into existence. As far as his position was from that of Wheaton on the question of the desirability of an international legal code enforceable on states, Gross held that the true interests of states – their well-being rightly understood – rested on adherence to reliable, objectively just law and that to accomplish this goal no 'super-state' – no world government dictating to states – was needed.

A second trait of the Anglo-American tradition may be found in its insistence on the centrality of liberty, both individual and national. 'To assert or develop its own freedom of action is the right and the duty of every separate community', wrote Lorimer in perhaps the clearest statement of this emphasis on liberty. 'To recognise this assertion and to aid this development is the duty and the right of all the communities which recognise their several existence as States. The freedom of each is the object of all, and considered simply as jural entities it is their only object.'[30] In an influential article published in the year of the three-hundredth anniversary of the Treaty of Westphalia, Gross described the centuries-long breakdown of a fairly centralized system of international public law held together by the authority of the Papacy and the Holy Roman Empire and its replacement by an international 'law of coordination' created by states to fit within an international order marked by 'rugged individualism of territorial and heterogeneous states, balance of power, equality of states, and toleration'. In the mid-twentieth century, he deemed it necessary to find a replacement for the old reliance on 'right reason and natural law' that would serve as a new standard based on 'sources of objective ... validity', which would result in what he called 'the old-new doctrine ... a law of subordination, that is, a law above states'. Still, he recognized the power of 'the national will to self-control which after a prolonged struggle first threw off the external shackles of Pope and Emperor [and] *mutatis mutandis* persists today in declining any far-reaching subordination to external controls'. The very most that he thought might be achieved would be some method of 'harmonizing the will of major states to self-control with the exigencies of an international society which by and large yearns for order under law'.[31] Gross realized that in yearning for order under a law of subordination, he was opposing the predominant current in Anglo-American legal thinking, which favoured instead 'the international law of political liberty'.[32]

Almost simultaneously with the appearance of Gross's article, Jessup published his book, making many of the same arguments in favour of 'a modern law of nations' whereby international law would be made applicable directly to individual persons and not to states, and 'breaches of the law [would] no longer be considered the concern of only the state directly and primarily affected', but would instead be considered similar to the domestic institution of criminal law, 'in which the community as such brings its combined power to bear upon the violator'. Yet Jessup had to admit that 'the traditional legal foundations' of what he called 'unilateralism' 'remain largely unshaken'.[33]

In his identification of an international society guided by an international law of 'subordination' that was, beginning in the Renaissance, replaced by one wedded to a law of 'coordination' among free, equal and sovereign political entities that came to be called states, and the subsequent elaboration of the rules regarding collaboration and conflict among these juridically equal states, which remained free to alter the rules they had created, Gross may have been thinking of Wheaton, who, in his preface to the third edition of his study of international law, published in 1845, referred approvingly to the fact that 'the immunity of the national flag from every species and purpose of search, by the armed vessels of another State, in time of peace, except in virtue of a special compact, was maintained by an appeal to the oracles of public law both of Great Britain and the United States, and has since been solemnly sanctioned by the treaty of Washington [the Webster-Ashburton treaty], 1842'.[34]

Of course, the right of search to which Wheaton referred concerned the right to stop ships on the high seas suspected of carrying slaves, which could indicate that national liberty and individual liberty might not always coincide – a tension that persists in contemporary debates over the degree to which an international Responsibility to Protect should infringe on the traditional right under international law of non-intervention. Anglo-American thinking has been marked by its confidence that these two forms of liberty can indeed be reconciled – and that both can be advanced without the progress of either coming at the expense of the other. In that belief, Wheaton, Lorimer and others have been inheritors of Gibbons's claim that, unlike Rome, the independence of several polities in the Europe of his own day and their rivalry preserved individual liberty as well: 'The abuses of tyranny are restrained by the mutual influence of fear and shame.'[35]

The Role of Anglo-American States in International Law

Not unrelated to the disinclination to radically redistribute the resources of power in an effort to equalize the members of international society is the position of the United Kingdom and the United States in that society. Two aspects of this phenomenon may be mentioned, one having to do with the freedom of action of states under international law and the other with a sense of guardianship of the international legal order. It would be difficult to expect any state to completely divorce its views on any of the institutions of international life, including international law, from its own vantage point and interest, and the Anglo-American powers have been no exception in this regard.

First, as noted at the beginning of this essay, Wolfers has observed a difference between a Continental emphasis on 'necessity of state' (required by the constant threat of insecurity created by powerful neighbours) and an An-glo-American 'debate about the best way of applying accepted principles of morality to the field of foreign policy' (made possible by the greater protection provided by geographic remoteness and the greater degree of domestic har-mony, which allowed for growth in the role of law).[36] Observers should not draw this distinction too sharply, for there are exceptions in both the 'Conti-nental' and the 'insular' camps, yet the history of two countries separated from the main arenas of world conflict by the Channel and by the Atlantic has had an effect on the degree to which their scholars and their political leaders thought that the international realm could, to some degree, be tamed by law and legal institutions – and what they believed their part in such develop-ments should be.[37]

On the other hand, this sense of comparatively greater separation and secu-rity has led to a heightened emphasis on international freedom of action and a corresponding reluctance to subject national decision-making to supranational legal control. What Claude has called the role of the 'auxiliary' – a willingness to intervene to oppose threats to world order, but only at times and places of one's own choosing – has commonly been assumed in both countries.[38]

Wheaton's monumental mid-nineteenth-century compendium of interna-tional law is typical in this regard. Non-intervention is the general rule it supported and it was careful to highlight that 'the performance of the duties of international law [is] compelled by moral sanctions only, by fear on the part of nations of provoking general hostility, and incurring its probable evils in case they should violate this law'. The discussion of intervention recalls two instances in which Britain was urged to intervene in the Iberian Peninsula – the case of French intervention in Spain in 1822 and the case of Spanish intervention in Portugal in 1826. Wheaton summarized the response of the Foreign Secretary George Canning to the two crises with evident approval:

> The British government might lawfully have interfered [in 1822], on grounds of political expediency; but they were not bound to interfere, as they were now [in 1826] bound to interfere on behalf of Portugal, by the obligations of treaty. War might have been their free choice, if they had deemed it politic, in the case of Spain; interference on behalf of Portugal was their duty, unless they were pre-pared to abandon the principles of national faith and national honor.

The difference lay in the fact that Britain was a party to a treaty of alliance with Portugal, while it had made no such commitment to Spain; interna-tional law created no general obligations beyond what the state had chosen to accept.[39] Written commitments to act on behalf of a specific party were, under good faith and honour, binding, but otherwise intervention was to be guided by 'political expediency'. Not all state papers bring to their subject this degree of frankness, but Wheaton's distillation of Canning's statement was a concise description of the 'free hand' that both the United Kingdom and the United States have frequently sought from international law. Kent, writing earlier in the nineteenth century, laid down the dictum that interposition in a foreign civil conflict was a right, not a duty, and a right to be 'submitted to the guidance of eminent discretion and controlled by principles of justice and sound policy', making it not a matter of legal responsibility at all.[40] Theodore Woolsey, writing in 1879 following his time as president of Yale, suggested that sentiments of outrage against manifest injustices committed in the international realm could bring states to feel a moral duty to intervene even in actions that did not involve them directly, but he reminded his readers that international law 'is the most voluntary of codes' and he presented no argument that taking the decision on intervention out of the hands of each state and attempting to turn that sense of outrage into a binding legal obligation would be either consistent with the basic character of the law of nations or desirable for the progress of the world.[41] The scepticism among American senators in 1919 over the automaticity of the commitments of the United States under the collective security arrangements of the League Covenant would be another instance of this insistence upon retaining a free hand. Only six years later, London followed Washington's example in negotiating the Treaty of Locarno, which was a guarantee on Britain's part rather than a military alliance, 'which had the advantage of making Britain's commitments less rigid and automatic' and allowed her to retain 'her freedom to decide how to fulfill her pledge'.[42] Although in 1945, the United States made a choice contrary to the decision it had made after the First World War and joined the United Nations, similar concerns were voiced in the Senate over the obligations being assumed under the provisions concerning collective security in the Charter allowing the Security Council to 'determine the existence of any threat to the peace' and 'take such action by air, sea, or land forces as may be necessary to maintain or restore international peace', and similar assurances were given that the United States was undertaking no legal obligation that would vitiate the power of Congress to determine whether in any particular instance the United States would go to war. Even in the case of the closer alliance of the North Atlantic Treaty, the report of the Senate Committee on Foreign Relations in 1949 pointedly noted that Article 5 was 'absolutely clear that each party remains free to exercise its honest judgment in deciding upon the measures it will take' in the event of aggression against any NATO member state.[43] Gross disapprovingly termed this general attitude, displayed over centuries, 'rugged individualism', but he did not suggest that it had disappeared.[44]

A second aspect of Anglo-American thought on international law, beyond its concern not to extend legal obligations too far, stems from the fact that throughout much of the modern period, and particularly at the times at which each has contributed most powerfully to international consideration of the questions raised by the existence of a system of law in a states-system, each has reflected on these questions from a position of strength. British and American scholars and statesmen have approached the subjection of international politics to law in the knowledge that their countries have looked forward to or already held the role of a great power and often the role of an actual or would-be hegemon. The assumption that international institutions and the legal rules they created would, in general, support the well-being of their own national interests has encouraged British and American leaders to oversee the creation of new organizations formed to 'legalize' and thereby 'reform' international affairs, while also making them exceedingly careful to protect their own position of international leadership within these institutions. They have been solicitous of international law, both in the sense that they wished to promote this means of softening international behaviour and in the sense that they have seen themselves as the guardians and patrons of international law, with all the deference to their national interests that this guardianship role implies.

Such an attitude is, of course, the object of Carr's stinging criticism that London and Washington's proclaimed devotion to international law was only a cover for rather hard-boiled self-interest, in that both were satisfied powers. (At least, Carr made this argument when he was not castigating the United States and the United Kingdom for the shallow idealism they exhibited in actually believing what they said about the rule of law in international affairs.) Yet there seems to be more to this strand of the tradition than myopia or hypocrisy.

Anglo-American writers have, in general, voiced a clear view of what might be termed the 'scope' of international law – that is, the identification of the parties to whom international law applies and who can claim its rights and be subject to its duties. Their clarity allows the observer to discern the variation over time in the international social space within which international law operated. One might begin with Gentili's observation that 'the law of nations is that which is in use among all the nations of men, which native reason has established among all human beings, and which is equally observed by all mankind'.[45] Zouche follows this line rather closely in defining the law of nations as 'the law which is observed in common between princes or peoples of different nations', though he allows that variation in the closeness of relations, and therefore the thickness of ties, may occur among peoples depending on the similarity of their forms of government and 'on the ground of a common origin, nearness of territories, a common language, opportunity of rendering mutual services, and the like'.[46] What followed in the ensuing centuries as internal religious conflicts and encounters with other cultures slowly turned 'Christendom' into 'Europe' was the shrinking of the area within which international law was thought applicable to Europe and regions of European settlement. Kent noted that 'during the war of the American revolution, Congress, claiming cognizance of all matters arising upon the law of nations, professed obedience to that law "according to the general usages of Europe"'.[47] Wheaton insisted on both the distinctiveness and the superiority of European international practice and attributed much of this advance to the influence of international legal scholars:

> If the international intercourse of Europe, and the nations of European descent, has been … marked by superior humanity, justice, and liberality, in comparison with the usage of the other branches of the human family, this glorious superiority must be mainly attributed to these private teachers of justice, to whose moral authority Sovereigns and States are often compelled to bow, and whom they acknowledge as the ultimate arbiters of their controversies in peace; whilst the same authority contributes to give laws even to war itself, by limiting the range of its operations within the narrowest possible bounds consistent with its purposes and objects.[48]

Other writers laid greater stress on the development of a multi-state system in Europe, of which a system of law among the state-parties was a natural component; Westlake, for example, opened his study of international law with the statement that 'It is the experience of every man of European blood that he lives in a state, which in its turn lives among states'.[49] Still others preferred to refer to international law as a set of rules among 'modern civilised states', though in their discussion of the accomplished or anticipated entry of states like Japan or China into this order, they made it clear that the order originated in Europe.[50] Particularly since the second half of the twentieth century, the scope of international law has broadened again to resume something like its original application to all humanity, just as contemporary international society is said to be the first fully global society in history. Martin Dixon describes the provision of the Statute of the International Court of Justice authorizing the court to consider 'the general principles of law recognized by civilized nations' as an 'irrelevant' phrase that 'can be ignored'.[51]

Through all these fluctuations, one constant has been that Anglo-American thinkers have considered their countries to be a part of whatever community international law applied to. Gentili and Zouche had no doubt that the England of their day fell within the general bounds of 'all the nations of men' and Kent and Wheaton were certain that the new United States was a participant in the 'general usages of Europe'. Hall assumed that the United Kingdom was to be classed among 'modern civilized states' and Dixon equally assumed that both Britain and the United States were, of course, subject to contemporary international law embracing all states of whatever culture or level of economic development.

It is noteworthy that, whatever the breadth of the society of states to which international law has been thought to apply, Anglo-American thinkers have seen their countries as being at the heart of it. When London and Washington have disagreed, as, for example, over some aspects of the post-Second World War economic order, at issue was the kind of rules and institutions that would advantage each party, as well as sincerely held beliefs on each side that its preferred form of order would be best for the entire society of states – a very typically Anglo-American attitude towards the compatibility of the just and the advantageous.

Conclusion

None of this seems likely to change in the foreseeable future – neither the history of these two societies that has left them with a frequently invoked though not absolutely unbroken dedication to the rule of law, nor the possession of the predominant power that leads them to appreciate law as a force for stability, nor the fortunate circumstances that give them faith that law can serve to soften the harsh contests for power in international life. In that very broad sense, the Anglo-American tradition of thinking about international law seems set to continue. None of these tenets is perhaps peculiar to an Anglo-American conception of international society and the place of law in it, but, looked at in toto, their combination seems almost unique.

It is also a combination that has, in the main, been fruitful for international society as a whole. Anglo-American influence has by and large been exerted in the direction of seeking the application of law to matters of mutual benefit that are suited to the voluntary adherence to legal principles in the loose community that is the society of states. This influence has also leant towards damping down expectations that law can be the sole guide to international conduct in matters in which prudence and statesmanship require more flexibility and creativity than a simple invocation of rules can allow. Put another way, the Anglo-American tradition has, in general, sought to delineate international law in a manner that makes room for states to defend their important interests and does not force them into crusades that could produce more human suffering than they would alleviate. Thus, prudence, as the application of good judgement to particular circumstances of time and place, seems to have been an Anglo-American contribution to international law. Neither dismissing law entirely nor demanding that it confront (much less solve) every problem on the world's agenda, this tradition, with collaboration from others in corresponding traditions elsewhere, has sought to maintain a principled distinction between those who have more right on their side and those who have less, while also accepting a responsibility to avoid the excessive harm that could result from the application of the principle of 'let justice be done though the heavens fall'. To advance the cause of justice incrementally while minimizing the possibility that the heavens will actually fall has been both an ambition and an attribute of the Anglo-American tradition of international law.

The tradition has been pragmatic, but not in the highly specialized sense of the philosophical pragmatism associated with William James, whereby the validity of any idea is to be judged solely by experience of the practical results of its adoption. Anglo-American thinking is too reliant on the assumption that there are ideas and associated behaviours that are inherently right or wrong, to go very far down the path that James described. Nor is the tradition reducible to the commonly employed usage of 'pragmatism' as whatever course of action may 'work', without any overly exacting standard of what it may mean for a social practice to 'work'. No tradition of thought that has come to fashion law as a means of managing conflicts among different culturally grounded views of 'working', or achieving some goal, could be so loose in its measure of success.[52]

The pragmatism of the Anglo-American tradition falls between the Jamesian requirement of theoretical precision and the everyday reliance on an ill-defined general notion of 'working'. Pragmatic Anglo-American legal prudence asks to know the consequences of any overall conception of the nature and role of law in international life and any particular application of international law, but within limits. That is, it would be guided by experience of the results, but not solely by that experience. Its foundation in and recent revival of a conception of natural law would prevent it from adopting the criterion of increased national power and plenty as the only test of the applicability of international law. That unwillingness to rely on pragmatism unreservedly causes adherents of the Anglo-American tradition to speak, write and act in terms of long-term self-interest. Just as Alexis de Tocqueville observed that Americans justified their conduct using the principle of 'self-interest rightly understood', or the belief that action in the common good was in the long run in their own good, through the preservation of societal mores that protected each party ultimately even if they balked its desires in the present, so those directed by the Anglo-American tradition have held out hope that adherence to a comparatively modest set of flexible rules will eventually be advantageous – working to their own advantage and to the advantage of the international society at large. Tocqueville suggested that Americans were, in reality, more virtuous and selfless than this idea justified, but in the less restrained circumstances of international life it may be a more accurate summary of the thinking behind the Anglo-American tradition of international law.

Tocqueville's own description of international politics as a great international society in which each people acts as an individual citizen, but a society with a less 'soft' character than that of a well-ordered domestic society, perhaps captures the essence of the Anglo-American tradition best. In conceiving of international law as operating within a society rather than a jungle, it establishes limits on national self-seeking that go beyond the purely pragmatic or instrumental. In casting a sceptical eye over plans for the wholesale replacement of international politics by law, whether that law is imposed and enforced by a world state or voluntarily accepted by every individual state, it establishes room for law to operate alongside politics, for general norms to exist within which states still seek their own advantage and make provision for their own security. It is not a conception marked by clean lines of philosophical consistency. Yet, in its very mixed nature, it may best reflect the complex essence of international relations.

David Clinton is a professor of political science at Baylor University in Waco, Texas, where he has taught for fifteen years. He previously taught at Kansas State University, Colgate University, Hamilton College, Union College and Tulane University. His teaching and research interests centre on diplomacy, ethics in international relations and the history of international thought. His publications include *Tocqueville, Lieber, and Bagehot: Liberalism Confronts the World* (Palgrave Macmillan, 2003); *The Realist Tradition and Contemporary International Relations* (edited, Louisiana State University Press, 2007); *Realism and the Liberal Tradition* (co-edited, Palgrave Macmillan, 2016); 'Les Etats-Unis', in Thierry Balzacq and Frédéric Ramel (eds), *Traité de Relations Internationales*; 'Diplomacy and International Law', in Costas Constantinou, Pauline Kerr and Paul Sharp (eds), *The SAGE Handbook of Diplomacy* (SAGE, 2016); and 'Nicholas Murray Butler and "The international mind" as the Pathway to Peace', in Molly Cochran and Cornelia Navari (eds), *Progressivism and US Foreign Policy between the World Wars* (New York: Palgrave Macmillan, 2017).

Notes

1. A. Wolfers and L. Martin (eds), *The Anglo-American Tradition in Foreign Affairs: Readings from Thomas More to Woodrow Wilson* (New Haven, CT: Yale University Press, 1956), xix–xx.

2. A. Gentili, *De Jure Belli* (1598), in M.G. Forsyth, H.M.A. Keens-Soper and P. Savigear (eds), *The Theory of International Relations: Selected Texts from Gentili to Treitschke* (New York: Atherton Press, 1970), 20–21.

3. H. Halleck, *International Law; or, Rules Regulating the Intercourse of States in Peace and War* (San Francisco, CA: H.H. Bancroft, 1861), 43–44.

4. M. Dixon, *Textbook on International Law* (Oxford: Oxford University Press, 2000), 17.

5. J. Abdy (ed.), *Kent's Commentary on International Law* (Cambridge: Deighton, Bell and Co., 1878), 33.

6. J. Westlake, *International Law* (Cambridge: Cambridge University Press, 1910), 1.

7. R. Phillimore, *Commentaries on International Law* (Philadelphia, PA: T. & J.W. Johnson, 1854), v.

8. J. Lorimer, 'The German War: Introductory Lecture Delivered to the Class of Public Law, 5th November 1866', Yale Law School Library, retrieved 4 July 2018, 30–31.

9. J. Brierly, *The Law of Nations: An Introduction to the International Law of Peace* (London: Oxford University Press, 1928), 45.

10. For a discussion of this interplay between the two 'doctrines', one being 'an objective approach to the problem of the binding force of international law and … an organic conception of the international community of states' and the other a 'voluntaristic conception of the binding force of international law [and] … the liberty of states', or international law as 'a law of coordination' made by states and international law as 'a law of subordination, that is, a law above states', see L. Gross, 'The Peace of Westphalia, 1648–1948', *The American Journal of International Law* 42(1) (1948), 38–40.

11. I. Claude, *Swords into Plowshares: The Problems and Progress of International Organization* (New York: Random House, 1971).

12. An exception could be thought to exist in E. Reves, *The Anatomy of Peace* (New York: Harper & Brothers, 1945), but even here, when Reves contends that 'the problem of peace in our time is the establishment of a legal order to regulate relations among, beyond and above the nation-states', which 'requires transferring parts of the sovereign authority of the existing warring national institutions to universal institutions capable of creating law and order in human relations beyond and above the nation-states', he is arguing that present international law is not really 'law', but only diplomatic contrivance, which should be replaced with the true law enacted by a sovereign global authority. Reves thus maintains the distinction between existing international law and a world government. (See Reves, *Anatomy of Peace*, 254–55.)

13. R. Zouche, *Iuris et Indici Fecialis, Sive, Iuris Inter Gentes, et Quaestionum de Eudem Explicato* (1650) (Miami, FL: Forgotten Books, 2017), 1–3.

14. Phillimore, *Commentaries on International Law*, v, ix.

15. Westlake, *International Law*, 7.

16. But see P. Jessup, *A Modern Law of Nations: An Introduction* (New York: Macmillan, 1949).

17. See M. Wight, *International Theory: The Three Traditions* (New York: Holmes & Meier, 1992), 233–34.

18. H. Bull, *The Anarchical Society: A Study of Order in World Politics* (New York: Columbia University Press, 1977), 127–61, 200–29.

19. The phrase 'give the law to nations' comes from Alexander Hamilton's criticism of the actions of the French First Republic and defence of the Adams administration's naval quasi-war

against France in 1798. See A. Hamilton, *The Papers of Alexander Hamilton* (New York: Columbia University Press, 1961), XXI, 408.

20. S. Hoffmann, *Janus and Minerva: Essays in the Theory and Practice of International Politics* (Boulder: CO: Westview Press, 1987), 4.

21. The distinction Carr draws between the stability of law and the dynamism of politics may be found in E. Carr, *The Twenty Years' Crisis, 1919–1939: An Introduction to the Study of International Relations* (New York: Harper Torchbooks, 1964), 190–207.

22. C. Manning, 'The Legal Framework in a World of Change', in B. Porter (ed.), *The Aberystwyth Papers: International Politics 1919–1969* (London: Oxford University Press, 1972), 305. Manning goes on to assert that this uncertainty, while 'inevitable and only to be expected', is not unique, 'since international law is like any other kind of law'. In other words, it is *law*, and not *international* law, that is uncertain, since no law ever goes completely unviolated.

23. Abdy, *Kent's Commentary on International Law*, 8, 30.

24. H. Wheaton, *Elements of International Law* (Boston, MA: Little, Brown, and Company, 1866), xiii, xv.

25. J. Lorimer, *Studies National and International* (Edinburgh: W. Green, 1890), 148–49, 151. For a somewhat similar contemporary account employing the terms 'naturalists' and 'positivists', see M. Akehurst, *A Modern Introduction to International Law* (London: Allen and Unwin, 1987), 13–15.

26. W. Hall, *A Treatise on International Law* (Oxford: Clarendon Press, 1924), quoted in Jessup, *A Modern Law of Nations*, 8. Jessup's citation of the Privy Council refers to British practice.

27. Jessup, *A Modern Law of Nations*, 8.

28. G. Kennan, *American Diplomacy, 1900–1950* (Chicago: The University of Chicago Press, 1951), 95.

29. H. Wheaton, *Elements of International Law*, xix; J. Lorimer, 'Prolegomena to a Reasoned System of International Law: Introductory Lecture Delivered to the Class of Public Law, November 1878', Yale Law School Library, accessed 4 July 2018, 152–53.

30. Lorimer, 'Prolegomena', 157.

31. Gross, 'The Peace of Westphalia', 40–41.

32. Ibid., 38–39.

33. Jessup, *A Modern Law of Nations*, 2, 11.

34. Wheaton, *Elements of International Law*, xviii.

35. E. Gibbon, *History of the Decline and Fall of the Roman Empire*, ed. David Womersley (London: The Penguin Press, 1994), III: XXXVIII, 513.

36. A. Wolfers, *Discord and Collaboration: Essays on International Politics* (Baltimore, MD: The Johns Hopkins Press, 1962), 233–51.

37. H. Kissinger, *A World Restored: Metternich, Castlereagh and the Problems of Peace* (Boston, MA: Houghton Mifflin, 1973), 7–40.

38. I. Claude, *American Approaches to World Affairs* (Lanham, MD: University Press of America, 1986), 3–17.

39. Wheaton, *Elements of International Law*, 77, 94–95. See also 100.

40. Abdy, *Kent's Commentary on International Law*, 83.

41. T. Woolsey, *Introduction to the Study of International Law* (New York: Charles Scribner & Co., 1879), 116, 222.

42. A. Wolfers, *Britain and France between Two Wars: Conflicting Strategies of Peace from Versailles to World War II* (New York: W.W. Norton, 1966), 259.

43. R. Bartlett (ed.), *The Record of American Diplomacy: Documents and Readings in the History of American Foreign Relations* (New York: Alfred A. Knopf, 1964), 735–36.

44. Gross, 'The Peace of Westphalia', 40.
45. Gentili, in Forsyth, Keens-Soper and Savigear, *The Theory of International Relations*, 21.
46. Zouche, *Iuris et Iudici Fecialis*, 2.
47. Abdy, *Kent's Commentary on International Law*, 2.
48. Wheaton, *Elements of International Law*, xx.
49. Westlake, *International Law*, 1.
50. Hall, *A Treatise on International Law*, 1.
51. Dixon, *Textbook on International Law*, 38. The provision of the Statute of the International Court of Justice in question is para. 1(c) of Art. 38.
52. For an expression of concern that international law may not be up to this task from within the Anglo-American tradition, see A. Bozeman, *The Future of Law in a Multicultural World* (Princeton, NJ: Princeton University Press, 2016).

Bibliography

Abdy, J. (ed.). *Kent's Commentary on International Law*. Cambridge: Deighton, Bell and Co., 1878.

Akehurst, M. *A Modern Introduction to International Law*. London: Allen & Unwin, 1987.

Bartlett, R. (ed.). *The Record of American Diplomacy: Documents and Readings in the History of American Foreign Relations*. New York: Alfred A. Knopf, 1964.

Bozeman, A. *The Future of Law in a Multicultural World*. Princeton, NJ: Princeton University Press, 2016.

Brierly, J. *The Law of Nations: An Introduction to the International Law of Peace*. London: Oxford University Press, 1928.

Bull, H. *The Anarchical Society: A Study of Order in World Politics*. New York: Columbia University Press, 1977.

Carr, E.H. *The Twenty Years' Crisis, 1919–1939: An Introduction to the Study of International Relations*. New York: Harper Torchbooks, 1964.

Claude, I. *American Approaches to World Affairs*. Lanham, MD: University Press of America, 1986.

———. *Swords into Plowshares: The Problems and Progress of International Organization*. New York: Random House, 1971.

Dixon, M. *Textbook on International Law*. Oxford: Oxford University Press, 2000.

Gentili, A. *De Jure Belli*, in M.G. Forsyth, H.M.A. keen-Soper and P. Savigear (eds), *The Theory of International Relations: Texts from Gentili to Treitschke*. New York: Atherton, 1970.

Gibbon, E. *History of the Decline and Fall of the Roman Empire*, ed. David Womersley. London: The Penguin Press, 1994.

Gross, L. 'The Peace of Westpalia, 1648–1948', *American Journal of International Law* 42(1) (1948), 20–41.

Hall, W. *A Treatise on International Law*. Oxford: Clarendon Press, 1924.

Halleck, H. *International Law; or, Rules Regulating the Intercourse of States in Peace and War*. San Francisco, CA: H.H. Bancroft, 1861.

Hamilton, A. *The Papers of Alexander Hamilton*. New York: Columbia University Press, 1961, XXI.

Hoffmann, S. *Janus and Minerva: Essays in the Theory and Practice of international Politics*. Boulder, CO: Westview Press, 1987.

Jessup, P. *A Modern Law of Nations: An Introduction*. New York: Macmillan, 1949.

Kennan, G. *American Diplomacy, 1900–1950.* Chicago: University of Chicago Press, 1951.

Kissinger, H. *A World Restored: Metternich, Castlereagh and the Problems of Peace.* Boston, MA: Houghton-Mifflin, 1973.

Lorimer, J. 'The German War: Introductory Lecture Delivered to the Class of Public Law, 5th November 1866'. Retrieved 4 July 2018 from Yale Law School Library.

_____. 'Prolegomena to a Reasoned System of International Law: Introductory Lecture delivered to the Class of Public Law, November 1878'. Retrieved 4 July 2018 from Yale Law School Library.

_____. *Studies National and International* Edinburgh: W. Green, 1890.

Manning, C. 'The Legal Framework in a World of Change', in B. Porter (ed.), *The Aberystwyth Papers: International Politics 1919–1969.* London: Oxford University Press, 1972.

Phillimore, R. *Commentaries on International Law.* Philadelphia, PA: T. & J.W. Johnson, 1854.

Reves, E. *The Anatomy of Peace.* New York: Harper & Brothers, 1945.

Westlake, J. *International Law.* Cambridge: Cambridge University Press, 1910.

Wheaton, H. *Elements of International Law.* Boston, MA: Little, Brown, 1866.

Wight, M. *International Theory: The Three Traditions.* New York: Holmes & Meier, 1992.

Wolfers, A. *Britain and France between Two Wars: Conflicting Strategies of Peace from Versailles to World War II.* New York: W.W. Norton, 1966.

_____. *Discord and Collaboration: Essays on International Politics.* Baltimore, MD: The Johns Hopkins Press, 1962.

Wolfers, A., and L. Martin (eds). *The Anglo-American Tradition in Foreign Affairs: Readings from Thomas More to Woodrow Wilson.* New Haven, CT: Yale University Press, 1956.

Woolsey, T. *Introduction to the Study of International Law.* New York: Charles Scribner, 1879.

Zouche, R. *Iuris et Iudicii Fecialis, Sive, Iuris inter Gentes, et Quaestionum de Eodem Explicatio* (1650). Miami, FL: Forgotten Books, 2017.

PART IV

Distinctive Features of an Anglo-American Tradition

Chapter 8

Reformulating Anglo-Saxon Identity

Intersections of Racism, National Identities and Transatlantic Stereotypes in the Nineteenth Century

Robert M. Hendershot

Anglo-Saxonism emerged gradually in the sixteenth and seventeenth centuries as both a field of study and a cultural identity among those who could trace their descent from the people of Anglo-Saxon England. Anglo-Saxonists envisioned their pre-Norman ancestors as lovers of liberty, free institutions and religious purity, and derived from this construction of identity a justification for England's break with Rome, an increasingly empowered Parliament and resistance to royal overreach.[1] However, Anglo-Saxon identity went through an important metamorphosis in the nineteenth century, as it was explicitly racialized, used as a rationale for conquest and imperial rule, and harnessed to justify systems of inequality in both the United Kingdom and the United States. But in order for this new racialized Anglo-Saxonism to become one of the factors influencing the relationship between these two nations, former patterns of collective identity within both populations would have to be realigned. Each nation's practice of viewing the other as a diametric enemy, which had become well established during the American Revolution (1775–83) and the War of 1812, complicated the process of identity realignment associated with Anglo-Saxonism. Accordingly, this chapter casts light upon a decades-long process in the mid-nineteenth century during which shifts in racial theory, national identities and transatlantic stereotypes slowly but persistently intersected to produce a new cultural environment wherein Anglo-American war would be considered as inconceivable as Anglo-American co-operation was natural.

There has been much discussion among historians of Anglo-American relations regarding precisely when Anglo-Saxonism began to exert an influence on diplomacy. For example, Iestryn Adams and Charles Kupchan have both contended that it did not become a significant factor until after the Great

Rapprochement of the 1890s[2] and David Haglund has argued that America's overwhelmingly negative opinion of the British did not change until the era of the First World War.[3] While these works have added to our understanding of how identity shifts have both impacted and been impacted by policy shifts, the rise of Anglo-Saxonism in both nations was neither sudden nor limited to one particular contingent moment or crisis. A wider scope is required to fully understand the causative factors involved, for this was an identity shift that began much earlier than the 1890s and required decades to become predominant. Consequently, this chapter aligns its analysis with another group of specialists[4] who argue that the earlier emergence of Anglo-Saxonism in both nations was a main cause of the Great Rapprochement rather than a consequence of it. In the analyses put forward by this group, a central principle propounded by social and cultural historians such as E.P. Thompson and Natalie Davis – that cultural changes are always a driving force of history[5] – is clearly evident. Furthermore, Thompson's critique of Antonio Gramsci is particularly influential. Believing that Gramsci overestimated the power of elites to rule though 'cultural hegemony', Thompson emphasized that lower social classes have the ability to limit and reformulate cultural control from above.[6] Put another way, widely held identities within national populations have the power to put limitations on, as well as direct, the policies of nations, particularly democracies, and thus, as Srdjan Vucetic has written, 'foreign policy can be said to follow the dominant discourse of identity'.[7]

The brief section below introduces the British and American stereotypes and biases that have long animated transatlantic discourse and that have played important roles in the national identities of both countries. Subsequent sections explain how and why the nineteenth-century evolution of these identities and stereotypes was associated with the rise of racialized Anglo-Saxonism and enhanced Anglo-American perceptions of coidentity. The final section explores how these dynamics, by altering the social reality and political culture of both Britain and the United States, made an essential contribution to the emergent Anglo-American friendship of the 1890s.

Understanding Anglo-American Stereotypes:
The Other and the Brother

To understand how Anglo-Saxonism helped alter Anglo-American relations and why this process took decades, it is crucial to acknowledge that Americans and Britons have historically known not one but two distinct stereotypes of one another over the last few hundred years. The first of these, referred to in this chapter simply as the other, functioned as a classic heterostereotype, a derogatory collective perception of an external group.[8] As Eric Hobsbawm argued, there is no more effective way of bonding together a nation's diverse communities 'than to unite them against outsiders'.[9] For this reason, the British often perceived the American people as an other. Depicted as uncultured, rash, brutish, ungrateful, smug and undistinguished, the American other represented what the British themselves were not, at least in the collective construct of their own national consciousness. Americans stereotyped the British other, for the same essential reason, as an arrogant aristocratic snob with a predilection for tyranny and the exploitation of hard-working peoples around the world. The British other served as a powerful juxtaposition that defined everything Americans perceived themselves not to be.[10]

But these heterostereotypes have not existed alone in the respective British and American worldviews. Another has existed there too, sometimes simultaneously, often producing a degree of cognitive dissonance that ultimately proved problematic. This was the brother stereotype, the mirror image of either a British or American autostereotype, or self-perception. The British stereotype of the American brother and the American stereotype of the British brother were essentially the same: a strong, good-hearted, freedom-loving, Anglo-Saxon, English-speaking, natural ally who shares our own blood, race, culture, values and divinely ordained civilizing mission. The label 'brother' is not used here to imply that this stereotype was only held by or applied to men. Indeed, Americans and Britons used the terms 'mother', 'daughter', 'sire', 'son', 'brethren', 'cousin', 'kinfolk' and other family-centric terms interchangeably when describing this perception, but all such terms were employed to express the core idea of Anglo-American likeness and unity. While usage of feminine and gender-neutral labels was by no means rare, it should be noted that these patriarchal cultures gravitated towards the use of masculinist language, as when British Secretary of State for the Colonies Joseph Chamberlain argued that war between the United States and the United Kingdom would be a 'fratricidal strife' in 1896,[11] when Foreign Secretary Lord Lansdowne described Americans as 'our brothers across the ocean' in 1901[12] and when Prime Minister Winston Churchill called for a 'fraternal association of English-speaking peoples' in 1946.[13] Accordingly, using the label 'brother' to refer to this concept serves as an allusion to the evident gender bias in the primary sources as well as a general reflection of period discourse.

Both stereotypes, the other and the brother, existed throughout the history of Anglo-American relations, but specific historical circumstances have served to make either the other or the brother dominant at particular times due to changes in their respective social or political utility. Significantly, these shifts occurred in tandem in both countries. For example, from the Revolutionary War and well into the first half of the nineteenth century, the other was dominant in both nations – justifying and reinforcing their state of mutual enmity.

Early Dominance of the Other

As Linda Colley has explained, prior to the American Revolution, 'many Englishmen and women had been accustomed to viewing [American colonists] as mirror images of themselves'.[14] Alike in language and religion, sharing family identities and as subjects of the same monarch, many American colonials shared a similar sense of coidentity with the British, which helps explain why the war initially divided public opinion on both sides of the Atlantic. As hostilities began, pro-peace and pro-war petitions with thousands of signatures were submitted to newspapers and governments throughout Britain and the colonies.[15] But as violence escalated, these divisions of public opinion began to erode and the other gained utility and prominence. For example, after Bostonian rebels tarred and feathered a British tax collector, a broadside published in London in 1774 popularized an early but vivid image of the American other. The artist, Philip Dawe, portrayed the Americans as lawless, uncultured, destructive villains who wore maniacal grins as they tortured their helpless British victim and contemptuously dumped tea into his mouth, as well as into the city's harbour.[16]

As the American revolutionaries allied themselves first with France in 1778 and then with Spain and Holland in, respectively, 1779 and 1780, support for the colonies faded in Britain as the experience of being betrayed by their colonies and surrounded by continental enemies produced a stronger sense of national unity within the United Kingdom.[17] As a consequence of bitter warfare and as a politically advantageous source of unity, the American other became a fixture of British national identity in this period. It was useful for Britain to gain a new external other at the end of the eighteenth century. As a consequence of the Act of Union with Ireland in 1800 and the accelerating political process of Catholic emancipation, previous others that had long been used to define Britishness grew problematic. Furthermore, after the Napoleonic threat ended in 1815 and as Spain's power diminished after the loss of its vast American empire in the 1820s, the new American other helped fill important voids.[18]

Meanwhile, the United States needed to construct a national identity and strengthen perceptions of unity among the former colonies. Key characteristics that defined 'Americans' needed to be popularly understood and internalized. However, this would not be easy, as much of what was thought to unite the new states could also unite them with Britain. Many white Americans had never abandoned their Anglo-Saxon identity; indeed, they believed that their actions in the revolution were justified because they were seeking to have their proper Anglo-Saxon rights and liberties maintained. Similarly, though enemies of Britain, early Americans would not wholly dissociate themselves from British culture and history. Like many of his contemporaries in Britain, Thomas Jefferson was convinced that the study of Anglo-Saxon history and language instilled valuable political and social principles.[19] For men like Jefferson, political separation from Britain was necessary and just, but cultural separation was unthinkable. On a joint mission to the United Kingdom in 1786, Jefferson and John Adams were enthusiastic tourists as well as diplomats, travelling widely and often feeling deeply connected to places they visited. After visiting Edgehill and Worcester, important sites in the English Civil War, Adams noted in his diary that these places were holy ground 'where freemen had fought for their rights'. Stratford upon Avon, the birthplace of William Shakespeare, was also a must-see for these Founding Fathers. Upon being shown a wooden chair upon which the playwright had once sat, a souvenir was necessary: 'We cutt [*sic*] off a Chip according to the Custom.'[20] Jefferson visited no less than sixteen famous gardens throughout the country, took copious notes and later incorporated British ideas at Monticello.[21]

In this way, othering the British required a degree of cognitive dissonance. Anglo-American cultural connections, while undeniable, were also unhelpful when it came to constructing American nationalism. Uniquely American identity markers, such as the experience of the war itself and particularly the country's political values, were more useful. As John Jay explained in the *Federalist Papers* in 1787, 'Providence' had given 'one connected country to one united people ... attached to the same principles of government, very similar in their manners and customs, and who, by their joint counsels, arms, and efforts, fighting side by side throughout a long and bloody war, have nobly established their general liberty and independence'.[22] In this context, the British represented the other half of a dichotomy that reinforced what made Americans a separate people. Where Britain was a monarchy, the United States was a democracy; where British society was aristocratic, America was egalitarian; where the British were greedy, the Americans were hard-working and resourceful.

Continuing animosity and another Anglo-American confrontation, the War of 1812, intensified the othering process in both countries and prompted frequent negative depictions of the enemy.[23] Two generations of Americans and Britons had grown accustomed to using such comparisons to the other to assert their respective identities by the time a peace treaty was signed in Ghent in 1814 and the end of open warfare had little impact on the other's dominance. British travelogues of America, for example, became an industry in the early decades of the nineteenth century. Depictions of the American other reverberated among British audiences during what Allan Nevins termed the age of 'Tory condescension', a literary era in which a harsh critique of the Americans became a trope that correlated with successful book sales.[24] After travelling in the United States for several years, Francis Trollope launched her successful writing career by publishing *Domestic Manners of the Americans* in 1832. The title itself was a jibe; as her book made clear, they had none. Americans lacked all social graces, led joyless lives, spurned culture, indulged in jingoism and openly insulted the British. This description was repeated in numerous similar works. Other popular British writers such as Fanny Kemble and Frederick Marryat also found utility in the American other, and their graphic accounts of American incivility and boorishness served to reinforce their own conservative politics and warn British readers about the dangers of parliamentary reform and democratization.[25] British radicals likewise found ideological value in the American other, as exemplified in Harriet Martineau's *Society in America* (1837), which argued that the United States had failed to live up to its republican ideas, citing political corruption and the cruelty of slavery as evidence.[26]

American audiences were outraged by such portrayals and viewed the authors as archetypes of British villainy. Retaliatory mudslinging was common in the American press. The Baltimore *Chronicle*, for example, dehumanized Marryat personally and labelled him an '*unmitigated blackguard*. His awkward, unwieldly misshapen body, was but a fair lodging for a low, depraved, licentious soul ... he is a beast.'[27] But it was Charles Dickens's critique that proved most hurtful to America pride. An admired celebrity in the United States when he first arrived there in 1842, he became a nationally reviled figure following the publication later that year of his *American Notes*, which described his travel experiences, and *Martin Chuzzlewit*, a novel serialized in 1843–44 and partly set in America. The United States as described by Dickens was a land of greedy scoundrels and corrupt buffoons who, almost universally, lacked table manners and were unhygienic. American anger grew so potent that Dickens feared for his safety and warned friends that if they should visit the United States, 'Never claim me for your friend, or champion me in any way.'[28]

Americans incensed by such British portrayals could, at least, take some comfort in the work of a different outsider, Alexis de Tocqueville. Not only had the famous French writer praised the American experiment in general, but he also, after visiting London in 1833, confirmed that he saw there only aristocratic people, institutions, and homes. Nowhere 'do I find our America'.[29] Such continuing comparisons served to further entrench the other stereotypes within American and British worldviews. However, even while these critiques and insults remained dominant in transatlantic discourse, new catalysts were emerging by mid-century to help alter this state of affairs.

The Other and Brother in Competition

As established in the works of historians such as Ernest Gellner and Benedict Anderson, modern nation-states were constructed upon popular notions of imagined community in the century following the American and French revolutions.[30] This rise of modern nationalism occurred alongside the emergence of scientific racism in both Europe and America and these two historical developments fed off one another. Nationalisms were increasingly based upon ethnic homogeneity and racial purity, as advocated by famous promoters of scientific racism such as Louis Agassiz and Arthur Gobineau.[31] In both Britain and America, the early nineteenth century witnessed a sharp increase in ethnologists, philologists and phrenologists who merged science with pseudoscience to 'prove' that perceived racial differences resulted in a natural hierarchy, with Anglo-Saxon peoples at the top and either African or Native American peoples at the bottom.[32] As Eduardo Bonilla-Silva has argued, though such racial identities and hierarchies are subjective and artificial, once constructed and institutionalized they produce a new social reality in which people and organizations must operate.[33] In both the United Kingdom and the United States, the emergence of a new social reality based on Anglo-Saxon racial supremacy produced a new challenge to the dominance of the others discussed above.

American and British thinkers effectively nourished and reinforced mutual biases as they published their philosophies of racial hierarchy. British surgeon William Lawrence first published his *Lectures on ... the Natural History of Man* in England in 1819, but his work, which argued that Caucasians were far superior to the 'dark-coloured people of the globe', found a keen readership in both nations and had appeared in numerous editions by the 1840s.[34] Lawrence's ideas of race were key to the development of ethnology in the United States and provided inspiration to doyens of American racism such as Samuel Morton and Josiah Nott, physicians who in turn achieved renown within the British ethnological community in the 1830s and 1840s as they helped disseminate a new racialized doctrine of Anglo-Saxon superiority.[35]

By mid-century, this concept, which effectively merged older ideas of Anglo-Saxon excellence and freedom with scientific racism, was gaining high-profile supporters, including renowned historians and essayists Thomas Carlyle and Thomas Arnold, Prime Minister Benjamin Disraeli and the noted clergyman and social reformer Charles Kingsley. Their shared creed was that race was the key to understanding history as well as the future, which belonged not to one nation, but rather to the superior Anglo-Saxon race. Among this race, as Carlyle wrote to his friend Ralph Waldo Emerson in 1839, they counted the Americans. Carlyle, whose literary career had made him famous throughout the transatlantic world, envisioned a future in which the United States would become the main meeting point of 'All-Saxondom'.[36] Like many nineteenth-century white Americans, British proponents of Anglo-Saxonism clearly conceived of the United States as a white nation, the country's actual diversity notwithstanding. In this way, the constructed identity of race had the power to produce more than nationalisms. It also led to the formation of a transatlantic and supranational imagined community: a racially superior and united Anglo-Saxon people.

This is, of course, not to argue that racism was universal in these nations – the philosopher John Stuart Mill, for example, valiantly and publicly denounced many of Carlyle's racial arguments in the mid-1800s[37] – but racialized Anglo-Saxonism nevertheless continued to gain influence. As the British Empire expanded across much of Asia and Africa and American settlement thrust westward, the doctrine of Anglo-Saxon superiority was useful as a justification for conquest and imperial control. As Reginald Horsman has argued, American expressions of Anglo-Saxon pre-eminence first gained popularity in the wake of the War of 1812 as the country made peace with Britain and turned its attention towards Native American lands, but this process accelerated in the 1830s and 1840s as white Americans thoroughly weaponized an established doctrine of Anglo-Saxon racial supremacy to justify the policy of Indian Removal, the Mexican–American War and the expansionism of the 1850s.[38]

As the British Empire grew during the same period, British national identity depended less upon the Catholic others of the past (French and Irish) and, as Colley has explained, 'allusions to the presumed otherness of imperial spaces and cultures were frequently utilized as a means of highlighting, by contrast, the distinctive and distinguished qualities of Britishness itself'.[39] Race gained new prominence in this process. Establishing control over the darker-skinned peoples of Australia, Africa and India justified Victorian pseudoscientific delusions of Anglo-Saxon racial supremacy and the biological inferiority of colonial others. This view was well represented by the noted English biologist Thomas Huxley when, in 1865, he explained to his readers:

> No rational man, cognizant of the facts, believes that the average negro is the equal, still less the superior, of the average white man. And if this be true, it is simply incredible that, when all his disabilities are removed, and our prognathous relative has a fair field and no favour, as well as no oppressor, he will be able to

compete successfully with his bigger-brained and smaller-jawed rival, in a contest which is to be carried out by thoughts and not by bites.[40]

The growth of racialized Anglo-Saxon identity in Britain and the United States also impacted the previous hegemony of the other in their national perceptions of one another by the mid-nineteenth century. Americans embracing Anglo-Saxonism, for example, had to contend with an unspoken but key question looming in the background: how could Britain, with its people descended from the same superior racial stock and as the epicentre of Anglo-Saxon history, culture and tradition, also be the opposite of all things American? British Anglo-Saxonists had to cope with a similarly circuitous line of logic: if Americans were members of the same race as the British and that race was superior, how could the image of the American other be true? In both countries, as scientific racism grew more important to identity and as an imperial justification, the other, though well entrenched in each nation's culture, grew increasingly problematic and the brother stereotype began to challenge its dominance.

Post-1850: Decline of the Other, Rise of the Brother

In the four decades preceding the Great Rapprochement, several concurrent developments culminated in the dominance of the brother stereotype. Governmental reforms, new reactions to immigration trends, more calls for a 'Greater Britain', and continuing territorial expansion contributed to the increasing supremacy of racialized Anglo-Saxonism. The expansion of this identity would, in turn, promote perceptions of Anglo-American similarity and unity, as well as reduce the utility and popularity of stereotypes of the other.[41]

In terms of government reform, this was a period of dramatic change for both the United States and Britain. As Alan Dobson has written, 'Politically, Britain underwent various reforms that made her more democratic and diluted the importance of birth and status. Such changes brought her closer to the more egalitarian American system.'[42] The 1832 Reform Act made the British cabinet responsible to Parliament instead of the monarch, and the British Reform Act of 1884 enlarged the voting franchise as well as the powers of Parliament.[43] Such reforms widened the gap between political reality and the aristocratic and tyrannical themes central to American perceptions of the British other. The British monarchy had become a curiosity rather than a threat by the time Prince Albert Edward, later King Edward VII, successfully toured the United States in 1860 and was mobbed by fans in Detroit, Albany and Chicago.[44] Similarly, changes in the American legal system undermined

key components of the American other in British perceptions – the end of
slavery after 1865 made it more difficult for Britons to see Americans as hypo-
critical in their pretensions of liberty.[45] With their laws and socioeconomic
systems standing on more common ground, the nations could more easily
style themselves and one another as lands of freedom and liberal progress who
were less likely than ever to go to war with one another, a reality attested to by
the fact that the US–Canadian border went largely undefended after 1865.[46]
It was equally significant, however, that the Anglo-American liberalism of this
era, though advancing universal claims about humanity, made little political
headway in the field of racial equality. Slavery, for example, was denounced as
an obstacle to the liberal principles of freedom and progress, but the end of
slavery in the nineteenth century did not mean the end of racism and views of
racial hierarchy, which, in many ways, grew more intense and institutionalized
following Reconstruction.[47]

Responses to increasing immigration also illustrate how perceptions of
identity were shifting in both countries. The United States, for example, experienced a 433 per cent immigration increase from 1830 to 1860. The majority
of new arrivals were Catholic and one third of them Irish.[48] As these groups
dispersed throughout the eastern seaboard and into the Midwest, resentment
of the immigrant other rose. Working-class and middle-class native-born
white people more frequently claimed their birthright as members of the
superior Anglo-Saxon race to differentiate themselves from the immigrants
with whom they competed for jobs and housing, and consequently the stereotype of the brother gained utility among larger sections of society. New York's
Protestant nativist societies demonstrated this in 1858 when, in response to
the parading of Irish American and other ethnic groups, the St Nicholas, St
George, St Andrew, St David and Scottish societies staged a parade of their
own. While ostensibly held to celebrate the completion of the transatlantic
telegraph cable, the parade allowed participants to openly taunt the Irish and
revel in their Anglo-Saxon supremacy, with banners and slogans such as 'Severed July 4, 1776, united August 12, 1858' and 'There is no such word as fail
for Saxon Blood'.[49]

Whereas Irish immigrants and Irish Americans continued to embrace the
image of the British other, nativists embraced the idea of shared blood and
unity with Britain. Racial identities and ethnic tensions were powerful enough
to divide those who might otherwise have been united by social class. Anti-
immigrant Anglo-Saxonism remained formidable in the United States for
many decades, inspiring fears of miscegenation and 'race suicide' as well as
promises of unity with other Anglo-Saxon peoples into the twentieth century.[50] British Anglo-Saxonists shared these views: for instance, the journalist
W.T. Stead praised the United States as 'one of the finest stud farms in the

world for the production of human beings' while simultaneously warning Americans not to 'to spoil their breed of pedigree stock' by admitting a 'mass of crude, undigested, and indigestible foreigners'.[51]

Victorian Britain likewise experienced rising immigration as groups were drawn to the country by the prospect of jobs in its industrial cities. Coming largely from Ireland, Germany and the Russian Pale, these newcomers faced poverty, religious bias and, increasingly, scientific racism as they struggled for acceptance and social mobility. As Panikos Panayi has written, any depiction of multicultural Victorian Britain 'needs balancing against the vicious and violent xenophobia which accompanied it'. In studying the history of Irish immigrants in British cities, Panayi notes that sectarian violence became regular, and even as anti-Catholicism declined during the nineteenth century, various periodicals, under influence of Social Darwinism, began 'racialising the Irish, which meant depicting them as apes contrasted with the English'.[52] As race was used to dehumanize the immigrant other in communities across Britain, the concept of Anglo-Saxon superiority was simultaneously emphasized.

With similarities between the British and US governments rising and the doctrine of racial superiority gaining importance amid intensifying immigration, the British other and the American other became less useful and less frightening. These stereotypes continued to exist, but, in contrast to the menacing character they had possessed in the past, they could now be viewed as quaint or amusing in the right cultural context, a phenomenon observable through the lens of popular culture as early as the late 1850s. *Our American Cousin*, written by English playwright Tom Taylor, provides a vivid snapshot of the era's Anglo-American stereotypes. The play premiered in New York in 1858 and quickly became a commercial success in an impressive five-month run on Broadway. In 1861, the comedy moved to the Theatre Royal Haymarket in London and ran for nearly five hundred performances, to the equal delight of British audiences.[53]

As perhaps the most famous and successful transatlantic crowd-pleaser of the mid-nineteenth century, it is useful to note that the play's plot and humour were largely inspired by American and British stereotypes. Asa Trenchard, the central character, is a personification of British perceptions of the American other – a rustic and vulgar Yankee who inherits an ancestor's estate in England. After arriving at the estate, Asa meets his English cousins, the most notable of whom is Lord Dundreary, an eccentric and dandyish aristocrat exemplifying the American image of the British other. However, as the play unfolds and these characters attempt to understand one another's unfamiliar ways, Anglo-American conflict is not the outcome. Rather, as their true natures are established, themes of family, likeness and love become dominant as the brother stereotype surfaces. Asa, for example, though still rustic and unable to master the concept of taking a shower, proves that his true nature is heroic, selfless and honest, and ends up happily married to a kind-hearted English milkmaid.[54]

Audiences were entertained by this comedic portrayal of their respective others and found satisfaction in the play's resolution of family strife; in consequence, the play spawned several sequels, including *Our Female American Cousin* (1859) and *Our American Cousin at Home, or, Lord Dundreary Abroad* (1860).[55] The evident consumer demand for these productions, in which the other and brother stereotypes were always central to the plot, character development and comedy, indicates that such stereotypes were widely understood. Indeed, authors and actors had to depend upon the audience to bring these notions of identity with them into the theatre, for without them much of the dialogue would cease to make sense and the humour would fall flat. That the other had become a basis for comedy rather than conflict testifies to the changing roles of transatlantic stereotypes in this era of expanding Anglo-Saxonism.

The shifting utilities of the other and the brother were tapped by more than playwrights after 1850 and themes of Anglo-American family and unity also appeared in discussions of foreign policy. In 1857, the *Manchester Guardian* described Americans as 'our transatlantic cousins' and argued that 'their language, their race, their institutions should render them our natural allies'.[56] Arguments claiming cultural and racial likeness as the axis of Britain's future international relationships became increasingly common in subsequent decades and merged with the concept of Greater Britain advocated by the British politician and author Charles Dilke in the late 1860s. Greater Britain, a vast political, economic and linguistic society of Anglo-Saxons, was envisioned as a union of the United Kingdom and its settler colonies made possible by democratization as well as technological advancements.[57]

Dilke and many of his contemporaries expected that this geopolitical community would also include the United States. Indeed, Dilke believed that the process of Anglo-American unification had already begun. In a book recounting his travels through English-speaking countries in 1868, he explained that the increasing power of the United States was best embraced as an opportunity: 'as the English element has given language and history to that land, America offers the English race the moral directorship of the globe, by ruling mankind through Saxon institutions and the English language. Through America, England is speaking to the world.'[58] Those who shared Dilke's beliefs could take satisfaction from developments in contemporary Anglo-American diplomacy. As Vucetic has written, the 1871 Treaty of Washington was an important development 'in the sense that this peaceful resolution of the American Civil War-era disputes between London and Washington added grist to the mill of those who claimed that Anglo-American commonalities –

language, literature, lineage, etc. – facilitated Anglo-American cooperation'.[59] Stereotypes of the other continued to fade in transatlantic discourse as perceptions of shared culture and race promoted a modern story of Anglo-American brotherhood, with notable figures, such as American industrialist Andrew Carnegie and British historian John Robert Seeley, publicly calling for Anglo-American union in the 1880s[60] in much the same way as Winston Churchill and H.G. Wells would do in the twentieth century.[61]

Perceptions of Anglo-American connection were simultaneously advanced by the popular doctrines of manifest destiny and the White Man's Burden, which cast Anglo-Saxons in the mould of history's great protagonists, spreading their superior civilization across the planet. Just as the British found utility in this notion as a justification for empire, Americans found justification for westward expansion. Since journalist John O'Sullivan had coined the term 'manifest destiny' in 1839, the concept of America's divinely ordained growth had become thoroughly intertwined with American racism. John Gast's *American Progress* (1872), among the most widely reproduced American artworks of the century, gave the nation a powerful visual portrayal of this merger. An angelic, pale-skinned Columbia, with a schoolbook in one hand and a telegraph wire in the other, guides America's white pioneers westward as Native Americans and wild animals flee before the juggernaut of civilization.[62]

Figure 8.1. John Gast, *American Progress*, 1872, Library of Congress, https://www.loc.gov/pictures/item/97507547/.

As white Americans became accustomed to seeing themselves as part of a superior race bringing the light of progress to the primitive and dark lands of the world, Britain and its empire seemed less a threat and more a partner in creating a world dominated by Anglo-Saxons.

This is not to argue that the other disappeared completely, only that it lost its former dominance within mainstream British and American worldviews. For example, when British writers Oscar Wilde and Rudyard Kipling published accounts of their respective travels in the United States in the 1880s, these contained more than a few patronizing depictions of the American other. Each author described the United States as a cultural desert, mocked American speech patterns and condemned the nation's crass commercialism. But as Anna Pochmara has noted in her intertextual analysis of these works, such 'residual colonial condescension' was diluted amid expressions of Anglo-Saxon race unity and rising esteem for America and its growing empire.[63] Both writers perceived the United States as a white nation whose greatness stemmed from its Anglo-Saxon origins and its fundamentally English character. Kipling was explicit in his account of race in America, arguing that the growing populations of African-Americans and immigrants threatened the vast potential of Anglo-Saxon America's otherwise bright future.[64] Unlike the early nineteenth-century British accounts of America, Kipling and Wilde expressed powerful elements of coidentity with America and their works helped punctuate the slow-burning but nevertheless dramatic shift in transatlantic identities that occurred before, and would ultimately help facilitate, the Great Rapprochement.

1890s: Supremacy of the Brother

As the final decade of the nineteenth century began, essential components of identity required to transform the diplomatic relationship between Britain and the United States were already in place. Racialized Anglo-Saxonism had become an essential doctrine in both countries. Each relied upon this ideology to justify the social status quo of their domestic hierarchies and the expansion of their respective empires.[65] Similarly, scientific racism had trickled down through public education and into popular culture, entering, as Peter Conlin has written, the realm of 'common knowledge'.[66] Theories of racial superiority had also synced through the popular doctrines of manifest destiny and the White Man's Burden to further foreground national similarities, strengthen the brother stereotype and erode the previous utility of the other.

Though the period that followed the peaceful resolution of the Venezuelan border dispute in 1896 would witness a great outpouring of Anglo-Saxon sentiments in both nations, it would be a classic logical error to believe that such expressions were caused by the increase in diplomatic friendship. Rather, the elimination of diplomatic tensions was a product of the reconciliation of foreign policies and major shifts in transatlantic identity, racialized Anglo-Saxonism having led the brother stereotype to slowly displace the other over the previous decades. The 1890s began with influential and insistent views of Anglo-American unity, which, when considered in their historical context, illustrate the continuation of an earlier trend rather than a rapid shift. For example, the significant *Influence of Sea Power upon History* (1890), written by US naval officer and historian Alfred Thayer Mahan, reflected the author's personal Anglo-Saxonism. While Mahan identified Japan and Germany as potential naval rivals of the United States, his belief in racial bonds led him to foresee no future confrontation between his native United States and the British Empire.[67] American minister Josiah Strong went further, merging Christianity and evolution to claim God had ordained the superiority of Anglo-Saxon peoples and chosen them to bring civilization and Protestantism to the world, as proven by both nations' successful expansion.[68]

Like Strong, the influential British journalist W.T. Stead believed the growing power of the United States would lead that nation to primacy among the Anglo-Saxons and that this was nothing for Britons to fear. The inevitable outcome, he told his readers in 1893, would be a 'great race alliance' benefitting the British, the Americans and, indeed, the world.[69] Advocating this argument throughout the decade, he took the US victory in the Spanish–American War as an opportunity to hail America in the tradition of the brother stereotype, stressing that the United States and Britain were mirror images of one another: 'As the English have been, the Americans are; and as we English did, so will these stout sons of ours do. Our own history in the past is the prophecy of their future.'[70]

The brother stereotype remained dominant in British and American worldviews even during fraught diplomatic episodes, such as the 1895 British–Venezuela border dispute. When the United States invoked the Monroe Doctrine to demand that Britain submit to arbitration and the British government initially dismissed that demand, tension mounted as both sides appeared intractable. Yet, where once such Anglo-American crises had prompted ubiquitous incarnations of the other, recent shifts in transatlantic identities mandated a very different reaction. In the following months, both governments backed away from their initial hard-line positions when it became clear that their respective publics would not support confrontation. Each nation's press was overwhelmingly opposed to any Anglo-American conflict and petitions with thousands of signatures denounced the idea. These appeals were filled with both references to racial unity and the family-centric language of

the brother stereotype, and, as in the case of a large British petition, demanded that foreign policy be aligned with identity: 'All English-speaking peoples
united by race, language and religion, should regard war as the only absolutely
intolerable mode of settling the domestic differences of the Anglo-American
family.'[71]

As these ideas permeated public discourse, they reverberated in British
Prime Minister Lord Salisbury's cabinet, with Colonial Secretary Joseph
Chamberlain and First Lord of the Treasury Arthur Balfour describing the
notion of Anglo-American conflict as 'unnatural', 'absurd' and 'fratricidal'. In
Parliament, Liberal Party leaders William Harcourt and the Earl of Rosebery
paraphrased authors such as Stead and Strong when they declared that peace
between the 'mighty nations of the Anglo-Saxon race' was essential to the
future of the Christian world and civilization itself. Just as British racial identities and perceptions of the American brother made Salisbury's initial refusal
of arbitration untenable, the same dynamic led President Grover Cleveland to
abandon conflict as an option.[72] Following the peaceful resolution and arbitration of the Venezuela crisis in 1896, both governments remained keenly aware
of the power of transatlantic Anglo-Saxonism and diplomacy continued in accordance with this identity trend. Britain's support for the United States in the
1898 Spanish–American War, for example, was in tune with public celebra-
tions of the Fourth of July in England, articles in *The Times* that stressed the
'bonds of blood' that made Americans 'kinfolks' and Lord Coleridge's speech
at an Anglo-American banquet, saluting 'a common kinship of race'.[73] Reflective statements flowed from America as well – Senator Henry Cabot Lodge
noted in relation to Britain's support that 'race, blood, language, identity of
beliefs & aspirations, all assert themselves' and, in a speech at Harvard, Secretary of State Richard Olney declared that the United Kingdom was America's
'best friend' and explained 'there is such a thing as patriotism for race as well
as for country'. The same year, the US branch of the Anglo-American Committee publicized a letter, signed by over one thousand of the country's leading
opinion makers, that called for 'an intimate and enduring friendship between
these two kindred peoples'.[74]

While such public and elite statements grew more effusive towards the
century's end, the ideas expressed were not new. The *longue durée* analysis
of history reveals that a common transatlantic identity based on notions of
family and race had been growing steadily since mid-century and had now
become powerful enough to influence policy as well as discourse. For example,
when the Second Boer War split American public opinion in 1899, the old
conflict between the other and the brother stereotypes was briefly revived.
American supporters of the Boers tended to see the conflict as a relatable
struggle for independence from tyranny and some three hundred Americans

even volunteered to fight the British on behalf of the Boers. But not all critics went to such extremes. For example, the humourist Mark Twain opposed the war but also felt that recent British actions in South Africa were strikingly similar to the simultaneous American conflict in the Philippines. As he told Winston Churchill in 1900, 'England and America were kin in almost everything; now they are kin in sin.'[75] An objective analysis of both nations' foreign policies made it difficult for an American to criticize Britain, and Twain was no hypocrite. While the other never fully disappeared, it had lost its former supremacy in public opinion, as well as its ability to inspire government action. The United States took no official stance on the war and many of its Anglo-Saxonist leaders declared their approval of British policy. As Secretary of State John Hay wrote in 1900, the 'fight of England is the fight of civilization and progress and all our interests are bound up in her success'.[76]

The British, for their part, tended to take American inaction as a sign of support, as attested to by the popular Boer War-era music hall piece titled 'America Looking On', which declared, 'though America stands by, it's you she's standing by'.[77] Assumptions of axiomatic American support fit a pattern in contemporary music, as evidenced by other popular songs of the era such as 'It's the English-Speaking Race against the World' and 'John Bull's Letter Bag', which included the lyric: 'Though they may think us "lax-uns", / Thank God we're Anglo-Saxons, / And the Anglo-Saxon race shall rule the world.'[78]

Figure 8.2. William Allan, 'John Bull and Uncle Sam [sheet music]' (Chicago, S. Brainard's Sons Co., 1898), Library of Congress, M1644.H.

The most overt musical expression of Anglo-American unity was 'John Bull and Uncle Sam', written by William Allan, Member of Parliament, in 1898. This cheerful transatlantic singalong, copyrighted in London and published in Chicago, told the story of how 'John Bull once had a little boy who ran away from home' and though Sam separated from 'his sire', he had since matured into a strong freedom-loving man, until one day John Bull, 'with proud and loving heart', admitted 'of me you are a part'. The song ends with the two shaking hands and unifying against the world, a point emphasized by the sheet music's cover art, as well as by its final refrain of 'Stars and Stripes and the Union Jack shall rule o'er land and sea!'[79]

As indicated by these types of songs, themes of Anglo-Saxon racial unity and Anglo-American family had become well established in popular culture. By the late 1890s, depictions of America and Britain as unified mirror images of one another had achieved widespread resonance, becoming a trope in popular publications as well as in diplomatic rhetoric. America's *Puck* magazine, for example, made frequent use of John Bull and Uncle Sam to illustrate Anglo-American unity, as on the cover of a June 1898 issue depicting the national symbols as brothers-in-arms, standing shoulder to shoulder above the words, 'United we stand for civilization and peace!'[80]

As the twentieth century began, the security of the brother stereotype remained assured through each nation's continuing reliance upon Anglo-Saxon superiority and civilization as their justification for empire. For example, with

Figure 8.3. Louis Dalrymple, 'United we stand for civilization and peace!' *Puck* (New York, Keppler & Schwarzmann, 8 June 1898), Library of Congress, https://www.loc.gov/item/2012647570/.

his nation in the midst of conquering the Philippines, Theodore Roosevelt's December 1901 presidential message explained that it was America's 'duty toward the people living in barbarism to see that they are freed of their chains, and we can free them only by destroying barbarism itself'. He concluded by stressing that 'peace cannot be had until the civilized nations have expanded in some shape over the barbarous nations'.[81] Britain, though unmentioned, was nevertheless positioned as an American partner within the global dichotomy of civilization/barbarism. With such similar racist principles, as well as foreign policies, the other stereotypes of the past had lost their former utility and grew rare in mainstream discourse. *Puck*, once again, cleverly portrayed the dominant perception of Britain for an American popular audience with the two-page illustration, 'From the Cape to Cairo', in 1902.[82]

Waving the flag of civilization, Britannia leads British soldiers and settlers into battle against dark-skinned peoples of Africa under their banner of barbarism. The caption beneath the artwork's title reads, 'Though the process be costly, the road to progress must be cut.' Though subtlety was not a goal and the artist may have lacked the talent of Gast, this 1902 work is far too similar to the famous 1872 painting *American Progress* for its similarity to be a coincidence. In this way, *Puck* offered yet another portrayal of the British as the mirror image of America's national self-perception, emphasizing the Anglo-Saxon whiteness and civilizing mission thought to unite the Anglo-American family. British Anglo-Saxonists would doubtless have been pleased with such portrayals, for they fit well with their own observations. As Stead, perhaps the most eloquent writer to describe the mirroring component of the brother, wrote in 1901, 'as the creation of the Americans is the greatest achievement of our race, there is no reason to resent the part the Americans are playing in fashioning the world in their image, which, after all, is substantially the image of ourselves'.[83]

Figure 8.4. Udo Keppler, 'From the Cape to Cairo', *Puck* (New York, Ottmann Lith. Co., 10 December 1902), Library of Congress, https://www.loc.gov/pictures/item/2010652189/.

Conclusion

In American and British worldviews, a competition between the other and brother stereotypes had occurred over the nineteenth century. Though perceptions of the other had permeated Anglo-American relations in its early decades, multiple concurrent trends, including accelerating immigration, the expansion of both countries' empires and the institutionalization of scientific racism, had caused the brother stereotype to gain popularity and ultimately dislodge the other from its dominant position. Racial concepts of national destiny and purpose grew so important and similar in the second half of the nineteenth century that it became difficult and counterproductive for the nations to maintain older heterostereotypes of one another. The racialized identity of Anglo-Saxonism thoroughly merged with the brother stereotype, enhancing the reach and influence of both. This process of identity realignment spanned much of the century, but through their perceptions of racial unity, white Americans and Britons increasingly found utility in coidentity.

Entrenched in popular culture as well as the elite circles of government, a common mythology that cast the Anglo-Saxon race as the enemy of barbarism and as the champion of civilization made a significant contribution to emergent Anglo-American friendship by the 1890s. No longer others, the dominant perception of Britain and America had become sire and son, mother and daughter, cousins and kinfolk, in all ways a transatlantic family of race, blood and culture. To be sure, diplomatic rifts and squabbles would continue to be a part of their story in the decades ahead, but the deeply entrenched racist worldviews of the nineteenth century would live on into the twentieth century, continuing to influence each population's social reality and each nation's political culture. As a result, perceptions of Anglo-American unity would endure and conflict would remain a 'fratricidal' proposition as the next century of Anglo-American diplomacy began.

Robert M. Hendershot is Professor of History in the Department of Social Sciences at Grand Rapids Community College, Michigan. Specializing in the historical influence of culture, identity and public opinion upon Anglo-American relations, his works include *Gerald Ford and Anglo-American Relations: Re-Valuing an Interim Presidency* (co-authored with Steve Marsh and Tia Culley, University of Michigan Press, forthcoming), *Culture Matters: Anglo-American Relations and the Intangibles of 'Specialness'* (co-edited with Steve Marsh, Manchester University Press, 2020) and *Family Spats: Perception, Illusion, and Sentimentality in the Anglo-American Special Relationship* (VDM Verlag, 2008).

Notes

1. R. Horsman, 'Origins of Racial Anglo-Saxonism in Great Britain before 1850', *Journal of the History of Ideas* 37(3) (1976), 387–88; also see L. Curtis, *Anglo-Saxons and Celts: A Study of Anti-Irish Prejudice in Victorian England* (New York: New York University Press, 1968).

2. I. Adams, *Brothers across the Ocean: British Foreign Policy and the Origins of the Anglo-American Special Relationship* (London: Tauris Academic Studies, 2005), 10–13; C. Kupchan, *How Enemies Become Friends: The Sources of Stable Peace* (Princeton, NJ: Princeton University Press, 2010), 68, 73, 402.

3. D. Haglund, 'Is There a "Strategic Culture" of the Special Relationship?', in A. Dobson and S. Marsh (eds), *Anglo-American Relations: Contemporary Perspectives* (London: Routledge, 2013), 33, 37.

4. See S. Vucetic, 'The Fulton Address as Racial Discourse', in Dobson and Marsh (eds), *Churchill in the Anglo-American Special Relationship* (London: Routledge, 2017); Vucetic, *The Anglosphere: A Genealogy of a Racialized Identity in International Relations* (Stanford, CA: Stanford University Press, 2011); Horsman, *Race and Manifest Destiny: The Origins of Racial Anglo-Saxonism* (Cambridge, MA: Harvard University Press, 1981); S. Anderson, *Race and Rapprochement: Anglo-Saxonism and Anglo-American Relations* (Rutherford, NJ: Fairleigh Dickinson University Press, 1981); S. Rock, *Appeasement in International Politics* (Lexington: University Press of Kentucky, 2000).

5. L. Hunt (ed.), *The New Cultural History* (Berkeley: University of California Press, 1989), 50.

6. E.P. Thompson, 'The Moral Economy of the English Crowd in the Eighteenth Century', *Past and Present* 50(1) (1971), 83.

7. Vucetic, *Anglosphere*, 11–12.

8. V. Glăveanu, 'Stereotypes Revised – Theoretical Models, Taxonomy and the Role of Stereotypes', *Europe's Journal of Psychology* 3(3) (2007), 1.

9. E. Hobsbawm, *Nations and Nationalism since 1780* (Cambridge: Cambridge University Press, 1990), 91.

10. W. Mead, *God and Gold: Britain, America, and the Making of the Modern World* (New York: Alfred A. Knopf, 2008), 47–48.

11. C. Campbell, *Revolution to Rapprochement: The United States and Great Britain, 1783–1900* (New York: John Wiley, 1974), 183.

12. Adams, *Brothers across the Ocean*, 34.

13. Truman Presidential Library, Independence, Missouri, Papers of Harry S. Truman, President's Secretary's Files, Box 99, W. Churchill, 'The Sinews of Peace', 1946.

14. L. Colley, *Britons: Forging the Nation, 1707–1837* (New Haven, CT: Yale University Press, 2009), 105.

15. Ibid., 139–43.

16. Gilder Lehrman Collection, New York, GLC04961.01, P. Dawe, 'The Bostonian's Paying the Excise-man, or Tarring & Feathering', London, 31 October 1774.

17. Colley, *Britons*, 143, 145–46.

18. For additional information, see Colley, *Britons*, 139–50.

19. J. Hall, 'The Question of Language', in A. Frantzen and J. Niles (eds), *Anglo-Saxonism and the Construction of Social Identity* (Gainesville: University Press of Florida, 1997), 134.

20. Massachusetts Historical Society, John Adams Diary 44, 'Notes on a Tour of English Country Seats, &C., with Thomas Jefferson', 4–10 April 1786, retrieved 19 February 2018 from http://www.masshist.org/digitaladams/archive/doc?id=D44.

21. R. Micsak, 'A Comparative Study of Thomas Jefferson's Travels to England and Their Influences on Monticello' (Honors Thesis, Cornell University, 2007); US National Archives, Washington, DC, Thomas Jefferson, 'Notes on a Tour of English Gardens', 2–14 April 1786, retrieved 19 June 2018 from https://founders.archives.gov/documents/Jefferson/01-09-02-0328.

22. C. Rossiter (ed.), *The Federalist Papers* (New York: New American Library, 2003), 32.

23. For example, *Library of Congress*, W. Charles, '*A Boxing Match, or Another Bloody Nose for John Bull'*, *1813*, retrieved 5 May 2018 from http://www.loc.gov/item/2002708982/.

24. A. Nevins, *America through British Eyes* (New York: Oxford University Press, 1948), 79–102; also see R. Frankel, *Observing America: The Commentary of British Visitors to the United States, 1890–1950* (Madison: University of Wisconsin Press, 2006), 3–5; N. Cliff, *The Shakespeare Riots* (New York: Random House, 2007), 110.

25. See F. Marryat, *Second Series of a Diary in America, with Remarks on its Institutions* (Philadelphia: Collin, 1840); F. Trollope, *Domestic Manners of the Americans* (London: Harmondsworth, 1997); F. Kemble, *Journal of a Residence in America* (Paris: W. Galignani and Co., 1835); Cliff, *Shakespeare Riots*, 111–15.

26. Frankel, *Observing America*, 6.

27. As quoted in Cliff, *Shakespeare Riots*, 118.

28. See C. Dickens, *American Notes for General Circulation* (London: Chapman & Hall, 1842); Dickens, *The Life and Adventures of Martin Chuzzlewit* (London: Chapman & Hall, 1842–44); Cliff, *Shakespeare Riots*, 108–9, 121–25; Frankel, *Observing America*, 7–11.

29. I. Burma, *Anglomania: A European Love Affair* (New York: Vintage Books, 2000), 91.

30. See B. Anderson, *Imagined Communities: Reflections on the Origin and Spread of Nationalism* (London: Verso, 1998); E. Gellner, *Nations and Nationalism* (Ithaca, NY: Cornell University Press, 2009).

31. W. Sollors (ed.), *The Invention of Ethnicity* (New York: Oxford University Press, 1989), xi–xii.

32. M. Krenn, *The Color of Empire: Race and American Foreign Relations* (Lincoln, NE: Potomac Books, 2006), 103–7; Horsman, 'Origins of Racial Anglo-Saxonism', 395, 398.

33. E. Bonilla-Silva, *Racism without Racists*, 5th edn (New York: Rowman & Littlefield, 2018), 8.

34. Horsman, 'Origins of Racial Anglo-Saxonism', 397.

35. Ibid., 397–98.

36. D. Scragg and C. Weinberg (eds), *Literary Appropriations of the Anglo-Saxons from the Thirteenth to the Twentieth Century* (Cambridge: Cambridge University Press, 2006), 163; Frankel, *Observing America*, 54; Horsman, 'Origins of Racial Anglo-Saxonism', 399–401.

37. M. Kohn, 'A Tale of Two Indias: Burke and Mill on Empire and Slavery in the West Indies and America', *Political Theory* 34(2) (2006), 192–228.

38. Horsman, *Race and Manifest Destiny*, 4.

39. Colley, *Britons*, xxii, 377.

40. T. Huxley, *Lay Sermons, Addresses and Reviews* (New York: D. Appleton and Company, 1870), ix, 20.

41. This chapter focuses on broad national factors leading to the dominance of the brother stereotype in the latter half of the 1800s, but regional trends also impacted this shift. See, for example, G. VanHoosier-Carey, 'Byrhtnoth in Dixie' in Frantzen and Niles, *Anglo-Saxonism*, 157–72.

42. A. Dobson, *Anglo-American Relations in the Twentieth Century* (London: Routledge, 1995), 15–16.

43. Kupchan, *How Enemies Become Friends*, 103–5.

44. A. Chernock, 'Why Do Americans Fawn over British Royalty?', *Conversation*, 27 November 2017, retrieved 4 May 2018 from http://theconversation.com/why-do-americans-fawn-over-british-royalty-39038.

45. Colley, *Britons*, 361.

46. Kupchan, *How Enemies Become Friends*, 105.

47. See H. Gates, *Stony the Road: Reconstruction, White Supremacy, and the Rise of Jim Crow* (New York: Penguin Press, 2019); S. Lyman, 'The Race Question in Liberalism', *International Journal of Politics, Culture and Society* 5(2) (1991), 183–247; T. Davis, '"I Long for My Home in Kentuck": Christy's Minstrels in Mid-19th-Century Britain', *TDR* 57(2) (2013), 38–65.

48. R. Daniels, *Guarding the Golden Door* (New York: Hill and Wang, 2005), 9–10.

49. M. Ryan, 'The American Parade: Representations of the Nineteenth-Century Social Order', in Hunt, *New Cultural History*, 146–47.

50. Daniels, *Guarding the Golden Door*, 30; Vucetic, *Anglosphere*, 31; A. Stern, *Eugenic Nation: Faults & Frontiers of Better Breeding in Modern America* (Oakland: University of California Press, 2016), 14; W.A. Williams, *The Tragedy of American Diplomacy* (New York: W.W. Norton, 2009, 46.

51. Frankel, *Observing America*, 55.

52. P. Panayi, 'Pride and Prejudice: The Victorian Roots of a Very British Ambivalence to Immigration', *The Independent*, 1 July 2010, retrieved 7 June 2018 from http://www.independent.co.uk/news/uk/this-britain/pride-and-prejudice-the-victorian-roots-of-a-very-british-ambivalence-to-immigration-2016353.html; also see Panayi, *An Immigration History of Britain: Multicultural Racism since 1800* (London: Routledge, 2010).

53. R. Cavanaugh, 'Our American Cousin', *The Guardian*, 6 April 2015, retrieved 15 February 2018 from http://www.theguardian.com/stage/2015/apr/06/our-american-cousin-lincoln-theatre-john-wilkes-booth; Morgen Stevens-Garmon, 'Lincoln's Last Play; or, the Continuing Fascination with "Our American Cousin"', Museum of the City of New York, 17 April 2012, retrieved 10 May 2018 from https://blog.mcny.org/2012/04/17/lincolns-last-play-or-the-continuing-fascination-with-our-american-cousin/.

54. T. Taylor, *Our American Cousin*, 1858, retrieved 18 May 2018 from Project Gutenberg, http://www.gutenberg.org/files/3158/3158-h/3158-h.htm.

55. 'Burton's New Theater', *New-York Daily Tribune*, 27 January 1859, 1; A. Brown, *A History of the New York Stage* (New York: Dodd, Mead and Co., 1903), 450.

56. Kupchan, *How Enemies Become Friends*, 96.

57. Vucetic, '*The Fulton Address*', 105; also see D. Bell, *The Idea of Greater Britain* (Princeton, NJ: Princeton University Press, 2011).

58. T. Machan, *What Is English?: And Why Should We Care?* (Oxford: Oxford University Press, 2013), 271; Burma, *Anglomania*, 129.

59. Vucetic, *Anglosphere*, 104.

60. Ibid., 105.

61. R. Toye, *Churchill's Empire: The World that Made Him and the World He Made* (New York: Henry Holt, 2010), 136; Frankel, *Observing America*, 246.

62. *Library of Congress, Washington, DC,* John Gast, *American Progress, 1872*, retrieved 26 May 2018 from http://www.loc.gov/pictures/item/97507547/.

63. A. Pochmara, 'Between Elysium and Inferno: The Rhetoric of Ambivalence in Oscar Wilde's and Rudyard Kipling's Writings about America', *Journal of Transatlantic Studies* 13(1) (2015), 71.

64. Ibid., 56–67.

65. Vucetic, *Anglosphere*, 28–29, 32.

66. P. Conlin, 'Victorian Racism: An Explication of Scientific Knowledge, its Social Character, and its Relation to Victorian Popular Culture', *Inquires Journal* 10(1) (2018), 1.

67. S. Geisler, *God and Sea Power: The Influence of Religion on Alfred Thayer Mahan* (Annapolis, MD: Naval Institute Press, 2015), 1; Vucetic, *Anglosphere*, 37–38.

68. J. Strong, 'The Anglo-Saxon and the World's Future', 1890, in J. Herbst (ed.), *Our Country* (Cambridge, MA: Belknap Press, 1963), 208; also see Williams, *The Tragedy*, 60.

69. Frankel, *Observing America*, 58.

70. Ibid., 63.

71. Kupchan, *How Enemies Become Friends*, 91; Vucetic, *Anglosphere*, 34.

72. Vucetic, *Anglosphere*, 33–34.

73. Kupchan, *How Enemies Become Friends*, 90–91, 97.

74. Ibid., 97.

75. Toye, *Churchill's Empire*, 80–81.

76. Vucetic, *Anglosphere*, 39

77. B. Murdoch, *Fighting Songs and Warring Words: Popular Lyrics of Two World Wars* (London: Routledge, 2018), 65.

78. D. Russell, *Popular Music in England 1840–1914* (Manchester: Manchester University Press, 1997), 152; Toye, *Churchill's Empire*, 22.

79. Library of Congress, M1644.H., W. Allan, 'John Bull and Uncle Sam' (Chicago: The S. Brainard's Sons Co., 1898).

80. *Library of Congress*, L. Dalrymple, 'United we stand for civilization and peace!' *Puck* (*New York:* Keppler & Schwarzmann, 8 June *1898)*, retrieved 1 June 2018 from http://www.loc.gov/item/2012647570/.

81. Williams, *The Tragedy*, 63

82. *Library of Congress*, U. Keppler, 'From the Cape to Cairo', *Puck* (*New York:* Ottmann Lith. Co., 10 December *1902)*, retrieved 1 June 2018 from http://www.loc.gov/pictures/item/2010652189/.

83. W.T. Stead, *Americanization of the World* (New York: H. Markley, 1901), 1–2.

Bibliography

Adams, I. *Brothers across the Ocean: British Foreign Policy and the Origins of the Anglo-American Special Relationship*. London: Tauris Academic Studies, 2005.

Anderson, B. *Imagined Communities: Reflections on the Origin and Spread of Nationalism*. London: Verso, 1998.

Anderson, S. *Race and Rapprochement: Anglo-Saxonism and Anglo-American Relations*. Rutherford, NJ: Fairleigh Dickinson University Press, 1981.

Bell, D. *The Idea of Greater Britain*. Princeton, NJ: Princeton University Press, 2011.

Bonilla-Silva, E. *Racism without Racists*. 5th edn. New York: Rowman & Littlefield, 2018.

Brown, A. *A History of the New York Stage, Volume I*. New York: Dodd, Mead and Co., 1903.

Burma, I. *Anglomania: A European Love Affair*. New York: Vintage Books, 2000.

Campbell, C. *Revolution to Rapprochement: The United States and Great Britain, 1783–1900*. New York: John Wiley, 1974.

Cavanaugh, R. 'Our American Cousin'. *The Guardian*, 6 April 2015, http://www.theguardian.com/stage/2015/apr/06/our-american-cousin-lincoln-theatre-john-wilkes-booth.

Cliff, N. *The Shakespeare Riots: Revenge, Drama, and Death in Nineteenth-Century America*. New York: Random House, 2007.

Colley, L. *Britons: Forging the Nation, 1707–1837*. New Haven, CT: Yale University Press, 2009.

Conlin, P. 'Victorian Racism: An Explication of Scientific Knowledge, its Social Character, and its Relation to Victorian Popular Culture', *Inquires Journal* 10(1) (2018), http://www.inquiriesjournal.com/a?id=1719.

Curtis, L. *Anglo-Saxons and Celts: A Study of Anti-Irish Prejudice in Victorian England*. New York: New York University Press, 1968.

Daniels, R. *Guarding the Golden Door: American Immigration Policy and Immigrants since 1882*. New York: Hill and Wang, 2005.

Davis, T. '"I Long for My Home in Kentuck": Christy's Minstrels in Mid-19th-Century Britain'. *TDR* 57(2) (2013), 38–65.

Dickens, C. *American Notes for General Circulation*. London: Chapman & Hall, 1842.

Dobson, A. *Anglo-American Relations in the Twentieth Century*. London: Routledge, 1995.

Dobson, A., and S. Marsh (eds). *Anglo-American Relations: Contemporary Perspectives*. London: Routledge, 2013.

———. *Churchill and the Anglo-American Special Relationship*. London: Routledge, 2017.

Frankel, R. *Observing America: The Commentary of British Visitors to the United States, 1890–1950*. Madison: University of Wisconsin Press, 2006.

Frantzen, A., and J. Niles (eds). *Anglo-Saxonism and the Construction of Social Identity*. Gainesville: University Press of Florida, 1997.

Gates, H. *Stony the Road: Reconstruction, White Supremacy, and the Rise of Jim Crow*. New York: Penguin Press, 2019.

Geisler, S. *God and Sea Power: The Influence of Religion on Alfred Thayer Mahan*. Annapolis, MD: Naval Institute Press, 2015.

Gellner, E. *Nations and Nationalism*. Ithaca, NY: Cornell University Press, 2009.

Glăveanu, V. 'Stereotypes Revised – Theoretical Models, Taxonomy and the Role of Stereotypes', *Europe's Journal of Psychology* 3(3) (2007), https://ejop.psychopen.eu/article/view/409/308.

Herbst, J. (ed.) *Our Country*. Cambridge, MA: Belknap Press, 1963.

Hobsbawm, E. *Nations and Nationalism since 1780*. Cambridge: Cambridge University Press, 1990.

Horsman, R. 'Origins of Racial Anglo-Saxonism in Great Britain before 1850'. *Journal of the History of Ideas* 37(3) (1976), 387–410.

———. *Race and Manifest Destiny: The Origins of Racial Anglo-Saxonism*. Cambridge, MA: Harvard University Press, 1981.

Hunt, L. (ed.). *The New Cultural History*. Berkeley: University of California Press, 1989.

Kemble, F. *Journal of a Residence in America*. Paris: W. Galignani and Co., 1835.

Kohn, M. 'A Tale of Two Indias: Burke and Mill on Empire and Slavery in the West Indies and America', *Political Theory* 34(2) (2006), 192–228.

Krenn, M. *The Color of Empire: Race and American Foreign Relations*. Lincoln, NE: Potomac Books, 2006.

Kupchan, C. *How Enemies Become Friends: The Sources of Stable Peace*. Princeton, NJ: Princeton University Press, 2010.

Lyman, S. 'The Race Question in Liberalism', *International Journal of Politics, Culture and Society* 5(2) (1991), 183–247.

Machan, T. *What Is English?: And Why Should We Care?* Oxford: Oxford University Press, 2013.

Marryat, F. *Second Series of a Diary in America, with Remarks on its Institutions*. Philadelphia, PA: Collin, 1840.

Mead, W. *God and Gold: Britain, America, and the Making of the Modern World*. New York: Alfred A. Knopf, 2008.

Murdoch, B. *Fighting Songs and Warring Words: Popular Lyrics of Two World Wars*. London: Routledge, 2018.

Nevins, A. *America through British Eyes*. New York: Oxford University Press, 1948.

Panayi, P. *An Immigration History of Britain: Multicultural Racism since 1800*. London: Routledge, 2010.

Panayi, P. 'Pride and Prejudice: The Victorian Roots of a Very British Ambivalence to Immigration'. *The Independent*, 1 July 2010, http://www.independent.co.uk/news/uk/this-britain/pride-and-prejudice-the-victorian-roots-of-a-very-british-ambivalence-to-immigration-2016353.html.

Pochmara, A. 'Between Elysium and Inferno: The Rhetoric of Ambivalence in Oscar Wilde's and Rudyard Kipling's Writings about America', *Journal of Transatlantic Studies* 13(1) (2015), 56–75.

Russell, D. *Popular Music in England 1840–1914*. Manchester: Manchester University Press, 1997.

Sollors, W. (ed.). *The Invention of Ethnicity*. New York: Oxford University Press, 1989.

Stead, W.T. *Americanization of the World; or, the Trend of the Twentieth Century*. New York: H. Markley, 1901.

Stevens-Garmon, M. 'Lincoln's Last Play; or, the Continuing Fascination with "Our American Cousin"'. Museum of the City of New York, 17 April 2012, https://blog.mcny.org/2012/04/17/lincolns-last-play-or-the-continuing-fascination-with-our-american-cousin/.

Thompson, E.P. 'The Moral Economy of the English Crowd in the Eighteenth Century', *Past and Present* 50(1) (1971), 76–136.

Toye, R. *Churchill's Empire: The World that Made Him and the World He Made*. New York: Henry Holt, 2010.

Trollope, F. *Domestic Manners of the Americans*. London: Harmondsworth, 1997.

Vucetic, S. *The Anglosphere: A Genealogy of a Racialized Identity in International Relations*. Stanford, CA: Stanford University Press, 2011.

Chapter 9

The Anglosphere
Rise and Demise of an Anglo-American Policy Idea

David G. Haglund

Introduction

Among the various policy ideas to have circulated in the transatlantic political arena in recent years, few have been as charged with controversy as the notion of the 'Anglosphere' – a notion that began to attract a good deal of attention early in the first decade of the twenty-first century.[1] This ideational construct has been interpreted as representing either something wonderful or something terrible. At one extreme, it has been viewed as representing the fullest flowering of the venerated Anglo-American tradition of liberty, the ideational underpinning of the West's liberal-democratic 'zone of peace'.[2] Conversely, it has been said to signify nothing so much as the continuation of a pattern of ethnic (some say even racial) self-promotion that makes a mockery of those very same liberal-democratic norms and values.[3] It has even been mustered, by one of its detractors, into the service of justifying Scotland's leaving the United Kingdom and joining – wait for it – *Canada*, as the latter's eleventh province. For Ken McGoogan, who was evidently serious in advancing this policy idea, among its merits would be the clearly normative one of situating both Scotland and its new 'country' on the right side of justice, because 'while the Tories in Britain and the Republicans in the United States set about creating a neo-liberal Anglosphere – anti-egalitarian, avowedly Christian, pro-Big Business, pro-military – Scotland becomes part of Canada and helps lead the way to a more progressive world'.[4]

Nor is the debate simply limited to the normative meaning and consequences of the Anglosphere, as important as these may be. Scholars, policymakers and political activists have also disputed the postulated sources of this policy idea. Some argue that its origins can be found in the realm of linguistics; in so doing, they merely use different formulations to echo Otto von Bismarck's famous remark about how English being the predominant tongue in two very powerful transatlantic countries would be the determinative geopolitical feature of the twentieth century, a consequence of the 'logic of history'.[5] Or, as the same thought was expressed in more cultural than geopolitical terms shortly after the First World War, 'a language, of course, is more than words. It is a body of literature, it is a method of thinking, it is a definition of emotions, it is the exponent and the symbol of a civilization. You cannot adopt English without adapting yourself in some measure to the English, or the Anglo-American tradition.'[6] Others, however, put the emphasis not so much upon the tongue as upon the 'blood', taken by them to represent not only the speaking of a common language, but also the sharing of a 'biological' common past.[7]

This chapter examines the rise and apparent demise of enthusiasm for the Anglosphere. To reiterate, the rubric itself may be of recent vintage, but the concept has its roots in a more distant period, one in which talk of Anglo-American amity and (who could say?) possibly even 'reunion' was being heard in certain quarters on both sides of the Atlantic. Eventually, there would develop a stitching together, of sorts, of the first British Empire, made manifest through an alliance between the United States and its former mother country, and enshrined in a bilateral relationship whose qualities were deemed to be unprecedentedly 'special' in world affairs. And while the Anglosphere and the Anglo-American special relationship (AASR) may not be identical constructs, they possess obvious common features. Accordingly, this chapter's next section embeds the current debate over the Anglosphere in an anterior discussion on that geopolitical dispensation we know as the AASR. Following this, the focus shifts to the business of trying to define the Anglosphere and identifying its two principal significations. The chapter's fourth section zeroes in on the most controversial matter of all, namely whether the Anglosphere countries have a propensity towards military intervention and, if so, why. The concluding section explores the current state and future prospects of the Anglosphere.

Is the Anglosphere Just Another Way of Saying, 'Anglo-American Special Relationship'?

The volume in which this chapter is found constitutes a broad historical, cultural and philosophical overview of Anglo-American political traditions, some of which date from a moment in the eighteenth century preceding America's departure from the first British Empire and some of which are much more recent. Among the conceptual parvenus in international relations (IR) lore, few, it would seem, have attained the celebrity (if not infamy) so recently associated with the Anglosphere, an apparent, and novel, derivative of that older geostrategic institution known as the Anglo-American special relationship, with which it shares a certain lustre or, as the case may be, notoriety. Although the two geopolitical conceptualizations are obviously related, they are not identical. Thus, it is important to draw attention to a couple of differences between the Anglosphere and the AASR at the outset. To start with the obvious, the membership of the latter is more restricted than that of the former: by definition, the AASR involves two states, the United States and the United Kingdom, while the Anglosphere constitutes an assumed identity-based community embracing, depending on how it is construed (see below), anywhere from a minimum of three members to upwards of a dozen or more. Then there is the second distinction, functional in scope, that sets the AASR apart from the Anglosphere. The former must logically connote as its *raison d'être* the cultivation and sustaining of a highly co-operative political relationship between two state actors, each of which seeks to derive benefit from their co-operative interaction; it is, in a word, a *purposive* enterprise, intended to effect, at its most ambitious, nothing short of the construction and maintenance of 'world order'.[8] The Anglosphere, by contrast, is a looser grouping and – again depending upon its definition – it can embrace states or societies, or a combination of the two, and can exist for some purpose, or for no particular purpose at all.

These differences being noted, there are nevertheless some commonalities between the two conceptual entities. Most importantly, each has spawned queries as to whether it even *exists* or is simply a geopolitical conceit, with the more familiar AASR presenting itself as a useful proxy for the Anglosphere in this matter of existential contestation. This is to suggest that there is a natural comparability between what has been said of the AASR's existence and that of the Anglosphere, save that not enough time has passed to enable a full-throated airing of the contestation of the latter. Nevertheless, existential questions that have been posed regarding the AASR can, *mutatis mutandis*, find applicability in respect of the Anglosphere. So let us see what has been said of the AASR, as a surrogate for what might be said of the Anglosphere.

Like Caesar's Gaul, the interpretive school of the AASR can be divided into three parts. The first part consists of the sceptics, scholars who are blunt in their insistence that to the extent there might be anything deemed particularly 'special' about the AASR, it inheres in how lousy an arrangement it has been for one, if not both, of the transatlantic partners. For the sceptics, the so-called merits of the AASR have been an overhyped and oversold potion, a kind of geostrategic snake oil that has been poured down the gullets of a credulous transatlantic public for far too long. These scholars include those whom the editors of this volume have labelled AASR 'terminalists'.[9] Among the sceptics (indeed, cynics), we find Erwan Lagadec and Edward Ingram. For Lagadec, the only thing 'special' about the relationship between the United States and the United Kingdom is its dysfunctionality – a relationship 'only "special" insofar as it has been *more* contentious than any other in the recent past. As a result, the political "special relationship" is but a futile exercise in deluded nostalgia. It leans on the altar of a past that never was, though it yields but the flimsiest results in the present, and is a useless tool to shape the future.'[10] Ingram goes one step further than Lagadec and considers the AASR to be nothing other than a sinister means by which the United States ensnared a hapless Britain into its orbit of satellites, blinding gullible British decision-makers to reality, such that '[a]lthough the United States did not formally declare war against Britain during World War II, it did destroy Britain and may have done so deliberately'.[11]

Against the sceptics are two other categories of analyst, each of which professes to discern utility in the AASR for both members, albeit for different reasons. One group, let us call them the 'Palmerstonians',[12] understands the AASR to be held together purely on the basis of rational calculations of interest in both the United Kingdom and the United States. They agree that there is logical and empirical substance to this geostrategic institution and they also think it has served each country reasonably well ever since it came into existence. But they insist, in the manner of most (though not all) 'realist' analysts of IR, that self-interest constitutes the AASR's bonding agent, especially as that interest gets manifested through the pursuit of power. In the words of one such analyst, the AASR is nothing more or less than 'an element in the central power-balance, ... [therefore] the failure to see it in this context leads to its either being sentimentalized or (and this comes to much the same thing) being written down as of no account'.[13]

The third group, whom we are going to meet again later in this chapter, represents both a new and an old tradition in IR and foreign-policy theorizing. In its newest guise, it reflects an interest in 'collective identity' and emotion as factors in policymaking.[14] In its older guise, it associates both of those phenomena with a policy construct once known as the 'Anglo-Saxon' idea. Importantly, it is possible to describe both the AASR and, *a fortiori*, the Anglosphere as having been built upon cultural foundations predicated upon a transatlantic, 'racialized', collective identity.[15] But even if one dismisses the emotional appeal of this postulated racial identity, there still remains a theoretically interesting, also 'counter-Palmerstonian', claim with which to contend – namely the claim, advanced by certain constructivist theoreticians, that states can indeed be 'friends' for reasons derived as much from affect as from interest, and possibly even more from affect than from interest.[16]

Prior to getting to this counter-Palmerstonian inquiry, let's return to the question, adumbrated earlier, of how we might actually go about defining the

Anglosphere, as well as illuminating its principal denotative qualities. That is the task of the next section of this chapter.

Conceptual Foray: The Two Faces of the Anglosphere

A convenient, likely even necessary, point of embarkation for this definitional foray is the 2003 Iraq War, concerning which a few commentators both at the time and since have professed to detect a definite, if dimly understood, connection between one 'cultural' attribute and one particular foreign-policy output. The attribute was language and the output a willingness, if not a keenness, to undertake military interventions. Because the big three of the interventionist coalition mustered to topple Saddam Hussein – the United States, the United Kingdom and Australia – were all populated mainly by native English speakers, some imagined they detected evidence of a linguistic connection, even if no one could actually be sure how a common language was supposed to stimulate a proclivity towards interventionism. It was at this time that, suddenly, media pundits and celebrity-happy scholars began to talk up the prowess of the Anglosphere. But what was the Anglosphere supposed to mean and who was in it?

To begin to answer this, we need to back up a few years, to the middle of the previous decade, for it was in the 1990s that our concept got its name, in a science-fiction novel penned by Neal Stephenson, entitled *The Diamond Age*.[17] Stephenson's Anglosphere was one of three large cultural groupings in a future world order organized more on civilizational than on traditional Westphalian (i.e. state-centric) lines. There was no apparent connection between the word and the policy orientation until the Iraq War and certainly there was none with martial connotations. But even the Iraq conflict, which saw some analysts attempting to discern an Anglospheric element of great significance, cannot be said to have settled the question of how to define the word.

That is because, in addition to, and in many ways more persuasive than, the protagonists of the Anglosphere-as-intervention thesis was a second group of thinkers, for whom the Anglosphere was more likely to conjure up Kantian visions of perpetual peace than Hobbesian ones of recurrent bellicosity. If the militaristic version could be termed 'Anglosphere heavy', then its more irenic conceptual cousin can be labelled 'Anglosphere lite'.[18] The chief intellectual luminary of this second variant of the Anglosphere is James C. Bennett, president of the Anglosphere Institute in Virginia, although it need hardly be said that Bennett himself would not, and did not, use the adjective 'lite', with its potentially pejorative connotations.[19] Bennett's Anglosphere has two 'nodes': the United States and the United Kingdom. But that is not all it has, for its membership includes some 'powerful and populous outliers': Australia, New Zealand, Ireland and the Anglophone portions of Canada and South Africa. He calls this group a 'network commonwealth'. Importantly, it is a non-interventionist kind of community, a gathering of like-minded countries and societies that 'concentrates on tending and perfecting our own garden first, on creating deep and strong ties between highly similar nations and cultures, and seeking to help other nations by serving as an example (and sometimes, as a caution). It does not impose solutions on nations and cannot benefit thereby'.[20]

There are two ironies associated with this clustering of Anglosphere adherents. One concerns the label. It could be remarked that there must be something derogatory in likening what is, after all, the most highly refined of the two Anglosphere variants to an insipid brew, lite beer, which many Americans and Canadians seem to enjoy quaffing. My purpose here is not to demean, but to describe, and I use the modifier in somewhat the same way that, for instance, Michael Ignatieff employed the notion of 'empire lite', as a means of drawing attention to policy implications that are thought to be rather admirable.[21]

The other irony concerns not the label applied to the deed, but the deed itself. In this connection, those who imagine culture and intervention somehow to be positively correlated must be disappointed, for this Anglosphere, sometimes also known as the 'English-using' community, turns out to be very much a stay-at-home phenomenon. It is also the most 'inclusionary', and therefore the most territorially expansive, variant of the Anglosphere – indeed, some have come close to making it virtually synonymous with the entire West.[22] It represents a security dispensation associated with a liberal-democratic set of transnational values of unmistakable Anglo-American rootage – a dispensation known as a 'security community', which is to say an international order informed and sustained by 'dependable expectations of peaceful change', meaning that members of the community neither make war on each other nor *threaten* so to do.[23] If this were all that we could say about the Anglosphere, namely that it was the throbbing heart of the Western 'zone of peace', then our concept would lose much of the normative sting associated with it – except, of course, for those excluded from membership in the zone, or conversely, those critics ('populists' and otherwise) who see little worth cheering about in the liberal international order of the post-Second World War decades.[24]

It is no small matter to contemplate a world – or at least a portion of a world – from which the use or threat of force has been banished as a means of international dispute settlement. This is indeed an accomplishment worth celebrating. But *this* Anglosphere, founded as it is upon collective identity derived above all else from shared political values of a British provenance, seems to be a particularly inert beast when it comes to the issue of actually using, instead of refraining from using, military force. In other words, Anglosphere lite may be a marvellous device for getting its members to abstain from physically bashing each other, but it is not such a good mechanism if the challenge at hand is to impel them to intervene *outside* their zone of peace. If culture is somehow correlated with interventionist preferences on the part of members of the Anglosphere, we will have to turn to the alternative variant, because, in this respect, lite can at best whet, but cannot slake, a thirst for military expeditions. For quenching that thirst, we have to turn to 'Anglosphere heavy'.

This higher-octane concoction has been responsible for generating the most criticism of the Anglosphere concept, as evinced by the widespread opposition to the 2003 invasion of Iraq. It is also the variant that puzzles us the most. For at the core of Anglosphere heavy, there must be assumptions about the Anglo-American 'character' that can somehow be credibly linked to interventionism. Though it might discomfit proponents of Anglosphere lite, who want to insist upon the *non*-racial content of their concept, in a very real sense the current discussion of Anglosphere heavy is but a continuation of a debate harking back more than a century, concerning the meaning of 'Anglo-Saxon' identity for international peace and security. On this issue, Owen Harries is correct: the term itself might have been new, emerging as it did in discussions of a latter-day 'English-speaking union', which began to surface in in the late 1990s,[25] but there was nothing new in the aspiration contained within the Anglosphere rubric. '[W]hat some are now referring to as a political "Anglosphere" … [is a] line of argument almost exactly replicat[ing] one advanced by a group of highly intelligent, well-educated and well-connected young men at the beginning of the last century.'[26]

Those who articulated and advanced that vision were identified by a series of appellations during the first third of the twentieth century, ranging from 'Milner's Kindergarten' through the 'Round Table' and eventually even the 'Cliveden Set' (though this latter is typically associated with pro-appeasement enthusiasts of the mid- to late 1930s, so much so that it is easy to forget the group's principal focus at its founding, namely the fostering of closer Anglo-American strategic ties). Regardless of the name they bore, they preached the same message about the singular promise of English-speaking unity as a necessary and quite possibly sufficient condition of international peace and stability.[27] Panegyrists of this earlier collective identity appealed to cultural solidarity, specifically to the once and future co-operative vision of a great *Volk*, the Anglo-Saxons, destined to prevail over the international political system.

To be sure, what was sought by the Anglo-Saxon unity enthusiasts in that earlier era is precisely what the more recent Anglosphere heavy enthusiasts have wanted: peace through strength, that is, through *Anglospheric* strength. As there is a separate chapter in this volume that is specifically focused on

'Anglo-Saxonism', it suffices here simply to highlight one essential unity of aspiration between the earlier and later champions of peace through English speakers. In that earlier period, commencing towards the end of the nineteenth century and picking up steam in the first decade of the twentieth century, the quest for 'universal peace' was predicated upon the fomenting of the 'Anglo-Saxon alliance' – that is, progression of Anglo-American comity from the Great Rapprochement of 1898 to the cementing of a bilateral alliance.[28] For some time, there had been discussion, within the transatlantic world, of the wonderful benefits that could be enjoyed, for it as well as for the entirety of humankind, should the formerly antagonistic English-speaking powers not only bury the hatchet, but also take the next step in fashioning a co-operative relationship. That step was the forging of a military alliance.

Such a mighty alliance between the international system's two leading economic powers had already begun to be bruited by policy intellectuals even prior to 1898. Much of this advocacy stemmed from enthusiasts based in the United Kingdom, but some Americans also happily drank the Kool-Aid of 'universal peace' through Anglo-American strategic union.[29] No one quite captured the uplifting vision with as much verve as British mining potentate, Cecil Rhodes, who knew what the reassembly of the first British Empire could achieve; it would lay the 'foundation of so great a power as to hereafter render wars impossible and promote the best interests of humanity'.[30] Imagine, Rhodes enthused, what could be accomplished through the combined might of these two great powers: 'What an awful thought it is that if we had not lost America, or if even now we could arrange with the present members of the United States Assembly and our House of Commons, the peace of the world is secured for all eternity!'[31]

It is easy enough for us to grasp, at the remove of a century, the geostrategic logic of this policy aspiration. IR theorists have long been convinced, after all, that the source of state power must ultimately be found in economic strength, and the United States and the United Kingdom happened to be the first- and second-ranking economies during the era of enthusiasm for the Anglo-Saxon alliance. By 1880, America's GDP already exceeded that of *any* of the European powers; by 1910, it was 10 per cent larger than the combined GDPs of Britain and Germany.[32] Today, so many are convinced that the big story of the twenty-first century must be the implications for global security of China's 'rise' – and this big story betrays logic identical to power-transition assumptions from that earlier period. With economic strength, it was maintained, came military power; with military power came military *threat*, all things being equal.[33] But, of course, ceteris was not paribus for champions of Anglo-Saxon universal peace. They knew that, in this specific case, cultural affinity could corrode the logic of inexorable great-power war, at least between members of the cultural in-group (the United States and the United Kingdom). This was not all that cultural affinity could accomplish, however; it was also said to be capable of serving as a mighty spur to collective militarized statecraft vis-à-vis members of out-groups. Thus, these debates prefigured those that, a century later, would transpire regarding the Anglosphere, especially in its 'heavy' aspect.

Anglosphere and Affect: The Impact of Character, Identity and Folkways

One should always approach the concept of 'culture' with trepidation, as it is one of the most slippery categories upon which political analysts find themselves forced to tread. Although Raymond Williams was neither a specialist in, nor particularly fond of, the scholarly discipline of international relations, his assessment of the concept of culture was spot on, insofar as concerns IR theorists: to him, the word ranked as one of the two or three most difficult to define in the entire English language (and, he could have added, in any other language).[34] Yet, it is also an apparently indispensable concept in IR, as evidenced by the attention allocated, over the past generation, to the notion of 'strategic culture', which, to quite a few analysts, holds the key to unlocking the secrets of state behaviour.[35] If culture is valuable to that end, it is even more valuable as a tool for contemplating the Anglosphere, which, in both its lite and heavy variants, pays homage to the impact that 'cultural' variables have had upon the ability of countries sharing a common language to adopt qualitatively different – and, it is said, healthier – patterns of interaction than is the case for states that do not share cultural attributes. Cultural commonality, the argument runs, counteracts the otherwise iron grip of international anarchy on the behaviour of states, forcing them to constantly be on the *qui vive* for security challenges, no matter from which direction they originate.

Illustratively, and to advert to the concluding paragraph in the above section of this chapter, it is sometimes remarked that the perils of the so-called 'Thucydides Trap' in IR can be obviated through cultural commonality and the 'affect' associated therewith. Adherents of a school of thought known as power-transition theory insist that whenever there is so great a reduction in the margin separating the leading power in the international system from the second-ranking power as to bring about near-parity, the risk of war between them vastly increases.[36] If there is a glimmer of light on an otherwise dismal theoretical horizon, some descry it in the manner in which Britain managed not only to 'accommodate' the rise of the United States, but even incorporate it into its security network, thereby making it a buttress of the AASR, to the benefit of both countries.[37] However, a serious reading of the

Anglo-American transition would suggest more caution than celebration, at least when analogical utility is being sought to help us contemplate the future course of Sino-American relations; there is just too little cultural commonality between the United States and China to ensure a smooth transition of power from the former to the latter.[38]

And *this* thought brings us back to how culture might be said to relate to the Anglosphere, particularly in its heavy variant. Analysts who seek guidance from the strategic-culture paradigm tend to be divided into two clusters. One group puts a premium on the myths, symbols and associated metaphors through which the purposes of statecraft are known and expressed; they are cognitivists before they are anything else and set great store by the investigation of symbolism. The other group holds culture to be tantamount to 'context' and, for them, the challenge is to discover what it is about the identity or character of a state (or a group of states) that might be said to propel it (or them) along certain policy paths. This kind of strategic-cultural inquiry into Anglosphere heavy could feature, for instance, an examination of 'national character' – or would do so had that particular rubric not fallen out of favour as a result of one serious distortion of it during the Second World War, when some (wrongly) held it to represent an apologia for Nazism.[39] These days, scholars seem to prefer what they consider to be a very different rubric, 'national identity', over which they fawn in their bid to provide insight into foreign-policy making.

Some analysts have detected an unmistakable 'ethnic' quality in the national identity of Americans and they have traced this back to the former mother country. Despite the 'multicultural' appearance of today's America, they say, the country remains very much what it has been all along, a chip off the ancestral (British) block. Moreover, the 'ethnocultural continuity'[40] on display on both sides of the Atlantic tells us a lot, not just about Anglo-American relations, but also about the Anglosphere when this latter is said somehow to be predisposing certain countries towards interventionism. For those who subscribe to the thesis that there is a transatlantic 'Anglo' identity and that it corresponds with a propensity to undertake military interventions (which is, of course, the gravamen of the Iraq War/Anglosphere linkage), the task before them is to demonstrate how culture and intervention go hand in hand.

One would think this a daunting task, and it is. But some have risen to the challenge of trying to make the connection between transatlantic 'Anglo' identity (character, really) and the use of military force. They do so, in the first instance, by invoking, implicitly more often than explicitly, the notion of an *ethnie*, that is a collective identity predicated in some way upon ethnicity. To be sure, ethnicity is, in its own right, a large and controversial topic, but for my purposes here I rely upon Anthony Smith's understanding of this version of

collective identity that presupposes an affixation to a 'named human population with a myth of common ancestry'.[41] And while many things can sustain
the myth of common ancestry, three constituent elements of identity stand
out. One is religion. Another is language. A third is a shared political history.
The second of these must, by definition, be of more than passing interest to
students of the Anglosphere; indeed, we have already seen in the preceding
section how important language can be for adherents of the Anglosphere lite
category, not only when this latter is conceived as a network commonwealth,
but also when it is seen to be the embodiment of a political-cultural legacy
handed down through generations of English-speaking political leaders and
theoreticians.

For Anglosphere heavy adherents, enthusiasm for practices of English
origins transcends the linguistic dimension of ethnicity, incorporating other
cultural phenomena as well. What is sought is the establishment of a connection between political values and a cultural identity that, at the extreme, can
be and sometimes has been invested with some of the 'racial' (or biological)
qualities mentioned above, in the discussion of Anglo-Saxonism. But culture
hardly derives its meaning from race alone and while it is true that the earlier
Anglo-Saxonist vogue *was* suffused with a great deal of bunkum associated
with the 'blood', there were always other policy advocates who placed the
spotlight on culture as a *sociological* rather than biological phenomenon. To
put it in contemporary terminology, not even in the heyday of Anglo-Saxonism did 'essentialism' (or, 'primordialism') rule the roost completely; there
were plenty of 'circumstantialists' lurking in the conceptual bushes, folk who,
in a later age, would wear the label of social-constructivists.[42] This is especially
so true today, among scholars or enthusiasts of the Anglosphere, who direct
their gaze towards non-racial, yet still eminently cultural, sources of foreign-
policy behaviour.

So, how might a case for culturally conditioned interventionism be made,
in the context of this section's emphasis upon Anglosphere heavy? To start
to answer this question, we need to ask a different one: is there something
uniquely warlike about native speakers of English? Do they, to borrow a
phrase employed by a recent Chinese ambassador to Canada, possess a 'gene
of aggression'?[43] Needless to say, proponents of the Kantian Anglosphere that
I have been calling 'Anglosphere lite' would scoff contemptuously at the very
posing of such a query, for what is being suggested is that there could be
something singular about a social grouping that expresses itself in English as
a mother tongue, no matter what its ostensible racial origins may be – namely,
that it has a propensity towards military interventionism! Putting things in
this way seems, on the surface, absurd, or if not absurd, then so fraught with
stereotyping as to arouse our immediate suspicions.

Well might we laugh today at stories such as one told by an English travel-ler in Holland a little more than a century ago about the cleanliness of Dutch cities and towns: 'Spring cleaning goes on here ... all the year round ... Every bulwark has a washing tray that can be fixed or detached in a moment. "It's a fine day, let us kill something", says the Englishman; "Here's an odd moment, let us wash something", says the Dutch.'[44] Amusing as this remark might seem to us now, we would do well to recall that it was not so very long ago that many English-speaking policy analysts put a great deal of stock in the notion that one *could* ascribe martial (hence, interventionistic) qualities to a people who spoke a certain language. We called those people *Germans* and thought them to be a particularly bellicose crowd, so much so that to the extent that the international system had a security problem, one could do much worse than to refer to it as the 'German problem'. It is true that even when such a problem was taken to be the principal source of upset in European and global politics, there had always been some who were prepared to concede that it may have been Germany's geopolitical setting and not the Germans' national character that lay at the root of things, but there never was any shortage of English-speaking biographers, historians, political scientists and even prime ministers who could assure you that most of what was wrong with the planet had to be traced to the individual and social demerits of Germans qua Germans.[45]

Similarly, there are some writers who will tell you that Anglosphere states *do* have a propensity towards military interventionism such as that glimpsed in the Iraq War, in the sense that there exist societally conditioned traits pos-sessed by denizens of the English-speaking world that put a cultural impress upon interventionist practices. How so? In a word, it is a function of the kind of ethnocultural 'continuity' we glimpsed above, in which social practices de-veloped in one part of the world get reproduced in another part, pari passu with the processes of demographic transfer associated with long-term migra-tory trends.[46] This is certainly a claim that has been advanced in respect of Anglo-American relations and since those relations form the central pillar of the Anglosphere, at least in its heavy variant, it is well worth taking a closer look at those processes of demographic transfer.

A superficial observer might remark, of the United States, that it has never been less 'Anglo' than it is today, or – more to the point – than it was more than fifteen years ago, at the time of the Iraq War. It would follow, from this observation, that British-inherited cultural attributes must have little or noth-ing to do with America's foreign policy, not least when it comes to the business of projecting military force abroad. Indeed, decennial census results would appear to validate this assumption regarding US demography, given the slight share (less than 10 per cent) of the country's population that today self-identi-fies as 'English' (by which they really mean 'British').[47] But the numbers mask a deeper reality, according to some scholars. One such scholar is David Hackett Fischer, who advances a modified form of 'germ theory' expressive of a very old idea that America's political and social virtues derived from its 'Teutonic' ancestry; instead, in Fischer's view, it is specifically to *British* sources that one must look in order to understand contemporary America, census figures to the contrary notwithstanding.

America, according to Fischer, remains very much what it has been for centuries. It is 'Albion's seed'.[48] Transatlantic 'folkways' of British provenance have endowed American political culture with inexpungible sociological qualities, down to the present time. Importantly, these characteristics are not, themselves, *homogeneous* inheritances from the former mother country, but are rather variegated legacies dependent upon where in the British Isles the emigrants to America originated. That is why, Fischer explains, there are four relatively *distinct* British folkways, each associated with one of the great waves of immigration to colonial America. Singly and collectively, these have been much more responsible for giving American political (and we could also say strategic) culture its peculiar stamp than any competing sources of American identity, whether those competing sources are anchored in environmental factors (viz. the Turner, or 'frontier', thesis) or are 'pluralistic' in nature (e.g. the [s]melting pot metaphor).[49]

For Fischer, America's having been born 'British' does not in the slightest translate into its being a socio-demographic monolith. Because those who arrived in America from the British Isles were so unlike each other politically, their possession of a common language could not be expected to generate social conformity in their new country, any more than it had in their old one. Those four waves of immigration to colonial America brought 1) Puritans from East Anglia to Massachusetts between 1629 and 1640; 2) a royalist elite from the south of England, along with their indentured servants, to Virginia between 1642 and 1675; 3) emigrants from the North Midlands and Wales to the Delaware Valley between 1675 and 1725; and 4) a very interesting, if excitable, group of borderers from the northern counties of England and the southern ones of Scotland, who came, some after a sojourn in the north of Ireland, to settle down in the Appalachian back country between 1718 and 1775. Fischer's thesis is that, thanks to these four groups, British folkways have remained the single most important determinant of America's voluntary society down to the present day.

For this section's inquiry into Anglosphere heavy, it is only the last group that stands out as a potential link between affect and intervention, and even then only in a qualified way. These are the folk who became known as the 'Scotch-Irish' (sometimes 'Scots-Irish') and what makes them so interesting is both their peculiar value set and their recent, and surprising, rebound as one of contemporary America's dominant subcultures – if not its *dominant* subculture. The borderers had known little but conflict for some seven hundred years prior to their arrival in America and the constant warfare left an indelible mark on their group identity. They fought in the old country and they continued to fight in the new one. *Lex talionus* was their quotidian rule and their golden rule was 'do unto others as they threaten to do unto you' – only do it first, if you can.[50] In the words of their principal contemporary chronicler, Walter Russell Mead, the value set of the borderers constitutes America's 'folk ideology' and, to the surprise of many, not only did they *not* get subsumed by the great waves of continental European migration to hit America throughout the nineteenth and into the early twentieth centuries, but they actually managed to expand their cultural reach from its original heartland in the 'Southern Highlands' to vast swathes of America, more or less coterminous with the 'red-state' America of recent electoral maps (so called for the colour assigned on televised depictions of states carried by Republican candidates, in contradistinction to the blue states taken by Democrats). These borderers are, today, the solid core of support for Donald Trump.[51]

They are also the people Mead calls the 'Jacksonians'.[52] This Weberian ideal type is one of four great schools, or 'paradigms', of American foreign policy (the other three being the Hamiltonians, Jeffersonians and Wilsonians). The Jacksonians are America's martial caste, its warriors par excellence, and they abide by a code of values that accords pride of place to virtues imported from the ancestral borderlands, among which is a willingness to kill, and die, for country and kinfolk, possibly including those still resident in the ancestral homeland.[53] There is no reason to challenge Mead's assessment of this *ethnie's* impact upon American foreign policy, but we do well to ask to what extent Jacksonianism in one country can be constitutive of a transnational collective identity worthy of the descriptive 'Anglosphere heavy'.

The concluding section of this chapter begins with an explanation of why Jacksonianism really cannot be taken seriously as a vector for the kind of transnational collective identity subsumed under that descriptive. It ends with some observations regarding the impact of Trump upon the Anglosphere, in either of its two main variants.

Conclusion: Jacksonianism, Trump and the Demise of the Anglosphere

If there is any ethno-cultural correlation to be made between English-speaking countries and a fondness for military interventionism, then the Jacksonian category is the place to begin the search. What one would need to establish, in order to sustain the Anglosphere-heavy thesis, is an evidentiary link between ethnicity (in this case, Scots-Irish) and foreign-policy behaviour. Even if we accept the validity of the Fischer–Mead hypothesis for America's Scots-Irish, and by extension *its* foreign policy, it does not follow that the other assumed core members of the interventionist Anglosphere, so hotly debated a decade or so ago, can and do boast their own ethno-cultural 'martial caste'. In the case of the two other active interventionists of 2003, the United Kingdom and Australia, it really would be a wild stretch of the imagination to make a claim about Scots-Irish ethnicity somehow having contributed to interventionist zeal.

For the United Kingdom itself, the Scots-Irish ethnic factor obviously matters, given the sempiternal Ulster problem, but it matters primarily for reasons relating to domestic politics, not foreign policy. As far as Australia is concerned, while there is a considerable (albeit declining) proportion of the population that can trace its ancestry to Ireland, it is not with Ulster but with the other three provinces of the Emerald Isle (Leinster, Munster and Connaught) that the ancestral sentimentalities are mainly associated. If one were permitted to add to the small group of Anglosphere-heavy countries some of Bennett's 'outliers' – for instance, Canada, New Zealand and South Africa – the search for anything remotely approaching a Jacksonian strain in foreign and defence policies would be even more fruitless. Therefore, while the Jacksonian 'contribution' to American national character may indeed be formidable, it is not exportable; it cannot and does not serve as the basis of any transnational collective identity within the English-speaking world that corresponds with what I have been terming 'Anglosphere heavy'.

But what about Anglosphere lite? Is it the default option for those who wish to believe in the continuing relevance of the Anglosphere? This variant, it will be recalled, is the one Bennett had in mind when he spoke of the Anglosphere as a network commonwealth. It is also one that many others might regard as being virtually indistinguishable from the liberal international order created by the United States and the United Kingdom following the destruction of the Second World War. But why label this the Anglosphere, when we have far superior, and more familiar, descriptive terms at our disposal? Why not just say the liberal international order (LIO), or, even better, the West?

Admittedly, the state of health of both the LIO and the West is in no small way a function of the quality of co-operation between the United States and United Kingdom. This, then, obliges us to think about the recent Trump administration and its impact upon transatlantic relations in general, and Anglo-American relations in particular, upon which topic this chapter concludes. It is hardly original or provocative to assert that of the forty-four individuals to have served as US president since the inception of the republic, Donald Trump has been a case apart.[54] Never has there been anyone quite like him. For both his admirers and critics, he was a president cut from a decidedly different bolt of cloth from that of any predecessor.[55] What admirers like to stress, namely Trump's willingness to shatter taboos and venture where no others have dared to go, his detractors chalk up to his simply being out of control.[56]

Shocking, for many observers, was the manner in which he seemed to delight in irritating key allies, countries that, these observers would argue, can and do contribute to America's overall image and its power ranking.[57] In early 2019, two former US ambassadors to NATO, Douglas Lute and Nicholas Burns, issued a sombre report on the alliance's state of health during what was its seventieth anniversary year. NATO, they said, confronted a range of daunting and complex challenges, with the biggest one of all coming from the Trump White House, which appeared to revel in flaunting an 'absence of strong American presidential leadership'.[58]

Without any doubt, there has been a sharp degradation in America's image in many allied countries ever since Donald Trump's assumption of power. Once again, during his tenure in office, talk of 'friendly-fire' anti-Americanism was on everyone's lips, just as it had been during the Iraq War.[59] Public opinion polls in most NATO countries revealed a worrisome degree of distrust in the quality of American leadership, even and especially among such close allies as Canada and the countries of Western Europe (though farther to the east in Europe, the populations of allied countries seemed to like the president well enough).[60] The AASR did not escape this affective downturn. This is somewhat ironic, given that following the November 2016 election of Trump there was a flurry of excitement in some quarters about a rekindling of American enthusiasm for both the AASR and the Anglosphere, with some analysts being quick to note that a bust of Winston Churchill had been restored to prominence in the White House. The new president's gesture was supposed to signify, particularly for Brexiteers such as Boris Johnson, the UK prime minister, and Nigel Farage, the head of the country's Brexit Party, an American recommitment to its 'Anglo' heritage, following the administration of Barack Obama, considered by them to have been insufficiently attentive to that same heritage, in large part because the president's Kenyan ancestry was said to have instilled in him an abiding distrust of Britain, stemming from its colonial record in Africa. Indeed, Farage went so far as to proclaim Obama the most anti-British president ever![61]

Yet this rebirth in enthusiasm for the AASR, and by extension the Anglosphere, proved to very short-lived. Instead, we saw in Washington more than a bit of schadenfreude at the heartburn Brexit visited upon Theresa May, rather than any committed initiatives to buttress the beleaguered British ally. Even worse, when I wrote the first draft of this chapter, Jeremy Corbyn was pawing the ground for an election that some pundits thought might return Labour to power. Understandably, AASR watchers were nervous about the short-term future of bilateral relations. Withal, the AASR has been pronounced dead on so many previous occasions that its obituary notices have a way of inducing reader fatigue; that is why two scholars have sagely described it as the 'Lazarus' of the international system.[62] Yet it remains far from obvious that the Anglosphere possesses a similar ability to arise from the dead. There are many reasons for this, the most important of which is that it remains extremely difficult to imagine how the conditions that *temporarily* gave rise to this Anglo-American policy idea we call the Anglosphere can be replicated. That policy idea, it bears recalling, was a feature of the uniquely 'unipolar' structural context of the post-Cold War period.

Consider, illustratively, the impact that China's current challenge to America has had upon both that structural context and the so-called core Anglosphere members. Some analysts would tell us to forget about sophistical notions such as Anglosphere lite or Anglosphere heavy, and concentrate instead upon the 'one true' Anglosphere, considered by them to be that group of five English-speaking countries who share the most top-secret intelligence only among themselves. They are called, strangely, the 'five eyes'[63] (which conjures up images of cyclopes or pirates, rather than two-eyed officials in close consultation with their counterparts). To the extent that *this* is the Anglosphere, then its immediate future is foreshadowed by the manner in which the group responds to Huawei's bid to be the dominant company in 5G networks worldwide. The Huawei controversy elevates the notion of a 'network commonwealth' to a new, and more complicated, level than even James Bennett could have imagined. As of this writing, the group suffers a severe case of Huawei-induced geostrategic amblyopia, with the eyes of the United States, the United Kingdom, Australia and New Zealand focused upon blocking the Chinese tech giant on the grounds of national security, while Canada stares off at different horizons.

But as this chapter has argued, the Anglosphere was more than a set of eyes, no matter how they are counted or where they are looking. Yet, at the same time, it was much less than the AASR. The latter will almost certainly rebound from its current moribund condition, just as it has done on similar occasions over the past several decades. But it is doubtful that the structure of the international system in the post-unipolar era could ever result in the re-emergence of the Anglosphere, in either of the variants described in this chapter. Both lite and heavy were products of the unique structural configuration that arose in the wake of the Cold War's ending and the USSR's demise. Therefore, it seems only fitting to close this chapter's assessment of the Anglosphere with one of Alice Roosevelt Longworth's most memorable quips, apropos of New York governor Thomas Dewey's second try for the presidency in 1948: 'you cannot make a soufflé rise twice.'[64]

David G. Haglund is Professor of Political Studies at Queen's University (Kingston, Ontario). His research focuses on transatlantic security and Canadian and American international security policy. His books include *Latin America and the Transformation of U.S. Strategic Thought, 1936–1940* (University of New Mexico Press, 1984); *Alliance Within the Alliance? Franco-German Military Cooperation and the European Pillar of Defense* (Westview Press, 1991); *Will NATO Go East? The Debate Over Enlarging the Atlantic Alliance* (Center for International Relations, Queen's University, 1996); *The North Atlantic Triangle Revisited: Canadian Grand Strategy at Century's End* (Irwin Publishing, 2000); *Ethnic Diasporas and the Canada-United States Security Community: From the Civil War to Today* (Rowman & Littlefield, 2015); and *The US "Culture Wars" and the Anglo-American Special Relationship* (Springer, 2019). His current research project focuses on strategic culture and the France–US security and defence relationship.

Notes

1. James C. Bennett, 'The Emerging Anglosphere', *Orbis* 46(1) (2002), 111–26.

2. Though not employing the 'Anglosphere' label, the following works clearly reflect the assumption of close affinity between Anglo-American political traditions and the Western zone of peace: Niall Ferguson, *Empire: The Rise and Demise of the British World Order and the Lessons for Global Power* (New York: Basic Books, 2002) and James E. Cronin, *Global Rules: America, Britain and a Disordered World* (New Haven, CT: Yale University Press, 2014).

3. See Srdjan Vucetic, 'A Racialized Peace? How Britain and the US Made Their Relationship Special', *Foreign Policy Analysis* 7(4) (2011), 403–21.

4. Ken McGoogan, 'It's Time for Scotland to Find a New Home – in Canada', *Globe and Mail* (Toronto), 5 April 2017, A11.

5. Quoted in William Clark, *Less than Kin: A Study of Anglo-American Relations* (Boston, MA: Houghton Mifflin, 1958). 2. On language as a shaper of identity, a phenomenon sometimes called 'linguistic nationalism', see John R. Edwards, *Language, Society and Identity* (Oxford: Blackwell, 1985).

6. Henry Seidel Canby, 'Anglomania', *Harper's* 143 (November 1921), 710.

7. Christopher Hitchens, *Blood, Class, and Empire: The Enduring Anglo-American Relationship* (New York: Nation Books, 2004).

8. See, especially, Walter Russell Mead, *God and Gold: Britain, America, and the Making of the Modern World* (New York: Alfred A. Knopf, 2008) and Or Rosenboim, *The Emergence of Globalism: Visions of World Order in Britain and The United States, 1939–1950* (Princeton, NJ: Princeton University Press, 2017).

9. Alan P. Dobson and Steve Marsh, 'Anglo-American Relations: End of a Special Relationship?' *International History Review* 36(4) (2014), 682–83.

10. Erwan Lagadec, *Transatlantic Relations in the 21ˢᵗ Century: Europe, America and the Rise of the Rest* (London: Routledge, 2012), 80.

11. Edward Ingram, 'The Wonderland of the Political Scientist', *International Security* 22(1) (1997), 56–57. For a similar view, see Guy Arnold, *America and Britain: Was There Ever a Special Relationship?* (London: Hurst, 2014). Somewhat more constrained versions of the 'nothing-special' thesis are Andrew Mumford, *Counterinsurgency Wars and the Anglo-American Alliance: The Special Relationship on the Rocks* (Washington, DC: Georgetown University Press, 2017); James Barr, *Lords of the Desert: The Battle Between the United States and Great Britain for Supremacy in the Modern Middle East* (New York: Basic Books, 2018); and Derek Leebaert, *Grand Improvisation: America Confronts the British Superpower, 1945–1957* (New York: Farrar, Straus and Giroux, 2018).

12. So termed because of Lord Palmerston's oft-cited 1848 comment in the House of Commons about Britain's having neither eternal friends nor perpetual adversaries, but only eternal and perpetual interests.

13. Coral Bell, *The Debatable Alliance: An Essay in Anglo-American Relations* (London: Oxford University Press, 1964), 129–30.

14. Representative of this recent trend in IR scholarship are Neta C. Crawford, 'The Passion of World Politics: Propositions on Emotion and Emotional Relationships', *International Security* 24(4) (2000), 116–56; Roland Bleiker and Emma Hutchison, 'Fear No More: Emotions and World Politics', *Review of International Studies* 34 (2008), 115–35; Jean-Marc Coicaud, 'Emotions and Passions in the Discipline of International Relations', *Japanese Journal of Political Science* 15(3) (2014), 485–513; and Andrew Linklater, 'Anger and World Politics: How Collective Emotions Shift over Time', *International Theory* 6(3) (2014), 574–78.

15. As does, for instance, Srdjan Vucetic, *The Anglosphere: A Genealogy of a Racialized Identity in International Relations* (Stanford, CA: Stanford University Press, 2011).

16. To take some examples, Andrew A.G. Ross, 'Coming in from the Cold: Constructivism and Emotions', *European Journal of International Relations* 12(2) (2006), 197–222; Felix Berenskoetter, 'Friends, There Are No Friends? An Intimate Reframing of the International', *Millennium: Journal of International Studies* 35(3) (2007), 647–76; and Heather Devere and Graham M. Smith, 'Friendship and Politics', *Political Studies Review* 8(3) (2010), 341–56.

17. *The Diamond Age: Or, a Young Lady's Illustrated Primer* (New York: Bantam Books, 1995).

18. I have introduced these rubrics in my article, 'Relating to the Anglosphere: Canada, "Culture," and the Question of Military Intervention', *Journal of Transatlantic Studies* 3(2) (2005), 179–98. Portions of this section have been drawn from that article.

19. See James C. Bennett, *The Anglosphere Challenge: Why the English-Speaking Nations Will Lead the Way in the Twenty-First Century* (Lanham, MD: Rowman & Littlefield, 2004).

20. Bennett, 'Emerging Anglosphere', 122. Also see this same author's 'Networking Nation-States: The Coming Info-National Order', *National Interest*, no. 74 (2003/4), 17–30.

21. Save that, as Ignatieff used it, lite is code for a politically acceptable species of interventionism, which he calls 'temporary imperialism'; my usage of the descriptor tends in the other direction, away from the willingness to project military force. See Michael Ignatieff, *Empire Lite: Nation-Building in Bosnia, Kosovo and Afghanistan* (Toronto: Penguin Canada, 2003), vii.

22. See, for instance, Peter J. Katzenstein, 'The West as Anglo-America', in Katzenstein (ed.), *Anglo-America and Its Discontents: Civilizational Identities beyond West and East* (London: Routledge, 2012), 1–30; and John Bew, 'Pax Anglo-Saxonica', *American Interest* 10(5) (2015), 40–49.

23. See Emanuel Adler and Michael N. Barnett, 'Governing Anarchy: A Research Agenda for the Study of Security Communities', *Ethics & International Affairs* 10 (1996), 73; idem, *Se-*

curity Communities (Cambridge: Cambridge University Press, 1998); and Adrian Hyde-Price, 'Security and Integration in Mitteleuropa: Towards a New Research Agenda' (Stockholm: Swedish Institute of International Affairs, 1997).

24. On this debate, see Jeff D. Colgan and Robert O. Keohane, 'The Liberal Order Is Rigged: Fix It Now or Watch It Wither', *Foreign Affairs* 96(3) (2017), 36–44; Edward Luce, *The Retreat of Western Liberalism* (New York: Atlantic Monthly Press, 2017); Bill Emmott, *The Fate of the West: The Battle to Save the World's Most Successful Political Idea* (New York: PublicAffairs Press, 2017); Patrick J. Deneen, *Why Liberalism Failed* (New Haven, CT: Yale University Press, 2018); and Michael Kimmage, *The Abandonment of the West: The History of an Idea in American Foreign Policy* (New York: Basic Books, 2020).

25. Robert Conquest, 'Toward an English-Speaking Union', *National Interest*, no. 57 (1999), 64–70; idem, *Reflections on a Ravaged Century* (New York: W.W. Norton, 2000); and Conrad-Black, 'Britain's Atlantic Option, and America's Stake', *National Interest*, no. 55 (1999), 15–24.

26. Owen Harries, 'The Anglosphere Illusion', *National Interest*, no. 63 (2001), 130.

27. This epistemic community originated with the group of young, mainly Oxford-bred, enthusiasts working on post-war reconstruction for Lord Alfred Milner, British high commissioner in South Africa, in the immediate aftermath of the Boer War. See Norman Rose, *The Cliveden Set: Portrait of an Exclusive Community* (London: Jonathan Cape, 2000) and Andrea Bosco, 'From Empire to Atlantic "System": The Round Table, Chatham House, and the Emergence of a New Paradigm in Anglo-American Relations', *Journal of Transatlantic Studies* 16(3) (2018), 222–46.

28. On the dramatic improvement in relations between the United States and United Kingdom, see Bradford Perkins, *The Great Rapprochement: England and the United States, 1895–1914* (New York: Atheneum, 1968).

29. For one particularly eupeptic recitation of the manifold benefits such a combination could bestow, not just upon the two participating states, but upon the entire planet, see Andrew Carnegie, 'A Look Ahead', *North American Review* 156(439) (1893), 685–710. Expressive of the same sentiment, and longing for the day when the two countries could be reunited in alliance, was James Bryce, 'The Essential Unity of Britain and America', *Atlantic Monthly* 82 (1898), 22–29. Also see Duncan Bell, 'Before the Democratic Peace: Racial Unionism, Empire, and the Abolition of War', *European Journal of International Relations* 20(3) (2014), 647–70.

30. Frank Aydelotte, *The Vision of Cecil Rhodes: A Review of the First Forty Years of the American Scholarships* (London: Oxford University Press, 1946), 5.

31. William T. Stead (ed.), *The Last Will and Testament of Cecil John Rhodes* (London: Review of Reviews, 1902), 73.

32. See John M. Owen IV and Richard Rosecrance, *International Politics: How History Modifies Theory* (New York: Oxford University Press, 2019), 109, and Richard N. Cooper, 'Economic Interdependence and War', in Richard N. Rosecrance and Steven E. Miller (eds), *The Next Great War? The Roots of World War I and the Risk of U.S.–China Conflict* (Cambridge, MA: MIT Press, 2014), 57–69.

33. For instance, see Graham Allison, *Destined for War: Can America and China Escape the Thucydides Trap?* (Boston, MA: Houghton Mifflin Harcourt, 2017). Also see idem, 'China vs. America: Managing the Next Clash of Civilizations', *Foreign Affairs* 96(5) (2017), 80–89.

34. Williams, cited by William H. Sewell Jr, 'The Concept(s) of Culture', in Victoria E. Bonnell and Lynn Hunt (eds), *Beyond the Cultural Turn: New Directions in the Study of Society and Culture* (Berkeley: University of California Press, 1999). 35–61. For an extensive catalogue of culture's many, and at times contradictory, meanings, see Alfred L. Kroeber and Clyde

Kluckhohn, *Culture: A Critical Review of Concepts and Definitions* (New York: Vintage Books. 1963).

35. See David G. Haglund, 'What Good Is Strategic Culture? A Modest Defence of an Immodest Concept', *International Journal* 59(3) (2004), 479–502.

36. The logical foundations of power-transition theory have been explicated by A.F.K. Organski, *World Politics*, 2nd edn (New York: Alfred A. Knopf, 1968; orig. pub. 1958), 364; as well as in Organski and Jacek Kugler, *The War Ledger* (Chicago: University of Chicago Press, 1980). But for a critique, cf. Richard Ned Lebow and Ben Valentino, 'Lost in Transition: A Critical Analysis of Power Transition Theory', *International Relations* 23(3) (2009), 389–410.

37. Especially Feng Yongping, 'The Peaceful Transition of Power from the UK to the US', *Chinese Journal of International Politics* 1 (2006): 83–108. Also see T.V. Paul (ed.), *Accommodating Rising Powers: Past, Present, and Future* (Cambridge: Cambridge University Press, 2016).

38. For this assessment, see Kori Schake, *Safe Passage: The Transition from British to American Hegemony* (Cambridge, MA: Harvard University Press, 2017).

39. An astringent criticism launched by Hamilton Fyfe, *The Illusion of National Character* (London: Watts, 1940). But for a sturdy rebuttal of the charge, see Dean Peabody, *National Characteristics* (Cambridge: Cambridge University Press, 1985).

40. The emphasis upon such continuity courses through the pages of Kevin P. Phillips, *The Cousins' Wars: Religion, Politics, and the Triumph of Anglo-America* (New York: Basic Books, 1999).

41. Anthony D. Smith, 'The Ethnic Sources of Nationalism', *Survival* 35(1) (1993), 50.

42. See, for this terminological distinction, Francisco Gil-White, 'How Thick Is Blood? The Plot Thickens…: If Ethnic Actors Are Primordialists, What Remains of the Circumstantialist/Primordialist Controversy?', *Ethnic and Racial Studies* 22(5) (1999), 789–820.

43. Lu Shaye, China's ambassador to Canada, explaining to a Toronto audience that his own country's geostrategic DNA, naturally, lacks such a 'gene'. Robert Fife, Steven Chase and Nathan VanderKlippe, 'Chinese Envoy Says It's Up to Canada to Thaw Diplomatic Relations', *Globe and Mail*, 24 May 2019, A1, 7.

44. E.V. Lucas, *A Wanderer in Holland* (London: Methuen, 1905), 5.

45. Balanced discussions of the issue are provided in David Calleo, *The German Problem Reconsidered* (Cambridge: Cambridge University Press, 1978) and Dirk Verheyen, *The German Question: A Cultural, Historical, and Geopolitical Exploration* (Boulder, CO: Westview Press, 1991). For a less balanced account that stresses national character, see A.J.P. Taylor, *The Course of German History* (New York: Coward-McCann, 1946).

46. See note 40 above.

47. The numbers are necessarily imprecise, given that many, if not most, of those who self-identify on the census as 'Americans' are themselves of British extraction, so adding these self-identifiers to the English category results in around 13 per cent of Americans claiming in 2010 that they are of British descent (excluding all parts of Ireland). The leading 'ethnic' self-identification choice remains what it has been ever since 1980, when Americans were first given the chance to declare what they thought their ethnicity was: German (14.7 per cent), followed closely by African-American (12.3 per cent) and Mexican (10.9 per cent). See 'Largest Ethnic Groups and Nationalities in the United States', available at https://www.worldatlas.com/articles/largest-ethnic-groups-and-nationalities-in-the-united-states.html.

48. David Hackett Fischer, *Albion's Seed: Four British Folkways in America* (New York: Oxford University Press, 1989).

49. The 'frontier' thesis held that geography, not demography, was most responsible for the development of American political culture; see Frederick Jackson Turner, *The Frontier in*

American History (New York: H. Holt, 1921). By contrast, 'pluralist' theory put the emphasis upon demography, and in particular upon the processes of 'Americanizing' a multicultural demographic flow. Ralph Waldo Emerson was the first to popularize the 'smelting pot' metaphor, but over time it ceded its place to the related, though somewhat different, image of the 'melting pot'. Technically, the former is used to separate a metal from its mineral, while the latter is used to blend metals into alloys. For the metaphor and its evolution, see Denis Lacorne, *La Crise de l'identité américaine: du melting-pot au multiculturalisme* (Paris: Fayard, 1997), 198–203.

50. James Webb, *Born Fighting: How the Scots-Irish Shaped America* (New York: Crown, 2004).

51. See J.D. Vance, *Hillbilly Elegy: A Memoir of a Family and Culture in Crisis* (New York: HarperCollins, 2016). Their geographical centre of gravity initially comprised three zones, running from east to west: the Blue Ridge Belt, the Greater Appalachian Valley and the Cumberland Belt; it covered portions of Maryland, Virginia, North Carolina, South Carolina, Georgia, Alabama, Tennessee and Kentucky, as well as all of West Virginia. See John C. Campbell, *The Southern Highlander and His Homeland* (New York: Russell Sage Foundation, 1921).

52. Walter Russell Mead, 'The Jacksonian Revolt: American Populism and the Liberal World Order', *Foreign Affairs* 96(2) (2017), 2–7.

53. Walter Russell Mead, *Special Providence: American Foreign Policy and How It Changed the World* (New York: Alfred A. Knopf, 2001), 231–50.

54. See Arthur Paulson, *Donald Trump and the Prospect for American Democracy: An Unprecedented President in an Age of Polarization* (Lanham, MD: Rowman & Littlefield, 2018). Although there have been forty-five administrations, an enumerative oddity results in there having been only forty-four actual human beings presiding over these administrations, due to the manner in which Grover Cleveland's time in power is assessed. Because he served two *discontinuous* terms – elected in 1884, failing to be re-elected in 1888, and regaining the White House in 1892 – his reign is counted as two separate administrations, thus he is both America's twenty-second president and its twenty-fourth. In contrast, Franklin D. Roosevelt, who was elected *four* consecutive times from 1932 to 1944, is counted as only one president, the country's thirty-second.

55. For assessments, pro and con, see Victor David Hanson, *The Case for Trump* (New York: Basic Books, 2019) and Bob Woodward, *Fear: Trump in the White House* (New York: Simon & Schuster, 2018).

56. This latter is best exemplified in Michael Wolff, *Fire and Fury: Inside the Trump White House* (New York: Henry Holt, 2018).

57. In the understated words of one editorialist, President Trump 'tends to ignore how soft power cements alliances' (*Economist*, 18 May 2019, 9).

58. Douglas Lute and Nicholas Burns, *NATO at Seventy: An Alliance in Crisis*, A Report of the Project on Europe and the Transatlantic Relationship (Cambridge, MA: Harvard University Kennedy School, Belfer Center for Science and International Affairs, February 2019), 1–2. Also see Trine Flockhart, 'A Fractured Alliance in Good Shape? NATO at 70', *Atlantisch perspectief* 43(2) (2019), 10–14; and Celeste A. Wallander, 'NATO's Enemies Within: How Democratic Decline Could Destroy the Alliance', *Foreign Affairs* 97 (4) (2018), 70–81.

59. See Elizabeth Pond, *Friendly Fire: The Near-Death of the Transatlantic Alliance* (Pittsburgh, PA: European Union Studies Association; and Washington, DC: Brookings Institution Press, 2004) and Julia E. Sweig, *Friendly Fire: Losing Friends and Making Enemies in the Anti-American Century* (New York: Public Affairs, 2006). Also see, for that era's wave of

criticism of American foreign policy, Peter J. Katzenstein and Robert O. Keohane (eds), *Anti-Americanisms in World Politics* (Ithaca, NY: Cornell University Press, 2007).

60. An April 2019 poll in Canada found that only China, among a group of selected countries, had a more negative approval rating than America. Western European survey data reveal similar attitudes. See Michelle Zilio, 'Canadians More Positive about Ties with Europe than with the U.S., China: Poll', *Globe and Mail*, 3 May 2019, A6, and Richard Wike et al., 'Trump's International Ratings Remain Low, Especially Among Key Allies', Pew Research Center, October 2018.

61. See Michael D. Shear and Steven Erlanger, 'Obama Warns Britain That Trade Might Suffer if It Leaves European Union', *New York Times*, 23 April 2016, A9, and Estelle Shirbon, 'Brexit Figurehead Johnson Under Fire for "Part-Kenyan" Obama Comment', *Globe and Mail*, 23 April 2016, A9.

62. Steve Marsh and John Baylis, 'The Anglo-American "Special Relationship": The Lazarus of International Relations', *Diplomacy & Statecraft* 17(1) (2006), 173–211.

63. Jeffrey T. Richelson and Desmond Ball, *The Ties that Bind: Intelligence Cooperation Between the UKUSA Countries* (Sydney: Allen and Unwin, 1985).

64. Available at https://www.brainyquote.com/quotes/alice_roosevelt_longworth_398015.

Bibliography

Adler, Emanuel, and Michael N. Barnett. 'Governing Anarchy: A Research Agenda for the Study of Security Communities', *Ethics & International Affairs* 10 (1996), 63–98.

———. *Security Communities*. Cambridge: Cambridge University Press, 1998.

Allison, Graham. 'China vs. America: Managing the Next Clash of Civilizations', *Foreign Affairs* 96(5) (2017), 80–89.

———. *Destined for War: Can America and China Escape the Thucydides Trap?* Boston, MA: Houghton Mifflin Harcourt, 2017.

Arnold, Guy. *America and Britain: Was There Ever a Special Relationship?* London: Hurst, 2014.

Aydelotte, Frank. *The Vision of Cecil Rhodes: A Review of the First Forty Years of the American Scholarships*. London: Oxford University Press, 1946.

Barr, James. *Lords of the Desert: The Battle Between the United States and Great Britain for Supremacy in the Modern Middle East*. New York: Basic Books, 2018.

Bell, Coral. *The Debatable Alliance: An Essay in Anglo-American Relations*. London: Oxford University Press, 1964.

Bell, Duncan. 'Before the Democratic Peace: Racial Unionism, Empire, and the Abolition of War', *European Journal of International Relations* 20(3) (2014), 647–70.

Bennett, James C. *The Anglosphere Challenge: Why the English-Speaking Nations Will Lead the Way in the Twenty-First Century*. Lanham, MD: Rowman & Littlefield, 2004.

———. 'The Emerging Anglosphere', *Orbis* 46(1) (2006), 111–26.

———. 'Networking Nation-States: The Coming Info-National Order', *National Interest* 74 (2003/4), 17–30.

Berenskoetter, Felix. 'Friends, There Are No Friends? An Intimate Reframing of the International', *Millennium: Journal of International Studies* 35(3) (2007), 647–76.

Bew, John. 'Pax Anglo-Saxonica', *American Interest* 10(5) (2015), 40–49.

Black, Conrad. 'Britain's Atlantic Option, and America's Stake', *National Interest* 55 (1999), 15–24.

Bleiker, Roland, and Emma Hutchison. 'Fear No More: Emotions and World Politics', *Review of International Studies* 34(1) (2008), 115–35.

Bosco, Andrea. 'From Empire to Atlantic "System": The Round Table, Chatham House, and the Emergence of a New Paradigm in Anglo-American Relations', *Journal of Transatlantic Studies* 16(3) (2018), 222–46.

Bryce, James. 'The Essential Unity of Britain and America', *Atlantic Monthly* 82(7) (1898), 22–29.

Calleo, David. *The German Problem Reconsidered*. Cambridge: Cambridge University Press, 1978.

Campbell, John C. *The Southern Highlander and His Homeland*. New York: Russell Sage Foundation, 1921.

Canby, Henry Seidel. 'Anglomania', *Harper's* 143(11) (1921), 709–14.

Carnegie, Andrew. 'A Look Ahead', *North American Review* 156(439) (1893), 685–710.

Clark, William. *Less than Kin: A Study of Anglo-American Relations*. Boston, MA: Houghton Mifflin, 1958.

Coicaud, Jean-Marc. 'Emotions and Passions in the Discipline of International Relations', *Japanese Journal of Political Science* 15(3) (2014), 485–513.

Colgan, Jeff D., and Robert O. Keohane. 'The Liberal Order Is Rigged: Fix It Now or Watch It Wither', *Foreign Affairs* 96(3) (2017), 36–44.

Conquest, Robert. *Reflections on a Ravaged Century*. New York: W.W. Norton, 2000.

_____. 'Toward an English-Speaking Union', *National Interest* 57 (1999), 64–70.

Cooper, Richard N. 'Economic Interdependence and War', in Richard N. Rosecrance and Steven E. Miller (eds), *The Next Great War? The Roots of World War I and the Risk of U.S.–China Conflict*. Cambridge, MA: MIT Press, 2014, 57–69.

Crawford, Neta C. 'The Passion of World Politics: Propositions on Emotion and Emotional Relationships', *International Security* 24(4) (2000), 116–56.

Cronin, James E. *Global Rules: America, Britain and a Disordered World*. New Haven, CT: Yale University Press, 2014.

Deneen, Patrick J. *Why Liberalism Failed*. New Haven, CT: Yale University Press, 2018.

Devere, Heather, and Graham M. Smith. 'Friendship and Politics', *Political Studies Review* 8(3) (2010), 341–56.

Dobson, Alan P., and Steve Marsh. 'Anglo-American Relations: End of a Special Relationship?', *International History Review* 36(4) (2014), 673–97.

Edwards, John R. *Language, Society and Identity*. Oxford: Blackwell, 1985.

Emmott, Bill. *The Fate of the West: The Battle to Save the World's Most Successful Political Idea*. New York: PublicAffairs Press, 2017.

Ferguson, Niall. *Empire: The Rise and Demise of the British World Order and the Lessons for Global Power*. New York: Basic Books, 2002.

Fife, Robert, Steven Chase and Nathan VanderKlippe. 'Chinese Envoy Says It's Up to Canada to Thaw Diplomatic Relations', *Globe and Mail* (Toronto), 24 May 2019.

Fischer, David Hackett. *Albion's Seed: Four British Folkways in America*. New York: Oxford University Press, 1989.

Flockhart, Trine. 'A Fractured Alliance in Good Shape? NATO at 70', *Atlantisch perspectief* 43(2) (2019), 10–14.

Fyfe, Hamilton. *The Illusion of National Character*. London: Watts, 1940.

Gil-White, Francisco. 'How Thick Is Blood? The Plot Thickens …: If Ethnic Actors Are Primordialists, What Remains of the Circumstantialist/Primordialist Controversy?', *Ethnic and Racial Studies* 22(5) (1999), 789–820.

Haglund, David G. 'Relating to the Anglosphere: Canada, "Culture," and the Question of Military Intervention', *Journal of Transatlantic Studies*, 3(2) (2005), 179–98.

_____. 'What Good Is Strategic Culture? A Modest Defence of an Immodest Concept', *International Journal* 59(3) (2004), 479–502.

Hanson, Victor David. *The Case for Trump*. New York: Basic Books, 2019.

Harries, Owen. 'The Anglosphere Illusion', *National Interest* 63 (2001), 130–36.

Hitchens, Christopher. *Blood, Class, and Empire: The Enduring Anglo-American Relationship*. New York: Nation Books, 2004.

Hyde-Price, Adrian. 'Security and Integration in Mitteleuropa: Towards a New Research Agenda'. Stockholm: Swedish Institute of International Affairs, 1997.

Ignatieff, Michael. *Empire Lite: Nation-Building in Bosnia, Kosovo and Afghanistan*. Toronto: Penguin Canada, 2003.

Ingram, Edward. 'The Wonderland of the Political Scientist', *International Security* 22(1) (1997), 53–63.

Katzenstein, Peter J. 'The West as Anglo-America', in Katzenstein (ed.), *Anglo-America and Its Discontents: Civilizational Identities beyond West and East*. London: Routledge, 2012, 1–30.

Katzenstein, Peter J., and Robert O. Keohane (eds). *Anti-Americanisms in World Politics*. Ithaca, NY: Cornell University Press, 2007.

Kimmage, Michael. *The Abandonment of the West: The History of an Idea in American Foreign Policy*. New York: Basic Books, 2020.

Kroeber, Alfred L., and Clyde Kluckhohn. *Culture: A Critical Review of Concepts and Definitions*. New York: Vintage Books, 1963.

Lacorne, Denis. *La Crise de l'identité américaine: du melting-pot au multiculturalisme*, Paris: Fayard, 1997.

Lagadec, Erwan. *Transatlantic Relations in the 21st Century: Europe, America and the Rise of the Rest*. London: Routledge, 2012.

Lebow, Richard N., and Benjamin Valentino. 'Lost in Transition: A Critical Analysis of Power Transition Theory', *International Relations* 23(3) (2009), 389–410.

Leebaert, Derek. *Grand Improvisation: America Confronts the British Superpower, 1945–1957*. New York: Farrar, Straus and Giroux, 2018.

Linklater, Andrew. 'Anger and World Politics: How Collective Emotions Shift over Time', *International Theory* 6(3) (2014), 574–78.

Lucas, E.V. *A Wanderer in Holland*. London: Methuen, 1905.

Luce, Edward. *The Retreat of Western Liberalism*. New York: Atlantic Monthly Press, 2017.

Lute, Douglas, and Nicholas Burns. *NATO at Seventy: An Alliance in Crisis*. A Report of the Project on Europe and the Transatlantic Relationship. Cambridge, MA: Harvard University Kennedy School, Belfer Center for Science and International Affairs, February 2019.

Marsh, Steve, and John Baylis. 'The Anglo-American "Special Relationship": The Lazarus of International Relations', *Diplomacy & Statecraft* 17(1) (2006), 173–211.

McGoogan, Ken. 'It's Time for Scotland to Find a New Home – in Canada', *Globe and Mail*, 5 April 2017.

Mead, Walter Russell. *God and Gold: Britain, America, and the Making of the Modern World*. New York: Alfred A. Knopf, 2008.

_____. 'The Jacksonian Revolt: American Populism and the Liberal World Order', *Foreign Affairs* 96(2) (2017), 2–7.

_____. *Special Providence: American Foreign Policy and How It Changed the World*. New York: Alfred A. Knopf, 2001.

Mumford, Andrew. *Counterinsurgency Wars and the Anglo-American Alliance: The Special Relationship on the Rocks*, Washington, DC: Georgetown University Press, 2017.

Organski, A.F.K. *World Politics*. 2nd edn. New York: Alfred A. Knopf, 1968.

Organski, A.F.K., and Jacek Kugler. *The War Ledger*. Chicago: University of Chicago Press, 1980.

Owen, John M. IV, and Richard N. Rosecrance. *International Politics: How History Modifies Theory*. New York: Oxford University Press, 2019.

Paul, T.V. (ed.). *Accommodating Rising Powers: Past, Present, and Future*. Cambridge: Cambridge University Press, 2016.

Paulson, Arthur. *Donald Trump and the Prospect for American Democracy: An Unprecedented President in an Age of Polarization*. Lanham, MD: Rowman & Littlefield, 2018.

Peabody, Dean. *National Characteristics*. Cambridge: Cambridge University Press, 1985.

Perkins, Bradford. *The Great Rapprochement: England and the United States, 1895–1914*. New York: Atheneum, 1968.

Phillips, Kevin P. *The Cousins' Wars: Religion, Politics, and the Triumph of Anglo-America*. New York: Basic Books, 1999.

Pond, Elizabeth. *Friendly Fire: The Near-Death of the Transatlantic Alliance*. Pittsburgh, PA: European Union Studies Association; and Washington, DC: Brookings Institution Press, 2004.

Richelson, Jeffrey T., and Desmond Ball. *The Ties that Bind: Intelligence Cooperation Between the UKUSA Countries*. Sydney: Allen and Unwin, 1985.

Rose, Norman. *The Cliveden Set: Portrait of an Exclusive Community*. London: Jonathan Cape, 2000.

Rosenboim, Or. *The Emergence of Globalism: Visions of World Order in Britain and The United States, 1939–1950*. Princeton, NJ: Princeton University Press, 2017.

Ross, Andrew A.G. 'Coming in from the Cold: Constructivism and Emotions', *European Journal of International Relations* 12(2) (2006), 197–222.

Schake, Kori. *Safe Passage: The Transition from British to American Hegemony*. Cambridge, MA: Harvard University Press, 2017.

Sewell, William H., Jr. 'The Concept(s) of Culture', in Victoria E. Bonnell and Lynn Hunt (eds), *Beyond the Cultural Turn: New Directions in the Study of Society and Culture*. Berkeley: University of California Press, 1999, 35–61.

Shear, Michael D., and Steven Erlanger. 'Obama Warns Britain That Trade Might Suffer if It Leaves European Union', *New York Times*, 23 April 2016.

Shirbon, Estelle. 'Brexit Figurehead Johnson Under Fire for "Part-Kenyan" Obama Comment', *Globe and Mail*, 23 April 2016.

Smith, Anthony D. 'The Ethnic Sources of Nationalism', *Survival* 35(1) (1993), 48–62.

Stead, William T. (ed.). *The Last Will and Testament of Cecil John Rhodes*. London: Review of Reviews, 1902.

Stephenson, Neal. *The Diamond Age: Or, a Young Lady's Illustrated Primer*. New York: Bantam Books, 1995.

Sweig, Julia E. *Friendly Fire: Losing Friends and Making Enemies in the Anti-American Century*. New York: Public Affairs, 2006.

Taylor, A.J.P. *The Course of German History*. New York: Coward-McCann, 1946.

Turner, Frederick Jackson. *The Frontier in American History*. New York: H. Holt, 1921.

Vance, J.D. *Hillbilly Elegy: A Memoir of a Family and Culture in Crisis*. New York: HarperCollins, 2016.

Verheyen, Dirk. *The German Question: A Cultural, Historical, and Geopolitical Exploration.* Boulder, CO: Westview Press, 1991.

Vucetic, Srdjan. *The Anglosphere: A Genealogy of a Racialized Identity in International Relations.* Stanford, CA: Stanford University Press, 2011.

_____. 'A Racialized Peace? How Britain and the US Made Their Relationship Special', *Foreign Policy Analysis* 7(4) (2011), 403–21.

Wallander, Celeste A. 'NATO's Enemies Within: How Democratic Decline Could Destroy the Alliance', *Foreign Affairs* 97(4) (2018), 70–81.

Webb, James. *Born Fighting: How the Scots-Irish Shaped America.* New York: Crown, 2004.

Wike, Richard, et al. 'Trump's International Ratings Remain Low, Especially Among Key Allies', Pew Research Center, October 2018.

Wolff, Michael. *Fire and Fury: Inside the Trump White House.* New York: Henry Holt, 2018.

Woodward, Bob. *Fear: Trump in the White House.* New York: Simon & Schuster, 2018.

Yongping, Feng. 'The Peaceful Transition of Power from the UK to the US', *Chinese Journal of International Politics* 1 (2006), 83–108.

Zilio, Michelle. 'Canadians More Positive about Ties with Europe than with the U.S., China: Poll', *Globe and Mail*, 3 May 2019.

Chapter 10

Anglo-American Relations

A Political Tradition of Special Relationship(s)

Steve Marsh

Scholars, commentators and policymakers have long agonized over whether Anglo-American relations are or ever have been special, what makes/made them special and even how 'special' itself is to be defined. Consequently – and inconclusively – the essence of the special relationship has been sought in comparative analysis, criteria-based examination and alliance theory.[1] Those of a functionalist disposition attribute 'specialness' primarily to calculations of mutual utility that throw the balance of advantage in favour of unique co-operation. Cast in this light, special relations carry a clear, if temporally undefined, expiry date.[2] At some point, they will not recover from a Suez, a Skybolt or a Trump.[3] In contrast, critics of this functionalist reductionism of specialness point out, as Thomas L. Hughes of the State Department's Intelligence and Research Bureau did in February 1968, that 'The special relationship has been pronounced dead as often as Martin Bormann has been reported alive. Indeed, perhaps the best evidence that it is still alive is the fact that that its detractors feel obliged to re-announce its death every few months.'[4] For the likes of H.C. Allen, Churchillian rhetoric of 'fraternal association' and 'kindred systems of society' was truth rather than diplomatic art. Anglo-American relations were special because, as well as encompassing shared interests, they were imbued with a natural, reflexive and unique emotional underpinning that drew its strength from the commonalities of a shared language, Anglo-Saxon heritage and the perceived special responsibilities of these two great powers within international relations.[5]

These debates are significant for what follows, but this chapter is concerned less with debating the special relationship – its fluctuating fortunes and its very existence (or otherwise) – than with how it might be *perceived* as a unique political tradition between the United Kingdom and the United States. It should be noted, too, that a temporal incongruity is in play. Former British prime minister and honorary American citizen Winston Churchill introduced the nomenclature 'special relationship' to the vernacular of Anglo-American relations in 1946.[6] Yet what has been termed the 'apogee'[7] of that relationship is normally considered to be the wartime experience of fighting the Axis powers. Epitomized by the Combined Boards, co-development of the atomic bomb and the exercise of command over each other's troops, Anglo-American relations attained a depth and breadth of co-operation never previously, or since, experienced by two world powers.

At first sight, it therefore seems somewhat odd to speak of a political tradition that became established after the height, at least in functional terms, of what it represented had passed. So how might this be explained? This chapter begins by arguing that the special relationship, regardless of what it is thought to comprise, was established as a perceived political tradition during the Cold War and has retained purchase through to the present. It then goes on to consider three interpretations of the special relationship as a political tradition. The first is that it is a political tradition contrived by the British to help mask and manage Britain's relative decline as a world power. The second views the special relationship as an elite political tradition facilitated by communities of practice, which provide for mutual learning and modes of operation. Finally, the special relationship might be seen as a discursive construct comprised in part of a coalescence of other British and American political traditions.

The Special Relationship: A Socioculturally Embedded Tradition

In Britain especially, the special relationship is a political tradition that has, over time, become embedded in the sociocultural fabric of the country. A sweeping statement, perhaps, but it is possible to demonstrate the strength of elite and popular attachment to the nomenclature – irrespective of what it is believed to comprise or to signify. Two examples are sufficient to testify to the strong British association with this political tradition.

The first example is the acute sensitivity of media to suggestions, particularly but not exclusively when they arise from American behaviour, that the special relationship has run its course. This is often evidenced in the surge of coverage of the special relationship that accompanies changes of US administrations. For instance, when the Obama administration assumed office in 2009, Richard LeBaron, US diplomat and chargé d'affaires at the American embassy in London, reported that 'British media and contacts are busy over-reading perceived signals for evidence of tensions in the relationship. This over-reading would often be humorous, if it were not so corrosive.'[8]

Another example, this time originating from the British side, is the outcry in response to a House of Commons Foreign Affairs Committee (HCFAC) report in 2010 that concluded that the special relationship was 'over'.[9] The BBC online news service led with a report entitled 'Special Relationship between UK and US is Over, MPs Say'.[10] British broadsheets and tabloids provided variants of the same theme. Michael Smith in the *Sunday Times* headlined with 'It's Over: MPs Say the Special Relationship with US Is Dead';[11] the *News of the World* declared provocatively, 'UK & US Love KO: Special Relationship Is Over so It's Time to Stop Sucking Up to the US, Say MPs'.[12] An era of global media helped ensure that commentary on the HCFAC-inspired end of the special relationship appeared as far afield as Africa, the Middle East and China. Even in the United States, where such speculation about the special relationship often fails to excite, elements of the report seeped into media and political commentary.[13]

Also indicative of popular attachment to the special relationship tradition is the fate of government initiatives to change the narrative. The first sustained attempt at this was made under the leadership of Prime Minister Edward Heath in the early 1970s. Heath tried to retitle the special relationship the 'natural relationship'. His terminological preference for the nomenclature 'natural relationship' has attracted much comment, especially in terms of whether it indicated a downgrading of UK–US relations or whether it simply constituted a linguistic sop to France intended to ease British entry into the European Economic Community.[14] Regardless of the rationale, though, the fact remains that it was a failure. Neither in Britain nor the United States did the term 'natural relationship' gain traction and once the Labour government returned to power under Prime Minister Harold Wilson, the nomenclature 'special relationship' once more became the staple vernacular of media and politicians on both sides of the Atlantic.

Some forty years later, another attempt was made to rebrand Anglo-American relations. According to the aforementioned 2010 HCFAC report, 'the use of the phrase "special relationship" in its historical sense, to describe the totality of the ever-evolving UK–US relationship, is potentially misleading, and we recommend that its use should be avoided'.[15] The following May, Prime Minister David Cameron and President Barack Obama tried to push an alternative nomenclature. In an open joint letter to *The Times*, the two leaders opined that 'the reason why this is such a natural partnership, is because it advances our common interests and shared values ... And the reason it remains strong is because it delivers time and again. Ours is not just a special relationship, it is an essential relationship – for us and for the world.'[16]

This attempt to rebrand Anglo-American relations quickly drew forth a stalwart defence of the special relationship.[17] After denouncing the 'essential relationship' as a weakening of UK–US relations, media ignored it and instead elected simply to continue frequently and indiscriminately using the term 'special relationship', which the HCFAC had rejected. Tellingly, Obama and Cameron retreated before political tradition. During Obama's state visit to Britain in May 2011, both president and prime minister emphasized the values, sentimentality and atmospherics of the special relationship. Cameron explicitly used the term 'special relationship' during the joint press conference, as did Obama in his address to Parliament in Westminster Hall. The 'essential relationship' was not mentioned and, by February 2012, it had slipped from the agenda. The White House Press Office release announcing that Cameron would visit Washington in March for an official visit and state dinner featured archetypal special relationship prose:

> The visit will highlight the fundamental importance of the U.S.–U.K. special relationship and the depth of the friendship between the American people and the people of the United Kingdom, as well as the strong personal bond that has developed between the two leaders and their families. It will also be an opportunity to recall the valor and sacrifice of the U.S. and British armed forces and their long tradition of standing shoulder-to-shoulder beside each other in defense of our liberties and shared values.'[18]

When the furore over the HCFAC report broke, a Foreign and Commonwealth Office spokeswoman tried to assure people that in Anglo-American relations all was business as usual: 'It doesn't really matter whether someone calls it "the special relationship" or not …What matters is that the UK's relationship with the US is unique, and uniquely important to protecting our national security and promoting our national interest.'[19] This was indeed a reasonable defence of the everyday transaction of Anglo-American affairs. British officials have often maintained that they do not use the term 'special relationship' when dealing with their American counterparts;[20] former British ambassador to Washington Sir Jeremy Greenstock asserted emphatically to the HCFAC that 'British officials do not use the term "special relationship"', although they might have to respond to the term 'special relationship' 'in public if it is thrown at us by the Americans'.[21] Nevertheless, as the media outcry indicated, the spokeswoman's assurance also totally missed the point. Anglo-American relations might be natural. They may even be essential. But the usage of the term 'Anglo-American relations' in lieu of the nomenclature 'special relationship' was perceived as nothing less than an assault on an Anglo-American political tradition.

Fiction as Fact: Political Tradition as a Diplomatic Construct

The idea that the British established a political tradition of a special relationship as a diplomatic device has its origins in the very different wartime
fortunes of Britain and the United States. The former ended the war with the
largest external debt in history, was forced to accept unpalatable terms in the
1946 Anglo-American loan and had incurred substantial damage to the homeland at the hands of the Luftwaffe. In addition, traditional British supply routes
had been badly disrupted, expensive overseas commitments leeched the Treasury
and signs of imperial overstretch were soon evident.[22] Indian independence in
1947, withdrawal from the Palestine Mandate and the nationalization of Iranian
oil in 1951 all evidenced Britain's new-found woes. In contrast, the United States
emerged from the war with its homeland unscathed, a monopoly on the atomic
bomb, and possession of 50 per cent of the world's manufacturing capacity, 40
per cent of global wealth and two thirds of the world's monetary gold. Moreover,
it largely determined a post-war international infrastructure that protected and
leveraged this new-found American supremacy.

From these different fortunes flowed domestic political repercussions too.
In the United States, internationalism triumphed over isolationism in post-war
planning, although rapid military demobilization from Europe and Congress's
rejection of the International Trade Organization in 1949 demonstrated that
this was neither a complete nor necessarily indefinite victory. Preserving America's new-found status meant global interests and engagement; US support for
the United Nations and its Security Council constituted an acknowledgement
of spheres of influence, as well as being a nod to American idealism. More importantly, during the war, the Roosevelt administration had decided that the
New Deal needed to be internationalized if the United States – and the wider
capitalist world – were to avoid a repeat of the interwar depression. International free-market capitalism with the United States at its heart promised to
empower the United States structurally, whilst also bringing prosperity and
access to both key strategic goods and markets sufficient to absorb America's
heightened productive capacity and its reversion to peacetime production.

Britain was much different. Its people were accustomed to global engagement – political, military and economic – and British leaders still thought in
terms of traditional global strategy and, often, imperial power. However, the
sacrifices of the wartime effort and newly straitened economic circumstances
gave rise to foreign-policy constraints on more than simply resources; they
changed political priorities. The British electorate removed Churchill from
power in favour of Clement Attlee and the Labour Party. Health, education,
housing, economic recovery – these were the pressing public concerns of the
day. And that meant intense intra-government competition for resources,

pressure for budgetary rebalancing and a rearguard defence of as many revenue sources as possible. When the Korean War broke out, Attlee committed British troops alongside the United States, but with rationing still in force and popular domestic priorities elsewhere, the political cost was substantial. In April 1951, the popular Minister of Labour Aneurin Bevan, architect of the National Health Service, resigned from an already weakened government over the imposition of health service charges to help fund the expanding defence budget and took with him other talented junior officials – including Harold Wilson and John Freeman.

Britain was thus dependent on international trade and had extensive overseas commitments and an imperial tradition, but it had insufficient resources to preserve any of them. Some officials initially considered this to be a temporary state of affairs. Foreign Secretary Ernest Bevin, for instance, argued in October 1948 that 'if we only pushed on and developed Africa, we could have the United States dependent on us, and eating out of our hand, in four or five years'.[23] Others were less sanguine. In November 1951, Roger Makins, British ambassador to Washington, mourned that Britain was 'back in the breadline for the third time in six years'.[24] Whatever the case, though, traditional British foreign policy had to change.

Churchill's 'Three Circles' concept, unveiled in a speech on 9 October 1948, is one of the best-known examples of this rethinking to preserve Britain's great power status. Indeed, it has persisted as a broad characterization of Britain's foreign-policy approach through to the present, with the relative importance of the North American, European and Commonwealth/empire circles fluctuating over time. However, the general predominance of the relationship with America was presaged as early as 1944. In a paper entitled 'The Essentials of an American Policy', the Foreign Office recognized a 'Changing of the Guard'[25] within Anglo-American relations. British governments needed to adjust interaction with their American counterparts to the new reality of asymmetric relations. Still more importantly, the traditional policy of balancing British power against that of America was no longer appropriate and now that the United States was unlikely to return fully to isolationism there were new possibilities for Anglo-American co-operation.[26] Five years later, the prioritization of the Anglo-American relationship was cemented when the Foreign Office dismissed Britain heading a 'Third Power' grouping as an alternative to close partnership with the United States. It deemed that 'the partnership with the United States is essential to our security' and that Britain's wider objectives would best be promoted by establishing a position 'closely related to the U.S.A., and yet sufficiently independent of her, to be able to influence American policy in the directions desired'.[27]

The principal challenge was how to do this and, for David Reynolds and others of a like mind, the answer lay in 'a tradition invented as a tool of diplomacy'.[28] A political tradition of a special relationship would give British policymakers preferential access to Washington decision-makers. It would give Britain an additional claim to a seat at the top table of world powers. It would encourage third parties to tread cautiously when challenging British interests lest American power be brought to bear in support of the Anglo-Saxon cousin. And it would give the overt semblance of an equal Anglo-American partnership; this would play well with British public opinion, preserving the self-image of Britain as a great power and encouraging the people to bear sacrifices necessary to help maintain the overseas assets that the economy needed and the commitments that the Americans expected.

Cast in this light, what mattered was not of what the special relationship was confected but that it was perceived by elites and publics to be unique. British Foreign Secretary David Owen once spoke directly, albeit negatively, to the manufactured nature of the special relationship when he argued that it was a dangerous intellectual concept that 'gave us a distorted perception of our power and influence in the world'.[29] Consider, too, how British pursuit and public representation of the special relationship changed between the time of hope that Britain's wartime setbacks were temporary and the era of its reluctant settling into second-class power status.

When Churchill was re-elected as British prime minister in October 1951, he was convinced that the Labour government had neglected the special relationship. By January 1952, he was in Washington for bilateral talks with President Harry S. Truman, determined to improve 'the tone' of diplomatic relations[30] and to develop a stage for Anglo-American relations that, as Truman administration officials recognized, would 'strengthen and re-emphasize the partnership between the United States and the United Kingdom in world affairs'.[31] However, Churchill's ambitions were even greater than this. First, he wanted to emphasize that Anglo-American relations constituted a partnership and not a dependency relationship. To this end, he publicly cast US aid to Britain as a trade – he had come to America 'not for gold, but for steel' so that they might work for a common defence. Privately, he sent signals that British support could not be assumed by US officials, refusing, for instance, until the last moment to acquiesce to Atlantic command arrangements (SACLANT), despite heated exchanges with American policymakers and his own officials' advice.[32] Second, Churchill used a prestigious joint address to Congress on 17 January 1952 to reintroduce ideas of 'fraternal association' and a common Anglo-American fate. As he told the assembled representatives and senators, 'Bismarck once said that the supreme fact of the 19th century was that Britain and the United States spoke the same language. Let us make sure that the supreme fact of the 20th century is that they tread the same path.'[33] Finally, Churchill wanted a lasting rather than transitory impact in terms of establishing the impression of a special

Anglo-American relationship. One of his most important legacies in this respect was the establishment of regular bilateral summitry between British prime ministers and American presidents; he secured three summits within three years. These events guaranteed international attention and would provide an opportunity to send key messages about Anglo-American understanding and amity.

Anglo-American leader summits have continued to be one of the principal vehicles for rehearsing the trappings and pageantry of the special relationship through to the present day. However, the presentation of that relationship by British officials has changed. Churchill, fighting to keep Britain at the top table of power, sought an exclusive Anglo-American relationship and overt demonstrations of this. Prior to his summit with Truman, he made it clear that 'It would not be worthwhile going unless we were "à deux".'[34] Similarly, he later told President Dwight D. Eisenhower that 'Two is company; three is hard company; four is a deadlock.'[35] As a tool of policy, the special relationship generally worked best for the British at this time when publicly demonstrated to be strong and unique. This was the most effective way of reassuring British public opinion and suggesting to third parties the expectation of US support for British interests.

By the 1970s, things were different. Britain had ceased being an imperial power and was in the process of redefining itself as a medium-sized power 'punching above its weight' – or what Prime Minister Tony Blair later called a 'pivotal power'.[36] The imagery of a special relationship remained important, but it was no longer possible to maintain credible claims that it was an exclusive relationship. Moreover, overt demonstrations of UK–US bilateralism were now complicating Britain's other relationships. This was one of the reasons why Prime Minister Heath had sought to recast the special relationship as the natural relationship, a nomenclature that was less abrasive to Britain's other partners. Subsequent British governments maintained a commitment to the practice and nomenclature of the special relationship, but they, too, took a step back from Churchill's insistence on overt Anglo-American bilateralism. The British claim to exclusivity through the special relationship was dropped. The relationship was represented instead as an established friendship that benefitted others and supported the institutions that provided for public goods. Consider, in this light, Harold Wilson's speech prepared for delivery at the University of Texas in April 1971. Discussing explicitly whether Anglo-American relations were a special case, Wilson opined:

> Special? No, if that means we have inherited an intellectual or diplomatic capital on which we can draw, if a sense of common purpose is lacking…
>
> No, if that means exclusive…
>
> No, if in its content it is living in the past, whether in the age of imperialism that has gone, as even the more recent era of the cold war…

No, if it is merely a medium in which politicians and diplomats posturise and strike attitudes...

No, if we fail to recognise the political realities of our two countries, and those others with whom we are associated.[37]

Communities of Practice: An Elite Political Tradition

The special relationship is sometimes likened to a layer cake, with personal leader relations at its apex, bureaucratic interweaving in the middle and public-level cultural interactions at its base.[38] In considering the special relationship as an elite political tradition, it is the habits of co-operation and complex bureaucratic interpenetration that are of primary concern. How, in these activities, might Anglo-American relations differ from other international relationships?

Epistemic communities have been seen as one reason why the special relationship has its particular character and stability. According to Peter M. Haas, members of these epistemic communities share normative and principled beliefs that provide a value-based rationale for community action, notions of validity that enable agreement on internally defined criteria for measuring and validating knowledge, and causal beliefs that help identify a central set of problems in their domain.[39] Members themselves are knowledge-based professionals in scientific and technological areas, work closely together in a common enterprise and engage in shared learning. Crucially, they have the capacity to influence policy and, within an Anglo-American context, have helped US and UK governance and societies to evolve broadly in tandem. Consider, for instance, Anglo-American planning for a revised post-Second World War international economic order based upon the Bretton Woods system.[40]

However, to capture the wider elite levels of the layer cake, it is necessary to consider also Anglo-American interpenetration outside of the exacting epistemic community criteria. Here, it is useful to think in terms of Anglo-American communities of practice. The concept of communities of practice derives from learning theory, but social scientists have increasingly applied it to help analyse, for instance, business, organizational design and development projects. The basic idea is that communities of practice are formed when people engage in a process of collective learning in a shared domain of activity. In identifying a community of practice, Etienne Wenger argues that three characteristics are essential: domain, community and practice. Domain derives its identity from the shared interest and commitment of members and their shared competence distinguishes members from other people. Community is formed by domain members engaging in joint activities and discussions, relationship-building and mutual learning. The practice results from domain members being practitioners who, over time and through sustained interaction, develop a bank of shared resources. These include experiences, tools and modes of operation.[41]

H.C. Allen once observed of Anglo-American relations that 'It is a problem throughout their history to determine whether common or analogous courses of actions in the two countries are due to direct influence of the one upon the other, or to similar responses to similar stimuli. There are certainly many examples of both ... But even to the casual glance there are broad parallels in the two histories which cannot possibly be ascribed merely to coincidence.'[42] Communities of practice facilitate both of these possibilities and there are numerous examples of Anglo-American mutual learning and common problem-solving – even within domains central to national sovereignty. The early evolution of the American intelligence establishment drew heavily upon the British model, and the British army's tactical doctrine manual *Keeping the Peace* was important in the US development of counter-insurgency operations. Conversely, US sharing of nuclear technology following the 1958 Mutual Defence Act was essential in maintaining Britain's nuclear deterrent. Specific Anglo-American objectives have also encouraged complementary and sometimes co-ordinated responses. Consider, for example, the development of military doctrine and procurement choices in support of the interoperability of British and American armed forces. Similarly, Christopher Finn and Paul D. Berg emphasize that 'combined planning, personnel exchanges, and training events like bombing competitions and Red Flag war games have honed US–UK co-ordination to a fine edge'.[43] There are instances, too, of particular actors sharing information and co-operating more closely across the British and American governments than they do within their own governments. Service-to-service relations are a good example of this. As Christopher J. Bartlett explains, during the Falklands Crisis, for instance, the US navy played an especially sympathetic and helpful role in terms of service-to-service naval relations.[44] Likewise, John Dickie argues that the closeness of the Anglo-American intelligence community meant that '[s]ome of the most crucial assistance came clandestinely on the Old Pals network between senior members of the Intelligence Service'.[45]

Beyond functionally driven domains, communities of practice have been influential in encouraging Anglo-American elites to respond in similar ways to different challenges. One example of this is the organizational and institutional reactions of British and American governments to the erosion of the traditional distinction between internal and external state affairs. In 2006, the British and American governments unveiled 'Active Diplomacy for a Changing World' and 'Transformational Diplomacy' within weeks of each other – both strategies were designed to adjust national diplomacy to evolving challenges and were in many respects strikingly similar, despite making no direct references to each other.[46] Then, to improve co-ordination of external and internal security infrastructures, the British introduced in 2008 a counterpart to the US National Security Strategy and created in 2010 an American-style National Security Council (NSC) and a National Security Advisor.[47] American and British governments have also responded to the need for greater co-ordination and oversight of internal and external affairs by centralizing power. Prime Minister Blair, for example, was regularly accused of the 'presidentialisation' of British politics[48] and although Britain's NSC goes some way towards democratizing matters, there is no doubt regarding the central position of the prime minister.

Finally, it is possible to see communities of practice as driving and reinforcing unique aspects of Anglo-American diplomatic interaction. Alison Holmes, for instance, argues that an infrastructure has developed between the US State Department and the British Foreign and Commonwealth Office that 'can operate jointly, in parallel or at tangents when the need arises, while remaining largely enmeshed'.[49] This enmeshing is borne out, for example, in British reactions to the secretive policymaking style adopted by the Nixon White House. In November 1971, the British ambassador to Washington, Lord Cromer, advised the Foreign and Commonwealth Office that 'No disinterested observer could possibly maintain that it [US foreign policy] is being well made and many of the Washington professionals, inside and outside the Government, think it is a mess'. He went on to caution that 'State Department officials often do not know what is going on, even as well as we do'. The consequent upset to normal channels of communication was obvious in his warning that on one occasion Henry Kissinger had 'delivered a specific rebuke to the Embassy for having mentioned to the State Department that Sir Burke Trend had accompanied Mr Harold Wilson, as Prime Minister, in a discussion à *quatre* with the President'.[50]

It is the case, too, that the conduct of diplomacy between Britain and America has acquired particular characteristics as a result of officials building relationships, sharing experiences and developing modes of operation over time. Nowadays, it is common for presidents and prime ministers, and other senior officials, to speak of the open and intimate style of diplomatic exchange that they maintain with one another. However, it was not always that way, despite the shared English language and cultural familiarity making 'US and UK officials feel more comfortable and cooperative with each other, more respectful and more trusting of each other'.[51] Convinced of the value of personal diplomacy, Churchill set the tone for intimate Anglo-American discussion. For instance, at his summit meeting with Truman in January 1952, he expressed his wish to 'reach a good understanding of each other's point of view over the whole field, so that we can work together easily and intimately at the different levels as we used to do'.[52] He also wanted a relaxed atmosphere, favouring 'a few informal meetings or meals' rather than an agenda meeting,[53] and he was particularly scornful of a proposed arrangement whereby he would meet Secretary of Defence Robert A. Lovett for the first time in the company of three Secretaries of the Army, Navy and Air Force, Secretary of State Dean Acheson, Ambassador Walter Gifford, General Omar Bradley and the three Joint Chiefs of Staff:[54] 'I do not see how a parade of this character would give an opportunity for an "undisturbed informal talk".'[55]

Over time, an expectation of open and intimate conversations in the quest for understanding and addressing common problems became established within Anglo-American relations. This was reflected in communications between British and American officials and in the practice of their exchanges. For instance, Kissinger once confided to Cromer that it was 'inconceivable' that he would be able to have the type of conversation he and the ambassador had with any other European colleagues.[56] Similarly, within days of his inauguration in January 1969, President Richard Nixon dispatched a letter to Prime Minister Wilson in which he demonstrated another facet of elite Anglo-American bureaucratic intermeshing – the open president–prime Minister direct line of communication – and foregrounded the equality and intimacy of their partnership:

> For many decades one of the great sources of strength in the cause of freedom has been the close relationship between Prime Ministers of the United Kingdom and Presidents of the United States. This is as it should be, for it but reflects the depth of feeling and kinship existing between our two nations. I intend, in the years ahead, to see that this tradition is upheld and nourished. I ask, therefore, that you feel free at all times to let me know of your concerns, and to give me your wise advice and council. I hope, for my part, that I am [to] have equal freedom to tell you what is on my mind.[57]

The number, range and subject matter of communities of practice within Anglo-American relations are remarkable and have helped to establish and maintain an elite political tradition of special relations. Under normal circumstances, communities of practice even within governments are often hindered by the formality of and competition between different bureaucratic actors, which impede open knowledge sharing. The development of communities of practice between governments is still harder because countries operate within a competitive and anarchic international system and the flow of information outside of government is consequently carefully controlled and restricted.

Communities of practice within Anglo-American relations are therefore an exception rather than the norm in interstate relations and they owe their number and existence to unusually high levels of reciprocal trust, an assumption of common ambitions, a wide range of common problems and sustained and proven engagement over a significant period of time. Furthermore, they, in turn, facilitate the habits of co-operation and complex bureaucratic interpenetration that characterize the special relationship at its apex and middle levels. As former US Secretary of State Kissinger revealed in 1982, the British 'became a participant in internal American deliberations, to a degree probably never before practiced between sovereign nations'.[58]

A Tradition of Traditions: The Discursive Special Relationship

Speaking before the Pilgrims Society in March 1975, Elliot Richardson, the US ambassador to the United Kingdom, noted that 'these special relationships of ours of language, of culture, of cast of mind become vital, because however power shifts, whatever the complexities of balance between nations and forces, the value of an old and easy partnership away from the conference-table, sharing the same assumptions and aspirations, is inestimable'.[59] It is these assumptions and aspirations that have allowed British and American policymakers to enjoy an ease of exchange and higher levels of policy congruence than they have with any of their other partners. For instance, describing his summit talks with President Gerald Ford at the White House as 'very, very relaxed' and 'free flowing', Prime Minister Wilson explained in January 1975 that 'We don't have, you know, to spend about fifty minutes in every hour arguing about first principles, arguing about trying to convince one another. They are thoroughly practical and that's why you get six times as much results out of an hour of discussions such of the kind we've had.'[60]

There is an important difference, though, between what the special relationship enables and the assumptions and aspirations that underpin it. To understand the latter, it is necessary to return the debate about the special relationship to first principles – or shared political traditions. Whether one regards the special relationship as a tool of British diplomacy, as a nomenclature that captures a genuinely unique international relationship or simply as a myth, the evidence demonstrates that from the Second World War onwards the special relationship has been perceived to exist. As such, a common denominator of these perspectives is that the relationship has been constructed in and through discourse.

Consider the weakest of acknowledgements of the existence of a special relationship. Max Beloff bemoaned dressing up a perfectly good international relationship in the garb of sentimentality but conceded a myth of a special relationship.[61] This raises the issue of how the myth first developed and then continued. According to Roland Barthes, a myth is a system of communication, a mode of signification. A core function of myth is to give an historical intention a natural justification and to make contingency appear eternal. This means that the consumer of the myth reads what is actually a semiological system as a factual system, rather than as a system of values. Fact is thereby constructed at a remove from 'truth'. Furthermore, a myth needs to be animated – or, as Barthes puts it, 'it is human history which converts reality into speech, and it alone rules the life and the death of mythical language'.[62]

How, then, was the special relationship first animated and then maintained? The answer lies in discourse and the conscious choices made in the creation of selective narratives of Anglo-American relations. Churchill, of course, was the first major narrator of special Anglo-American relations and Isaiah Berlin once noted of him that he had 'an historical imagination so strong, so comprehensive, as to encase the whole of the present and the whole of the future in a framework of a rich and multicolored past'. For Berlin, this approach was 'dominated by a desire – and a capacity – to find fixed moral and intellectual bearings to give shape and character, color and direction and coherence, to the stream of events'.[63] When, in 1946, Churchill rhetorically launched the special relationship in his famous 'Sinews of Peace' speech, he chose a narrative that blended sentiment and interest and glossed over past Anglo-American divisions. But, more than that, the narrative was timeless in the sense that he drew selectively from entwined histories to imbue Anglo-American relations with a natural specialness and to maintain this specialness ad infinitum by establishing sentiment and interest as joint Anglo-American holdings and responsibilities.[64]

Upon examining this speech carefully, one can discern that, from the onset, other Anglo-American political traditions were central to the establishment of the special relationship itself. The sentimentality of 'fraternal association' was anchored in references to 'kindred systems of society', a democratic 'othering' of communism and a call to 'the great principles of freedom and the rights of man'. These were, he reminded his audience, the 'joint inheritance of the English-speaking world and which through Magna Carta, the Bill of Rights, the Habeas Corpus, trial by jury, and the English Common Law find their most famous expression in the American Declaration of Independence'.[65]

As the nomenclature 'special relationship' gained traction, it needed to be kept relevant and maintained in the public consciousness. What evolved was a mythologized special relationship co-authored by British and American political and media elites and disseminated widely to their publics through film, literature, media, commemoration, memorials, photography and so forth.

These narratives continually spoke not only to common Anglo-American interests and sacrifice but also to shared ideals of governance, economic and
political systems, international norms, individual rights and so on; in short, a
shared way of life. Indeed, Prime Minister Blair explicitly spoke of 9/11 as an
attack on a shared way of life in the same way as Churchill had spoken of the
looming Cold War threat: 'The target of the terrorists was not only New York
and Washington but the very values of freedom, tolerance and decency which
underpin our way of life.'[66]

As the apogee of Anglo-American co-operation in the Second World War
faded from public consciousness, the special relationship narrative was adapt-
ed. For instance, speeches by British prime ministers and US presidents began
to rhetorically connect Anglo-American relations past, present and future and
to almost always reference shared political traditions. Of the bountiful examples that exist of these discursive choices, consider the following extract from
an address by President Bill Clinton to the British Parliament in 1995. Note
especially how memory of the Placentia Bay meeting that enshrined Anglo-
American aims and ideals in the Atlantic Charter is invoked, how the Second
World War is connected to present/future Anglo-American relations, how
joint sacrifice is represented as being made in the interests of shared ideals
and how the Anglo-American alliance is heralded as a model for democratic
governance:

> When President Roosevelt and Prime Minister Churchill first met on the deck
> of the HMS *Prince of Wales* in 1941 at one of the loneliest moments in your na-
> tion's history, they joined in prayer, and the Prime Minister was filled with hope.
> Afterwards, he said, 'The same language, the same hymns, more or less the same
> ideals. Something big may be happening, something very big.'
>
> Well, once again, he was right. Something really big happened. On the basis of
> those ideals, Churchill and Roosevelt and all of their successors built an endur-
> ing alliance and a genuine friendship between our nations. Other times in other
> places are littered with the vows of friendship sworn during battle and then aban-
> doned in peacetime. This one stands alone, unbroken, above all the rest, a model
> for the ties that should bind all democracies.[67]

Cast in this light, the discursive political tradition of the special relationship is, in part at least, a tradition of traditions. Democracy, capitalism, individual rights, the rule of law and so on; these Anglo-American political
traditions are a staple diet in the discursive construction and ongoing renewal of the special relationship. Moreover, they are timeless and removed
from functionalist concerns for relative Anglo-American power and calculations of mutual utility. This is precisely what US Ambassador Richardson

was referring to in March 1975 when he spoke of Anglo-American special relationships being independent of 'power shifts' and 'the complexities of balance between nations and forces'.[68] It also resonates strongly with H.G. Nicholas's argument that 'a common historical inheritance of "Anglo-Saxon" polity' helped establish 'a set of immediately recognizable and axiomatically accepted [Anglo-American] habits of thought and behaviour' that led to 'a common cast of mind, parallel styles of action and reaction at both the popular and higher levels of government.'[69]

Conclusion

The special relationship is an Anglo-American political tradition – albeit an odd and perhaps analytically perplexing one. It can and does exist as a political tradition, regardless of whether it is interpreted as a British diplomatic creation, a co-authored discursive construct or a unique international relationship in which communities of practice have helped break down traditional interstate behaviour. It is the case, too, that the special relationship is a political tradition that has grown out of and come to represent other shared British and American political traditions. This is evident not only in the ongoing narrative of the special relationship but also in the common 'cast of mind'.

Anglo-American officials routinely affirm in public speeches their commitment to shared principles of democracy, liberal free-market capitalism, an international rules-based order, respect for the rights of the individual and so forth. Privately, their commitment to these ideals and the aspirations they engender are assumed rather than debated. This does not mean harmony, as evidenced by American anti-colonialism and suspicion of British socialism. But it does mean a shared platform from which to try to direct the traffic of international affairs. As President Ford observed in 1975, 'Britons and Americans communicate effectively because we share a common background of understanding ... each of us is aware that behind these few words lie volumes of thought and experience which do not need to be articulated, and of course, this is a priceless asset to both our nations and our enduring friendship.'[70]

Analytically, this view of the special relationship as a political tradition is perplexing in that it transcends rather than resolves extant debates about 'specialness'. It is the case, too, that there are contradictions in the different representations of the special relationship as a tradition. For example, the idea that the special relationship is a tradition invented as a tool of British diplomacy sits awkwardly with that of a mythologized special relationship, in Barthes's sense, that was authored by British *and* American political and

media elites and echoed in the cultural interactions of publics at the base of
the Anglo-American 'layer cake'.

However, many political traditions suffer – or even thrive upon – internal contradiction. The special relationship is no different. What, if anything,
is unique to Anglo-American relations remains contested and yet the special relationship exists nonetheless because it is perceived to exist. The failed
attempts, first by Heath and then by Cameron and Obama, to rebrand the
special relationship, as the natural and essential relationship respectively, demonstrate this. To bridge the tension between these two realities, it is necessary
to recognize that, at the discursive level of construction, it does not matter
to the special relationship, for example, whether claims of uniqueness are accurate, whether it was a British diplomatic device or whether 'specialness' is
proportionate to mutual utility. What matters is that the political tradition
of a special relationship was, and remains, a co-constructed Anglo-American
enterprise that embodies other shared political traditions and that blends interest and sentiment in a living narrative.

Steve Marsh is Reader in International Politics at Cardiff University, United
Kingdom. His principal research interests lie in post-Second World War in-
ternational politics, with a particular focus on American foreign policy and
Anglo-American relations. His latest book, co-edited with Robert M. Hen-
dershot, is *Culture Matters: Anglo-American Relations and the Intangibles of
Specialness* (Manchester University Press, 2020).

Notes

1. J. Dumbrell and A. Schafer (eds), *America's 'Special Relationships': Foreign and Domestic Aspects of the Politics of Alliance* (London: Routledge, 2009); A. Danchev, 'On Specialness', *International Affair* 72(4) (1996), 737–50; R. Dawson and R. Rosecrance, 'Theory and Reality in the
Anglo-American Alliance', *World Politics* 19(1) (1966), 21–51; J. Baylis, 'Anglo-American Relations and Alliance Theory', *International Relations* 8(4) (1985), 368–79.

2. J. Dickie, *'Special' No More. Anglo-American Relations: Rhetoric and Reality* (London: Weidenfield & Nicolson, 1994); A. Danchev, *On Specialness: Essays in Anglo-American Relations* (Basingstoke, MacMillan, 1998); C. Coker, 'Britain and the New World Order: The Special Relationship
in the 1990s', *International Affairs* 68 (1992), 407–21.

3. K. Kyle, *Suez* (London: Weidenfeld & Nicolson, 1992); W.S Lucas, *Divided We Stand: Britain, the US and the Suez Crisis* (London: Hodder & Stoughton, 1991); R. Sanghro, J. Chandio
and S. Soomro, 'The Special Relationship: The US, Great Britain and Egypt over the Suez Canal',
Journal of History Culture and Art Research 7 (2018), 127–35; N. Ashton, 'Harold Macmillan and
the "Golden Days" of Anglo-American Relations Revisited, 1957–63', *Diplomatic History* 29(4)
(2005), 691–723; I. Clark, *Nuclear Diplomacy and the Special Relationship: Britain's Deterrent and
America, 1957–1962* (Oxford: Oxford University Press, 1994), chapter 10; K. Young, 'The Sky-

bolt Crisis of 1962: Muddle or Mischief?, *Journal of Strategic Studies* 27(4) (2004), 614–35; S. Marsh, 'The US, BREXIT and Anglo-American Relations', *Journal of Transatlantic Studies* 16 (2018), 1–23; Peter Harris, 'A Not-So-Special Relationship: Why Britain Is Becoming Divided Over the Atlantic Alliance', *The National Interest*, 17 July 2019; A.A. Michta, 'The US–UK Special Relationship and the "Principled Realism" of the Trump Administration', in R. Johnson and J. Matlary (eds), *The United Kingdom's Defence After Brexit* (London: Palgrave Macmillan, 2019), 59–74.

4. To: The Secretary Through: S/S From INR – Thomas L. Hughes, 7 February 1968, 'Subject: What Now for Britain? Wilson's Visit and Britain's Future', J. Colman, 'Communication: "What Now for Britain?" The State Department's Intelligence Assessment of the "Special Relationship", February 7, 1968', *Diplomacy & Statecraft* 19(2) (2008), 351.

5. H.C. Allen, *The Anglo-American Predicament* (London: Macmillan, 1960); H.C. Allen, *Great Britain and the United States: A History of Anglo-American Relations* (London: Odhams, 1955); H.G. Nicholas, *The United States and Britain* (London: University of Chicago Press, 1975); B. Brogan, *American Aspects* (New York: Harper and Row, 1964); A.C. Turner, *The Unique Partnership, Britain and the United States* (New York: Pegasus, 1971).

6. Although the 'Sinews of Peace' speech is often regarded as the first articulation of the term 'special relationship' by Churchill, he had in fact used it previously. For instance, *The New York Times Herald* included the following quotation from Churchill in a news feature dating from November 1945: 'We should not abandon our special relationship with the United States and Canada about the atomic bomb and we should aid the United States to guard this weapon as a sacred trust for the maintenance of peace.'

7. From an interview with James Callaghan conducted by A.P. Dobson, February 1987, in A.P. Dobson, *Anglo-American Relations in the Twentieth Century* (London: Routledge, 1995), 72.

8. Le Baron to Washington, 9 February 2009, cited in 'The British Ask, Is Our Special Relationship Still Special in Washington', *The Telegraph*, 4 February 2011, http://www.telegraph.co.uk/news/wikileaks-files/london-wikileaks/8305152/THE-BRITISH-ASK-IS-OUR-SPECIAL-RELATIONSHIP-STILL-SPECIAL-IN-WASHINGTON.html.

9. House of Commons Foreign Affairs Committee – Sixth Report Global Security: UK-US Relations (HCFAC), 18 March 2010, https://publications.parliament.uk/pa/cm200910/cmselect/cmfaff/114/11402.htm.

10. BBC News, 28 March 2010, http://news.bbc.co.uk/1/hi/uk/8590767.stm.

11. M. Smith, 'It's Over: MPs Say the Special Relationship with US Is Dead', *The Sunday Times*, 28 March 2010, http://www.timesonline.co.uk/tol/news/politics/article7078844.ece.

12. *News of the World*, 28 March 2010, http://www.newsoftheworld.co.uk/news/765588/Special-relationship-is-over-so-its-time-to-stop-sucking-up-to-the-US-say-MPs.html.

13. Examples include: Unattributed, 'End Nears for "Special Relationship" of UK and US', The Associated Press, 28 March 2010; D. Goure, 'The Trans-Atlantic Alliance: Going, Going, Gone', States News Service, 1 April 2010; S. Goldstein, 'British Parliamentary Members: Don't Use "Special" to Describe U.S. Relations', Marketwatch (distributed by McClatchy-Tribune News Service), 28 March 2010; C. Bohlen, 'Obama's Foreign Relations: Cold, or Just Cool?', *The Star-Ledger* (Newark, NJ), 7 April 2010; C. Mayer, 'Why Britain's Affair with the U.S. Is Over', *Time*, 29 March 2010, http://www.time.com/time/world/article/0,8599,1976102,00.html.

14. A. Spelling, 'Edward Heath and Anglo–American Relations 1970–1974: A Reappraisal', *Diplomacy and Statecraft* 20(4) (2009), 638–58; A. Scott, *Allies Apart: Heath, Nixon and the Anglo-American Relationship* (Basingstoke: Palgrave Macmillan, 2011); N. Rossbach,

Heath, Nixon and the Rebirth of the Special Relationship: Britain, the US and the EC, 1969–74 (London: Palgrave Macmillan, 2009).

15. HCFAC 2010, pt 4, p. 3.

16. 'Prime Minister and President Obama Article: An Essential Relationship', 24 May 2011, http://www.number10.gov.uk/news/statements-and-articles/2011/05/prime-minister-and-president-obama-article-an-essential-relationship-64103.

17. Nile Gardiner, 'The Special Relationship Doesn't Need a Makeover: David Cameron Should Dump the Phrase "Essential Relationship"', 24 May 2011, http://blogs.telegraph.co.uk/news/nilegardiner/100089145/the-special-relationship-doesn%E2%80%99t-need-a-makeover-david-cameron-should-dump-the-phrase-%E2%80%9Cessential-relationship%E2%80%9D/.

18. Official White House announcement, cited in 'Obama to Host State Dinner for Cameron, 3 February 2012', http://content.usatoday.com/communities/theoval/post/2012/02/obama-to-host-state-dinner-for-cameron/1.

19. BBC News, 28 March 2010, http://news.bbc.co.uk/1/hi/uk/8590767.stm.

20. British Ambassador Sir Christopher Meyer, for instance, famously banned the term from the Washington Embassy and Foreign Secretary Robin Cook once said of the term 'special relationship' "'It's not a phrase that I use"'. Cook cited in R. Lister, 'US and the UK: Special Relationship?', BBC News, 23 February 2001, available at http://news.bbc.co.uk/1/hi/world/americas/1185177.stm.

21. Evidence provided by Jeremy Greenstock, HCFAC 2010, EV34.

22. For more details, see A. Cairncross, *Years of Economic Recovery: British Economic Policy 1945–51* (London: Methuen, 1985), 7.

23. J. Gallagher, *The Decline, Revival and Fall of the British Empire: The Ford Lectures and Other Essays*, ed. Anil Seal (Cambridge: Cambridge University Press, 1982), 146.

24. United Kingdom National Archives (UKNA), FO 371/90838, paper Makins, 'Objectives in the Washington Talks', 29 November 1951.

25. R.B. Woods, *A Changing of the Guard: Anglo-American Relations 1941–46* (Chapel Hill: University of North Carolina Press, 1990).

26. UKNA, FO 371 38523, 'The Essentials of an American Policy', 21 March 1944.

27. This paper was first drafted in March 1949 but was initially considered too sensitive to circulate. The original document is UKNA, FO371/76384, 'Third World Power or Western Preponderance', 23 March 1949. The revised paper is reprinted in Extract from Memo. for the Permanent Under-Secretary's Committee, 'Anglo-American Relations: Present and Future', 22 April 1950, in R. Bullen and M. Pelley (eds), *Documents on British Policy Overseas, Series 2, Vol. 2: The London Conferences, Anglo-American Relations and Cold War Strategy January–June 1950* (London: Her Majesty's Stationery Office, 1987), Doc. 27, 81.

28. D. Reynolds, 'Roosevelt, Churchill and the Wartime Anglo-American Alliance, 1935–1945: Towards a New Synthesis', in H. Bull and W.R. Louis (eds), *The 'Special Relationship': Anglo-American Relations since 1945* (Oxford: Clarendon Press, 1986), 85–86.

29. D. Owen, 'Britain and the United States', in W.E. Leuchtenburg et al., *Britain and the United States: Four Views to Mark the Silver Jubilee* (London: Heinemann, 1979), 63.

30. UKNA, FO 371/90838, paper Makins, 'Objectives in the Washington Talks', 29 November 1951; *Foreign Relations of the United States (FRUS)* 1952–54, vol. 6, part one, Gifford to State Dept., 28 December 1951, 720–23.

31. Harry S. Truman Library (HST), PSF, box 116, papers prepared for general information, Steering Group preparation for President and PM talks, 'Approach and Objectives for the Churchill Talks', u.d., 1.

32. A.P. Dobson and S. Marsh, 'Churchill at the Summit: SACLANT and the Tone of An-glo-American Relations in January 1952, *International History Review* 32(2) (2010), 211–28.

33. UKNA, CAB 21/3057, Churchill speech to Congress, 17 January 1952.

34. UKNA, FO 371/90937, Hunt to Wilford, 15 November 1951.

35. Dwight D. Eisenhower Library (DDE), Ann Whitman File, International Series, box 18, Churchill visit June 1954(3), memo of conversation, 26 June 1954, 2.

36. Speech by Tony Blair, Lord Mayor's banquet, 22 November 1999.

37. Bodleian Library, MS Wilson, 1179, Wilson speech at University of Texas, master copy, 'Anglo-American Relations – A Special Case?', 30 April 1971.

38. J. Dumbrell, 'Personal Diplomacy: Relations between Prime Ministers and Presidents', in A.P. Dobson and S. Marsh (eds), *Anglo-American Relations: Contemporary Perspectives* (London: Routledge, 2013), 82.

39. P.M. Haas, 'Introduction: Epistemic Communities and International Policy Coordination', Special Issue: Knowledge, Power, and International Policy Coordination, *International Organization* 46(1) (1992), 1–35.

40. See, for instance, G.J. Ikenberry, 'A World Economy Restored: Expert Consensus and the Anglo-American Postwar Settlement', in *International Organization* 46(1) (1992), 289–322; P. Hall, *The Politics of Political Power of Economic Ideas: Keynesianism across Nations* (London: George Phillip Publishers, 1988), 361–91; R. Hulme, 'The Role of Policy Transfer in Assessing the Impact of American Ideas on British Social Policy', *Global Social Policy* 6(2) (2006), 173–195; U. Lehmkuhl, 'Still Special! Anglo-American Relations since the End of the Cold War', in K. Oppermann (ed.), *British Foreign and Security Policy. Historical Legacies and Current Challenges* (Augsburg: Wißner, 2012), 13–30.

41. E. Wenger, *Communities of Practice: Learning, Meaning, and Identity* (Cambridge: Cambridge University Press, 1998); Etienne Wenger and William Snyder, 'Communities of Practice: The Organizational Frontier', *Harvard Business Review*, January–February 2000, 139–45.

42. H.C. Allen, *Great Britain and the United States*, 120.

43. C. Finn and P.D. Berg, 'Anglo-American Strategic Air Power Co-operation in the Cold War and Beyond', *Air and Space Power Journal*, Winter 2004, http://www.airpower.maxwell. af.mil/airchronicles/apj/apj04/win04/finn.html#finn, n.p.

44. Caspar Weinberger even tried to offer Britain a loan of an American aircraft carrier, which Thatcher found encouraging, if impractical. M. Thatcher, *The Downing Street Years* (London: Harper Collins), 226–27; C. Weinberger, *Fighting for Peace: Seven Critical Years at the Pentagon* (New York: Warner Books, 1991), 203–17; L. Richardson, *When Allies Differ: Anglo-American Relations during the Suez and Falklands Crises* (Basingstoke: Macmillan, 1996); C.J Bartlett, *'The Special Relationship': A Political History of Anglo-American Relations since 1945* (New York: Longman, 1992), 156.

45. Dickie, *'Special' No More. Anglo-American Relations: Rhetoric and Reality*, 5.

46. Foreign and Commonwealth Office, 'Active Diplomacy for a Changing World', March 2006, https://www.gov.uk/government/uploads/system/uploads/attachment_data/file/272260/6762.pdf; Condoleezza Rice, 'Transformational Diplomacy', speech at Georgetown University Washington, DC, 18 January 2006, https://2001-2009.state.gov/secretary/rm/2006/59306.htm.

47. For more details of the development of the NSC, see J. Devanny and J. Harris, 'National Security at the Centre of Government', Institute for Government's Centre of Government Project, https://www.instituteforgovernment.org.uk/sites/default/files/publications/NSC%20final%202.pdf.

48. See, for instance, M. Foley, *The British Presidency: Tony Blair and the Politics of Public Leadership* (Manchester: Manchester University Press, 2000).

49. A. Holmes, 'Transatlantic Diplomacy and "Global" States', in A.P. Dobson and S. Marsh (eds), *Anglo-American Relations: Contemporary Perspectives*, 122.

50. UKNA, FCO 82/66, 10763732, Memo Cromer to Greenhill, 'The Making of American Foreign Policy', 12 November 1971.

51. To: The Secretary Through: S/S From INR – Thomas L. Hughes, 7 February 1968, 'Subject: What Now for Britain? Wilson's Visit and Britain's Future', J. Colman, 'Communication', 351.

52. *FRUS* 1952–54, vol. 6, part one, Churchill to Truman, 10 December 1951, 704–5. Churchill rated not going to see Truman after Roosevelt's death as his biggest mistake during the Second World War. Lord Moran, *Winston Churchill: The Struggle for Survival, 1940–1965* (London: Constable, 1966), diary entry, 15 October 1951, 47.

53. *FRUS* 1952–54, vol. 6, part one, footnote 4, 699.

54. UKNA, FO 371/90938, Washington Embassy to FO, 28 December 1951.

55. *FRUS* 1952–54, vol. 6, FO to Washington Embassy, personal from Churchill, 29 December 1951.

56. UKNA, PREM 15/712, 10763422, Cromer to FCO, c.13 November 1971.

57. Richard Nixon Library, National Security Council Files, President's Trip Files, President's February–March 1969 Trip to Europe, Richard Nixon to Harold Wilson, 11 January 1969.

58. Text of Henry Kissinger's 10 May 1982 speech to the Royal Institute of International Affairs, http://www.larouchepub.com/other/2002/2901_kissinger.html.

59. 'US-British Relations "Were Never Better"', *The Times*, 12 March 1975, 9.

60. Bodleian Library, MS Wilson, 1263, Transcript of Prime Minister's Q&A session at the National Press Club Luncheon, 31 January 1975.

61. Max Beloff, 'The Special Relationship: An Anglo-American Myth', in M. Gilbert (ed.), *A Century of Conflict, 1850–1950: Essays for A.J.P. Taylor* (London: Hamish Hamilton, 1966), 170.

62. R. Barthes, 'Myth Today', in John Storey ed., *Cultural Theory and Popular Culture: A Reader* (Harlow: Pearson, 2006), 293; R. Barthes, *Mythologies*, trans. Annette Lavers (New York: Hill and Wang, 1984).

63. Isaiah Berlin, 'Mr Churchill', *The Atlantic*, September 1949, http://www.theatlantic.com/magazine/archive/1949/09/mr-churchill/303546/.

64. A. Marchi and S. Marsh, 'Churchill, Fulton and the Anglo-American Special Relationship: Setting the Agenda?', *Journal of Transatlantic Studies* 14(4) (2016), 365–82.

65. Winston Churchill, 'Sinews of Peace', 5 March 1946, https://www.nationalchurchillmuseum.org/sinews-of-peace-iron-curtain-speech.html.

66. 'Attacks Remembered: In Quotes', BBC News, 11 September 2002, http://news.bbc.co.uk/1/hi/world/americas/2251406.stm.

67. Of course, the two actually first met at the peace negotiations after the First World War. *President Clinton's speech to the Houses of Parliament, 29 November 1995, http://www.johnmajor.co.uk/page1367.html.*

68. 'US-British Relations "Were Never Better"', *The Times*, 12 March 1975, 9.

69. H. Nicholas, *The United States and Britain* (Chicago: University of Chicago Press, 1975), 1.

70. Gerald R. Ford, 'Toasts of the President and Prime Minister Wilson of the United Kingdom', 30 January 1975, *The American Presidency Project*, http://www.presidency.ucsb.edu/ws/?pid=5305.

Bibliography

Allen, H.C. *The Anglo-American Predicament*. London: Macmillan, 1960.

———. *Great Britain and the United States: A History of Anglo-American Relations*. London: Odhams, 1955.

Ashton, N. 'Harold Macmillan and the "Golden Days" of Anglo-American Relations Revisited, 1957–63', *Diplomatic History* 29(4) (2005), 691–723.

Barthes, R. *Mythologies*, trans. Annette Lavers. New York: Hill and Wang, 1984.

———. 'Myth Today', in J. Storey (ed.), *Cultural Theory and Popular Culture: A Reader*. Harlow: Pearson, 2006.

Bartlett, C.J. *'The Special Relationship': A Political History of Anglo-American Relations since 1945*. New York: Longman, 1992.

Baylis, J. 'Anglo-American Relations and Alliance Theory', *International Relations* 8(4) (1985), 368–79.

Beloff, M. 'The Special Relationship: An Anglo-American Myth', in M. Gilbert (ed.), *A Century of Conflict, 1850–1950: Essays for A.J.P. Taylor*. London: Hamish Hamilton, 1966, 151–71.

Brogan, B. *American Aspects*. New York: Harper and Row, 1964.

Bullen, R., and M. Pelley (eds). *Documents on British Policy Overseas, Series 2, Vol. 2: The London Conferences, Anglo-American Relations and Cold War Strategy January–June 1950*. London: Her Majesty's Stationery Office, 1987.

Cairncross A. *Years of Economic Recovery: British Economic Policy 1945–51*. London: Methuen, 1985.

Clark, I. *Nuclear Diplomacy and the Special Relationship: Britain's Deterrent and America, 1957–1962*. Oxford: Oxford University Press, 1994.

Coker, C. 'Britain and the New World Order: The Special Relationship in the 1990s', *International Affairs* 68 (1992), 407–21.

Colman, J. 'Communication: "What Now for Britain?" The State Department's Intelligence Assessment of the "Special Relationship", February 7, 1968', *Diplomacy & Statecraft* 19(2) (2008), 350–60.

Danchev, A. *On Specialness: Essays in Anglo-American Relations*. Basingstoke: MacMillan, 1998.

———. 'On Specialness', *International Affairs* 72(4) (1996), 737–50.

Dawson, R., and R. Rosecrance. 'Theory and Reality in the Anglo-American Alliance', *World Politics* 19(1) (1966), 21–51.

Dickie, J. *'Special' No More. Anglo-American Relations: Rhetoric and Reality*. London: Weidenfield & Nicolson, 1994.

Dobson, A.P. *Anglo-American Relations in the Twentieth Century*. London: Routledge, 1995.

Dobson, A.P., and S. Marsh. 'Churchill at the Summit: SACLANT and the Tone of Anglo-American Relations in January 1952', *International History Review* 32(2) (2010), 211–28.

Dumbrell, J. 'Personal Diplomacy: Relations between Prime Ministers and Presidents', in A.P. Dobson and S. Marsh (eds), *Anglo-American Relations: Contemporary Perspectives*. London: Routledge, 2013.

Finn, C., and P.D. Berg. 'Anglo-American Strategic Air Power Co-operation in the Cold War and Beyond', *Air and Space Power Journal*, Winter 2004, http://www.airpower.maxwell.af.mil/airchronicles/apj/apj04/win04/finn.html#finn, n.p.

Foley, M. *The British Presidency: Tony Blair and the Politics of Public Leadership*. Manchester: Manchester University Press, 2000.

Gallagher, J. *The Decline, Revival and Fall of the British Empire: The Ford Lectures and Other Essays*, ed. A. Seal. Cambridge: Cambridge University Press, 1982.

Haas, P.M. 'Introduction: Epistemic Communities and International Policy Coordination', Special Issue: Knowledge, Power, and International Policy Coordination, *International Organization* 46(1) (1992), 1–35.

Hall, P. *The Politics of Political Power of Economic Ideas: Keynesianism across Nations.* London: George Phillip Publishers, 1988, 361–91.

Holmes, A. 'Transatlantic Diplomacy and "Global" States', in A.P. Dobson and S. Marsh (eds), *Anglo-American Relations: Contemporary Perspectives.* London: Routledge, 105–28.

Hulme, R. 'The Role of Policy Transfer in Assessing the Impact of American Ideas on British Social Policy,' *Global Social Policy* 6(2) (2006), 173–195.

Ikenberry, G.J. 'A World Economy Restored: Expert Consensus and the Anglo-American Postwar Settlement', *International Organization* 46(1) (1992), 289–322.

Kyle, K. *Suez.* London: Weidenfeld & Nicolson, 1992.

Lehmkuhl, U. 'Still Special! Anglo-American Relations since the End of the Cold War', in K. Oppermann (ed.), *British Foreign and Security Policy. Historical Legacies and Current Challenges.* Augsburg: Wißner, 2012, 13–30.

Lucas, W. Scott. *Divided We Stand: Britain, the US and the Suez Crisis.* London: Hodder & Stoughton, 1991.

Marchi, A., and S. Marsh. 'Churchill, Fulton and the Anglo-American Special Relationship: Setting the Agenda?', *Journal of Transatlantic Studies* 14(4) (2016), 365–382.

Marsh, S. 'The US, BREXIT and Anglo-American Relations', *Journal of Transatlantic Studies* 16 (2018), 1–23.

Michta A.A. 'The US–UK Special Relationship and the "Principled Realism" of the Trump Administration', in R. Johnson and J. Matlary (eds), *The United Kingdom's Defence After Brexit.* London: Palgrave Macmillan, 2019, 59–74.

Moran, Lord. *Winston Churchill: The Struggle for Survival, 1940–1965.* London: Constable, 1966.

Nicholas, H.G. *The United States and Britain.* London: University of Chicago Press, 1975.

Owen, D. 'Britain and the United States', in W.E. Leuchtenburg et al., *Britain and the United States: Four Views to Mark the Silver Jubilee.* London: Heinemann, 1979, 61–78.

Reynolds, D. 'Roosevelt, Churchill and the Wartime Anglo-American Alliance, 1935–1945: Towards a New Synthesis', in H. Bull and W.R. Louis (eds), *The 'Special Relationship': Anglo-American Relations since 1945.* Oxford: Clarendon Press, 1986, 17–41.

Richardson, L. *When Allies Differ: Anglo-American Relations during the Suez and Falklands Crises.* Basingstoke: Macmillan, 1996.

Rossbach, N. *Heath, Nixon and the Rebirth of the Special Relationship: Britain, the US and the EC, 1969–74.* London: Palgrave Macmillan, 2009.

Sanghro, R., J. Chandio and S. Soomro. 'The Special Relationship: The US, Great Britain and Egypt over the Suez Canal', *Journal of History Culture and Art Research* 7(3) (2018), 127–35.

Scott, A. *Allies Apart: Heath, Nixon and the Anglo-American Relationship.* Basingstoke: Palgrave Macmillan, 2011.

Spelling, A. 'Edward Heath and Anglo–American Relations 1970–1974: A Reappraisal', *Diplomacy and Statecraft* 20(4) (2009), 638–58.

Thatcher, M. *The Downing Street Years.* London: Harper Collins.

Turner, A.C. *The Unique Partnership, Britain and the United States.* New York: Pegasus, 1971.

Weinberger, C. *Fighting for Peace: Seven Critical Years at the Pentagon.* New York: Warner Books, 1991.

Wenger, E. *Communities of Practice: Learning, Meaning, and Identity.* Cambridge: Cambridge University Press, 1998.

Wenger, E., and W. Snyder. 'Communities of Practice: The Organizational Frontier', *Harvard Business Review*, January–February 2000, 139–45.

Woods, R.B. *A Changing of the Guard: Anglo-American Relations 1941–46*. Chapel Hill: University of North Carolina Press, 1990.

Xu, R. *Alliance Persistence within the Anglo-American Special Relationship: The Post-Cold War Era*. London: Palgrave Macmillan, 2017.

Young, K. 'The Skybolt Crisis of 1962: Muddle or Mischief?', *Journal of Strategic Studies* 27(4) (2004), 614–35.

Index

CPSIA information can be obtained
at www.ICGtesting.com
Printed in the USA
BVHW050907230522
637277BV00021B/9